iMovie '11 & iDVD

the missing manual®

The book that should have been in the box®

iMovie '11 & iDVD

the missing manual®

The book that should have been in the box·

David Pogue and Aaron Miller

O'REILLY®

Beijing | Cambridge | Farnham | Köln | Sebastopol | Tokyo

iMovie '11 & iDVD: The Missing Manual

by David Pogue and Aaron Miller

Printed in Canada

Published by O'Reilly Media, Inc., 1005 Gravenstein Highway North, Sebastopol, CA 95472.

O'Reilly Media books may be purchased for educational, business, or sales promotional use. Online editions are also available for most titles: *http://my.safaribooksonline.com*. For more information, contact our corporate/institutional sales department: 800-998-9938 or *corporate@oreilly.com*.

Printing History:

March 2011:   First Edition.

ISBN: 978-1-449-39327-4

[TI]

Table of Contents

The Missing Credits xvii

Introduction 1

Part One: Editing in iMovie

Chapter 1: Importing Video **27**

iMovie: The Application 27
    iMovie on a New Mac 27
    iMovie for an Existing Mac 28
    ".0.1" Updates 28
Getting into iMovie 29
Importing Footage from a Tape Camcorder 31
    Automatic Scene Detection 36
Importing from Tapeless Camcorders 36
Importing from an iPhone or iPod Touch 44
Importing from DVD Camcorders 45
Recording Live from a Camcorder or iSight Camera 45
Importing Old iMovie Projects 47
Dragging Video In from the Finder 49
Importing with iMovie's Drop Box Folder 50
Importing Footage from Old Analog Tapes 51
    Approach 1: Use a Camcorder with Pass-Through Conversion 51
    Approach 2: Record onto Your DV Camcorder 51
    Approach 3: Use a Media Converter 52
    Approach 4: Use a Digital8 Camcorder 53

Chapter 2: The Lay of the Land 55

The Concept of Movie Projects 55
The Project Library 57
    Creating a Project 57
    Duplicating a Project 58
    Renaming a Project 58
    Project Folders 59
    Deleting a Project 59
    Undeleting a Project 60
    Moving a Project 60
    Consolidating Project Media 61
Aspect Ratios: The Missing Manual 62
    Mismatched Aspect Ratios 63
    Changing Your Project's Aspect Ratio 64
All About Events 65
    Fine-Tuning the Events List 65
    Splitting Events 66
    Merging Events 68
    Renaming an Event 68
    Deleting an Event 69
Five Ways to Remodel Your Workspace 69
    Hide the Projects or Events List 69
    Make the Clips Smaller 70
    Adjust or Relocate the Viewer 70
    Swap the Two Clip Areas 71
    Single-Row Editing: Return of the Timeline 72

Chapter 3: Building the Movie 75

Phase 1: Review Your Clips (Skim + Play) 75
    Filmstrips 76
    Skimming 77
    Playback 78
Phase 2: Select the Good Bits 79
    Select by Dragging 80
    Select 4-Second Chunks 80
    Selecting Entire Clips 81
    Selecting Multiple Clips 82
    Adjusting a Selection 82
    Playing a Selection 83
    Deselecting 84
    Selecting Specific Project Elements 84
Phase 3: Build the Storyboard 85
    Adding to the End of the Storyboard 85
    Adding to the Middle 87
    Advanced Insert Options 87
    The Orange Stripe 91
    Don't Remember to Save 91

Phases 2 to 3 (Alternate): Paint-to-Insert 91
Phase 4: Fine-Tune the Edit 93
Storyboard Playback 93
Full-Screen Playback 94
Rearranging Video 95
Copying and Pasting Video 96
Shortening or Lengthening Clips 97
    Select a Piece to Delete 98
    Select the Piece to Keep 99
    Use the Clip Trimmer 100
    Fine-Tuning with the Extendo Buttons 101
Splitting a Clip 102
Cutaways 103
    Adjusting a Cutaway 104
    Removing a Cutaway 105
The Precision Editor 105

Chapter 4: Video Chunks: Keywords, People, Favorites, and Rejects 109

Marking Favorites and Rejects: The Two-Step Method 110
Marking Favorites and Rejects: The One-Step Method 110
Unmarking 112
Selecting Marked Footage 112
Hiding and Showing Favorites and Rejects 112
Keywords 113
    Editing the Keyword List 115
    "Painting" Keywords onto Clips 115
    The Select-then-Apply Method 116
    Removing Keywords from Filmstrips 116
People 117
    Analyzing for People 117
    People Keywords 118
The Keyword/People Filter 118
Deleting Footage for Good 119
Space Saver 121

Chapter 5: Transitions, Themes, Travel Maps, and Animatics . . 125

About Transitions 125
When Not to Use Transitions 126
Two Ways to "Transish" 127
Creating Individual Transition Effects 127
    Changing or Deleting a Transition 129
A Long Discussion of Transition Lengths 129
    Why You Don't Always Get What You Want 131
    How Transitions Affect the Length of Your Movie 132

Automatic Transitions 133
   Adjusting Automatic Transitions 134
   Turning off Automatic Transitions 134
Transitions: The iMovie Catalog. 135
   Circle Open, Circle Close. 135
   Cross Blur 136
   Cross Dissolve 136
   Cross Zoom 136
   Doorway 136
   Fade Through Black, Fade Through White 136
   Mosaic 137
   Page Curl 137
   Ripple. 138
   Spin In, Spin Out 138
   Swap 138
   Wipe Down, Up, Left, Right. 138
Themes 139
   Choosing a Theme 139
   Custom Theme Transition and Titles. 141
   Changing a Theme 141
   Adjusting Theme Transitions 142
   Customizing the Sports Theme. 144
   Removing a Theme 146
Travel Maps 146
   Adding a Travel Map 146
   Changing Travel Points 147
   Changing a Map's Style 148
   Changing a Map's Timing 148
   Removing a Map 149
Animatics 150
   Building a Storyboard with Animatics 150
   Print Your Storyboard for Filming 151
   Build Your Movie from Your Storyboard 151

Chapter 6: Video Effects **153**
Video Effects. 154
   The Effects 154
   Applying a Video Effect. 155
   Adjusting a Video Effect 157
   Removing a Video Effect 157
Fast/Slow/Reverse. 157
   Changing a Clip's Speed 157
   Reversing a Clip's Playback Direction 158
   Removing Speed and Direction Changes 159

Green Screen/Blue Screen 159
   Preparing a Green Screen 161
   Getting the Shot 162
   Inserting a Green Screen Effect 163
   Adding Effects to a Green Screen Effect 165
   Removing a Green Screen Effect 165
Picture-in-Picture (PiP) 165
   Inserting a PiP 166
   Adjusting the PiP Size and Position 166
   Changing the PiP Appearance 167
   Mixing PiP Audio 168
   Moving and Trimming a PiP Clip 169
   Removing a PiP Clip 169
Side-by-Side 169
   Changing the Side-by-Side Appearance 170
One-Step Effects 170

Chapter 7: Stabilization, Color Fixes, Cropping, and Rotating . . 175

Video Stabilization 176
   Four Ways to Trigger Stabilization Analysis 176
   Fixing Shaky Footage 178
   Jellyroll Footage 181
Color Fixes 182
   Phase 1: Select the Clip, Find the Frame 182
   Phase 2: The Video Adjustments Panel 183
   Three Channels 184
   Exposure 184
   Adjusting the Levels 185
   Brightness and Contrast Sliders 186
   Automatic Correction 187
   Color Balance 188
   Individual Channel Sliders 189
   Removing or Adjusting Adjustments 190
   Copying and Pasting Adjustments 191
Cropping Video 191
   Adjusting or Removing a Crop 195
Rotating Video 195
   Adjusting or Removing the Rotation 197

Chapter 8: Titles, Subtitles, and Credits 199

Setting Up a Title 199
   Choose a Title Style 200
   Drag the Title into Position 204
   Adjust the Timing 207
   Type the Text 208
   Special Notes on Scrolling Credits 209

Font, Size, and Style 210
   The iMovie Font Panel 212
   The System Font Panel 213
   General Guidelines 216
   Add Your Own Custom Title 217
Checking the Result 219
Editing or Deleting a Title 220

Chapter 9: Narration, Music, and Sound 223

Three Kinds of Audio 223
   Audio Sources 224
Adding Audio to the Storyboard 225
   The Music and Sound Effects Browser 225
   Adding Audio from the Finder 227
Background Music 228
   Pinning and Unpinning Background Music 229
   Rearranging Unpinned Background Music 232
   Deleting Background Audio 234
Sound Effects (Pinned Music) 234
Editing to the Beat 235
   Phase 1: Add Your Background Music 236
   Phase 2a: Insert Beat Markers 236
   Phase 2b: Tapping Out Beats 237
   Phase 3: Add Your Video Clips 238
   Snap to Beats in Your Project 238
   Beat Markers in the Precision Editor 239
   The Beat Warning 240
Recording Narration 240
Extracting Audio from Video 244
Volume Adjustments 246
   The Rubber Band: A Re-Introduction 247
   Using the Other Volume Tools 249
   Adjusting Overall Clip Volume 249
Multiple Clip Adjustments 252
Removing Audio Adjustments 253
Audio Effects, Enhancements, and Equalizers 253
   Audio Effects 253
   Enhance Audio 255
   The Equalizer 256
Editing Audio in GarageBand 257
   GarageBand Basics 257
   Scoring in GarageBand 259

Chapter 10: Photos **261**

Importing Still Images 261

The Photo Browser 263

    Photos from the Finder 265

    iMovie Backgrounds 266

Two Ways to Add Photos 267

    Photo Filmstrips 267

    Photo Cutaways 268

    Timing Changes 271

The Dimensions of an iMovie Photo 272

Crop, Fit, Rotate 272

The Ken Burns Effect 273

    Applying the Ken Burns Effect 274

Creating Still Images from Footage 276

    Creating a Still Frame 277

    Creating a Freeze Frame 278

Exporting a Still Frame 279

    The Resolution Problem 279

    The Long Way 280

Chapter 11: Movie Trailers **283**

Trailers Basics 284

    Starting a Trailer Project 284

    The Outline 285

    The Storyboard 286

    The Shot List 286

The Trailers Catalog 287

Building Your Trailer 289

Customizing Your Trailer 290

    Converting to a Project 292

Chapter 12: Advanced Editing **295**

The Power of Editing 295

    Modern Film Theory 296

    Maintaining Continuity 297

    When to Cut 298

    Choosing the Next Shot 298

Popular Editing Techniques 299

    Tight Editing 299

    Variety of Shots 299

Back and Forth to iMovie 6 302

    Transferring Your Project, iMovie '11→iMovie 6 303

    Transferring Your Project, iMovie 6→iMovie '11 304

Part Two: Finding Your Audience

Chapter 13: Exporting to iPod, iPhone, iPad, Apple TV,
or Front Row **309**
Exporting the Movie to iTunes 309
From iTunes to iPod, iPhone, and So On 311

Chapter 14: Exporting to YouTube and the Web **313**
iMovie to YouTube 314
Posting to YouTube (The First Time) 314
Posting to YouTube (After the First Time) 317
After the YouTube Movie Is Up 317
iMovie to MobileMe 319
After Your MobileMe Movie Is Up 321
iMovie to Facebook 322
Posting to Facebook 322
After the Facebook Movie Is Up 322
iMovie to Vimeo 323
Uploading to Vimeo 324
After the Vimeo Movie Is Up 324
iMovie to CNN iReport 324
Uploading to iReport 326
After the iReport Is Up 327
Custom Web Pages: Two Roads 327
iMovie to iWeb 328
Posting a Movie on Your Site 331

Chapter 15: From iMovie to QuickTime **333**
Understanding QuickTime 333
A Crash Course in Video Compression 335
About Codecs 338
The Export Pop-up Menu 338
The Video Settings Button 340
The Filter Button 344
The Size Button 345
Audio Settings 346
The Video Codecs: A Catalog 348
Saving a QuickTime Movie 350

Chapter 16: QuickTime Player **353**
QuickTime Player X 354
Sharing with QuickTime Player X 354
Trimming Your Movies 356
Recording in QuickTime Player X 357
QuickTime Player 7 (Free Version) 358
Hidden Controls 360
Fancy Playback Tricks 360

QuickTime Player Pro 362
    Presenting Your Movies 363
    Editing Movies 363
    Exporting Edited Movies 366
Advanced QuickTime Pro: Track Tricks 367
    Flip a Clip 369
    The Video Wall 369

Part Three: iDVD '11

Chapter 17: iDVD Basics 373
Why iDVD? 373
    Getting iDVD 374
What You're in For 374
Phase 1: Prepare Your Video 375
    Overscanning and You 375
Phase 2: Insert Chapter Markers 378
    Markers in iMovie '11 380
Phase 3: Export from iMovie '11 381
    Export Your Movie as a File 382
Phase 4: Design the Menu Screen 382
    All About Themes 385
    Choosing a Theme 386
    The Inevitable Paragraphs About Aspect Ratio 388
    Drop Zones: The Basics 389
    Redesigning the Theme 391
Phase 5: Add Your Movies 391
Phase 6: Burning Your DVD 391
    Previewing Your Project 391
    Checking for Errors 392
    Maximum DVD Playback Time 392
    One Last Techie Look 395
    Shopping for Blank DVDs 396
    The Burn 396
OneStep DVDs and Magic iDVDs 397
    OneStep DVD 398
    Magic iDVDs 399

Chapter 18: DVD Menus, Slideshows, and the Map 403
Adding Movies 403
    The Import Command 404
    The Finder 404
    The Media Browser 404
Submenus ("Folders") 406
    Navigating Submenus 406

The DVD Map—and Autoplay 408
   Editing in the Map 410
   Autoplay 410
   Looping 412
DVD Slideshows 412
   iPhoto Albums 413
   Drag Folders from the Finder 414
   Add a Slideshow, Worry About the Pictures Later 415
   The Slideshow Editor 415
   Slideshow Settings 416
   Slideshow Options 417
   Leaving the Slideshow Editor 419
   Burning Your Slideshow 419

Chapter 19: Designing iDVD Themes 421

iDVD's Built-In Themes 421
Editing Buttons 422
   Changing Button Names and Fonts 422
   Button Styles 423
   Justification, Drop Shadows, and Thumbnail Size 425
   Repositioning Buttons 425
   Removing Buttons 426
   Editing Picture and Movie Buttons 426
Editing Text 427
Editing Backgrounds 428
   A Still Photo 429
   A Group of Photos 430
   A Movie 431
   Some Notes 432
Menu Audio 432
   What to Drag 432
   Where to Drag 433
   Replacing Menu Audio 434
   Removing Menu Audio 434
   Adjusting Menu Audio Volume 435
Saving Favorites 435

Chapter 20: Advanced iDVD **437**

iDVD: The DVD-ROM Maker 437
   Adding Files to the DVD-ROM Area 438
   Organizing DVD-ROM Contents 438
Uncover Your DVD Project File 439
Automator and iDVD 441
Archiving Your Project 442
   Copying an Archive to a Different Mac 444
Disk Images 444
Professional Duplicating 446
   Prepare to Copy 447
   Choosing a Replicator 448
   Working with Replicators 448
   Fulfillment 448

Part Four: Appendixes

Appendix A: iMovie '11, Menu by Menu **453**

Appendix B: Troubleshooting **477**

Appendix C: Master Keyboard Shortcut List **485**

Appendix D: Visual Cheat Sheet **489**

Index **493**

The Missing Credits

About the Authors

David Pogue (original author, editor) is the weekly tech columnist for the *New York Times*, an Emmy-winning correspondent for *CBS News Sunday Morning*, weekly CNBC contributor, and the creator of the Missing Manual series. He's the author or co-author of 50 books, including 24 in this series and six in the *"For Dummies"* line (including *Macs, Magic, Opera*, and *Classical Music*). In his other life, David is a former Broadway show conductor, a piano player, and a magician. He lives in Connecticut with his three awesome children.

Links to his columns and weekly videos await at *www.davidpogue.com*. He welcomes feedback about his books by email at *david@pogueman.com*.

Aaron Miller (author, '09 and '11 updates) is a part-time lawyer and part-time professor. He also authors the blog Unlocking iMovie (*http://unlockingimovie.blogspot.com*), his own little way of trying to make the Mac world a better place. If he's not at his computer, he's probably playing Ultimate Frisbee or "tickle monster" with his kids. Email: *ilifer08@gmail.com*.

About the Creative Team

Peter McKie (editor) lives in New York City and can be found exploring abandoned buildings and researching the history of old structures. Email: *pmckie@oreilly.com*.

Dan Fauxsmith (production editor) lives in Belmont, Massachusetts. From time to time, he photographs and identifies plants for his website (*www.theplantbase.com*).

Julie Hawks (indexer) is an indexer for the Missing Manual series. She is currently pursuing a Masters degree in Religious Studies while discovering the joys of warm winters in the Carolinas. Email: *juliehawks@gmail.com*.

Acknowledgments

The Missing Manual series is a joint venture between Pogue Press (the dream team introduced on these pages) and O'Reilly Media (a dream publishing partner). I'm indebted, as always, to Tim O'Reilly, Laurie Petrycki, Peter Meyers, and the rest of the gang.

The book in your hands is an updated version of *iMovie '09 & iDVD: The Missing Manual,* so it represents a lot of effort from that earlier book's production staff. That includes copy editor Teresa Noelle Roberts, photographer Tim Geaney, layout designer Phil Simpson, iDVD guru Erica Sadun, and graphics goddess Lesa Snider King.

Thanks to Randy Ubillos, the creator of iMovie '11; David Rogelberg, my agent; and especially to Aaron Miller, who cheerfully undertook the challenge of updating this book to reflect the changes in iMovie '11 without making it sound like two different authors were at work. He did a seamless, witty, professional job.

Above all, thanks to Kelly, Tia, and Jeffrey, whose patience and sacrifices make these books—and everything else—possible.

—David Pogue

Many thanks to David Pogue for another great opportunity to collaborate and for his masterful writing and editing (even if keeping up with his writing prowess felt like chasing an Olympic sprinter). Thanks as well to Peter McKie for expert support and guidance, and to the O'Reilly professionals behind the scenes who make it all look incredible.

Thanks to Peter Miller for great advice, and to all the friends and family members whose smiling faces appear throughout the book. Great thanks as well to my colleagues in the Romney Institute of Public Management and the Marriott School of Management at BYU, where I am surrounded by great thinkers and talented writers.

I also join with Mac users everywhere in giving thanks to Randy Ubillos and the entire iMovie team, whose abilities turn our home movies into treasures. Warmest thanks, in particular, to Randy for kindly and patiently answering questions.

Finally, my deepest gratitude to Katie, Luke, Sam, Thomas, and Seth for love, support, and antics that make great home movies.

—Aaron Miller

The Missing Manual Series

Missing Manuals are witty, superbly written guides to computer products that don't come with printed manuals (which is just about all of them). Each book features a handcrafted index and cross-references to specific pages (not just chapters).

Recent and upcoming titles include:

Access 2007: The Missing Manual by Matthew MacDonald

Access 2010: The Missing Manual by Matthew MacDonald

Buying a Home: The Missing Manual by Nancy Conner

CSS: The Missing Manual, Second Edition, by David Sawyer McFarland

Creating a Web Site: The Missing Manual, Second Edition, by Matthew MacDonald

David Pogue's Digital Photography: The Missing Manual by David Pogue

Droid X: The Missing Manual by Preston Gralla

Dreamweaver CS4: The Missing Manual by David Sawyer McFarland

Dreamweaver CS5: The Missing Manual by David Sawyer McFarland

Excel 2007: The Missing Manual by Matthew MacDonald

Excel 2010: The Missing Manual by Matthew MacDonald

Facebook: The Missing Manual, Second Edition, by E.A. Vander Veer

FileMaker Pro 10: The Missing Manual by Susan Prosser and Geoff Coffey

FileMaker Pro 11: The Missing Manual by Susan Prosser and Stuart Gripman

Flash CS4: The Missing Manual by Chris Grover with E.A. Vander Veer

Flash CS5: The Missing Manual by Chris Grover

Google Apps: The Missing Manual by Nancy Conner

The Internet: The Missing Manual by David Pogue and J.D. Biersdorfer

iMovie '08 & iDVD: The Missing Manual by David Pogue

iMovie '09 & iDVD: The Missing Manual by David Pogue and Aaron Miller

iPad: The Missing Manual by J.D. Biersdorfer

iPhone: The Missing Manual, Fourth Edition, by David Pogue

iPhone App Development: The Missing Manual by Craig Hockenberry

iPhoto '11: The Missing Manual by David Pogue and Lesa Snider

iPod: The Missing Manual, Eighth Edition, by J.D. Biersdorfer and David Pogue

JavaScript: The Missing Manual by David Sawyer McFarland

Living Green: The Missing Manual by Nancy Conner

Mac OS X: The Missing Manual, Leopard Edition, by David Pogue

Microsoft Project 2007: The Missing Manual by Bonnie Biafore

Microsoft Project 2010: The Missing Manual by Bonnie Biafore

Netbooks: The Missing Manual by J.D. Biersdorfer

Office 2007: The Missing Manual by Chris Grover, Matthew MacDonald, and E.A. Vander Veer

Office 2010: The Missing Manual by Nancy Connor, Chris Grover, and Matthew MacDonald

Office 2008 for Macintosh: The Missing Manual by Jim Elferdink

Office 2010 for Macintosh: The Missing Manual by Chris Grover

Palm Pre: The Missing Manual by Ed Baig

PCs: The Missing Manual by Andy Rathbone

Personal Investing: The Missing Manual by Bonnie Biafore

Photoshop CS4: The Missing Manual by Lesa Snider

Photoshop CS5: The Missing Manual by Lesa Snider

Photoshop Elements 7: The Missing Manual by Barbara Brundage

Photoshop Elements 8 for Mac: The Missing Manual by Barbara Brundage

Photoshop Elements 8 for Windows: The Missing Manual by Barbara Brundage

Photoshop Elements 9: The Missing Manual by Barbara Brundage

PowerPoint 2007: The Missing Manual by E.A. Vander Veer

Premiere Elements 8: The Missing Manual by Chris Grover

QuickBase: The Missing Manual by Nancy Conner

QuickBooks 2010: The Missing Manual by Bonnie Biafore

QuickBooks 2011: The Missing Manual by Bonnie Biafore

Quicken 2009: The Missing Manual by Bonnie Biafore

Switching to the Mac: The Missing Manual, Leopard Edition, by David Pogue

Switching to the Mac: The Missing Manual, Snow Leopard Edition, by David Pogue

Wikipedia: The Missing Manual by John Broughton

Windows Vista: The Missing Manual by David Pogue

Windows 7: The Missing Manual by David Pogue

Word 2007: The Missing Manual by Chris Grover

Your Body: The Missing Manual by Matthew MacDonald

Your Brain: The Missing Manual by Matthew MacDonald

Your Money: The Missing Manual by J.D. Roth

Int

iMovie is
corder or

That's a bi
You know
some neig
a trip to M

Deep dow
improved
along, edi
worth of c
horsepowe
editing foc

Then alon
pros call *n*
a videotap
through ev
rewinding
you put yo

The world
ing cards.
quit their c
weddings a
ing a new s

If you have

improve the quality of that footage. And using iMovie, you can delete all but the best scenes (and edit out those humiliating parts where you walked for 20 minutes with the camcorder filming the ground bouncing beneath it).

This, too, is where iMovie's Internet smarts come into play. Instead of burning and shipping a DVD of your home movies, you can shoot the finished product to the Web, where your lucky, lucky family and friends can enjoy them.

- **Web movies**. But why limit your aspirations to people you know? This is the YouTube Era, dude. If you've got something funny or interesting on "film," why not share it with the Internet population at large? In iMovie, YouTube, Vimeo, MobileMe, and Facebook are only one menu command away—and that's just the beginning. New film festivals, websites, and magazines are springing up everywhere, all dedicated to independent makers of *short* movies.

- **Business videos**. It's very easy to post video on the Internet or burn it onto a cheap, recordable CD or DVD, as described in Part 3 of this book. As a result, you should consider video a useful tool in whatever you do. If you're a real estate agent, blow away your rivals (and save your clients time) by showing movies, not still photos, of the properties you represent. If you're an executive, quit boring your comrades with stupefying PowerPoint slides and make your point with video instead.

- **Video photo albums**. A video photo album can be much more exciting, accessible, and engaging than a paper one. Start by filming or scanning your photos. Assemble them into a sequence, and add some crossfades, titles, and music. The result is a much more interesting display than a book of motionless images, thanks in part to iMovie's Ken Burns effect (see "Crop, Fit, Rotate" on page 272). This emerging video form is becoming very popular—videographers charge a lot of money to create "living photo albums" for their clients.

- **Just-for-fun projects**. Never again can anyone over the age of 8 complain that there's "nothing to do." Set them loose with a camcorder and instructions to make a fake rock video, commercial, or documentary.

- **Training films**. If there's a better use for video than how-to instruction, you'd be hard-pressed to name it. Make a video for new employees to show them the ropes. Create a video that ships with your product to give a humanizing touch to your company and help the customer make the most of her purchase. Make a DVD that teaches newcomers how to play the banjo, grow a garden, kick a football, use a computer program—and then market it.

- **Interviews**. You're lucky enough to live in an age where you can manipulate video clips in a movie just as easily as you do words in a word processor. Capitalize on this fact. Create family histories. Film relatives who still remember the War, the Birth, the Immigration. Or create a time-capsule, time-lapse film: Ask your kid or your parent the same four questions every year on his or her birthday (such as, "What's your greatest worry right now?" or "If you had one wish…?" or "Where do you want to be in five years?"). Then, after 5 or 10 or 20 years, splice together the answers for an enlightening fast-forward through a human life.

Introduction

iMovie is video-editing software. It grabs a copy of the raw footage on your camcorder or camera and lets you edit it easily, quickly, and creatively.

That's a big deal, because over the years, home movies have developed a bad name. You know what it's like watching other people's camcorder footage. You're captive on some neighbor's couch after dessert to witness 60 excruciating, unedited minutes of a trip to Mexico, or 25 too many minutes of a baby wearing a spaghetti bowl.

Deep down, most people realize that the home-movie viewing experience could be improved if the video were edited down to just the good parts. But until iMovie came along, editing camcorder footage on a computer required several thousand dollars' worth of digitizing cards, extremely complicated editing software, and the highest-horsepower computer equipment available. Unless there was a paycheck involved, editing footage under those circumstances just wasn't worth it.

Then along came iMovie, the world's least expensive version of what Hollywood pros call *nonlinear* editing software. In the old days, your recorded footage sat on a videotape, and you edited it in linear fashion—you rewound and fast-forwarded through every frame of the tape to get to the parts you wanted. Nowadays, there's no rewinding or fast-forwarding; you jump instantly to any piece of footage you want as you put your movie together.

The world of video is exploding. People give each other DVDs instead of greeting cards. People watch each other via video on their websites. And some people quit their daily-grind jobs to become videographers for hire, making money filming weddings and creating living video scrapbooks. Video, in other words, is fast becoming a new standard in communication for the new century.

If you have iMovie and a camera, you'll be ready.

The Difficult Birth of the New iMovie

Within six months of its release in October 1999, iMovie had become, in the words of beaming iMovie papa (and Apple CEO) Steve Jobs, "the most popular video-editing software in the world."

Apple only fanned the flames when it released iMovie 2 in July 2000 (for $50), iMovie 3 in January 2003 (for free), and then—as part of the iLife software suite—iMovie 4, iMovie HD, and iMovie 6 in successive Januaries.

Then, in August 2007, Apple dropped a bombshell. Or, rather, it dropped iMovie.

The company's new consumer video-editing program, called iMovie '08, was, in fact, not iMovie at all. It was a totally different program, using all-new code and a different design, and built by different people. It was conceived, according to Steve Jobs, by Randy Ubillos, an Apple programmer who wanted to edit down his vacation footage—but found the old iMovie too slow and complicated. So the guy sat down and wrote his own little program, focused primarily on editing speed above all. Steve loved it, and decided that it would replace the old iMovie.

Many people were stunned by Apple's move—and I, your humble author, was among them. In my *New York Times* email column, I wrote about just how different iMovie '08 was from its predecessors:

> iMovie '08 has been totally misnamed. It's not iMovie at all. It's designed for an utterly different task.
>
> The new iMovie, for example, is probably the only video-editing program on the market with no timeline—no horizontal, scrolling strip that displays your clips laid end to end, with their lengths representing their durations. You have no indication of how many minutes into your movie you are.
>
> The new iMovie also gets a D for audio editing. You can't manually adjust audio levels during a scene (for example, to make the music quieter when someone is speaking). All the old audio effects are gone, too. No pitch changing, high-pass and low-pass filters, or reverb.
>
> The new iMovie doesn't accept plug-ins, either. You can't add chapter markers for use in iDVD, which is supposed to be integrated with iMovie. Bookmarks are gone. Themes are gone. You can no longer export only part of a movie. And you can't export a movie back to tape—only to the Internet or to a file.
>
> All visual effects are gone—even basic options like slow motion, reverse motion, and fast motion. Incredibly, the new iMovie can't even convert older iMovie projects. All you can import is the clips themselves. None of your transitions, titles, credits, music, or special effects are preserved.
>
> On top of all that, this more limited iMovie has steep horsepower requirements that rule out most computers older than about two years old.

Pretty harsh, I know. But listen, I was an absolute whiz at iMovie 6. I knew it like the back of my mouse. And it looked to me like Apple was junking that mature, powerful program for what amounted to a video slideshow program.

Fortunately, Apple restored many of those "doesn't haves" in iMovie '09. The last major missing feature, detailed audio editing, showed up in your version of the program, iMovie '11. Furthermore, iMovie '11 comes with so many useful features of its own, it's far more difficult to resist.

It's more modern than the old iMovie, for example. It's equally adept at importing video from tapeless camcorders (DVD, hard drive, or memory-card models)—and from digital still cameras—as it is at importing from tape. And it's all hooked up to the Web, so you can post your masterpiece on YouTube, MobileMe, or Vimeo with a single command.

Then there are the cool features that the old iMovie could only dream about. Image-stabilizing, color-correction, and frame-cropping tools are unprecedented in a consumer program. The new trailers builder is downright awesome. You can really, truly delete unwanted pieces of your clips, thus reclaiming hard drive space. (iMovie HD, on the other hand, preserved an entire 20-minute clip on your hard drive even if you used only 3 seconds of it.)

iMovie '11 also creates titles, crossfades, and color adjustments instantly. There's no "rendering" time, as there was in the old iMovie. So you gain an exhilarating freedom to play, to fiddle with the timing and placement of things, without having to watch your computer crunch the effect for 5 minutes only to decide you don't like it.

So, no, iMovie '11 is not a descendant of the old iMovies. It's the latest generation of a different program, with a different focus and a different audience. But it's here to stay, and it has plenty of charms of its own.

iDVD

As you may have noticed, this iMovie book comes with a free bonus book: *iDVD: The Missing Manual*, which constitutes Chapters 17 through 20. iDVD can preserve your movies on home-recorded DVDs that look and behave amazingly close to the commercial DVDs you rent from Netflix or Blockbuster.

iDVD '11 isn't what you'd call a huge update from the previous version; in fact, this is the second time it's been put into iLife without *any* updates. (That's right, this is the same iDVD you would have bought over *three* years ago.) Be grateful that Apple even kept it alive, considering how strongly it feels about the DVD being a dead technology.

iMovie: What's It Good For?

If you're reading this book, you probably have some ideas about what you'd do if you could make professional-looking videos. Here are a few possibilities that may not have occurred to you. All are natural projects for iMovie:

- **Home movies**. Plain old home movies—casual documentaries of your life, your kids' lives, your school life, your trips—are the single most popular creation of camcorder owners. Using the suggestions in the following chapters, you can improve the quality of that footage. And using iMovie, you can delete all but the best scenes (and edit out those humiliating parts where you walked for 20 minutes with the camcorder filming the ground bouncing beneath it).

This, too, is where iMovie's Internet smarts come into play. Instead of burning and shipping a DVD of your home movies, you can shoot the finished product to the Web, where your lucky, lucky family and friends can enjoy them.

- **Web movies**. But why limit your aspirations to people you know? This is the YouTube Era, dude. If you've got something funny or interesting on "film," why not share it with the Internet population at large? In iMovie, YouTube, Vimeo, MobileMe, and Facebook are only one menu command away—and that's just the beginning. New film festivals, websites, and magazines are springing up everywhere, all dedicated to independent makers of *short* movies.

- **Business videos**. It's very easy to post video on the Internet or burn it onto a cheap, recordable CD or DVD, as described in Part 3 of this book. As a result, you should consider video a useful tool in whatever you do. If you're a real estate agent, blow away your rivals (and save your clients time) by showing movies, not still photos, of the properties you represent. If you're an executive, quit boring your comrades with stupefying PowerPoint slides and make your point with video instead.

- **Video photo albums**. A video photo album can be much more exciting, accessible, and engaging than a paper one. Start by filming or scanning your photos. Assemble them into a sequence, and add some crossfades, titles, and music. The result is a much more interesting display than a book of motionless images, thanks in part to iMovie's Ken Burns effect (see "Crop, Fit, Rotate" on page 272). This emerging video form is becoming very popular—videographers charge a lot of money to create "living photo albums" for their clients.

- **Just-for-fun projects**. Never again can anyone over the age of 8 complain that there's "nothing to do." Set them loose with a camcorder and instructions to make a fake rock video, commercial, or documentary.

- **Training films**. If there's a better use for video than how-to instruction, you'd be hard-pressed to name it. Make a video for new employees to show them the ropes. Create a video that ships with your product to give a humanizing touch to your company and help the customer make the most of her purchase. Make a DVD that teaches newcomers how to play the banjo, grow a garden, kick a football, use a computer program—and then market it.

- **Interviews**. You're lucky enough to live in an age where you can manipulate video clips in a movie just as easily as you do words in a word processor. Capitalize on this fact. Create family histories. Film relatives who still remember the War, the Birth, the Immigration. Or create a time-capsule, time-lapse film: Ask your kid or your parent the same four questions every year on his or her birthday (such as, "What's your greatest worry right now?" or "If you had one wish…?" or "Where do you want to be in five years?"). Then, after 5 or 10 or 20 years, splice together the answers for an enlightening fast-forward through a human life.

- **Broadcast segments**. Want a taste of the real world? Call your cable TV company about its public-access channels. (As required by law, every cable company offers a channel or two for ordinary citizens to use for their own programming.) Find out the time and format restraints, and then make a documentary, short film, or other piece for actual broadcast. Advertise the airing to everyone you know. It's a small-time start, but it's real broadcasting.

  Of course, you could skip the small time and upload your videos straight from iMovie to CNN's iReport website. Here, amateur reporters post their own news items for all the world to watch. On occasion, CNN even turns to these videos for their nationwide broadcasts.

- **Analyze performances**. There's no better way to improve your golf swing, tennis form, musical performance, or public speaking style than to study footage of yourself. If you're a teacher, camp counselor, or coach, film your students, campers, or players so that they can benefit from self-analysis, too.

- **Turn photos into video**. Technically, you don't need a camcorder at all to use iMovie; it's equally adept at importing and presenting still photos from a scanner or digital camera. In fact, iMovie's Ken Burns effect brings still photos to life, gently zooming into them, fading from shot to shot, panning across them, and so on, making iMovie the world's best slideshow creator.

A Camcorder Crash Course

For years, when you said "camcorder," people understood that you meant *tape* camcorder. And until recently, that meant recording onto MiniDV cassettes.

The popularity of digital tape camcorders is crashing, however. Their sales have been declining 10 to 15 percent a year.

As you can imagine, these numbers caused some consternation at the headquarters of Sony, Canon, and other camcorder makers. What's going on? Don't people want to preserve memories of their lives anymore?

As best they can tell, the problem is the cassettes themselves. They're too hard to find in the drawer when the neighbors want to see highlights of your latest vacation, and they take too long to rewind and fast-forward.

What the world wants, the camcorder manufacturers realized, is *random access:* the ability to jump directly to any scene without having to wait. In theory, a tapeless camcorder also saves time because, when you transfer your video to your computer to edit it, you don't have to play the tape back from the camcorder start to finish in real time. The camcorder stores your video on a memory card, hard drive, or DVD as regular computer files, which you should be able to simply drag and drop onto your Mac's hard drive. (In practice, it doesn't quite work out that way—see page 36—but you get the idea.)

That's why the camcorder industry has been flooding the stores with tapeless cameras, ones that record onto memory cards, hard drives, or little DVDs—anything but tape.

The Downsides of Going Tapeless

It used to be that tapeless camcorders couldn't match the incredible video quality of MiniDV tape cameras. To store a reasonable amount of video on a tiny memory card, hard drive, or DVD, the camera has to *compress* it to an alarming degree, using less information to describe each frame of video. Video recorded onto MiniDV tapes, on the other hand, is essentially uncompressed. What you record is what you see on playback.

Everything changed with the advent of High Definition, or HD, compression techniques. Camera manufacturers figured out a multitude of ways to compress very high quality video onto small storage media. Today, most tapeless HD camcorders match or even surpass MiniDV quality. (Some HD cameras still use tape, but tapeless storage is fast becoming the standard.) The technological magic here doesn't come without consequence, however. Some HD formats, for example, require a fast computer to edit them. (You'll find more details about HD video and its significance in the next section.)

Remember, too, that each kind of tapeless camcorder has its own kinds of storage limitations:

- **DVD camcorders**. The miniature blank DVDs used by DVD camcorders generally hold only 20 minutes of video apiece—and only 15 minutes of high-definition video. (Some models can record onto the newer double-sided discs, which roughly doubles the recording time.) And you can't play the resulting disc in a regular DVD player unless you first "finalize" it, a sort of software shrink-wrapping process that can take 10 or 15 minutes inside the camcorder. In fact, you can't play the resulting DVDs on a *Mac* at all. Macs expect full-size DVDs; these miniature, 8-centimeter discs can literally trash your drive.

- **Hard-drive camcorders** can record several hours of video (say, 5 hours at the highest quality) before running out of space—but at that point, you're dead in the water. Your camcorder is useless until it has a date with your computer, so you can dump the video off the camcorder to empty its hard drive.

- **Memory-card camcorders** might be able to store, for example, 1 hour of video on a 4 gigabyte memory card. And you can carry a couple of extras around in case of emergency. But memory cards are still too expensive for long-term storage. In other words, nobody but Donald Trump can afford to buy a new memory card for every vacation, holiday, and wedding. Everybody else transfers their video to their computer when the memory card gets full.

Tip: The new world of tapeless camcorders is filled with exceptions, footnotes, and caveats. Apple notes a few of the iMovie/camera quirks here—*http://help.apple.com/imovie/cameras*—but the best advice is to run a Google search before you buy any camcorder to ensure it's compatible with iMovie. (Search for *Sony SR7 iMovie 11*, for example.)

High Definition

A growing number of camcorders film in gorgeous, widescreen, ultrasharp *high definition* format. The video looks absolutely incredible on an HDTV set. Your own life looks like a Hollywood movie crew filmed it.

If you're shopping for a camcorder now, you should seriously consider going high-def. High-definition camcorders are available in both tape and tapeless models. The really cool thing about the tape models, in fact, is that they record onto ordinary MiniDV cassettes, exactly the same ones used by regular tape camcorders. The signal recorded on these tapes is different, of course—it's in a format called HDV—but you still get the convenience and economy of those ordinary drugstore tapes (Figure I-1).

Figure I-1:
High-def camcorders, like the Canon HV40, record onto ordinary MiniDV tapes. The image quality is anything but ordinary, however.

You may as well start filming your life in high definition now, because, in a few years, standard definition will look as quaint as daguerreotype photographs.

AVCHD, MPEG-2, and Other Jargon

Tapeless camcorders store videos as ordinary computer files—on a DVD, hard drive, or memory card—that you can copy to your Mac and edit in iMovie. But what are those files? Every computer document gets stored in some kind of standardized format, whether it's JPEG (the usual format for photos) or TXT (text files). So what format do video files come in?

MPEG

Some digital camcorders, especially old ones, record in formats called MPEG-1 and MPEG-2. Many tapeless HD cameras, especially the smaller, less expensive ones, record in MPEG-4. (The abbreviation stands for Motion Picture Experts Group, the association of geeks who dream up these standards.) iMovie '11 recognizes and imports MPEG-2—usually. Unfortunately, there are multiple flavors of MPEG-2, and iMovie doesn't recognize them all.

iMovie can also work with movies created by most digital still cameras, like .mov, .avi, and MPEG-4 files. Here again, though, your mileage may vary.

Tip: It's worth repeating: If you're tempted to buy a certain camcorder but you're not sure if it uses a file format that iMovie works with, Google it.

You should also know that the MPEG-4 clips from an HD camera will play fine on modern Macs. A 3- or 4-year-old Mac, because of its older, slower processor, *can* edit these files, but things like iMovie's skimming feature and full-screen playback will be a bit choppy.

AVCHD

The good news is that iMovie also recognizes *AVCHD*, which is the most popular file format for high-definition tapeless camcorders. (It stands for Advanced Video Coding/High Definition, and yes, it's an annoying acronym. Do they really think they're going to make video editing more attractive by dreaming up names like this?)

Anyway, AVCHD is a high-def format concocted by Sony and Panasonic in 2006, and is now available on camcorders from Sony, Panasonic, Canon, Samsung, and others. It offers roughly the same video quality as MPEG-2 or MPEG-4, but takes up even less space on your camcorder's memory card, MiniDVD, or hard drive.

As it turns out, AVCHD cameras can produce the same quality video as H.264 movies, the video format Blu-ray high-definition DVD discs use (and also the format of videos from the iTunes Store). That's a handy feature for people who own both an AVCHD camcorder that records onto miniature DVDs and a Blu-ray DVD player (or Playstation 3), because you can pop the DVD right out of the camcorder and into the Blu-ray player to watch it on your TV.

That's the good news. The bad news is that AVCHD files take up a lot of space; an AVCHD DVD camcorder holds only 15 minutes of best-quality video per disc!

The bigger bummer is that AVCHD video doesn't take kindly to being edited. When you import an AVCHD video to iMovie, for example, your Mac first converts it to a format you can edit (see page 48), which takes a very long time. In fact, 1 hour's worth of video takes over 2 hours to convert, which neatly cancels out the time you'd save importing video from a tapeless camcorder instead of a MiniDV tape camcorder.

AVCHD Lite

AVCHD Lite, a newer format found in a lot of Panasonic cameras, is a slimmed-down version of AVCHD. Instead of recording full-blown 1080p HD video, it maxes out at 720p. That's still hi-def, but not quite as hungry for memory card and hard drive space as its big brother. And many HDTVs still max out at 720p, so you probably won't miss the drop in quality.

iFrame

Apple itself developed this video format in an effort to create easy-to-edit, reasonably sized video files. It doesn't record in HD (it composes the image from 540 rows of pixels instead of 720 or 1080) but you can immediately edit it in iMovie without any conversion. It also edits much more smoothly on slower Macs. The underlying format is based on industry standards, so you don't need any special software to play iFrame video on a computer. Even so, the industry hasn't exactly been jumping all over this new format; only a handful of cameras offer iFrame recording.

Camcorder Features: Which Are Worthwhile?

So how do you know which camcorder to buy? Here's a rundown of the most frequently advertised camcorder features, along with a frank assessment of their value to the quality-obsessed iMovie fan.

FireWire connector

FireWire is Apple's term for the tiny, compact connector on the side of most MiniDV tape camcorders—and most Macs. You link your camera and Mac using a FireWire cable that plugs into these connectors. Other companies have different names for this connector—you may see it called IEEE-1394, i.Link, DV In/Out, or DV Terminal.

Tapeless camcorders usually don't have a FireWire jack, which is OK because you can transfer your video from camera to Mac in other ways, described in Chapter 1.

Note: Since Apple thinks that tape camcorders are dead, it thinks FireWire is dead, too. Some recent Mac models, like the MacBook and MacBook Air, don't have FireWire jacks at all, and you can expect the trend of the disappearing connector to continue.

Analog inputs

Analog inputs let you connect older, pre-digital video equipment, such as your VCR, 8mm camcorder, and so on, to your camcorder (see Figure I-2).

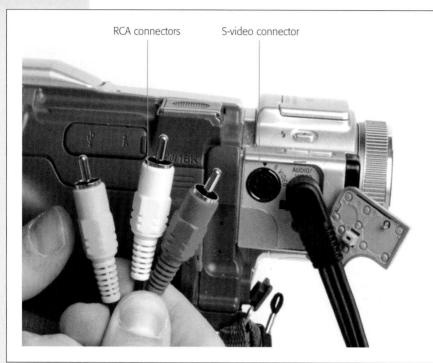

RCA connectors   S-video connector

Figure I-2:
Certain tape camcorders offer inputs for older, analog video. (Actually, what you'll probably get is a special cable with RCA connectors on one end and a miniplug on the camcorder end, like the one shown here. Don't lose this cable! You also need it to play your camcorder footage on TV.) A few older models offer an S-video connector too, for much higher-quality playback on TV.

Unfortunately, this is one of those features that camcorder makers have been quietly eliminating in an effort to shave costs. That's too bad, because there's no easier, less expensive way to transfer older footage into your digital camcorder—or directly into iMovie.

The transfer technique is described in more detail in Chapter 1. For now, note that the only other way to transfer pre-DV footage into digital format is to buy a $200 converter box.

HD inputs

Most HD camcorders now let you connect your camera directly to your HDTV. Using HD connections means you can see your camera's footage at full-quality resolution on your TV.

Some cameras have jacks for component cables, which look like the one pictured in Figure I-2, except that they have three cables (red, blue, and green) for the video signal and two (red and white) for the sound. The jacks on your HDTV, if there, will match in color.

More and more, HD camcorders have HDMI connectors, a convenient, high-quality connection that sends video and audio signals through a single cable. The connectors are flat and rectangular, and look like oversized USB ports.

Three chips (CCDs)

Professional camcorders offer three image sensors, one for each color component of a video picture: red, green, and blue. You'll see these camcorders advertised as having three chips, or CCDs (*charge-coupled devices*—electronic plates, covered with thousands of individual light sensors, that convert light rays into a digital signal). The result is even more spectacular picture quality, resolution, and color rendition than the less-expensive, one-CCD cameras.

Unfortunately, three-chip camcorders tend to be more expensive than one-chip cams—but they deliver much better color.

Not all three-chip models are big and pricey, though. Panasonic, in particular, has developed a line of three-chip camcorders that aren't much larger or more expensive than one-chip models. Note, however, that they usually contain three very *small* CCDs, so you'll notice the quality improvement primarily in bright, outdoor scenes.

Image stabilizer

Certain film techniques scream "Amateur!" to audiences. One of them is the instability of handheld filming. In a nutshell, directors shoot professional video using a camera on a tripod (Woody Allen's "handheld" period notwithstanding). Most home camcorder footage, in contrast, is shot from the palm of your hand.

A stabilizing feature (which may have a marketing name, such as Sony's SteadyShot) takes a half step toward solving that problem. As shown in Figure I-3, this feature neatly eliminates the tiny, jittery moves that show up in handheld video. (It can't do anything about bigger jerks and bumps, which are especially difficult to avoid when you zoom in on a subject.) The stabilizer also uses up your battery faster.

Figure I-3:
A digital stabilizer works by "taking in" more image than it actually uses in your final footage. The stabilizer analyzes your clip and identifies its subject. It then shifts the focus of the clip's individual frames to keep your subject centered and moving smoothly. To make this process work, the stabilizer zooms in on your image a bit. That's why you need the extra-large image capture—to compensate for the zoom-in. On less-expensive camcorders, unfortunately, this zooming in means that your clip's final frames will have less video information in them than normal, to the detriment of picture quality.

This kind of anti-shake feature comes in two forms:

- **Electronic, or digital, stabilization** is what you get on cheaper camcorders. Figure I-3 describes how it works.

- **Optical stabilization** is much preferable. It involves two transparent plates separated by a special optical fluid. As the camera shakes, these plates create a prism effect that keeps handheld shots clearer and steadier than electronic (digital) stabilizers. The images are clearer because optical stabilizers don't have to crop out part of the picture as a buffer, unlike the stabilizers illustrated in Figure I-3.

Tip: What could possibly be better than image stabilization on your camcorder? Image stabilization in your editing software. You'll find iMovie '11's amazing stabilizing feature described on page 176.

Manual controls

Better camcorders let you turn off the camera's automatic focus, automatic exposure control, automatic white balance, and even its automatic sound level. You'll find this feature useful in certain situations, like when you want to change focus from one object to another in the same shot (known to the pros as a focus-pull). If you decided to pay extra for this feature, look for a model that lets you focus manually by turning a ring on the lens casing, which is much easier than the alternative—sliders.

Optical zoom

When you read the specs for a camcorder—or read the logos painted on its body—you frequently encounter phrases like "12X/300X ZOOM!" The number before the slash tells you how many times the camera can magnify a distant image, much like a telescope does. That number measures the *optical* zoom, which is the amount of magnification you get through the camcorder lenses themselves. Such zooming, of course, is useful when you want to film something far away. (As for the number *after* the slash, see "Digital Zoom" on page 16.)

You should know, however, that the more you zoom in, the shakier your footage is likely to be, since the camera magnifies every microscopic wobble by, say, 12 times. You also have to be much more careful about focusing. When you're zoomed out all the way, everything is in focus—things near you, and things far away. But when you zoom in, very near and very far objects go out of focus. Put into photographic terms, the more you zoom in, the shorter the *depth of field* (the range of distance from the camera that can be kept in focus simultaneously).

Finally, remember that magnifying the picture doesn't magnify the sound. If you rely on your camera's built-in microphone for sound, always get as close as you can to the subject, both for the sound and for the wobble.

Tip: Professional video and film work includes very little zooming-in, unlike most amateur videos. The best zooming is subtle zooming, such as when you very slowly "move toward" the face of somebody you're interviewing.

For this reason, when you shop for a camcorder, test its zoom feature if at all possible. Find out if the camcorder has *variable-speed* zooming, where the zooming speed increases the harder you press the Zoom button. Some camcorders offer only two speeds–fast and faster–but that's still better than having no control at all. (The standard camcorder literature doesn't usually mention whether a camera has variable-speed zooming or not; you generally have to go to the store and try it out to see how it performs.)

Minutes-remaining readout

Fortunately, the problems exhibited by camcorder batteries of old—such as the "memory effect"—are a thing of the past. (When you halfway depleted an old camcorder battery several times in a row, the battery adopted that *halfway-empty* point as its new *completely* empty point, effectively halving the battery's capacity. The lithium-ion batteries today's camcorders use eliminate the problem.)

Some camcorders—mostly from Sony, JVC, and Canon—even display, in minutes, how much recording or playback time you have left—a worthy feature.

Note: The number of minutes' worth of recording time advertised for camcorder batteries is *continuous* recording time–that is, the time you'll get if you turn the camcorder on, press Record, and go out to lunch. If you stop and start the camera to capture shorter scenes, as almost everyone does, you'll get much less than the advertised time out of each battery charge.

Built-in light

Insufficient lighting is one of the leading causes of "amateuritis," a telltale form of poor video quality that lets viewers know that the footage is homemade. In the best—and most expensive—of all possible worlds, you'd get your scene correctly lit before filming, or you'd attach a light to the "shoe" (light connector) on top of the camera. Those few cameras that have such a shoe, or even have a built-in light, give you a distinct advantage in capturing colors accurately.

Scene modes

Many camcorders come with a number of canned focus/shutter speed/aperture settings for different indoor and outdoor environments: Sports Lesson, Beach and Snow, Twilight, and so on. They're a useful compromise between the all-automatic operation of less expensive models and the all-manual operation of professional cameras.

Remote control

Some camcorders come with a pocket-sized remote control. It serves two purposes. First, its Record and Stop buttons let you record *yourself,* with or without other people, in a shot. Second, when you play back footage with the camcorder connected to your TV or VCR, the remote lets you control playback without needing to have the camcorder on your lap. You may be surprised at how useful the remote can be.

FlexiZone or Push Focus

All camcorders offer automatic focus. Most work by focusing on the image in the center of your frame as you line up a shot.

That's fine if your subject is in the center of the frame. But if it's off-center, you have no choice but to turn off the autofocus feature and use the manual-focus ring. (Using a camcorder isn't like using a still camera, where you can point the camera directly at the subject for focusing purposes, and then—before taking the shot—shift the angle so that the subject is no longer in the center. Camcorders continually refocus, so pointing the camera slightly away from your subject makes you lose the off-center focus you've established.)

Some Canon, Sony, and Sharp camcorders let you specify the spot in a frame that you want to serve as the focus point, even if it's not the center of the picture. (Canon calls this feature FlexiZone; Sony calls it Push Focus. On Sony cams with touch-screen LCD panels, it's especially easy to indicate which spot in the frame should get the focus.) If the model you're eyeing has this feature, it's worth having.

Night-vision mode

Most Sony camcorders offer a mode called NightShot that works like night-vision goggles. You can actually film (and see, as you watch the LCD screen) in total darkness. The infrared transmitter on the front of the camcorder measures the heat given off by various objects in its path, letting you capture an eerie, greenish night scene. Rent *The Silence of the Lambs* for an idea of how creepy night-vision filming can be. Or watch any episode of *Survivor*.

The transmitter's range is only about 15 feet or so. Still, you may be surprised how often it comes in handy: on campouts, during sleepovers, on nighttime nature walks, and so on.

Still photos

All modern camcorders can take still photos. The camcorder freezes one frame of what it's seeing, and records it either on the tape (for, say, a 7-second stretch) or as a regular JPEG file on a memory card.

The still-photo image quality, unfortunately, is pretty terrible. The resolution may be OK (some camcorders offer 2- or even 3-megapixel resolution), but the quality isn't anywhere near what you'd get using a dedicated digital still camera.

Note: Newer hybrid cameras shoot OK stills, but the cameras themselves aren't ideal for still photography. Be sure to try out a camera or do thorough research. The last thing you need is a camera you never want to use.

If the camcorder you're considering offers the still photo feature, fine. But it may be redundant for the iMovie owner. iMovie can grab 1-megapixel still frames from *any* captured video, as described on page 280.

Progressive-scan CCDs

This special kind of image sensor is primarily useful for capturing still images. It ensures that the entire image is grabbed, not just one set of alternating, interlaced scan lines (the usual video signal). If you plan to catch still frames from your camcorder, a progressive-scan CCD will spare you some of the jagged lines that may appear. However, if your primary goal is to make movies, this expensive feature isn't worth paying for, especially since you can buy a digital *still* camera with much greater resolution for about the same added cost.

Useless Features

Here are some features you'll see in camcorder advertising that you should ignore (and definitely not pay extra for).

Title generator

Some camcorders let you superimpose *titles* (that is, text) on your video as you film. In your case, dear iMovie owner, a title-generating feature is useless. Your Mac can add gorgeous, smooth-edged type, with a selection of sizes, fonts, colors, and even scrolling animations, to your finished movies, with far more precision and power than the blocky text available on your camcorder. (Chapter 8 shows you how.)

Note: A title generator on a camcorder is actually *worse* than useless, because it permanently stamps your original footage with something you may wish you could amend later. In fact, as a general rule, you should avoid using (or paying for) *any* of the in-camera editing features described in this chapter—title generator, fader, special effects—because you can do this kind of editing much more effectively in iMovie. Not only are the in-camera features redundant, they commit you to an editing choice in advance, thus limiting how you can use your footage.

Special effects

Most DV camcorders offer a selection of six or seven cheesy-looking special effects. They can make your footage look solarized, or digitized, or otherwise processed (see Figure I-4).

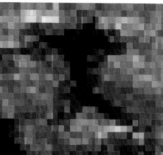

Figure I-4:
Using the stock collection of special effects built into your camcorder, you can create special, hallucinogenic visuals. The question is: Why?

Avoid using these effects. iMovie has its own special-effects options, and it gives you far greater control over when they start, when they end, and how intensely they affect the video.

In fact, unless you're shooting a documentary about nuclear explosions or bad drug episodes, consider avoiding these effects altogether.

Date/time stamp

Every camcorder offers the ability to stamp the date and time directly onto the footage. As you've no doubt seen (on *America's Funniest Home Videos* or *America's Scariest Cop Chases*), the result is a blocky, typographically hideous stamp that permanently mars your footage. Few things take the romance out of a wedding video, or are more distracting in spectacular weather footage, than a huge **20 NOV 11 12:34 PM** stamped in the corner.

Nor do you have to worry that you'll one day forget when you filmed some event. As it turns out, digital camcorders automatically and invisibly date- and time-stamp *all* your footage. You'll be able to see this information when you connect the camcorder to your Mac; then you can choose whether or not to add the stamp to the finished footage (and with much more control over its timing, location, and typography).

Digital zoom

Much as camera owners mistakenly jockey for superiority by comparing the megapixel rating of their cameras (more megapixels doesn't necessarily make sharper pictures), camcorder makers seem to think that what consumers want most in a camcorder is a powerful digital zoom. Your camcorder's packaging may "boast" digital zoom ratings of "50X," "100X," or "500X!"

When a camcorder uses its *digital* zoom—the number after the slash on the camcorder box tells you its maximum magnification—it simply enlarges the individual dots that compose an image. Yes, the image gets bigger, but it doesn't get any *sharper*. As the dots get larger, the image gets chunkier, coarser, and less recognizable, until it ends up looking like the blocky areas you see superimposed over criminals' faces to conceal their identity on *Cops*. After your digital zoom feature has blown up the picture by 3X, the image falls to pieces. Greater digital zoom is not something worth paying for.

The Long-Term Storage Problem

No matter which kind of camcorder you choose, you have more to think about more than just features and price; you have the future to consider. Every kind of camcorder presents serious challenges if you hope to preserve your video for future generations.

- **DVD camcorders**. Nobody has yet figured out how long those home-burned DVDs actually last. They don't last essentially forever, as Hollywood DVDs do. In Hollywood, they *stamp* DVDs, pressing a pattern of bits and bytes into the plastic. Home DVD burners, by contrast, record the pattern in a layer of organic dye on the bottom of the disc—a dye that can break down anywhere from several *months* to several *decades* later.

- **Memory-card and hard-drive camcorders**. Once the card or drive is full, you're finished shooting for the day. The camcorder is worthless until you offload the video to a computer, thereby freeing up space to continue shooting.

  But what then? Are you going to burn hour after hour of captured video onto DVDs? Not only is that practically a full-time job, but you're stuck with those homemade DVDs and their questionable lifespan.

  You could, of course, just keep the video on hard drives, even though that's a very expensive and bulky solution. Here again, though, you have to wonder: Will the hard drive you buy today still work 50 years from now?

- **Tape camcorders**. Digital tapes may deteriorate over a decade or two, just as traditional tapes do.

The solution to all these problems, of course, is simple vigilance. Every 10 or so years, you'll have to copy your masterworks onto newer tapes, discs, hard drives, or whatever the latest storage format happens to be.

About This Book

Don't let the rumors fool you. iMovie and iDVD may be simple, but they're not simplistic. Unfortunately, many of the best techniques aren't covered in the only "manual" you get with iLife—its electronic help screens.

This book is designed to serve as the iMovie/iDVD manual, as the book that should have been in the box. It explores each iMovie feature in depth, offers illustrated catalogs of the various title and transition effects, provides shortcuts and workarounds, and unearths features that iMovie's online help doesn't even mention.

Tip: Your camcorder and iMovie produce video of stunning visual and audio quality, giving you the *technical* tools to produce amazing videos. But most people don't have much experience with the *artistic* side of shooting–lighting, sound, and composition–or even how to use the dozens of buttons found on modern camcorders. If you visit this book's Missing CD at *http://tinyurl.com/33blf68* (see page 22), you'll find a bonus appendix in PDF form: three chapters designed to give you the basics of lighting, composition, and camera technique.

About the Outline

iMovie '11 & iDVD: The Missing Manual is divided into three parts, each with several chapters:

- Part 1, *Editing in iMovie*, is the heart of the book. It shows you how to transfer your footage into iMovie, edit your clips, pop them into a timeline, add cross-fades and titles, edit your soundtrack, and more.

- Part 2, *Finding Your Audience*, helps you take the cinematic masterpiece on your screen to the world. iMovie excels at exporting your work to the Web, to You-Tube, to an iPhone or an iPod, to an Apple TV, to a QuickTime file on your hard drive, or to iDVD for burning (your best bet for maintaining the visual quality of the original movie). This part of the book offers step-by-step instructions for each method, and shows you how you can use QuickTime Player Pro to supplement the editing tools in iMovie.

- Part 3, *iDVD*, is just what you'd expect: a bonus volume dedicated to the world's easiest-to-use DVD design and burning software. It goes way, way beyond the basics, as you'll see.

At the end of the book, four appendixes await:

- Appendix A provides a menu-by-menu explanation of iMovie menu commands.

- Appendix B is a comprehensive troubleshooting handbook.

- Appendix C is a master cheat sheet of iMovie's keyboard shortcuts.

- Appendix D is a visual reference to all of the little symbols, stripes, badges, and color-coded doodads that, sooner or later, will clutter up your iMovie window and leave you bewildered. Turn to this two-page cheat sheet in times of panic.

Technical Notes for PAL People

If you live in the Americas, Japan, or any of 30 other countries, your camcorder, VCR, and TV record and play back a video signal in a format known as *NTSC*. Even if you've never heard the term, every camcorder, VCR, TV, and TV station in your country uses this signal. (The following discussion doesn't apply to high-definition video, which uses the same signal across continents.)

What it stands for is National Television Standards Committee, the gang who designed this format. What it *means* is incompatibility with the second most popular format, which is called PAL (Phase Alternating Line, for the curious). In Europe,

Africa, the Middle East, Australia, and China (among other places), everyone's equipment uses the PAL format. You can't play an American tape on a standard VCR in Sweden—unless you're happy with black-and-white, sometimes jittery playback.

Note: France, the former countries of the Soviet Union, and a few others use a third format, known as SECAM. iMovie doesn't work with SECAM gear. To find out what kind of gear your country uses, visit a website like *www.vidpro.org/standards.htm*.

Fortunately, iMovie converses fluently with both NTSC and PAL camcorders. When you launch the program, it automatically studies the camcorder you've attached and determines its format.

However, most of the discussions in this book use NTSC terminology. If you're a friend of PAL, use the following information to translate this book's discussions.

The Tech Specs of NTSC

Whether you're aware of it or not, using the NTSC standard-definition format means that the picture you see is characterized like this:

- **30 frames per second**. A *frame* is one individual picture. Flashed before your eyes at this speed, the still images blend into what you perceive as smooth motion.
- **525 scan lines**. The electron gun in a TV tube paints the screen with this number of fine horizontal lines.
- **The DV picture measures 720×480 pixels**. This figure refers to the number of screen dots, or *pixels*, that compose one frame of image in the *DV* (digital video) version of the NTSC format.

The Tech Specs of PAL

When iMovie detects a PAL camcorder (or when you inform it that you're using one), it makes the necessary adjustments automatically, including:

- **25 frames per second**. Video fans claim that the lower frame rate creates more flicker than the NTSC standard. On the other hand, this frame rate is very close to the frame rate of Hollywood films (24 frames per second). As a result, many independent filmmakers find PAL a better choice when shooting movies they intend to convert to film.
- **625 scan lines**. That's 20 percent sharper and more detailed than NTSC. The difference is especially visible on large-screen TVs.
- **The DV picture measures 720×576 pixels**. This information may affect you as you read Chapter 12 and prepare still images for use with iMovie.

The Very Basics

You'll find very little jargon or nerd terminology in *iMovie '11 & iDVD: The Missing Manual*. You will, however, encounter a few terms and concepts you'll see frequently in your computing life. They include:

- **Clicking**. This book offers three kinds of instructions that require you to use the mouse or trackpad attached to your Mac. To *click* means to point the arrow cursor at something onscreen and then—without moving the cursor at all—press and release the clicker button on the mouse (or laptop trackpad). To *double-click*, of course, means to click twice in rapid succession, again without moving the cursor at all. And to *drag* means to move the cursor while keeping the button continuously pressed.

    When you're told to ⌘-*click* something, you click while pressing the ⌘ key (next to the space bar). Such related procedures as *Shift-clicking, Option-clicking*, and *Control-clicking* work the same way—just click while pressing the corresponding key on the bottom row of your keyboard.

Note: Apple has officially changed the name it uses for the little menu that pops up when you Control-click (or right-click) something on the screen. It's still a *contextual* menu, in that the menu choices depend on the context of what you click—but it's now called a *shortcut* menu. That term not only matches what Windows calls pop-up menus, but it's slightly more descriptive of its function. Shortcut menu is the term you'll find used in this book.

- **Menus**. The *menus* are the words at the top of your screen: File, Edit, and so on. Click one to make a list of commands appear, as though they're written on a window shade you've just pulled down. Some people click to open a menu and then release the mouse button; after reading the menu choices, they click the command they want. Other people like to press the mouse button and drag down the list of commands to the desired one; only then do they release the button. Both methods work, so use whichever you prefer.

Note: On Windows PCs, the mouse has two buttons. The left one is for clicking normally; the right one produces a tiny shortcut menu of useful commands. (See the previous Note.) But new Macs come with Apple's Mighty Mouse, a mouse that looks like it has only one button but can actually detect which side of its rounded front you press. If you turn on this feature in System Preferences, you, too, can right-click things on the screen.

That's why, all through this book, you'll see the phrase, "Control-click the photo (or right-click it)." That tells you that Control-clicking will do the job—but if you've got a two-button mouse or you turned on the two-button feature of the Mighty Mouse, right-clicking might be more efficient.

- **Keyboard shortcuts**. Every time you take your hand off the keyboard to move the mouse, you lose time and potentially disrupt your creative flow. That's why many experienced Mac fans use keystroke combinations instead of menu commands wherever possible. ⌘-P opens the Print dialog box, for example, and ⌘-M minimizes the current window to the Dock.

When you see a shortcut like ⌘-Q (which closes the current program), it's telling you to hold down the ⌘ key, and, while it's down, type the letter Q, and then release both keys.

If you've mastered this much information, you have all the technical background you need to enjoy *iMovie '11 & iDVD: The Missing Manual*.

About→These→Arrows

Throughout this book, and throughout the Missing Manual series, you'll find sentences like this one: "Open your Home→Library→Preferences folder." That's shorthand for a much longer instruction that directs you to open three nested folders in sequence, like this: "In the Finder, choose Go→Home. In your Home folder, you'll find a folder called Library. Open that. Inside the Library window is a folder called Preferences. Double-click to open it, too."

Similarly, this kind of arrow shorthand helps to simplify the business of choosing commands in menus, as shown in Figure I-5.

Figure I-5:
In this book, arrow notations simplify folder and menu instructions. For example, "Choose →Dock→Position on Left" is a more compact way of saying, "From the menu, choose Dock; from the submenu that then appears, choose Position on Left," as shown here.

Online Resources

As the owner of a Missing Manual, you've got more than just a book to read. Online, you'll find example files as well as tips, articles, and maybe even a video or two. You can also communicate with the Missing Manual team and tell us what you love (or hate) about the book. Head over to *www.missingmanuals.com*, or go directly to one of the following sections.

The Missing CD

This book doesn't have a CD pasted inside the back cover, but you're not missing out on anything. Go to *http://tinyurl.com/33blf68* to download additional information mentioned in this book. And so you don't wear down your fingers typing long web addresses, the Missing CD page also offers a list of clickable links to the websites mentioned in this book.

Registration

If you register this book at oreilly.com, you'll be eligible for special offers—like discounts on future editions of this book. Registering takes only a few clicks. Type *http://tinyurl.com/registerbook* into your browser to hop directly to the Registration page.

Feedback

Got questions? Need more information? Fancy yourself a book reviewer? On our Feedback page, you can get expert answers to questions that come to you while reading, share your thoughts on this Missing Manual, and find groups for folks who share your interest in iMovie. To have your say, go to *www.missingmanuals.com/feedback*.

Errata

To keep this book as up to date and accurate as possible, each time we print more copies, we'll make any confirmed corrections you suggest. We also note such changes on the book's website, so you can mark important corrections into your own copy of the book, if you like. Go to *http://tinyurl.com/296w6aa* to report an error and view existing corrections.

Newsletter

Our free email newsletter keeps you up to date on what's happening in Missing Manual land. You can meet the authors and editors, see bonus video and book excerpts, and more. Go to *http://tinyurl.com/MMnewsletter* to sign up.

Safari® Books Online

 Safari Books Online is an on-demand digital library that lets you easily search over 7,500 technology and creative reference books and videos to find the answers you need quickly.

With a subscription, you can read any page and watch any video from our library online. Read books on your cell phone and mobile devices. Access new titles before they are available for print, and get exclusive access to manuscripts in development and post feedback for the authors. Copy and paste code samples, organize your favorites, download chapters, bookmark key sections, create notes, print out pages, and benefit from tons of other time-saving features.

O'Reilly Media has uploaded this book to the Safari Books Online service. To have full digital access to this book and others on similar topics from O'Reilly and other publishers, sign up for free at *http://my.safaribooksonline.com*.

Part One: Editing in iMovie

Chapter 1: Importing Video

Chapter 2: The Lay of the Land

Chapter 3: Building the Movie

Chapter 4: Video Chunks: Keywords, People, Favorites, and Rejects

Chapter 5: Transitions, Themes, Travel Maps, and Animatics

Chapter 6: Video Effects

Chapter 7: Stabilization, Color Fixes, Cropping, and Rotating

Chapter 8: Titles, Subtitles, and Credits

Chapter 9: Narration, Music, and Sound

Chapter 10: Photos

Chapter 11: Movie Trailers

Chapter 12: Advanced Editing

1

Importing Video

L et's say you've filmed something. You've captured some video on your camcorder, digital camera, phone, or Flip, or maybe you've just assembled some videos on your hard drive. Now it's time for the heart of this book: editing your footage using iMovie on the Mac. This chapter introduces you to iMovie and its importing window, which slurps up video from tape camcorders, tapeless camcorders, and old iMovie projects. It can also record video live, in real time, from a camcorder or an iSight video camera.

iMovie: The Application

So far in your moviemaking adventures, you've probably thought about nothing but *hardware*—the equipment needed to edit your raw footage. In the end, however, the iMovie story is about *software*, both the footage as it exists on your Mac and the iMovie program itself.

iMovie on a New Mac

If you bought a Mac after October 2010, iMovie '11 is probably already installed on your hard drive. To see, open the Macintosh HD icon→Applications folder. Inside, you'll find the star-shaped icon for iMovie itself ( ). That icon is probably in your Dock, too.

iMovie for an Existing Mac

If your Mac didn't come with iMovie '11, you can buy it as part of Apple's $50 iLife '11 software suite. The suite comes on a single DVD and includes the latest versions of GarageBand, iMovie, iPhoto, iWeb, and iDVD. (It's available from Apple's website, Apple stores, Amazon.com, or popular Mac mail-order sites like *www.macmall.com* and *www.macwarehouse.com.*)

Apple says that iMovie requires an Intel-based Mac running Mac OS X version 10.6.3 or later. Apple also requires a machine with at least 1 gigabyte of memory. It goes without saying, of course, that the more memory you have, the bigger your screen, and the faster your processor, the happier you and iMovie will be. This program is *seriously* hungry for horsepower.

If you bought iLife, run its installer now and choose which of the programs listed above you want to install.

Tip: Consider installing GarageBand even if you're not a musician. You may use it to assist iMovie with things like editing sound.

When the installer finishes up, you'll find an icon called iMovie in your Applications folder and in your Dock.

Note: If you've got iMovie '08 or '09 on your Mac already, the '11 version replaces it. If you have iMovie HD (also known as iMovie 6), the installer thoughtfully preserves it (to find out why, see page 302). You'll find a folder called "iMovie (previous version)" in your Applications folder, ready to run when necessary.

".0.1" Updates

Like any other software company, Apple occasionally releases new versions of iMovie: version 9.1, version 9.2, and so on (or even 9.1.1, then 9.1.2, and so on). Each free upgrade improves the program's reliability. They're well worth installing for any program, but they're especially important for iMovie; Apple does more than squash bugs with these updates, it often adds features you'll want to use.

You don't have to look far to find these updates. One day you'll be online and the Mac's Software Update dialog box will pop up onscreen, letting you know there's a new version available and offering to install it for you. Alternatively, you can download any updates from within iMovie by choosing iMovie→Check for Updates.

When the updater finishes, your original copy of iMovie '11 has morphed into the newer version of the program. (One way to find out what version of iMovie you have is to open the program and then choose iMovie→About iMovie.)

This book assumes that you have at least iMovie 9.0.

Getting into iMovie

After you install iMovie, open it by double-clicking its icon in the Applications folder, or by single-clicking the star-shaped icon in the Dock (✭).

Now, just in case you had somehow forgotten that iMovie is a totally new program, a special starter screen appears to let you know (Figure 1-1).

Figure 1-1:
This window welcomes you to iMovie, although it doesn't tell you much more than to choose Help→iMovie Help if you're just figuring things out. Click Close to leave the welcome screen and get down to work.

When you click Close, you arrive at the main iMovie screen. Figure 1-2 is a cheat sheet for iMovie's various screen elements, but don't spend time memorizing their functions now; the rest of this book covers each tool in context and in depth:

- **Project Library**. If you're used to the old iMovie, the new iMovie's way of doing things may come as a shock. You create new movie projects the same way as always, by choosing File→New Project (or pressing ⌘-N). But now, after you type in a name for the movie you're about to create, iMovie doesn't ask where you want to save it. Instead, it adds your project's name to this Project Library list, alongside all your other projects, past and present. More on projects in the next chapter.

- **Project storyboard**. You'll spend most of your editing time in this window. Here's where you see your movie represented as filmstrips—short sequences of representative frames from each clip you shot. Parallel colored strips indicate blocks of sound that play simultaneously.

- **Viewer**. You watch your footage in this window.

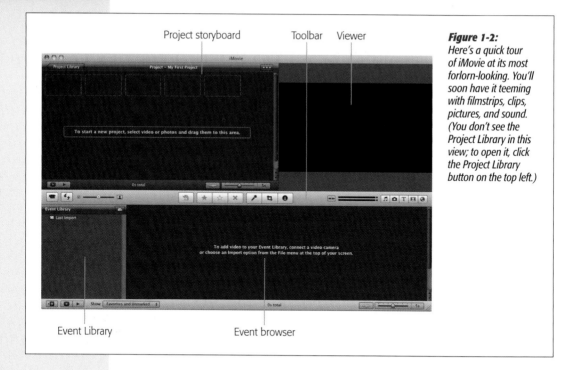

Project storyboard   Toolbar   Viewer

Event Library   Event browser

Figure 1-2:
Here's a quick tour of iMovie at its most forlorn-looking. You'll soon have it teeming with filmstrips, clips, pictures, and sound. (You don't see the Project Library in this view; to open it, click the Project Library button on the top left.)

- **Toolbar**. Here's where you'll find most of iMovie's onscreen controls.

- **Event Library**. In iMovie '11, *all* your raw footage is available to *all* your movie projects at *all* times. The Event Library lists all the video you've ever imported into iMovie, on all your hard drives. iMovie organizes the footage by *event*—Wedding, Vacation, Graduation, and so on. You'll read much more about Events on page 65, but for now, it's enough to know that iMovie lists your Events here, organized into folders by year.

- **Event browser**. This area stores your raw, unedited *clips*—"filmstrips" of footage and individual shots—that you'll rearrange into a masterpiece of modern storytelling. It displays the contents of the Event you choose in the Event Library, so exactly what you see here changes.

- **Playhead**. The playhead is like the little handle of a normal scroll bar. It shows exactly where you are in a piece of footage.

If you just opened iMovie for the first time, it probably looks pretty barren. But you'll fix that.

Importing Footage from a Tape Camcorder

If you have a MiniDV tape camcorder, high-def or not, transferring your recordings to the Mac is straightforward. All you have to do is connect the two machines—your camcorder and Mac—with a cable.

To do that, you use a *FireWire* cable, and it looks like the one in Figure 1-3. The big end of the cable goes into the FireWire jack on the front, side, or back of your Mac; it's marked by a radioactive-looking ⚛ symbol.

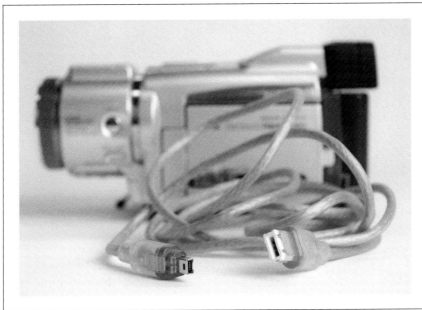

Figure 1-3:
Plug the larger end of the FireWire cable– the six-pin end, as Apple calls it–into the corresponding jack on your Mac. The tiny end may look almost square, but it's not–it plugs into your camcorder only one particular way, thanks to a little indentation on one side. Be gentle with it.

Note: Unfortunately, not all Mac models have FireWire jacks anymore, or they use a newer jack called FireWire 800. If your Mac has a FireWire 800 jack, you can find a cable that works with your camera (do a Google search or check the manufacturer's accessories web page). The MacBook Air and the regular aluminum MacBook, though, lack *any* FireWire jack. If you have MiniDV tapes full of recorded video, you're out of luck: There's no adapter box or converter that connects your camcorder's FireWire jack to a Mac that doesn't have this jack. Your best bet is to borrow a Mac that has a FireWire jack, dump all of your tapes onto it, and then sell your old camcorder.

On the other end is a much smaller, squarish plug (called the four-pin connector). Plug this tiny end into the FireWire connector on your camcorder, which, depending on the brand, may be labeled FireWire, i.Link, or IEEE 1394. It's almost always hidden behind a plastic or rubber door or flap on the camcorder.

This single FireWire cable communicates both sound and video from camcorder to Mac. Once you connect the cable, proceed like this:

1. **Turn on the camcorder. Switch it into Play mode (Figure 1-4).**

   The camcorder's playback mode may be labeled Play, VCR, VTR, or just ▶.

   At this point, iMovie's big blue Import window should open automatically. If it doesn't, run through the troubleshooting checks described on page 479.

Figure 1-4:
Your camcorder's Play mode should be a fairly prominent knob or menu setting. If you can't find it, check the manual.

Tip: You should open the camcorder's LCD screen, too, which also turns on its speaker. Otherwise, you'll have no way to hear the audio as you play back the tape.

2. **Specify what you want to import.**

   If you want to import the whole tape, make sure the Automatic/Manual switch (in the lower left of the Import From window) is on Automatic, and then click Import. This is a convenient feature, since you can walk away and do other things while iMovie works. Once iMovie finishes importing your footage, it displays a "Save to" dialog box (Figure 1-5); skip to step 3.

   If you want to import only *some* of what's on your camcorder, set the Automatic/Manual switch to Manual. At this point, iMovie's Import window sprouts a set of playback controls (Figure 1-6). Use them to control your camcorder as it scans the tape to find the sections you want to include in your movie.

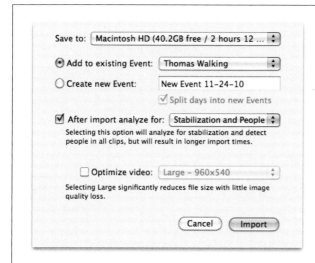

Figure 1-5:
This dialog box wants to know: Where do you want to save the incoming clips (on which hard drive)? What Event do they belong to? Do you want iMovie to stabilize your jerky camera work (page 176) and/or scan your footage for people? And at what resolution should iMovie import your clips (which also, of course, affects how much hard drive space your footage takes up)?

Figure 1-6:
There are no keyboard shortcuts for the playback buttons on the Import From screen. Use your mouse to operate the camcorder from iMovie, or use the playback controls on the camcorder itself.

Tip: You have to keep the mouse button down on the ◄◄ and ►► buttons continuously to make them work. If you use these buttons while the video is playing, you scan through the video; if you click Stop (■) first, these buttons zoom much faster through the tape, but of course you can't see where you are until you hit ► again.

When you find a shot worth bringing onto your Mac, click the Import button at the lower-right corner of the window. The "Save to" dialog box appears (Figure 1-5); read on.

3. **Tell iMovie where you want it to save the imported clips.**

   Most people, most of the time, save incoming video to their main Mac hard drive. But true iMovie addicts wind up buying additional hard drives to hold their movies. That's why the "Save to" pop-up menu appears here—so you can choose the hard drive you want to hold your video.

4. **Specify an Event.**

   The pair of choices shown in Figure 1-5 let you answer these questions: Were the scenes you're about to import filmed at a new Event? Or should iMovie file them along with scenes you already imported—as part of an existing Event, in other words?

   Selecting the right option, of course, requires that you know what Apple means by an Event. See "The Definition of an Event" on page 39.

Note: What you see in the "Add to existing Event" pop-up menu depends on which hard drive you select. That's because iMovie only "knows about" Events on the currently selected hard drive.

---

5. **Turn on "Analyze for stabilization and/or people," if you've got the time.**

   iMovie's built-in footage stabilizer is one of its most important and most effective features. It converts unsteady video into footage that looks as though the camera were on a tripod.

   The people analyzer scans all your footage for human faces, and then tags clips that include close-up, medium, and wide shots with people in them, as well as shots that include one, two, or more people. This way, you can go straight to footage that has people in it rather than wade through the junk footage of your foot, shot when you forgot to stop recording.

   The downside of these miraculous options is that your Mac requires a long period of thoughtful analysis before it can stabilize or people-find. It literally studies the first frame of video, compares each pixel to what's on the second frame, and so on. That takes a long time—hours, in some cases. (If you just analyze for people and not for stabilization, the process takes iMovie about one-tenth as long.)

   Fortunately, you can always apply these two features to individual parts of a movie, which saves huge amounts of time. In other words, the only reason to analyze for stabilization and/or people at this stage is because you intend to let the Mac crunch away for half a day (or night) after it finishes importing your footage.

6. **If you have a high-definition camcorder, optimize your video as either "Large – 960x540" pixels or "Full – 1920x1080" pixels.**

This option appears only if you import video from a high-definition camcorder, one that captures 720p, 1080i, or 1080p footage. (These terms refer to the number of horizontal lines that make up each frame of video. The more lines, the crisper your video. The "p" in 720p and 1080p means that each frame of video contains a full set of video-signal lines. The "i" in 1080i stands for "interlaced." That means that, instead of drawing each line of video from top to bottom one after the other, it splits the video signal into two sets of 540 lines each, one set odd and the other even. Your TV interlaces the odd and even lines, flashing them alternately on the screen.)

By giving you the Large and Full options, iMovie offers you the chance to import a smaller-scale version of that gigantic video canvas so you can save hard drive space. For assistance in making the Large vs. Full decision, see the box on page 37.

7. **Click Import.**

If you chose the Automatic option, iMovie rewinds the camcorder tape to the beginning, and then tells the camcorder to begin playback. As the video plays, iMovie captures it and stores it on your Mac. You can interrupt this process by clicking Stop if necessary; at this point, iMovie displays a little congratulations message, revealing how many minutes' worth of video you imported. You can click OK and then import some more, if you like, by starting from step 2 above.

Or you can click the Import button and walk away while iMovie works. You can surf the Web, crunch numbers, organize pictures in iPhoto, or whatever you like. Since iMovie is a Mac OS X program, your Mac doesn't have to devote every cycle of its processing power to capturing video. It continues to give priority to the video, so your other programs may act a little drugged. But you can get meaningful work done or read while iMovie works in the background.

If you let the Automatic import proceed without interruption, iMovie auto-rewinds the tape when it reaches the end.

If you chose the Manual setting, you can use iMovie's playback controls to operate the tape, shuttling through it to find the parts you want; use the Import button (and its alter ego, the Stop button) to capture only the good parts.

Tip: When you come to a scene you want to bring into iMovie, capture 3 to 5 seconds of footage before and after the interesting part. Later, as you edit, that extra leading and trailing video (called *trim handles* by the pros) gives you the flexibility to choose exactly the right moment for the scene to begin and end. Furthermore, you need extra footage at the beginning and end of your clips if you want to use transitions like crossfades to take viewers from one scene to another.

Unfortunately, the import process isn't the speedy joyride it was in the previous version of iMovie, where you could just tap the space bar (or click Import) every time you wanted to start or stop importing during playback.

In iMovie '11, each time you click Stop, iMovie locks you out for a minute or two while it displays the Generating Thumbnails message. That's iMovie's way of saying, "I'm processing this video and making some live, 'skimmable' filmstrips" (described on page 77).

Once that message disappears, you can use the playback controls to find the next bit of video worth importing—but you have to fill out the box shown in Figure 1-5 all over again, every time.

These frequent "Generating Thumbnails" and "Save to" interruptions are, for many people, a pretty strong argument for avoiding the Manual settings. The Automatic setting winds up saving you a lot of time—and doesn't cost you any extra disk space (see "Reclaiming Disk Space" on page 41).

8. **When you and iMovie are both finished, click Done.**

   The Import window goes away. You return to the iMovie screen, where you can click the name of the Event you specified in step 4 to see the newly imported clips. Proceed to Chapter 2.

Automatic Scene Detection

You'll notice a handy feature when iMovie finishes importing footage: The program automatically creates an individual filmstrip (clip) for each scene you shot. So an hour's worth of tape doesn't wind up as a single, mega-chunk of video—instead, you wind up with 30 or 40 individual clips, just the way you shot them.

You get these separate chunks of video because, behind the scenes, iMovie studies the *date and time stamp* that digital camcorders record with every frame of video. When iMovie detects a break in time, it assumes that you stopped recording, if only for a moment, and therefore considers the next piece of footage a new shot. It turns each new shot into a new clip.

In general, this feature doesn't work if you haven't set your camcorder's clock. Automatic scene detection also doesn't work if you're playing from a nondigital tape using one of the techniques described on page 51.

Importing from Tapeless Camcorders

The beauty of tapeless camcorders is that, because they store video as computer files on a hard drive, a DVD, or a memory card, you don't have to wait for the clips to play back in real time so iMovie can save them to your Mac. Instead, the importing process takes only as much time as iMovie needs to copy these files onto your Mac's hard drive. (At least in theory; read on.)

Note: If your camcorder records onto miniature DVDs, see page 45 for some additional notes.

Large vs. Full

High-def video is great and all. Truly it is. It's mind-blowingly sharp, clear, and colorful. One frame of a true high-def 1080p picture is made up of 1,920 pixels by 1,080 pixels. (Compare that with the pathetic dimensions of standard TV: 640 × 480 pixels.)

But high-def video also takes up a ridiculous amount of hard drive space: *26 gigabytes per hour*. (Standard-resolution DV video takes up less than half that.) Even the lesser versions of HD, like 720p and 1080i, take up a lot of space.

If your 500-gig drive is already half full with programs, photos, music, and other software, you've got room for only 9 hours of high-def video. And depending on how trigger-happy you are as a videographer (and how cute your kids are), that's not very much at all.

What Apple is subtly pointing out here, though, is that HD video is actually overkill for most of the things people do with their home movies. HD video is much too big for a standard DVD, for example, whose picture is only 640 × 480 pixels. It's way too big to stream from a web page, too. That size image may even be too big to fit on your monitor. (A 21.5-inch iMac has a maximum resolution of 1920 × 1080 pixels—just barely big enough for a 1080p movie. Among Mac laptops, only the 17-inch MacBook Pro has enough pixels.)

So Apple is offering you the opportunity to import your video at a *scaled-down* size: 960 × 540 pixels. If you do the math, you'll realize that that's actually only *one-quarter* the area of the original high-def picture (half the area in each dimension), which makes Apple's name for this option—Large—a little suspicious.

Still, importing your high-def video in the Large (quarter-size) format means that each hour of video takes up around 10 gigabytes of disk space instead of 26. You also get smoother playback on slower Macs. And for most end-result showcases—like a DVD, the Web, or computer-screen playback—the resolution is still sensational. It's unlikely that you'd see any difference between the Large and the Full settings in most cases.

There *are* times when the Full setting is appropriate, however: When you plan to export your edited movie to Final Cut Pro (Apple's professional video-editing program); when you intend to broadcast it on TV or use it in an actual, professional movie; or when you hope to burn it to a *high-definition* DVD someday (if such burners ever become available on the Mac). Also, video-sharing websites like YouTube and Vimeo can display full-HD videos for those movies that need to look especially great.

If you decide to optimize your video using the Full setting, you're basically converting the native HD footage to a very high-quality, but very large, format called Apple Intermediate Codec (AIC for short). (More on this codec and how it works on page 48.) HD footage in this setting is about as space-hungry as it can get, however, so make sure you have plenty of room on your hard drive. Of course, the huge file sizes beg the question, "Why the heck is this considered 'optimizing'?" The answer is that AIC is editing-friendly and preserves the quality of your video better than almost any other format.

Finally, as you weigh the Large versus Full decision, remember one thing: You're making this choice forever. Hard drives will get bigger and cheaper. High-def DVDs will eventually become commonplace. Computer horsepower will someday double or quadruple. If you're working with precious, important video that you want to last for decades to come, it might be worth keeping the full-resolution file just in case.

Note: Check your camcorder's manual. Not all camcorders advertised as "high-def" do, in fact, record at the full 1920 × 1080 pixels. And if yours *doesn't*, there's very little downside to using the Large option here.

Once you're ready to transfer video from your tapeless camcorder, here's what to do:

1. **Connect the camcorder's USB cable to your Mac.**

   Most tapeless camcorders connect to the Mac using a USB cable, which comes with your camcorder (see Figure 1-7). It connects to any of the Mac's skinny rectangular USB jacks. (If you have one of those tiny, very popular Flip camcorders, plug in its pop-out USB connector instead.)

Figure 1-7:
Tapeless camcorders generally come with a USB cable. The small end plugs into your camcorder (you may have to open some tiny plastic door on the camera to find the jack). The big end plugs into any of your Mac's USB jacks.

2. **Turn on the camcorder, and then switch it into PC mode.**

   The wording might vary, but every tapeless camcorder has a mode for making PC or Mac connections (Figure 1-8).

   If everything is going well, a message appears at the top of the screen that says, "Generating Poster Images." Then, after a minute, you see the Importing screen depicted in Figure 1-9.

Figure 1-8:
*Every camcorder has
a switch or command
that lets you connect
it to a PC (or, in this
case, a Mac). Most
tapeless camcorders
have a dedicated
position on the main
mode dial for this
purpose, like the
camera above.*

The Definition of an Event

In iMovie terms, an Event is an organizational tool, like a label or a desktop folder.

Sometimes, what constitutes an Event is obvious. A wedding, a graduation, a birthday party, and a ski trip, for example. You'd want all the clips from somebody's wedding filed under a single heading, even if you film them over the course of a whole weekend.

Sometimes, though, "Event" is a little nebulous. What if you film little scenes of your new baby every other day for a couple of months? Would they all be one Event called "August"? Or would you have a lot of little Events like "Overturned spaghetti bowl" and "First steps"?

Or what if you take a 10-day cruise featuring a stop every other day in a different port of call? Would the Event be "Mediterranean Cruise"? Or would you create individual Events for "Naples," "Monaco," and "Tunisia"?

The answer is, of course, "That's up to you." And that's why the options in Figure 1-5 appear at this point. If you want to create a new Event, type a name for it into the "Create new Event" box. But if you're importing footage into an Event category you already created, click "Add to existing Event," and then choose that Event from the pop-up menu.

Note: If you opt to create a new Event, iMovie also offers you a checkbox called "Split days into new Events." If you turn this option on, each day's worth of shooting becomes an Event all its own, even if you shot all the footage on the same vacation or wedding weekend. iMovie automatically adds day numbers to Event names, like "Wedding–Day 1" and "Wedding–Day 2."

Figure 1-9:
*You can import individual scenes from a tapeless camcorder without having to rewind or fast-forward through footage.
You can also preview the recorded scenes before you bother importing them (see step 3 below). If your intention is to bring in most of the clips, turn off the checkboxes under the scenes you don't want. If you want to import fewer than half of them, though, click Uncheck All, and then turn the checkboxes back on for the shots you do want.*

If iMovie *doesn't* open, or if the Importing screen doesn't appear, then choose File→Import From Camera, or run through the troubleshooting steps described on page 479.

You're about to experience one huge payoff of using a tapeless camcorder: instant access to individual scenes on the camcorder. That means, first of all, that you don't have to rewind or fast-forward to find a certain shot. Furthermore, as you can see in Figure 1-9, iMovie lets you import only the shots you want, leaving the duds behind. That feature alone can represent a huge time savings over the old "import the whole tape" method.

Tip: If your camcorder stores video on memory cards—SD cards, for example—you have another option at this juncture. You can remove the card from the camcorder and insert it into a *card reader* (which may even be built into your Mac laptop). The advantage of the card-reader method is that you don't use up the camcorder's battery power as you transfer your video.

---

3. **Review your shots before you import them.**

   To play a shot, click its thumbnail and then click the ▶ button. Click the ◀ or ▶|
   buttons to skip to the previous or next shot on the camcorder (or just click the
   thumbnails on the screen in front of you).

4. **Specify which shots you want to import.**

   If you want to import everything on the camcorder, click Import All and then
   skip to step 5.

   If you want to import only some of the shots, move the Automatic/Manual
   switch in the lower-left corner of the Import window to Manual. You'll see little
   checkboxes under the shot thumbnails. All of them start out with checkboxes
   turned on, meaning that iMovie intends to import all of them. See Figure 1-9
   for tips on selecting just the scenes you want. Once you specify your shots, click
   Import Checked.

   At this point, the top of the window displays a little sheet of options (see
   Figure 1-10).

5. **Tell iMovie where you want to save your imported clips.**

   Most people save incoming clips to their main Mac hard drive. But if you
   bought additional drives specifically for your movie files, use the "Save to" pop-
   up menu to choose a different drive.

6. **Specify an Event.**

   The pair of choices shown in Figure 1-10 lets you answer these questions: Are
   the scenes you're importing part of a new Event, or should iMovie file them with
   scenes you already imported, as part of an existing Event? See "The Definition
   of an Event" on page 39 for suggestions on what to choose here.

FREQUENTLY ASKED QUESTION

Reclaiming Disk Space

*I'm worried about using the Automatic importing option. It
seems like overkill if it brings in a whole hour of video, and
I wind up using only 10 minutes of it.*

Yes, it's true that imported digital video eats up 13 gigabytes
of disk space per hour of footage. (And that's standard-
definition video. High-definition video eats up 26 gigs.)

The good news: As you work on your project, you can
always delete the pieces you're not using—and reclaim
disk space in the process.

Details appear on page 119, but the point is that this iMovie
'11 feature is a big improvement over the previous incar-
nation of iMovie, where deleting part of a clip did not, in
fact, reclaim any disk space. (iMovie 6 hung onto the entire
clip, behind the scenes, just in case you ever changed your
mind about which piece you wanted to use in your movie.)

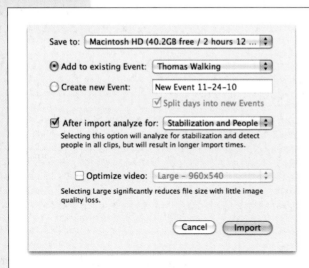

Figure 1-10:
This dialog box looks just like the one that appears when you import video from tape. Once again, it wants to know: Where do you want to save the incoming clips (on which hard drive)? What Event do they belong to? And how big do you really need the hard drive footage to be?

7. **If you have a high-def camcorder, optimize your video as either "Large – 960x540" or "Full – 1920x1080."**

   You may not see the final option shown in Figure 1-10. It appears only when you import video from a high-definition camcorder, one that captures 720p, 1080i, or 1080p video. See "Large vs. Full" on page 37 for a discussion of this option and advice on what to choose.

8. **Analyze for stabilization and/or people, if you've got the time.**

   iMovie's built-in footage stabilizer is one of its most important, and most effective, features. It converts unsteady video into footage that looks as though the camera were on a tripod. The people finder tags clips containing faces, making them easier to find later. But this "analysis" can take hours. See step 5 on page 34 for help in making this decision.

9. **Click Import.**

   Now iMovie swings into action. It begins slurping in video from the camcorder's hard drive, DVD, or memory card. As it works, a progress counter ticks off the remaining shots left to import (Figure 1-11).

   Considering that a tapeless camcorder is supposed to spare you the agony of importing footage from tape in real time, you may be surprised at how long it actually takes to import clips from a tapeless camera. AVCHD footage in particular (page 8) takes a long time because iMovie has to convert it into an editable format; depending on the speed of your computer, you may wind up waiting 2.5 minutes for each minute of video. An hour's worth of video, in other words, can take 2 and a half hours to import. You've been warned.

But never mind that; once iMovie is done, it displays a message to congratulate you. It lets you know how many minutes and seconds of video you imported in total, and how many clips you grabbed (Figure 1-12).

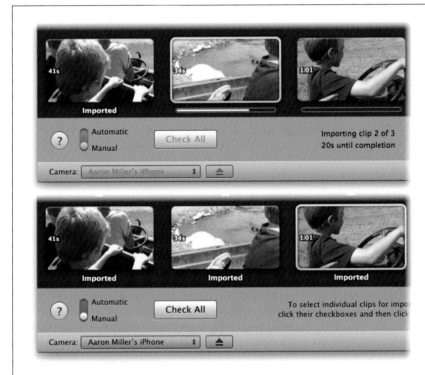

Figure 1-11:
Top: The time readouts here not only tell you how much longer it'll take to import a clip in "minutes:seconds" format, it also shows you how many clips iMovie still has to import.

Bottom: When it's all over, the word "Imported" appears under each thumbnail. That's a handy reminder when you've opted to import only some of your clips.

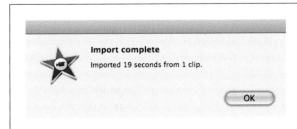

Figure 1-12:
Hey, you did it! You successfully imported some video from your camcorder to the Mac. You can now turn off the camcorder and put it away.

10. **Click OK.**

    The congratulations message goes away.

11. **Click ▲ to eject the camcorder, and then click Done.**

    The Import screen goes away. You arrive at the main iMovie screen, where your new video appears in the Events list at the left side of the screen. Page 65 describes this structure in more detail.

You can now turn off the camcorder to save battery power, if you like.

Importing from an iPhone or iPod Touch

If you have an iPhone (iPhone 3GS or later) or camera-equipped iPod Touch, you've probably been pulling it out of your pocket to shoot all kinds of great moments. Now you'd like to import those clips into iMovie to start editing.

In true, smooth Apple fashion, everything you read about importing video from tapeless cameras applies here. iMovie '11 automatically recognizes your iPhone or Touch, just as it does a regular tapeless camcorder. It also lets you select individual clips to import. iMovie even offers the same import options for analyzing and/or optimizing your footage.

The only real difference is that plugging in your iPhone or iPod Touch still opens iTunes automatically and starts syncing, even if you only want to import clips into iMovie (a minor annoyance that you can turn off in iTunes if you really want to).

UP TO SPEED

Camera Archives: The Quick-Camcorder-Dump Trick

One big problem with tapeless camcorders is that, well, they're tapeless. If you're on a four-day trip to Disneyworld and the camcorder fills up after one day, you're finished. You can't exactly duck into a drugstore and buy a new hard drive. Until you empty your camcorder footage onto your Mac (or start deleting stuff from the camcorder), you're dead in the water.

You could, of course, travel with a laptop, and import your footage into iMovie at the end of each day. The problem there is that if it's a high-def camcorder, iMovie will automatically convert the footage into the pared-down Apple Intermediate Codec (described in the box on page 48). This conversion takes forever—and eats up a lot more space on a hard drive than the original files from the camcorder did.

There's a cool, completely under-hyped feature in iMovie '11 that rather neatly solves these problems. It's called the Camera Archive, and it's designed to let you empty out your camera onto the Mac's hard drive in one simple step. There's no format conversion, no choices to make, no weeding out the bad clips; it just empties the camcorder in a hurry. You can open up the dumped footage in iMovie later, when you have more time and disk space.

To use this feature, begin by following steps 1 to 2 on page 38. But when the Import window appears, click the Archive All button at the bottom of the window. iMovie asks you to choose a folder location (your desktop is a good bet) and folder name (iMovie proposes the camcorder name and the current date)—and then gets right to work sucking in all the contents from your camcorder. When it's all over, you'll find a folder called Samsung 08-22-09 (or whatever), filled with video files in the camcorder's original format, like AVCHD. Nothing, at this point, has been imported into iMovie itself.

(Actually, the archive folder probably has other folders within it, containing still photos, audio files, and whatever else was on your camcorder. It's a great way to grab everything off the camcorder.)

Later, when you're back from Disneyworld and have more time, you can open up iMovie and choose File→ Import→Camera Archive. Click the archive folder and then click Import. iMovie opens up its standard Import window, exactly as though the camcorder were connected (which is pretty freaky). Proceed to import the video files into iMovie from step 3, exactly as described on page 41.

Importing from DVD Camcorders

In general, DVD camcorders are a mess. They're fussy, they take a long time to "initialize" and "finalize" a blank DVD, each disc doesn't hold very much footage, the recorded discs may not have a very long lifespan in your closet, and the miniature DVDs can actually damage your Mac.

If that's what you've got, though, the routine for importing video from a DVD camcorder—at this writing, the most popular format on the market—is exactly the same as it is for other tapeless camcorders. The instructions begin on page 36.

There are, however, a few caveats:

- iMovie can't import video from DVD camcorders that use the AVCHD video format (page 8). Unfortunately, that pretty much rules out all the *high-definition* DVD camcorders.

- Thanks to the hostility of the engineers who dreamed up the DVD camcorder disc, most DVD camcorders offer multiple recording *formats*, with such cheerful names as DVD-Video and DVD-VR. Each has tradeoffs: One plays back in a broader range of DVD players, another lets you erase scenes before committing them to plastic, and so on.

The thing is, you have to choose which format you want *when you put the blank DVD into the camcorder*. That's when the screen offers you the choice of formats. The key here is to choose the DVD-Video format, sometimes called Standard. If you choose VR or DVD-VR instead, iMovie won't be able to import your recorded video. (When you connect the camcorder, iMovie thinks you just inserted a DVD, rather than thinking that you attached a disk full of video.)

Recording Live from a Camcorder or iSight Camera

iMovie is also happy to capture live video straight from a tape camera, sending whatever it "sees" directly into iMovie. You can perform this stunt in either of two ways:

- **Using an iSight camera**. All recent Mac laptops and iMacs have this tiny Apple video camera built right in, just above the screen (Figure 1-13).

- **Using a camcorder**. Alternatively, you can connect a MiniDV camcorder to your Mac and use it as a glorified eyeball. (This doesn't work with tapeless and USB camcorders, and doesn't work if your Mac lacks a FireWire jack [page 9].)

Tip: You can even use an ordinary webcam, so long as it has a FireWire connector. Not many do.

Figure 1-13:
This tiny lens, in the top of every Mac laptop and iMac display frame, records live video with surprisingly good quality.

Here are the steps:

1. **If you're using a camcorder, set its mode switch to Camera or Record (rather than VCR or Play, as you would if you were importing something you'd already recorded).**

   If you're using an iSight camera or FireWire webcam, you can skip this step.

2. **Choose File→Import from Camera (⌘-I), or click the camcorder-shaped button at the left side of the screen.**

   Either way, the Import window opens. If everything's going your way, you'll see a live video image from your camera.

Note: If you have *more than one* camera connected—a camcorder connected to a Mac that has an iSight camera, for example—choose the camera you want to use from the Import From pop-up menu (at the lower-left corner of the Import window).

---

3. **Click Capture.**

   The usual "Save to" dialog box appears, just as shown in Figure 1-5.

4. **From the "Save to" pop-up menu, choose a hard drive's name.**

   Specify where you want iMovie to save your imported video.

5. **Specify an Event.**

   The pair of choices shown in Figure 1-5 lets you answer these questions: Were the scenes you're about to import filmed at a new Event, or should iMovie file them with scenes you already imported, as part of an existing Event? See "The Definition of an Event" on page 39 for details.

6. **Click OK.**

   iMovie begins importing the live video image.

7. **To end the recording, click Stop.**

   iMovie enters its usual "Generating Thumbnails" state of catatonia for a few minutes.

   To record more video, repeat these steps, starting at step 2.

8. **When you finish recording, click Done.**

   Your video appears in the Event you specified, ready for editing.

Importing Old iMovie Projects

Most software companies, most of the time, stick with certain time-honored traditions concerning software upgrades. One of them happens to be compatibility: If you release BeeKeeper Pro 7, it goes without saying that it can open files BeeKeeper Pro 6 created.

iMovie '08, '09, and '11, though, aren't updated versions of iMovie 6 (also known as iMovie HD); they're versions 1.0, 2.0, and 3.0 of a completely different program, written from scratch (see page 2 for details). Their ability to import older iMovie projects is extremely limited.

To bring in an older iMovie project, choose File→Import→iMovie HD Project. The dialog box shown in Figure 1-14 appears.

Here, you should make two decisions before choosing the old iMovie project you want to open:

- **Where do you want to save the imported, converted project?** The "Save to" pop-up menu lists your hard drives and shows you how much space is available on each.

- **How do you want iMovie to handle high-definition video projects?** See page 37 for details on making a choice here.

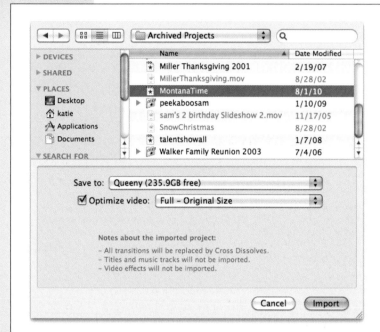

Figure 1-14:
In this dialog box, you specify what, where, and how you want to open an older iMovie project.

Apple Intermediate Codec

iMovie '11 can *edit* lots more formats than the old iMovie could, including MPEG-2 SD (from memory-card camcorders), MPEG-4, iSight video (Photo JPEG), H.264, and DV.

But if you import the two high-definition camcorder formats, HDV (high-def tape camcorders) and AVCHD (high-def tapeless), it must first convert them to AIC format.

A-I-what?

AIC stands for Apple Intermediate Codec. The conversion from high-def to AIC is what takes so bloomin' long when you import AVCHD clips.

There's a good reason for this: HDV and AVCHD are formats never intended for editing. They were meant to store a lot of video quality using very little camcorder space. So when you import them to the Mac, you're dealing with gigantic, unwieldy files that would make your processor wheeze and gasp.

Enter AIC. The AIC format retains all the quality of the original video, but is much faster to edit, play, copy, paste, and so on.

When Apple calls this converter "intermediate," it's not kidding; the video remains in this format only as you edit. When you finally *do* something with your finished movie, you usually convert it *back* into another format, like the H.264 format for YouTube or the MobileMe Web Gallery (Chapter 14).

All of this explains, by the way, why you can't drag movies into the main iMovie window to import them. You have to drag them into an *Event* or use the File→Import→Movies command. Both of those options trigger the conversion of incoming movies to the AIC format (and create filmstrip thumbnails for them) to prepare them for editing.

Once you make your choices, navigate to the iMovie project you want to import, and double-click its name or icon.

iMovie '11 springs into action, importing the video clips (making a new copy of them) and generating the filmstrip thumbnails you'll work with as you edit. This process can take a good long time.

When it's all over, whatever clips you had in your old project's iMovie timeline appear in the iMovie '11 Project (storyboard) area, in the correct sequence, correctly trimmed. iMovie imports leftover clips, too—the ones left unused in the Clips pane of your old project. They show up in the Event that holds your project, just in case you want to add them to the project later.

On the other hand, iMovie brings in only a few basic elements of the original iMovie project. To be precise:

- **You get only the clips**. iMovie '11 ignores all effects, titles, and credits. (Ouch.)
- **You lose all the audio work you did**. iMovie '11 ignores everything in the old iMovie's two audio tracks, including music, narration, sound effects, and any audio "paste-over" cutaways. The only audio that carries over is that in your project's video clips.
- **iMovie replaces all your scene transitions**. If you used any transitions in your old iMovie project, iMovie '11 replaces them all with generic crossfade dissolves.

If you really, truly want to go to all this trouble, you can now start over again, repairing and reconstructing the movie, restoring the elements that got lost during the import process. You might find the effort worthwhile if you want to use some iMovie '11 tools that weren't available in the old iMovie, like video cropping, stabilization, rotation, or one-click exporting to YouTube.

Otherwise, though, consider leaving your old iMovie projects just as they are. As Chapter 12 makes clear, the old iMovie version is still perfectly usable and freely available to you, so it might make more sense to leave it in its original format.

Dragging Video In from the Finder

iMovie can import movies directly from your hard drive, too—no camcorder needed. Position the iMovie window so you can see your movie files in the Finder, and then drag the files' icons directly onto an Event in iMovie's Event list. (Each clip icon is different—iMovie creates the icon still from actual footage.)

Alternatively, use the File→Import→Movies command to find and select the movies you want to import. iMovie asks which Event you want to save the imported flicks to.

Either way, you wind up with your digital movie files in an Event and ready to edit.

Importing with iMovie's Drop Box Folder

If you're short on time and you have a stack of videos you want to import, iMovie '11's new Drop Box folder is your friend. iMovie will import any video files in this folder the next time you open the program. This way, you can simply drop your movie files into the folder and forget about them. Then, the next time you launch iMovie, it imports the files. And if you're a pro with automation programs, like AppleScript or Automator, this folder becomes even handier (page 441).

Look in your iMovie Events folder (page 59) to find the folder called iMovie Drop Box. After you add files to this folder, iMovie displays a message like the one in Figure 1-15 the next time you open the program. Click Import Now; iMovie displays an Import window much like the one you saw in Figure 1-5. (For some reason, this window is missing the Stabilization checkbox. You'll have to analyze this footage later, as explained on page 176.)

Figure 1-15:
Top: If you have files lingering in your iMovie Drop Box folder, iMovie lets you know the next time you launch the software.

Bottom: Importing video files from the Drop Box works much the same way it does when you import files from your camera.

Note: If you notice that some of your Drop Box files didn't make it into iMovie for some reason, look in your iMovie Events folder for another folder called "Unused Drop Box Items."

Importing Footage from Old Analog Tapes

We live in a transitional period. Millions of the world's existing camcorders and VCRs require VHS, VHS-C, or 8mm cassettes—that is, analog tapes instead of digital.

These days, people buy only digital camcorders. But in the meantime, how are you supposed to import and edit the footage you shot before the digital era? Fortunately, this is fairly easy to do if you have the right equipment. You can take any of these four approaches, listed roughly in order of preference.

Note: When you use any of the approaches below, iMovie won't be able to chop the video into individual scenes automatically, as it does with digital video. That's because old analog camcorders didn't stamp every frame of every shot with an invisible time code, so iMovie doesn't know when you started and stopped your camcorder.

Approach 1: Use a Camcorder with Pass-Through Conversion

If you're in the market for a new digital camcorder, here's a great idea: Buy a Sony or Canon MiniDV tape camcorder that has analog-to-digital *pass-through conversion*. The camcorder itself acts as a converter—it turns the signal from your old analog tapes into a digital one that you can edit in iMovie. (Unfortunately, few modern camcorders have this feature, so ask before you buy. And on some models, you have to use the camcorder's own menu system to enable pass-through—and that process requires a Mac model that has a FireWire jack.)

Your old footage never hits a MiniDV tape. It simply plays from your older VCR or camcorder through the digital camcorder "converter" and into your Mac.

If you've got a drawer full of analog tapes, a pass-through camcorder is by far the most elegant and economical solution, especially if you're shopping for a new camcorder anyway.

Approach 2: Record onto Your DV Camcorder

Even if your newish digital camcorder doesn't offer *real-time* analog-to-digital conversion, it may have analog inputs that let you record your old material onto a MiniDV tape in your *new* camcorder. If so, your problem is solved:

1. **Unplug the FireWire cable from the DV camcorder.**

    Most camcorders' analog inputs automatically switch off if you have a FireWire cable hooked up.

2. **Connect RCA cables from the Audio Output and Video Output jacks on the side of your older camcorder or VCR. Connect the opposite ends to the analog inputs of your DV camcorder.**

    Put a blank tape in your DV camcorder.

Tip: If both your old camcorder and your DV camcorder have *S-video* connectors (round, dime-sized jacks), use them instead. S-video connections offer higher-quality video than RCA connections. (Note that an S-video cable doesn't conduct sound, however. You still have to connect the red and white RCA cables to carry the left and right stereo sound channels.)

3. **Switch both camcorders into VTR or VCR mode.**

   You're about to make a copy of the older tape by playing it into the camcorder.

   By now, every fiber of your being may be screaming, "But analog copies make the quality deteriorate!" Relax. You're only making a first-generation copy. Actually, since you're making a digital copy, you lose only half as much quality as you would with a normal VCR-to-VCR duplicate. In other words, you probably won't be able to spot any picture deterioration. And you'll have the footage in digital format forever, ready to make as many copies as you want with no further quality degradation.

4. **Press the Record button on the DV camcorder, and press Play on the older VCR or camcorder.**

   You can monitor your progress by watching your camcorder's LCD screen. Remember that a DV cassette generally holds only 60 minutes of video, compared with 2 hours on many previous-format tapes. You may have to change DV cassettes halfway through the process.

When it finishes the transfer, you can rewind the newly recorded DV cassette in the DV camcorder and import it into iMovie exactly as described in this chapter.

Approach 3: Use a Media Converter

If your digital camcorder doesn't have analog inputs, you can buy an *analog-to-digital converter*—a box that sits between your Mac and your VCR or older camcorder (Figure 1-16). It's an unassuming half-pound gray box, about 3 × 5 inches. Its primary features include analog audio and video (and S-video) inputs, which accommodate your older video gear, and a FireWire jack, whose cable you can plug into your Mac.

You'll be very pleased with the video quality. And when it comes to converting older footage, the media-converter approach has a distinct advantage over DV camcorders with analog inputs: You have to sit through the footage only once. As your old VCR or camcorder plays the tape through the converter, the Mac records it simultaneously. (Contrast that with Approach 2, which requires you to play the footage *twice*: once to the DV camcorder, and then from there to the Mac.)

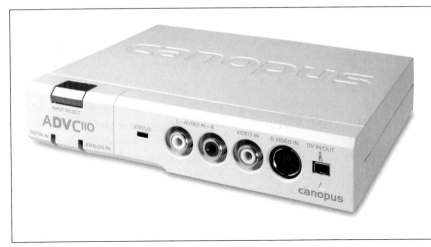

Figure 1-16:
*The Canopus ADVC-
110 (http://www.
grassvalley.com/
products/advc110,
about $210) requires
no external power
because it draws
its juice from your
Mac via the FireWire
cable. And it can
handle both NTSC
(North American)
and PAL (European)
video signals (see
page 19).*

Unfortunately, you can't control these devices using iMovie's playback controls, as described earlier in this chapter. Instead, you have to transfer your footage manually, by pressing Play on your old camcorder or VCR and then clicking Import on the iMovie screen. In that way, these converters aren't as convenient as an actual DV or Digital8 camcorder.

Approach 4: Use a Digital8 Camcorder

Sony's Digital8 family of camcorders accommodate 8mm, Hi-8, *and* Digital8 tapes, which are 8mm cassettes recorded digitally. (Low-end models may not offer this feature, however, so ask before you buy.) Just insert your old 8mm or Hi-8 cassettes into the camcorder and proceed as described in this chapter. iMovie never needs to know that the camcorder doesn't contain a DV cassette.

Actually, a Digital8 camcorder grants you even more flexibility: Most Digital8 camcorders also have *analog inputs*, which let you import footage from your VCR or other tape formats, as described in Approach 2.

The Lay of the Land

I f you're coming to iMovie '11 from iMovie HD (also known as iMovie 6), you're likely to be a bit confused; the design of '11 is completely different from HD. If you're coming to iMovie '11 from any *other* video-editing program, you'll be equally baffled. And if you've never used a video-editing program at all, well, you probably have no clue what's going on.

Before you delve into the actual experience of chopping and rearranging your video into a finished masterwork, therefore, it's worth sampling this brief chapter on what, exactly, iMovie is up to. Here's where you'll learn what's where on the screen, where iMovie actually stores your videos, and how to tailor the setup to your work habits.

The Concept of Movie Projects

A *project*, in iMovie lingo, is a movie you're editing. The reason you're learning iMovie in the first place is to create these projects.

In old versions of iMovie, projects showed up as icons on your desktop. They were really cleverly disguised folders, and inside, you'd find all the gigantic movie clips you used in your movie. This was convenient in one way: It made projects fully self-contained. So you could, for example, easily back up a project or move the whole thing to another computer.

But in another way, it wasn't ideal. If you wanted to use a particular piece of video in more than one project, you had to duplicate the clip (by pasting it into the second project), which ate up a lot more of your hard drive space.

iMovie '11 operates on a totally different system. In your Events list (click ⚡ in the lower-left of the iMovie window), the program displays every piece of video on your

Mac—even video on external hard drives. And all of that video is available to all your projects, all the time.

When you choose a video clip to use in a project, you're not moving the clip anywhere, you're just providing a *pointer* to it, so iMovie knows where to look for each piece of video in your project.

This new system has a number of implications:

- You can use the same video clip in dozens of movie projects, without ever eating up more disk space (see Figure 2-1).

Figure 2-1:
An orange line across the bottom edge of a source clip lets you know which chunks of the clip you used in your project. When you click a different project, you'll see the orange lines jump around. That's because you used a different chunk of the same source clip in the second project.

- You can create multiple versions of the same project—a long one and a short one, for example—without worrying about filling up your hard drive.

Note: Each project takes up disk space, but only an infinitesimal amount—about as much as a word processor document. It contains only a text list of *pointers* to bits of video on your hard drive.

- Backing up or moving a single project is no longer simply a matter of copying a file. Yes, there's a folder that contains your individual project files. (It's the Home→Movies→iMovie Projects folder.) But if you drag a project file from one disk to another, you'll have nothing, because you'll have left behind the raw video the project points to. (In iMovie '11, there is, however, a way to move or copy a project to another folder or disk, together with all the Event footage the project needs. Page 60 tells all.)

When you finish editing a project, you'll probably want to *send* it somewhere: to YouTube, to a DVD, to a QuickTime movie, or wherever. Only then does iMovie meld together the edits you specify in the project file with the video stored in the Events Library to produce a single, sharable movie file.

The Project Library

iMovie '11 keeps a handy list of all your projects in the *Project Library* (Figure 2-2). This list displays the name and a preview still of each project. It also displays the length and date of the project, plus a set of icons that indicate whether you shared your project to YouTube, MobileMe, iTunes, or the Media Browser. (Chapters 13 and 14 cover all these sharing options.)

Figure 2-2:
The Project Library shows your list of projects and project folders, along with a skimmable preview of your project and other useful information, like the project date, length, and shared status.

To begin editing an existing project, double-click the project name, or click the arrow-shaped Edit Project button in the top-left corner of the iMovie window. On the other hand, if you're already editing a project, you can go back to your Project Library by clicking the Project Library arrow (where the Edit Project button used to be).

Creating a Project

To create a new project, you have three choices:

- Choose File→New Project.
- Press ⌘-N.
- Click the + button beneath the Projects list.

In each case, the New Project screen appears, as shown in Figure 2-3. Here's where you name your project and choose its *aspect ratio* (see the explanation on page 62). You can also choose the theme and transitions you want iMovie to automatically apply. (You'll find themes covered on page 139 and transitions on page 125.) From here, you can also create a trailer project, discussed in detail in Chapter 11.

Figure 2-3:
Name your new project and specify the shape of the movie frame. In iMovie '11, you can also choose the frame rate (see page 342), along with a project theme and transitions. The project will appear in the list at lower left.

Duplicating a Project

It's often useful to create several versions of the same project. You could have a short and a long version, for example, or an R-rated and a PG-rated version, or several differently edited cuts so you can get feedback on which one works best.

The beauty of iMovie '11 is that you can duplicate a project easily and simply, without filling up your hard drive with duplicate video files. Each version of the project calls upon the *same* underlying video files.

To duplicate a project, click its name, and then choose File→Duplicate Project. You'll see the new project appear in the Project Library, complete with a temporary name (for example, if you called the original project "Baby Spaghetti on Head," iMovie calls the new one "Baby Spaghetti on Head 1." If you make a duplicate of the duplicate, iMovie is smart enough to call the newest copy "Baby Spaghetti on Head 2.") Feel free to rename your project using the method described next. Then you can get to work editing the new version of your project, independently of the original.

Renaming a Project

To give a project a new name, double-click the old name. The renaming rectangle opens so you can type in a new title.

Project Folders

It's great to have every project you've ever done right at your fingertips at all times. But when your projects start to pile up and the list gets unwieldy, you can create virtual folders to organize them—for example, a "2009 Movies" folder, a "2010 Movies" folder, and so on.

Click inside the Project list and then choose File→New Folder. iMovie creates a new folder icon in the list, much the way iPhoto creates albums or iTunes creates playlists. Conveniently enough, you'll see these folders any time you use the Media Browser (page 404) to incorporate your iMovie work into iDVD, Keynote, and so on.

You can rename a folder by double-clicking it, or delete it (*and* everything inside it, as described next) by choosing File→"Move Folder to Trash" (⌘-Delete).

Deleting a Project

To get rid of a project, click its name, and then choose File→"Move Project to Trash," or press ⌘-Delete.

Behind the scenes, iMovie moves the selected project to the *Macintosh* Trash. (To see for yourself, click 🗑 in your Dock and open the iMovie Temporary Items folder.) iMovie no longer lists the project, but it's not *completely* gone until you return to your desktop, choose Finder→Empty Trash, and click OK.

POWER USERS' CLINIC

Behind the Scenes at iMovie '11

In this chapter, you'll read about some sneaky ways to go behind iMovie's back. For example, if you delete a project or an Event by accident, you can rescue it by opening your Mac's Trash folder and manually restoring the files to their rightful place.

That's because, in the end, iMovie '11 is nothing more than a glorified front end for the files that actually sit on your hard drive. And knowing the relationship between what you see in iMovie and what you find in the Finder can be extremely useful.

It turns out that every project, Event, and camcorder clip you see in iMovie corresponds to an icon in the Finder. Want to see them? Open your Home folder (in the Finder, choose Go→Home), and then double-click the Movies folder. (Alternatively, click Movies in the sidebar at the left side of *any* Finder window.)

Here they are, the special folders iMovie '11 creates. One, called iMovie Projects, contains the icons for every project you've made in iMovie '11.

Another, called iMovie Events, contains individual folders for each set of clips you import. And inside *those* folders are the actual QuickTime video clips you imported that day. (It's here that you also find the iMovie Drop Box folder described on page 50.)

Every time you open iMovie '11, what you see in the Project Library and the Event Library is nothing more than a mirror of what's in the Finder, in the two iMovie folders within the Movies folder. (OK, you also see the videos you keep in iPhoto, but that's another story.)

Undeleting a Project

On the other hand, what if you delete a project and then change your mind? Or you delete the wrong one by accident? As long as you haven't yet emptied the Macintosh Trash, you can get that project back. Figure 2-4 shows the procedure.

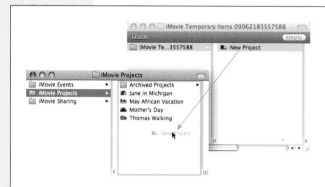

Figure 2-4:
Behind the scenes, iMovie represents every project with an icon in your Home→ Movies→iMovie Projects folder (front window). To rescue a project you deleted by accident, open the Trash (click its Dock icon 🗑), open the iMovie Temporary Items folder, and then drag the project's icon from the Trash back into the iMovie Projects folder. The next time you open iMovie, you'll find the project right back in the Projects list, ready to go.

Moving a Project

While in iMovie '11, you can copy an entire project to another hard drive. This comes in handy if, for example, you want to move a project to an external drive so you can edit it on another computer. Because iMovie automatically lists all your hard drives in the Project Library, moving a project is just a matter of dragging it to that drive's icon in the Project Library list.

At that point, iMovie shows a dialog box, pictured in Figure 2-5. If you choose "Copy project," iMovie makes a copy of the project—the pointers that describe the edits you've made—but *not* the Event footage that the project uses. You'd use this method *only* if the other computer or hard drive already contains a copy of all the video you're working with.

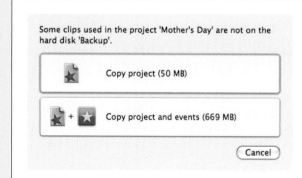

Figure 2-5:
If you move a project to another drive, iMovie lets you choose between moving just the project, or the project together with the Event footage it uses. Be sure to choose the latter if you want to edit the project on another computer. In most cases, therefore, you'll want "Copy project and events" instead. This option ensures that you take everything the project needs, including its source video, so you can continue to edit it.

Consolidating Project Media

Consolidating video is something like the opposite of moving a project; it keeps the *project* in place and moves the footage (and music) instead. Suppose, for example, you're editing a project on your computer's internal hard drive, and it incorporates raw video from an external drive. This is no big deal as long as the external drive *stays connected* to your computer. But what if you're using a laptop, and you take it on a trip without that external hard drive? You won't be able to edit the project, unless you used the Consolidate command first to copy all the necessary files to the laptop. (Nobody said this was going to be simple.)

iMovie knows this type of thing can happen and offers a convenient solution. Select the project in question by clicking its name in the Project Library. Then choose File→Consolidate Media. (This menu item is grayed out if the project footage and the project itself already reside on the same drive.) The dialog box in Figure 2-6 appears, giving you three options:

- **Copy the events**. This option copies *all* the footage from *all* the Events whose clips you used in the project, even clips or parts of clips that you haven't yet incorporated into your project. Use this option if you think you may want to use other bits from those Events during an editing session later.

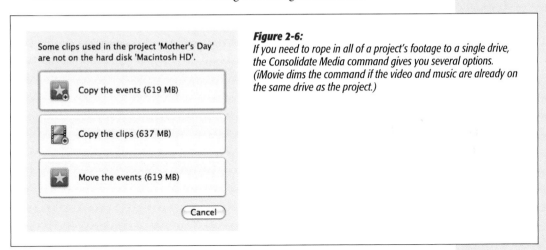

Some clips used in the project 'Mother's Day' are not on the hard disk 'Macintosh HD'.

Copy the events (619 MB)

Copy the clips (637 MB)

Move the events (619 MB)

Cancel

Figure 2-6:
If you need to rope in all of a project's footage to a single drive, the Consolidate Media command gives you several options. (iMovie dims the command if the video and music are already on the same drive as the project.)

- **Copy the clips**. Unlike the first option, clicking this button copies *only* the video you use in a project—just the pieces of just the clips—and not the surrounding Event footage. Use this option if you finished editing the project, but still want to be able to export it at full quality. (Clearly, this option requires a lot less hard-drive space than "Copy the events.")

- **Move the events**. This option is the same as "Copy the events," except that it *deletes* the Events video from the old drive after it moves the footage to the new drive.

All three options also copy any music files in the project to the new disk.

Tip: Remember, choosing Consolidate Media moves footage to the drive where your project currently resides. If you want the footage *and* the project on another drive, follow the instructions on page 60.

Aspect Ratios: The Missing Manual

Aspect ratio is an annoying geek term for *shape of the movie frame.* Having to learn about aspect ratios is an unfortunate requirement if you're going to master video editing.

A standard 1980 TV set's screen isn't the same shape as a movie screen. The TV is almost square but the movie is wide and short. They have different *aspect ratios* (see Figure 2-7).

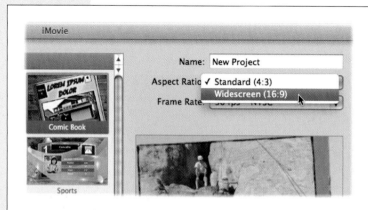

Figure 2-7:
iMovie offers you a choice of two aspect ratios: Standard (like a traditional TV) or Widescreen (like a high-def TV). You can always change your mind later.

Standard TVs have a 4:3 aspect ratio. Those are the horizontal:vertical proportions. So if your screen is 4 feet wide, it's 3 feet high.

High-def TV screens, on the other hand, are 16:9. If the width is 16 feet, then the height is 9 feet (and you have a heck of a big TV).

Note: Weirdly, 16:9 is *not* the standard aspect ratio for Hollywood movies! Those are usually 1.85:1 or 2.35:1. (Don't ask why movie aspect ratios always have 1 in the denominator. Nobody ever accused the video industry of being consistent.)

Believe it or not, those aren't even the only common aspect ratios. Consider the iPhone, which, of course, Apple hopes that *everybody* owns. Its screen is 3:2!

Every time you create a new project, iMovie asks you, "What aspect ratio would you like, O Master?"

If the result will play on a standard TV, choose Standard (4:3). If it will play on a high-def TV, choose Widescreen (16:9). The Widescreen setting is also the best match for the screen on an iPhone or iPod Touch.

And if it will play on the Internet or as a QuickTime movie, the aspect ratio really makes no difference. Choose the one that best fits the original video shape.

Mismatched Aspect Ratios

One cool thing about iMovie '11 is that it can handle *multiple* aspect ratios in the same movie. You can mix and match source video with different aspect ratios into a single, fixed-shape project.

How is this possible? Whenever iMovie encounters source video that doesn't fit a frame, it does one of two things:

- Adds black letterbox bars above and below the picture (or on either side).
- Blows up the video large enough to fill the frame. In the process, of course, some of the picture gets chopped off at the top and bottom of the frame, or on the right and left sides.

Figure 2-8 shows both situations.

Figure 2-8:
Top: If you choose the Standard frame for your movie, then standard video fits fine but widescreen video, shown here, has to be either cropped or letterboxed.

Bottom: If you choose Widescreen for your movie, then standard 4:3 video, shown here, also has to be either cropped or letterboxed. (Actually, when the black bars are vertical, some people call them pillarbox bars.)

So those are iMovie's two solutions: letterbox bars or cropping. But *you* have to tell iMovie which you prefer. To do that, click the name of the project, and then choose File→Project Properties (⌘-J). In the Project Properties dialog box (Figure 2-9), use the Initial Video Placement pop-up menu to choose either Crop (the misfitting video gets enlarged to fill the frame, even though you'll lose some video at the edges), or "Fit in Frame" (you get letterbox bars). Click OK.

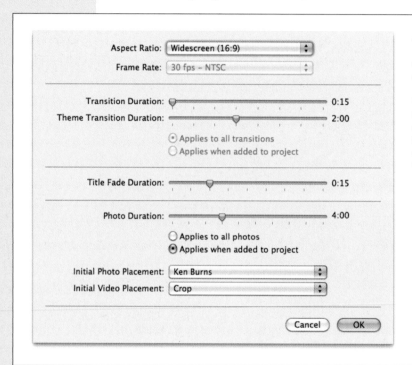

Figure 2-9:
The Project Properties dialog box lets you specify how you want misfitting video wedged into your chosen movie-frame shape: by cropping or by zooming. Here, you can also change the aspect ratio for a project—even one that's underway.

Changing Your Project's Aspect Ratio

Yes, iMovie asks you what aspect ratio you want when you first create a project. But you're not locked into it. You can change your mind at any moment.

Suppose, for example, you chose Widescreen when you created a project but later, after editing for a while, you realize that the vast majority of your footage is in standard-definition video. In that case, you'll probably want to make the whole project Standard, to minimize the amount of time your audience spends staring at letterbox bars.

To change aspect ratios for a project underway, click its name, and then choose File→Project Properties (⌘-J). In the window that appears, choose a new aspect ratio from the Aspect Ratio pop-up menu at the top, and then click OK.

iMovie dutifully reformats the movie, adding *different* letterbox bars as necessary, or zooming mismatched videos *differently*.

All About Events

At the lower-left corner of the iMovie window, you see the Events Library. It's supposed to be a massive repository of all the video on your entire computer, from all sources (Figure 2-10).

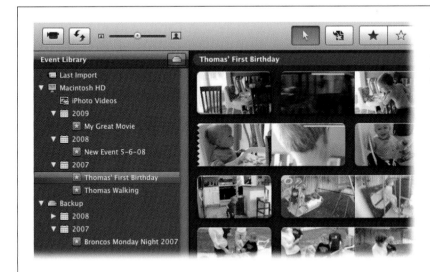

Figure 2-10:
When you click an Event name (left), iMovie shows you all the video clips it contains (right).

It's organized like this:

- **Last Import**. Click this heading to view, in the clips area, all the video clips *most recently* imported from your camcorder. Often, this is precisely what you want.

- **iPhoto Videos**. Click 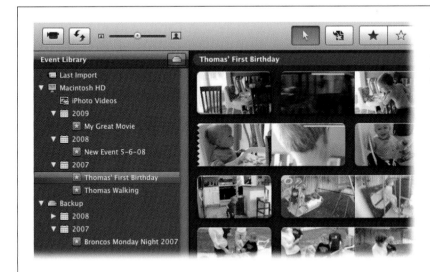 to see all the movie clips you shot with your digital *still* camera (not your camcorder). In the Great iLife Master Plan, of course, it's not iMovie that handles photos and videos from still cameras—it's *iPhoto*. So here, iMovie is giving you handy, one-click access to all the videos you imported into iPhoto from your still camera.

- **2010, 2009, 2008…** These year headings organize your camcorder video collection into annual clumps. Click the flippy triangle to expand or collapse the year heading, so you can see all the video batches within it.

These expanded lists actually show you all the individual import jobs you performed during that year, each with whatever name you gave it. If you click one of these Event names, the right side of the window displays all the video clips inside that Event.

Fine-Tuning the Events List

iMovie offers a slew of options designed to help you manage big video collections. (Some of them make it clear that Apple expects all of us to have multiple 2-terabyte hard drives in the very near future.)

- **Break it down by disk**. In the View menu, you'll find a command called Group Events By Disk. This command is made possible by iMovie's ability to see Events on multiple drives.

  If you choose View→Group Events By Disk, iMovie adds headings representing each of your hard drives, showing which videos you stored on each. Clicking the hard-drive-icon button at the top of your Event list does the same thing as the menu command, and the icon glows blue when you view your Events by disk.

- **Break it out by month**. You can also make iMovie break down each year's worth of Events by *month*. Just choose View→Group Events By Month. Now iMovie adds month subheadings within each year category: May, August, and so on. (To save space, it adds headings only for the months you actually shot video.)

- **Show days within Events**. Within an Event, or as you view multiple Events at once, you may have footage that spans several days. To see when one day ends and another begins, choose View→"Show Separate Days in Events." iMovie inserts dated, gray bars before each day's worth of clips.

- **Reverse the sort order**. Ordinarily, iMovie lists your Events in reverse chronological order, from oldest to newest. If you choose View→"Most Recent Events at Top," iMovie flips the sort order, and newest videos appear at the top.

- **Adjust the font size**. Out of the box, iMovie assumes you have a lot of video to manage. If you don't, or if you have a nice big monitor (or aging eyes), you can ask iMovie to enlarge the type size for the Events and Projects lists. Choose iMovie→Preferences, click the Browser tab, and then turn on "Use large font for Project Library and Event Library."

- **Add the dates**. Having your footage grouped by month is handy, but it can be even handier to see the exact *dates* you shot your clips. Once again, asking iMovie to display this information eats up screen space, but it's very helpful if your Events list isn't already sprawling off the screen.

  To make it so, choose iMovie→Preferences, and then, under the Browser tab, turn on "Show date ranges in Event Library." As shown in Figure 2-11, you now see little date ranges for your movies.

Splitting Events

You'll often want to split one Event into two. After all, a MiniDV tape holds an hour of footage; a harddrive camcorder holds 5 hours or more. On any given day, what you import to iMovie probably includes video you shot on different days. It will all wind up in one Event, unless you manually split it into different ones.

To split an Event, click its name in iMovie, and then proceed as shown in Figure 2-12.

Figure 2-11:
If you go nuts, you can add all kinds of useful information to the Events list: clumpings by hard drive, clumpings by month, individual date ranges, and more.

Hard drive subheads on/off

Larger type

Broken down by year

Date range

Broken down by hard drive

Figure 2-12:
To split an Event, inspect the video clips within it by skimming and playing. When you find a clip that was obviously shot on a different day, as part of a different real-life event, click it. Then choose File→Split Event Before Selected Clip. iMovie places that clip, and all later ones, into a new Event. (The Event browser is shown here, swapped to the top of the screen for clarity; see also Figure 2-13.)

Merging Events

You can combine Events, too. For example, if you import from your camcorder after each day at Disney World, you might want to combine all those clips into a single Event at the end of your three-day vacation. To do that, see Figure 2-13.

Figure 2-13:
To merge two Events, simply drag the name of one onto the name of another (top). iMovie asks what you want to name the newly merged Event; type a name, and then click OK. (Once again, the Events Library is shown here swapped to the top of the screen.)

Renaming an Event

You rename an Event the same way you rename a project—double-click its existing name so that the renaming rectangle appears.

Changing the Date of an Event

It could happen. Maybe your camcorder didn't date-stamp your video properly. Maybe you imported a bunch of analog VHS or Hi-8 videos, which show up as undated video clips. Or maybe you need an alibi. Either way, you'll be happy to learn that you can manually change the date and time stamps on your video clips, and, therefore, the way that iMovie sorts them. (This works with any video you import into iMovie '11—even, for example, movies you import that are hard drive files or from iMovie 6.)

To make the change, select the Events clips needing a new date, and then right-click (or Control-click) them. In the shortcut menu, choose "Adjust Clip Date and Time."

iMovie shows you a dialog box with the old date and time, labeled "From," and a chance to enter a new date and time, labeled "To." The date setting follows the American convention of Month/Day/Year, while the time setting lets you set the new clip time down to the second. Clicking OK applies the needed date and time changes.

Deleting an Event

You delete Events the same way you delete projects: highlight an Event's name, and then press ⌘-Delete (or choose File→"Move Event to Trash").

iMovie gets rid of the Event and moves it to the Trash. (You can even click 🗑 on your Dock and *see* it inside the iMovie Temporary Items folder.)

Be careful, though. When you delete an Event, you're also deleting *all the video inside it!* All of those clips you so carefully imported now sit in the Trash, poised for extinction.

In a pinch, you can rescue them. Just open the Trash, open iMovie Temporary Items, and drag the Event's folder back into your Home→Movies→iMovie Events folder. The procedure is almost identical to what's depicted in Figure 2-4.

If you decide you're really finished with those clips, return to your desktop, choose Finder→Empty Trash, and then click OK. Now they're really, truly gone.

Five Ways to Remodel Your Workspace

iMovie '11 is refreshingly respectful of your screen real estate. It offers a bunch of ways to maximize your work area without the hassle of buying a whole new monitor.

Hide the Projects or Events List

Once you're working on a movie, you don't need the list of your other projects staring you in the face. iMovie gets this. As soon as you open a project, iMovie hides the list of projects, giving you more space for the storyboard itself. (You can always bring the Projects list back by clicking the Project Library arrow in the top-left corner of your iMovie window.)

You can hide the Events list as well, and for the same reason: because when you're editing your Disney vacation video, you probably don't need to be staring at a list of other vacation footage. This time, choose Window→Hide Event Library, or click the Show/Hide Events List button (Figure 2-14). The list goes away, and the video-clip area expands.

To bring the Event list back, repeat this procedure. You can also use the Hide and Show commands in the Window menu to hide or show the Project Library and the Event Library.

Tip: You can also make the *font* bigger in the Projects and Events lists (see page 66).

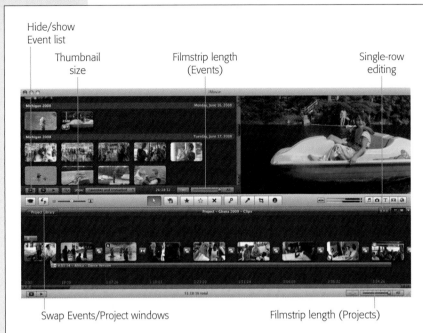

Hide/show
Event list

Thumbnail
size

Filmstrip length
(Events)

Single-row
editing

Figure 2-14:
*You can radically
change the look of
iMovie. You can hide
the Event list, for
example (top left). To
adjust the filmstrip
height, drag the
Thumbnail Size slider.
To adjust the horizon-
tal size of your film-
strips, drag the slider
at the lower-right
of the storyboard
or Events browser.
Swap the Projects and
Events lists by clicking
the Swap button, as
has been done here.
Finally, switch to
timeline editing by
clicking the Single-
Row button above the
storyboard.*

Swap Events/Project windows

Filmstrip length (Projects)

Make the Clips Smaller

iMovie '11 represents your video clips as *filmstrips*—multiframe horizontal strips whose lengths are proportional to the clip duration. You can read more about film-strips in Chapter 3.

For now, it's enough to note that you can adjust the size of these filmstrips, both verti-cally and horizontally. Making them smaller gives you less information about what's in a clip, of course, but it also increases the number of clips that fit on your screen.

See Figure 2-14 for instructions on making these adjustments.

Note: When you drag the filmstrip-length slider to its extreme-right position, iMovie represents every video clip by *one* frame; it no longer indicates the filmstrips' relative length, and every clip has just one icon. This arrangement makes clips easy to move around, resequence, and so on. It also makes this ver-sion of iMovie more familiar, if you're used to working in previous versions of the program.

Adjust or Relocate the Viewer

In iMovie, the *Viewer* is the playback window that sits in the upper-right corner of the screen. If you have a single monitor, the Viewer's always locked into the iMovie window. You can't drag it around freely, but you can change its size. If you have more than one monitor, you can use the second one to show the Viewer in full-screen mode.

To resize the Viewer, choose either Small, Medium, or Large from the Window→ Viewer submenu. Better yet, learn the keyboard shortcuts for the sizes so you can flip among them while you work: ⌘-8, ⌘-9, and ⌘-0.

The advantage of a large Viewer is, of course, that you get the best view of your movie as you work. The disadvantage is that a large Viewer eats up screen space. On smaller screens, it squishes down the Events area so much that you have to do more scrolling.

Tip: For more gradations of size and control, you can resize the Viewer by dragging the central, horizontal iMovie toolbar up or down. Use any blank spot as a handle.

If you're lucky enough to have a second monitor attached to your Mac, you can shove the Viewer out of the iMovie window altogether. Choose Window→"Viewer on Secondary Display." Now the preview fills the screen of your second monitor, giving you not only more editing room, but a much bigger Viewer as well. (Don't feel guilty if you buy a second monitor just for this feature. Many pro editors insist on a second display to preview their edits.)

Swap the Two Clip Areas

When you first fire up iMovie, the storyboard area, where you actually build your movie, is fairly small. It's wedged in between the Project Library and the Viewer.

The source-clips area, on the other hand, gets far more space, because it doesn't have the Viewer to contend with.

As you work on your movie, therefore, you may want to *swap* these two areas. You may wish that the *storyboard* could be the one with room to run, especially in the later stages of editing.

In that case, choose Window→"Swap Events and Projects," or click the *Swap button* shown in Figure 2-14. Once clicked, you get the cool, swoopy effect you see in Figure 2-15.

Tip: It probably goes without saying, but the first and most important step you can take to avoid having to use iMovie's scroll bars is to make the iMovie window itself as big as it can go! To do that, choose Window→Zoom, or click the little round, green Zoom button in the upper-left corner of the window.

Figure 2-15:
When you hit the Swap button, iMovie swaps the storyboard and Events browser areas, complete with an animated "funneling" effect to make sure you understand how you've just flopped the iMovie layout upside-down. (For slow-motion fun, press the Shift key while you click the Swap button.)

Single-Row Editing: Return of the Timeline

Few changes introduced in iMovie '08 upset more people than the unceremonious ditching of the timeline. If you've used any video-editing software other than iMovie '08, '09, or '11, then you've used a timeline before. Basically, it's a horizontally scrolling depiction of your movie, showing the video and audio tracks as long strips, punctuated by occasional transitions.

iMovie '08 dumped the timeline for something more like editing a text document. In the new design, the "filmstrips" representing your project wrap at the edge of the window, like sentences in a word processor. Now you have to scroll vertically to see the whole project instead of horizontally, and it's harder to get a mental picture of where you are in the whole thing.

This got under the skin of people who were accustomed to the traditional timeline. Now, in iMovie '11, two full versions of iMovie later, Apple has finally restored the basic timeline concept to iMovie.

A simple button click activates the timeline view, which Apple calls Single-Row Editing. (Maybe just calling it Timeline View would have been too obvious an admission of defeat.) The button lives just at the top-right of your project, next to the marker tray ( ). Clicking it morphs your movie into a horizontally scrolling version of your project, negating the need to scroll vertically. iMovie also inserts vertical timelines telling you where you are in your project. Everything else behaves the same way.

Tip: If you hide the Event list, swap the Project and Events areas, and then finally click the Single-Row Editing button, iMovie comes pretty dang close to looking like the iMovie of old (like in Figure 2-14). Ah, the memories!

To get the multiple-row editing back, click the Single-Row Editing button again. But if you were one of the vocal, timeline faithfuls, don't look back.

Building the Movie

Whether you work with video on your Mac or in a multimillion-dollar Hollywood professional studio, film editing boils down to three tiny tasks: selecting, trimming, and rearranging *clips*. Of course, that's like saying that painting boils down to nothing more than mixing various amounts of red, yellow, and blue. The *art* of video editing lies in your decisions about which clips you select, how you trim them, and in what order you put them.

You work with those clips in iMovie's two big storage areas. There's the *Event browser*, usually the bottom half of the screen, where all your raw, unedited video shots live. And there's the *storyboard*, usually the top half, where you assemble and edit your masterpiece.

At its simplest, then, iMovie editing is all about this three-step process:

1. **Review your video in the Event browser and find the good parts.**

2. **Add those chunks to the storyboard, where iMovie plays them in one seamless pass, from left to right.**

3. **Add crossfades, titles (credits), music, and effects.**

This chapter shows you the mechanics of the first two tasks: selecting raw footage, and adding it to your movie-in-progress. The following chapters cover the last step.

Phase 1: Review Your Clips (Skim + Play)

Video editing always starts with a pile of raw, unedited footage. In iMovie's case, that's the bunch of clips in the Event browser. Click an Event's name to see what video lurks inside.

Filmstrips

iMovie '11 represents every imported camcorder clip as a *filmstrip*—a horizontal bar whose length reflects the duration of the clip. The filmstrip is made up of individual sample frames from the clip.

Note: If a filmstrip is too wide for your iMovie window, it wraps around to the next line. A ragged filmstrip edge tells you that iMovie's wrapped your clip to the next line (think of that ragged edge as the video version of a hyphen). (The wrapping won't happen in your Project storyboard if you turned on Single-Row Editing as described on page 72.)

Each of these frames represents, for example, 5 seconds of actual video. So a 30-second video clip would appear as a filmstrip that's six frames long (Figure 3-1).

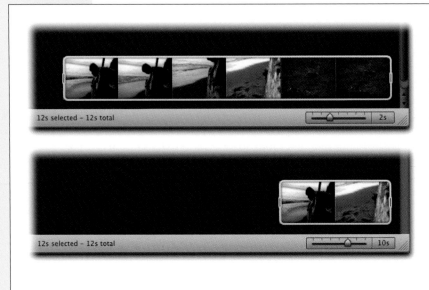

Figure 3-1:
Top: This filmstrip runs 12 seconds long, so with the "frames-per-thumbnail" slider set to "2 seconds," each frame represents 2 seconds of video. That's why you see six frames.

Bottom: If you adjust the slider, you change how many seconds of video each frame represents. Here, each frame represents a 10-second chunk of video (or a part thereof), which is why you now see only two frames.

Using the slider at the lower-right corner of the window, you can adjust the relative lengths of the filmstrips in your Event browser. An identical slider appears beneath the project storyboard area, meaning you can adjust the filmstrip lengths independently of each other.

So what's the right setting for these sliders? That's up to you, but here are some suggestions:

- At the slider's extreme-right position, iMovie represents every video clip by *one* frame. You can no longer tell the relative length of a clip; iMovie represents every clip as a single icon. This arrangement makes clips easy to move around, resequence, and so on. It makes a very long movie fit on your screen without scrolling. It also makes iMovie a lot more familiar if you're used to working in previous versions of the program.

- At the slider's extreme-left position, each frame of the filmstrip represents a *half second* of video. At this position, you can actually make frame-by-frame edits; see the box "Selecting Multiple Clips" on page 82.

- As you work, you can fiddle with the slider, zooming in and out as necessary. When you need to tweak the precise starting point of a piece of audio, for example, you might want to zoom in (drag the slider to the left); when you want to get a good overview of a long movie, you might want to zoom out (drag the slider to the right).

Skimming

At this point, you're about to learn the two iMovie skills you'll use most often: *skimming* and *playing*. Practice them, commit them to memory, make them automatic, and you'll absolutely fly through the editing process.

Skimming means moving your cursor across a filmstrip. Do not *click* or *drag* the strip, which would mean pressing the mouse button. Just *point* with the mouse.

The *playhead*—a vertical line, the height of the filmstrip—moves along with your cursor. And as you skim, the Viewer window plays back the underlying video at high speed—or medium speed, or slow speed, depending on your cursor speed. (You also see the same video playing within the filmstrip itself, beneath your cursor.)

Tip: Skimming also plays the *sound* of whatever clip you're examining–fast or slow, forward or reverse. Usually, that's helpful. But if the audio is driving you crazy, you can shut it up. Click the Audio Skimming button, shown in Figure 3-2, so that it turns into a faded version of itself. Or choose View→Audio Skimming (⌘-K) so that the checkmark disappears. Repeat the process to turn audio skimming back on.

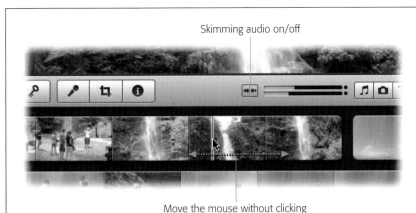

Skimming audio on/off

Move the mouse without clicking

Figure 3-2:
When you skim, you move your cursor across the face of a filmstrip without clicking your mouse button. It's a fast, simple way to find out what's in a clip without having to sit through a full playback. Click the Audio button to turn off the audio, which can be annoying.

Skimming may take some getting used to, because it's such an unusual computer technique; it's probably the first time in history that moving the mouse without clicking has done *anything* besides, well, moving the cursor to a new spot. But it means that you can control not only the speed of playback, but also the direction—forward or reverse—in real time, almost effortlessly.

Skimming works anywhere fine filmstrips are found—either in the Event browser or in the project storyboard (Figure 3-2).

Tip: You may sometimes wish that you could use the cursor as, well, a *cursor* instead of always making stuff play back. You may wish, for example, that you could freeze the frame as you skim–"Stay on this frame for just a sec"–while you go off to do something else with the cursor. You can. When you get to the spot you want to freeze, hold down the Control key. iMovie turns off skimming and leaves the same video frame on the screen until you release the Control key.

Playback

Skimming is great for quickly getting the gist of what's in your captured clips. But unless you're some kind of quasi-mechanical cyborg, you'll find it very difficult to skim at exactly the right speed for *real-time* playback.

Fortunately, iMovie can also play back clips all by itself, at the proper speed. To do that, use the space bar on your keyboard as the start/stop control. Hitting the space bar always begins playback at the position of your cursor, and it stops when you press the space bar again.

Once you master that difficult technique, you're ready for the real gem: using skimming and playback *together*. It works like this: Using your mouse, skim your footage, looking for the part you want to watch. When you get close to the right spot, tap the space bar. Playback begins from the precise position of your mouse.

UP TO SPEED

Secrets of the Filmstrip

When you stop and think about it, a filmstrip behaves just like a miniature QuickTime movie—and, in fact, that's precisely what it is.

You know how, after you import video, iMovie grinds to a halt and displays a message for several minutes that says, "Generating Thumbnails"? What it's actually doing is creating a little tiny QuickTime movie, 190 × 60 pixels, for use as the filmstrip for that clip. When you skim by moving your pointer, all you're really doing is playing back

that QuickTime movie. You can even see these thumbnail movies—they're sitting right there in your Movies→iMovie Events→[Name of the event]→Movie Thumbnails folder. (Look, but don't touch. Leave these miniatures alone.)

iMovie's most impressive stunt, in other words, is the way it lets you work with these miniatures as a representation for the enormous, full-frame clips—and plays the big ones back on command.

Tap the space bar to stop playback, then move your mouse to another spot, and then tap the space bar again. This way, you can jump around, spot-inspecting your clips, or even *pieces* of your clips, without ever touching the mouse button—and without ever having to wait.

Tip: Actually, there are four other ways to play back a source clip or your movie-in-progress, complete with corresponding keyboard shortcuts. Page 93 has details on all four:

- Play the selected chunk (/ key).
- Play from the beginning (\ key).
- Play the 2 or 6 seconds on either side of your cursor ([or] key, respectively).
- Play full-screen (⌘-G).

Phase 2: Select the Good Bits

The reason you're reviewing the clips in the Event browser, of course, is to find the good parts—the highlights, the pieces you want to include in your finished movie. Once you select a chunk of video, you can drag it into the storyboard to make it part of your movie.

Selecting comes in handy for other purposes, too. As you'll read in the next chapter, you can designate part of a clip as either a Favorite (a snippet you know you'll want to come back to later) or Reject (a worthless shot). These steps, too, require that you first *select* the piece of clip you want to tag.

GEM IN THE ROUGH

Playhead Info

One nice thing about working with *digital* video is that every frame of every shot is, behind the scenes, date- and time-stamped. (This presumes, of course, that you set your camcorder's internal clock when you bought it!) Years later, you can return to some captured video and see when, exactly, you filmed it.

Ordinarily, iMovie hides this information, on the assumption that the screen is busy enough already. (Besides, you may already have asked it to show the dates of your imports right in the Events list, as described on page 66.)

To see the dates of your video, choose View→Playhead Info, or just press ⌘-Y. Now when you skim, a handy info balloon floats above your playhead that says, for example,

"Sunday, February 10, 2008, 4:35 PM." It also shows how many seconds into the clip your pointer is. If you're skimming within a *project* (an assembled video), the balloon also tells you the timecode (in minutes:seconds:frames format) for that point in your project.

If iMovie has analyzed your video to correct stabilization or identify people (pages 176 and 117, respectively), the balloon tells you that, too. For example, the balloon for a particular shot might tell you, "One Person, Stabilization Analyzed, Wide," meaning that iMovie has stabilized the video and it's a wide shot of one person. It also tells you if the segment you're skimming is too shaky to stabilize. Press ⌘-Y again to hide the balloon.

Since selecting is such a critical step in iMovie moviemaking, Apple made sure you had all kinds of ways to do so. The following pages review them one by one.

Select by Dragging

The first selection method is the one you'll probably use most often: dragging. That is, slide the cursor across some footage while pressing the mouse button, just the way you'd select a phrase of text in a word processor.

iMovie indicates which part of a clip you selected by surrounding it with a yellow rectangle (Figure 3-3). The bottom edge of the iMovie window shows you how many seconds' worth of video you highlighted, relative to the original clip. Once you make a selection this way, you can adjust it; see page 82.

Figure 3-3:
You can highlight part of a clip by dragging across it. iMovie shows you what you selected by enclosing it in a yellow border.

Select 4-Second Chunks

iMovie makes it easy to build your movie from video snippets that are all exactly the same length—4-second chunks, for example. The iMovie online help says, over and over again, that using chunks of the same duration throughout your movie creates "an evenly paced project."

GEM IN THE ROUGH

The Mighty Undo

As programs go, iMovie is a forgiving one. Its Edit→Undo (⌘-Z) command is an *unlimited* one, meaning that you can retrace (undo) your steps, one at a time, working backward all the way back to the moment you opened iMovie. (You can even unimport a clip from your camcorder!)

There's an Edit→Redo command, too (Shift-⌘-Z), so you can undo your undoing.

Be warned: once you close iMovie, the program purges its Undo memory. It doesn't save a project's keystroke history so you can re-open the movie and start backtracking through your last session's commands.

Unless you're creating a music video of snowboarders, however, using all 4-second chunks also creates an artificially limiting project. Real-life events don't unfurl in consistent lengths. Still, having the ability to select tidy 4-second (or 2-second, or 10-second) chunks is occasionally handy—when you want to make the video match chord changes in a piece of background music, for example. To choose a 4-second chunk, click a filmstrip in the Event browser (without dragging). Your click marks the starting point; iMovie instantly selects the following 4 seconds of video.

Tip: You can change the factory setting, 4 seconds, to any length between 1 and 10 seconds. To do that, choose iMovie→Preferences, click the Browser tab, and then drag the "Clicking in Event browser selects" slider (Figure 3-4).

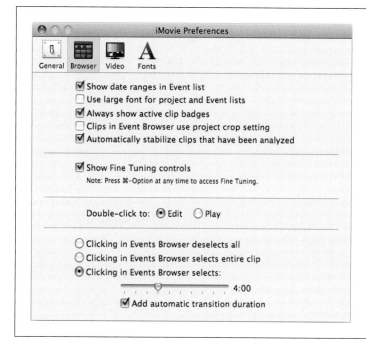

Figure 3-4:
What does a single click on a filmstrip in the Event browser mean? That's up to you. Out of the box, it means "Select 4 seconds" (or whatever duration you choose using the slider). But you can have it mean "Select the whole clip" if you prefer.

Selecting Entire Clips

In some cases, you may find that all this dragging or 4-second-clicking business is just too much fussiness—that you really want to select *entire clips* from the Event browser. Depending on the situation, you can select an entire clip in any of three ways:

- *Option-click* a filmstrip to highlight the whole thing.
- Click to select *part* of a clip, and then choose Edit→Select Entire Clip (⌘-A).

- Finally, if you *never* use that 4-second-clip selection feature, you can tell iMovie that one click on a filmstrip *always* selects the whole thing, even without the Option key. To do that, choose iMovie→Preferences, and then click the Browser tab. Turn on "Clicking in Events Browser selects entire clip" (Figure 3-4) and then close the Preferences window.

Note: These instructions apply only to selections in the Event browser. When you click a clip in your *project storyboard,* you *always* select the entire clip.

Selecting Multiple Clips

It's often useful to be able to select *more* than one clip at a time. Imagine how much faster you could work with clips—delete them, drag them, cut and paste them, mark them as Favorites or Rejects, and apply keywords to them—all at once.

Clips in the storyboard now behave just like icons in the Finder. For example, you can:

- **Highlight all the filmstrips**. Press ⌘-A (the equivalent of the Edit→Select All command).

- **Highlight random clips**. If you want to highlight, for example, only the first, third, and seventh clips in a storyboard, start by clicking clip icon No. 1. Then ⌘-click each of the others.

- **Remove a clip from the selection**. If you're highlighting a long string of clip icons and click one by mistake, you don't have to start over. Instead, just ⌘-click it again, so that the highlighting disappears. (If you *do* want to start over, you can deselect all selected clips by clicking any empty part of the window.)

  The ⌘ key trick is especially handy if you want to select *almost* all the icons in a window. Press ⌘-A to select everything in the storyboard, then ⌘-click any unwanted icons to deselect them.

- **Highlight consecutive clips**. Click the first clip you want to highlight, and then Shift-click the last one. iMovie automatically selects all the clips in between, along with the two you clicked. (This one works in both the storyboard *and* the Event browser.)

Adjusting a Selection

Once you highlight a portion of a filmstrip, you're not stuck with that yellow boundary just the way it is. You can adjust it within the filmstrip in any of four ways:

- Drag the vertical end handles of the yellow border to the right or left to select more or less of the clip.

- Shift-click another spot in the filmstrip. The nearest edge of the yellow border jumps to the location of your click, which makes the selection longer or shorter. Pressing Shift-arrow key (right or left) does the same thing.

- Drag the top or bottom edge of the yellow border to move the *entire* border on the filmstrip, sliding it around without changing its length. Use this technique to select a new chunk of footage.

- Press the right or left arrow keys to slide the selection border right or left one frame at a time.

Figure 3-5 shows these techniques.

Tip: These tips are great for making rough edits. For much finer control, get to know the new Precision Editor (page 105).

Playing a Selection

As you know, tapping the space bar always begins playing a video clip *at the position of the cursor*. But when you're making a selection, fiddling with that yellow border, that's not always what you want. In fact, it's probably *not* what you want.

A much more useful keystroke would be one that means, "Play what I've selected." And that's what the / key is for. (That's the slash next to the period key.) Tap it once to play whatever you selected; tap a second time to stop playback.

POWER USERS' CLINIC

Frame-Accurate Editing

If you're accustomed to a traditional timeline, like the kind found in iMovie HD, the storyboard in iMovie '11 could make editing feel fat-fingered. You might throw up your hands and decide that frame-precise editing is impossible. Happily, that isn't the case.

Modern digital video creates the illusion of motion by flashing about 30 pictures per second onscreen. If you want to be able to edit down to a specific frame, then you need to be able to zoom in close enough to see those 30 individual frames per second.

At first, it sure looks as though iMovie works in much larger chunks. But you can indeed make these precise adjustments. First, zoom way in, using the "frames-per-thumbnail" slider

at the lower-right corner of the window. In fact, if you drag this slider all the way to the left, each frame of the filmstrip represents a *half second* of video.

Then, if you drag the end of the yellow selection boundary carefully and slowly, you can actually feel it snap against *individual frames* of the recording—15 times for every filmstrip frame, in fact.

Let's see—each frame of your filmstrip represents half a second, and there are 15 snaps per frame. Sure enough, that's true frame-accurate editing. (The Shift-arrow key tip that appears on page 85 offers another method, one that doesn't require zooming in first.)

Figure 3-5:
Top: You can adjust the start or end points of a selection by dragging the side handles.

Middle: You can Shift-click to extend, or shrink, the right or left edge of the border. (iMovie adjusts whichever end of the border is closest to your Shift-click.)

Bottom: You can use the top or bottom edge of the yellow border as a handle to slide the entire selection area horizontally, without changing its duration. (You can also press the left or right arrow keys.)

Deselecting

To *deselect* whatever's selected—that is, to remove the yellow border entirely—use any of these three techniques:

- Click anywhere in the dark-gray background.
- Choose Edit→Select→None.
- Press Shift-⌘-A.

Actually, there's another way, too, but it involves a little backstory; see the box below.

Selecting Specific Project Elements

By the time you finish building a project, it might be full of all kinds of stuff—video clips, transitions, maps, and so on. In iMovie '11, you can select all the stuff of one type—for example, all the background images so you can change them from blue to black.

To do that, choose Edit→Select. iMovie shows you a long list of all the elements you can isolate in a project: Video Clips, Transitions, Photos, Maps, Backgrounds, and Animatics. Pretty handy.

Note: Unfortunately, titles and audio tracks are conspicuously missing from the Edit→Select list. For some reason, you can't select more than one of these at a time.

Phase 3: Build the Storyboard

The project storyboard is the large work area that starts out at the top of the screen, as shown in Figure 3-6. The key to building a movie is moving your selected video bits from the Event browser into this storyboard.

Adding to the End of the Storyboard

Most people, most of the time, build a movie by reviewing the raw footage from left to right—from beginning to end—and choosing bits, in sequence, to include in the edited movie. In such cases, you'll want to add your selected clip or clips to the *end* of your storyboard.

iMovie offers two ways to do that. Select some video in the Event browser, and then do one of these things:

- Press the letter E key.
- Click the Add Selection button (identified in Figure 3-6).
- If you have a Mac laptop with a multitouch trackpad (for example, a recent MacBook or MacBook Pro), swipe upward on your trackpad with three fingers.

GEM IN THE ROUGH

The Arrow-Key Trick

By tapping the right or left arrow keys, you can "walk" through a clip frame by frame, as though you're watching the world's least interesting slideshow. You'll even hear "one frame" of the audio, if you've got the audio turned on.

Hold down these arrow keys steadily to make the frame-by-frame parade go by faster—on a fast Mac, in fact, you get real-time playback when you hold down the arrow keys.

If you add the Shift key when you press the arrow, you make the nearest yellow border snap to your Playhead position. That's handy when you want to fine-tune a selection.

You can slap the yellow border around a certain clip, walk through it with the arrow keys to see if there might be a better ending point, and—when you're about to land on just the right frame—press *Shift*-arrow. The closest vertical end of the yellow border snaps to the current frame.

In time, you can get extremely good at finding or selecting exact frames in a particular piece of footage by just mastering the arrow-key shortcuts. (These shortcuts work only when a clip isn't playing.)

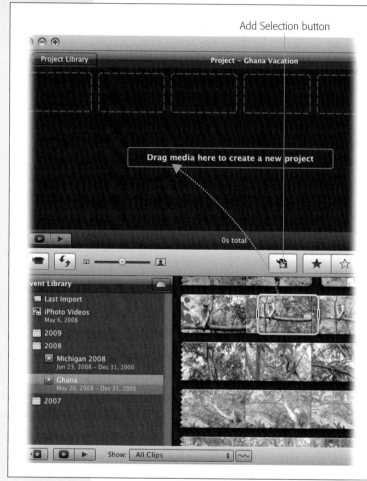

Add Selection button

Figure 3-6:
*When the storyboard area is fresh
and new, the message "Drag media here to create a new project"
appears. (It means "drag movies
here," of course.) But clicking the
Add Selection button, or pressing
the letter E, works just as well.*

In any case, you'll see the selected chunk(s) of video fly from the Event browser to
the *end* of your storyboard.

Tip: It's perfectly legal to add multiple clips to a storyboard at once; just Shift-click to select several
filmstrips in the Event browser first. But if you do so, iMovie scolds you: "You may achieve better results by
individually adding only the best segments of your video." Yeah, yeah, we get it—less is more.

To check the result, point to the storyboard (without clicking) just before the spot
where the new video has landed, and then press the space bar.

Adding to the Middle

You don't *have* to add selected video to the end of your storyboard. You can place it between two existing clips, smack in the middle of an existing clip, or even superimposed on a clip. These options are all part of a new feature in iMovie '11 called "Advanced Drag and Drop." (You can read more about it on page 88.)

To add a chunk of footage between two clips, drag the selected chunk (using anything inside the yellow border as a handle) right into the storyboard. When iMovie shows you a green vertical line indicating where the clip will go, release the mouse (Figure 3-7 shows what this green line looks like). The chunk of video slips right in between the surrounding clips.

If you drop your chunk *on top* of a clip in your storyboard rather than between clips, iMovie displays the "Drag and Drop" menu. Its options include Insert, which splits the underlying clip into two pieces, and drops your chunk between those pieces.

Advanced Insert Options

Suppose you're editing a project that has some music in it, and you worked hard to get the timing of the cuts to match up with the music. (Let's say you worked that hard because you haven't yet discovered the Beat Markers covered on page 235.) But as you preview your masterpiece, you realize that the clip of driving to the baseball game is just plain dull. You have something much more interesting to replace it with, but you know that unless your replacement is exactly the same length as the original shot, it will mess up the timing of your entire project.

WORKAROUND WORKSHOP

When One Click Means "Deselect"

The way iMovie comes from the factory, *one click* on any clip in the Event browser selects a piece of it. Four seconds of it, to be exact.

That's pretty unusual behavior, if you think about it. After all, one click in a word processor doesn't select four words; one click in Photoshop doesn't select four inches of a photo; and so on. In fact, what one click *usually* means in a creative program—word processor, Photoshop, and so on—is, "*deselect* everything."

Apple's programmers must have had quite a discussion about this point: What should a single click in the Event browser do? In the end, they went with the "4-second selection" thing, remaining true, as always, to the over-arching

goal of rapid movie assembly. But at least they've acknowledged the weirdness of that choice. And for anyone who's a little freaked out by the appearance of that 4-second yellow border every time you click, Apple has built a way out.

Choose iMovie→Preferences. In the Browser tab, turn on "Clicking in Event browser deselects all." Then close the Preferences dialog box. From now on, one click anywhere in the Event browser (except inside a yellow selection border) deselects everything. Of course, you can still select portions of clips (by dragging across them) or entire clips (by Option-clicking them); you just won't be surprised by the yellow border when you *don't* expect it.

Figure 3-7:
Once you highlight some video (bottom), you can drag it into position anywhere in the storyboard–in the gap between two existing clips, for example, or even in the middle of an existing clip. In the latter case, iMovie splits the existing clip in half, and puts the new footage between the split pieces.

POWER USERS' CLINIC

Show Advanced Tools

If your "Drag and Drop" menu gives you only four options, you're missing out on a bunch of iMovie '11's best features. Remember the green screen? Picture-in-picture? These, and many other handy doodads, become available only when you turn on Advanced Tools.

Evidently, iMovie's designer felt that revealing all of iMovie's goodies from the beginning would overwhelm the tremulous beginner and so he buried a lot of the good stuff. When you first run iMovie, a long list of buttons, commands, and features is hidden from you.

To make them appear, choose iMovie→Preferences. On the General tab, turn on Show Advanced Tools. Close the Preferences window.

You've just unleashed new iMovie capabilities all over the program; you'll read about them in the appropriate chapters of this book. Among them: iMovie now offers more than twice as many options when you drag footage or pictures on top of your project clips.

A cynic might complain that hiding half the features actually *creates* more confusion than it eliminates; in essence, there are two iMovies, and the novice may not realize that. But in any case, now you know how to turn those advanced features on or off.

---

iMovie offers three ways to replace a clip with a better one of the *exact same length*. If you haven't already done so, turn on the Advanced Tools (see the box on page 88). Select your replacement footage, drag it to your storyboard, and drop it onto the boring clip. In the "Drag and Drop" menu that appears, the following confusingly named options appear:

- **Replace** replaces the entire underlying clip with the selection you're adding, no matter how long either one is. This option does *not* match lengths, and will alter your project's timing.

- **"Replace from Start"** resizes the incoming clip to match the length of the re-placed clip—by adding, to the part you had selected, more footage to the *right*—in other words, it resizes the incoming clip by adding more footage to the end of it (see Figure 3-8).

  So if the soon-to-be-replaced clip is 8 seconds long, and your incoming clip is only 4 seconds long, iMovie extends the incoming video by another 4 seconds (if there's unused footage available). Alternatively, if the incoming selection is *longer* than 8 seconds, iMovie *cuts* from the end of it to make it match the dura-tion of the original clip.

Warning: If the incoming clip isn't long enough to be extended in this way, iMovie warns you that the result will shorten your movie.

- **"Replace from End"** is a lot like "Replace from Start," except that it resizes the incoming footage by extending your selection to the *left* (Figure 3-8, third from top). So if the clip being replaced is 8 seconds long, but the replacement selec-tion is only 4 seconds long, iMovie extends your selection by adding 4 seconds of footage to the *beginning* of the selection. If the incoming video is longer than the original, on the other hand, the first part of it gets lopped off.

- **"Replace at Playhead"** is the same as the other "Replace from" options, but uses the start of your selected footage as a sort of anchor. iMovie deposits this anchor at the Playhead, and then extends or shortens the selection in both directions, as necessary, to fill the space formerly occupied by the replaced clip.

Tip: If your resized footage doesn't display the moment just right, you can adjust it using the handy Clip Trimmer, covered on page 100.

Original selection

Replace from Start

Footage added to end

Replace from End

Footage added to beginning

Replace at Playhead

Footage added to both ends

Figure 3-8:
You can replace clips in your project without having to select exactly the right amount of video from a clip in the Event browser. In this example, you're replacing an 8-second project clip.

Top: You selected only 4 seconds of video in the Event browser.

Second from top: If you use "Replace from Start," iMovie adds four more seconds of footage to the end of your clip, so that it will have the same length as the clip it's replacing. (The little orange line shows what event footage has been added to your project.)

Third from top: If you use "Replace from End," instead of extending the selection by adding 4 seconds at the end of the clip, iMovie adds 4 seconds to the beginning of it.

Bottom: If you use "Replace at Playhead," iMovie adds footage to the front and the end of the incoming clip. The amount of footage added to either end depends on where your playhead is when you drop the incoming clip.

The Orange Stripe

Each time you add source video to your edited movie, iMovie slaps an orange stripe across the bottom of the original clip in the Event browser. That's a reminder that you've *used* this segment in your project. As your work proceeds, you'll be able to tell, with a glance at your Event browser, what proportion of the original video you used in your finished opus.

Now, remember that all your edited movies—your *projects*—draw upon the same well of source video on your computer. What's cool, therefore, is that iMovie memorizes the orange striping for every project. If you used a different set of Little League footage in each of three projects, you'll see the stripes jump around in the Event browser as you click each project in turn.

Tip: An easy way to select a chunk of Event footage already used in a project is to double-click the orange stripe. iMovie automatically selects *just* the striped footage.

Don't Remember to Save

You don't have to save your work. iMovie '11 automatically saves as you go. (It doesn't even have a Save command.)

Phases 2 to 3 (Alternate): Paint-to-Insert

Having slogged this far into the chapter, you might think that iMovie offers quite enough ways to drop footage into your movie. But believe it or not, there's yet another method.

This one makes throwing together a movie *crazy* fast. It turns your cursor into a sort of magic paintbrush. As you drag across filmstrips in the Event browser, any segment that you "paint across" with your mouse instantly becomes part of your movie. You'll never see any yellow borders. It's not select-and-then-place; it's *selectandplace*. One step, not two.

First, you need to turn on the Advanced Tools (page 88). You may not notice at first, but there are now several additional buttons in the toolbar across the center of the iMovie window (Figure 3-9).

Figure 3-9:
In paint-to-insert mode, the second toolbar icon ( ) is permanently selected. Now you can drag across bits of footage at high speed, each time adding it to the end of your storyboard.

Here's how to set up this advanced technique:

1. **Make sure you don't have any video selected in iMovie.**

   If you have video selected somewhere, some of the toolbar icons appear in washed-out light gray. In that case, try tapping the Esc key, and/or choose Edit→Select None. If you have no video selected, the toolbar tools are black and gray, ready to be used.

2. **Click the Edit tool, or press the letter E key.**

   The Edit tool, better described now as the Paint-to-Insert tool, is identified in Figure 3-9.

All the above is setup. Now you're ready to go to work.

From now on, forget everything you read about (1) selecting a chunk of video and then (2) adding it to the storyboard. Instead, any time you drag the mouse across a filmstrip, iMovie adds it *instantly* to the end of the storyboard. If you know what you're doing, you can whip together a movie made of 15 shots with only 15 swipes of the mouse. This trick takes some getting used to. You have to train yourself to never touch the mouse button except when you're prepared to commit something to the finished movie.

You should still use the skim-and-play technique to identify the chunks you want to add; performed correctly, skimming and playing doesn't involve the mouse button at all. (Point and tap the space bar; point and tap the space bar.) When you find a worthy chunk, *then* drag across it with the mouse button down. Or, faster still, Option-click a filmstrip to add the entire thing to the project.

If you add something by mistake, or if you undershoot or overshoot, remember iMovie's all-powerful Undo command. Hit ⌘-Z to rewind your last step and try again. To turn off paint-to-insert mode, press the letter E key (or click) again. You're back in yellow-border mode.

Phase 4: Fine-Tune the Edit

Once you've got a rough cut of your storyboard, you may consider the Event browser a lot less necessary. Your focus will probably shift to the storyboard from here on out. Now, in other words, might be a good time to hide the Projects list and move the whole storyboard to the wider space at the *bottom* of the iMovie window, as described in the previous chapter.

The rest of this chapter explores a few of the ways you can fine-tune your movie-in-progress.

Storyboard Playback

You can use instant playback to spot-check your storyboard work in the Viewer window. Since you'll probably be doing a lot of this, iMovie offers multiple techniques:

- **Anyplace playback**. Point (without clicking) to any spot; press the space bar to begin playback. Press the space bar again to stop.

Tip: As you near completion of your movie, you might want to make the Viewer bigger, so you see your work closer to full size. See page 70.

- **Selection playback**. Make a selection. (Either click a clip once to select the whole thing, or drag across it to choose just a part.) Then press the forward slash key (/, next to the period key) to play back *just that selection* from the beginning. Press / again to stop.

- **One-second (or 3-second) playback**. Here's a supremely handy feature: You can tap the [or] keys to play back the 1 or 3 seconds, respectively, immediately before and after the position of your cursor. It's sort of like a skim-and-play all at once.

  If the clip is highlighted with the yellow boundary, these keystrokes play back either the *first* second (or 3 seconds) of the selection, or the *last* second (or 3 seconds), depending on which is closer to your cursor.

Tip: You can press these bracket keys even when you have your mouse button clicked in the process of making a selection. That's a fantastic way to gauge whether you've selected exactly the right bit.

- **Whole-storyboard playback**. Press the backslash key (\, above the Return key) to play the *entire* storyboard from the beginning. Press \ again (or the space bar) to stop.

Note: There are menu equivalents for all three of these commands in the View menu: Play, Play Selection, and "Play from Beginning." But it's far more efficient to use the keyboard shortcuts.

No matter how you start playback, you can always stop it by clicking in the iMovie window or tapping the space bar.

Full-Screen Playback

You can make the Viewer window bigger to get a more detailed view of your video using the ⌘-8, ⌘-9, and ⌘-0 keystrokes; see page 70. But eventually, you'll want to treat yourself to iMovie's IMAX mode: *full-screen* playback. That's when all of iMovie's controls and menus disappear, and the video fills your entire monitor. Here again, iMovie offers different approaches:

- **Play from the pointer**. Point without clicking to any spot in the storyboard. Then press ⌘-G to begin *full-screen* playback of the selected video.

- **Play the entire storyboard**. Click the full-screen playback button (identified in Figure 3-10) to play your storyboard from the beginning. Choosing View→Play Full Screen does the same thing.

Figure 3-10:
Top: Click the "Play Project full-screen" button to begin playback of your entire storyboard from the beginning.

Bottom: During full-screen playback, if you wiggle your mouse, you get the navigation film-strip shown here at bottom. Click the filmstrip, and then skim it or drag the mouse to jump to a new spot without exiting full-screen mode.

Warning: In theory, ⌘-G is the keyboard equivalent of the View→Full Screen command. But they aren't, in fact, equivalent. ⌘-G is the *only* way to begin full-screen playback from a specific spot. If you choose View→Full Screen from the menu, iMovie begins playing the storyboard from the *beginning*. (It has to— since you moved your mouse to the menu, you're no longer pointing to a certain spot in the video!)

Once full-screen playback is underway, just moving your mouse produces the navigation strip shown in Figure 3-10. It starts out looking something like Cover Flow on the iPod or in iTunes, where all your projects (if you were previewing a project) or your events (if you were previewing an event) appear as though they're flipping album covers. Here are the basics of how it works:

- Press the space bar to start and stop playback without exiting full-screen mode. Or click the ▶ button at the left end of the navigation filmstrip.

- During playback, click another spot in the navigation filmstrip to jump there and pause playback.

- During playback, *double-click* another spot in the filmstrip to jump there *without* pausing playback.

- With playback paused, you can skim the navigation filmstrip (point without clicking) to explore the movie. Press the space bar to begin playback from any spot.

- Switch to a different event/project by either clicking one of the other filmstrips in the "cover flow," or by using the horizontal scrollbar underneath the clips.

You may have also noticed some other buttons on the left and right sides of the filmstrip. Their text labels don't appear unless you point to them without clicking, so here's a quick rundown of what they do:

- Switch between projects and events by clicking the 🔲 button on the left of the filmstrip.

- Turn the Cover Flow view (animated filmstrip-flipping) on or off by clicking the 🔲 button on the right of the filmstrip.

- The ⊕ button hides and shows the navigator filmstrip after your mouse starts moving. If you let iMovie hide it, you have more room to preview your video.

When you finish with full-screen playback, click the ✕ button, or press the Esc key, to return to the iMovie window. (Or, if you wish that iMovie would exit full-screen mode automatically after each playback, turn on that option by choosing iMovie→Preferences and visiting the General tab.)

Tip: Usually, your camcorder's video has lower resolution than your Mac's screen. To fill your screen for playback, iMovie *stretches* the picture, which lowers its quality slightly. In a few other cases (for example, high-def video on a small laptop), the video may actually be too *big* for the screen. In that case, iMovie has to scrunch it *down* to fit.

If you choose iMovie→Preferences and click the General tab, however, you can control all of this stretching and scrunching. The "Fullscreen playback size" pop-up menu lets you change the Entire Screen setting to Actual Size (the cleanest settings for video that's smaller than your screen) or Half Size (best-looking if the video is bigger than the screen). If you have HD video that plays back choppily on your computer, then choose "Entire Screen – Reduced Resolution." iMovie scales down the HD video so it doesn't require as much horsepower, but still fills the screen with your footage.

Rearranging Video

Unless your last name is Spielberg or Scorsese—and maybe even if it is—the first place you put a clip in the storyboard won't *always* be the best spot for it. Sooner or later, you'll wish you could move shots around in the film.

You can, if you know the secret.

1. **Select the part you want to move.**

   If it's an entire clip, simply click it in the storyboard. iMovie highlights the entire clip.

   If it's just part of a clip, drag to select the chunk you want. Fine-tune it with the arrow keys as described on page 85.

Tip: At this point, consider adjusting the storyboard's zoom level (page 76) so you'll have finer control over where you're about to place the moved video.

---

2. **Drag the selection to its new location.**

   Click carefully inside the outlined yellow-border area (shown in Figure 3-11) before you drag. When your cursor reaches the approximate destination, keep your finger on the mouse button, but move the cursor from side to side to find the precise target frame. Yes, you're actually skimming with the mouse button down, but don't let that confuse you.

   You can drop the dragged clip in between two clips in the storyboard, but *not* right in the middle of a clip, as you can when adding footage from an Event. If you want to take one project clip and insert it in the middle of another project clip, use the Copy or Cut commands discussed next.

Figure 3-11:
Rearranging scenes in the storyboard is a two-step process. First, select what you want to move, whether it's a full clip or just part of one (top). Second, drag it where you want it to go, whether it's in between two clips or right in the middle of another clip (bottom).

Copying and Pasting Video

Dragging isn't the only way to move footage around in iMovie; the Copy, Cut, and Paste commands can feel more precise. These commands are also the *only* way to copy edited footage from one project to another.

Note: When you copy and paste clips, you're never duplicating files on your hard drive, so don't worry about eating up free space.

You already know how to indicate *what* you want to cut or copy; just use the selection techniques described on page 79.

Then use the Edit→Cut or Edit→Copy command (⌘-X or ⌘-C). Point to where you want to paste the copied material (do not click), and then choose Edit→Paste (⌘-V). Presto! The cut or copied material appears at the position of your cursor, and shoves the rest of the movie to the right to make room.

Shortening or Lengthening Clips

Almost nobody hits the camcorder's Record button at the precise instant when the action begins, or stops recording the instant the action stops. Life (not to mention animals, geysers, and children) is just too unpredictable.

Most of the time, of course, you'll trim out the boring stuff in the Event browser before you add it to the storyboard. Sometimes, though, you'll discover—only *after* you put the clips into the storyboard, of course—that you didn't get the clip-editing process quite right. Maybe the shots are still *too* languorous, and should be shorter. Or the shots are *too* quick, and it's going to be hard for your audience to figure out what's going on.

In both cases, it would be nice to be able to lengthen or shorten a clip even after you place it in the storyboard.

Note: "Lengthen a clip?" That's right. iMovie is a *nondestructive* editing program. No matter how much editing you do, iMovie never, ever changes the original imported video on your hard drive. For example, if you shorten a clip by hacking a piece off the right end, you can later change your mind, even three Presidential administrations later. You can restore some or all of the missing footage, using the techniques described on these pages.

Fortunately, iMovie is crawling with ways to make these adjustments, even after you add the clips to the storyboard. They boil down to these approaches:

- Shorten a clip by selecting the part you want to *delete*.
- Shorten a clip by selecting the part you want to *keep*.
- Shorten, lengthen, or re-edit a clip in iMovie's Clip Trimmer window.
- Lengthen a clip by clicking iMovie's hidden Extend buttons.

Note: When you *shorten* a clip, all subsequent clips slide to the left to close the resulting gap. (That's called *ripple* editing.) On the other hand, when you lengthen a clip, exposing previously hidden footage, iMovie shoves all subsequent clips to the *right* to make room. Your movie, as a result, gets longer.

The following pages cover all four methods.

Select a Piece to Delete

Suppose you feel a clip is running too long in your edited movie. Fortunately, having mastered the art of selecting a portion of a clip as described earlier, you're ready to put that skill to work. You can shave off some footage from only one end of your clip, or even right from the middle. All you have to do is highlight the footage you want to delete, and then choose Edit→Cut (or press ⌘-X).

iMovie promptly trims away whatever was inside the yellow border. As a bonus, your invisible Clipboard now contains the snipped piece, which you're welcome to paste right back into the storyboard (at the position of your pointer) using the Edit→Paste command, in case you need that footage elsewhere.

Tip: You can also press the Delete key to get rid of the selected video. The difference is that the Delete key doesn't put the cut material into the Clipboard, ready for pasting, as the Cut command does. On the other hand, the Delete/Clear command doesn't replace what's *already* on the Clipboard, unlike the Cut command.

POWER USERS' CLINIC

Comment Markers

As you're rearranging the furniture, you may find it useful to insert reminders about the different clips in your project. This can be especially handy if a lot of your clips look alike, such as footage of Grandpa sharing stories from the army. As useful as the little filmstrips are, they all look the same while you shuffle clips around.

To limit potential confusion, iMovie offers you *comment markers*. These are little flags you can attach to any point in a project clip that let you type a brief note to yourself. They stay attached to the clip no matter where you move it, so you don't have to keep track of everything in your head.

Comment markers are considered an advanced feature, so you don't even see them until you turn on Advanced Tools (page 88). Now when you go into your project, you see a tiny box in the top left corner of your storyboard. The box contains comment markers (brown, as shown below) and chapter markers (orange with an arrow inside).

Just drag a comment marker from the little box onto any clip in your project. A text box becomes available inside the marker. Type in whatever words will help you remember;

the comment marker stretches to show you as much of your note as it can.

To edit a comment marker, double-click it to open its text box. To move a comment marker to a new spot, just drag it there.

If you're not prepared for it, the results can be startling. If you cut a chunk out of the middle of a clip, iMovie throws back at you the *two end pieces*—as two separate clips, side by side in the storyboard.

Select the Piece to Keep

If you want to trim some footage off *both* ends of a clip, it's quicker to highlight the part in the middle that you want to *keep* and then choose Clip→"Trim to Selection." (Or press ⌘-B. Why B stands for "trim to selection" is for you to figure out.) When you use this command, what used to be the selected part of the clip becomes, in effect, the *entire* clip. The clip is shorter now, as a tap on the space bar proves.

POWER USERS' CLINIC

The Shortcut Menu

A lot of great commands appear in iMovie's shortcut menu. This menu appears wherever you right-click (or Control-click); it offers different options depending on where your cursor is at the time.

For example, if you're pointing to a partially selected project clip, the shortcut menu lets you delete that portion (Delete Selection), or delete everything *but* the selection ("Trim to Selection").

Some commands are available *only* via the shortcut menu. That's logical, since certain commands involve a reference to the playhead, and so are useful only while skimming.

One such command is "Trim to Playhead." Think of this command as iMovie's very own guillotine. Any time you choose this from the shortcut menu, the part of a clip *to the right* of your cursor gets the axe.

Similar playhead-needy commands include Add Freeze Frame (page 278), "Add Still Frame to Project" (page 277), and a special version of Split Clip (page 102). Put the shortcut menu to use, and you can have all kinds of hidden powers.

Play
Play Selection
Loop Selection
Play from Beginning
Play full-screen
Cut
Copy
Paste
Delete Selection
Delete Entire Clip
Trim to Playhead
Split Clip
Detach Audio
Analyze Video ▶
Optimize Video – Full (Original Size)
Optimize Video – Large (960x540)
Add Comment Marker
Add Chapter Marker
Add Freeze Frame
Duplicate Last Title
Reveal in Event Browser
Reveal in Finder
Project Properties...
Project Theme...

Use the Clip Trimmer

All right, the Delete and Trim to Selection commands—mirror images of each other—are both quick, efficient ways to *shorten* a clip in the storyboard. But what if you decide you've cropped out *too much*, and you want to restore some footage? Or what if you can't even grasp what you're looking at, and wish you could see the entire original clip?

That's what the Clip Trimmer is all about. You can open it in either of two ways:

- Point to a clip without clicking. Click ✿ in its lower-left corner (Figure 3-12, top). Select Clip Trimmer from the list that appears.

- Click the clip in question and then choose Window→Clip Trimmer (⌘-R).

Figure 3-12:
Top: To open the Clip Trimmer, click the tiny gear button that appears when you point to a clip. (The number above it tells you how many seconds long the clip is at the moment.)

Bottom: In the Trim window, the yellow border shows which piece of the clip you're currently using in your movie. The extra, thin yellow borders show you what bits the transitions use on either end of the clip. The darkened portions are the ones you've so far eliminated. Above the Trimmer window, the arrow between two lines plays your selection. The left and right arrows refocus the Clip Trimmer on the project clip that comes just before or after the current clip.

iMovie replaces the entire Event Library area with a new display, labeled Clip Trimmer. You can see it at bottom of Figure 3-12.

In essence, what you're seeing here is the full-length clip, just as it originally appeared in the Event browser. The yellow border indicates which part you originally selected to include. You can use all the usual tricks to play back what's here, including skimming, hitting the space bar, or double-clicking. Or, in case you were just struck by a girder and have forgotten all of that, you can click the Play button that appears in the Trim window.

Your main business here is to readjust the selection border. Make it longer if you want to include more of the clip in your project, shorter if you want less. Or grab anywhere inside the yellow boundary and slide the entire thing horizontally to include an earlier or later portion of the same duration. Page 82 details all the fun you can have with the yellow border.

Tip: Press Option-left arrow or Option-right arrow to add one frame at a time to the video selection in the Trim window. (You're shifting either the beginning or the end of the yellow border, whichever is closest to your cursor.)

When you finish reselecting, click Done.

Fine-Tuning with the Extendo Buttons

The Trim window is a handy way to rechop a clip—especially if you want to *extend* the amount of footage you include in a project. But having to open a special editing window just to snap a few more frames onto a clip is a hassle.

Fortunately, there's another way to extend a cropped clip without having to bother with the Trim window: Use the Extendo buttons (what Apple calls the Fine Tuning buttons). To make them appear, you can use either the mouse or the keyboard:

- **Point to a clip** to make the tiny double-arrow icons (◄|►) appear in the corners (Figure 3-13) and then click one of them. (If you don't see the icons, you may have turned them off in Preferences.)
- **Point to either end of a clip**, and press ⌘-Option.

Extendo button

Figure 3-13:
Buttons appear in the corners of any storyboard clip you previously shortened from either end. Click one of these buttons to make the orange end-adjustment handles appear.

In either case, the ends of the selection border turn orange, and nearby filmstrips scoot away to make a little room. At this point, you can drag the orange handle to the left *or* right, either shortening the clip or (by revealing previously hidden footage) lengthening it by up to 1 second. As you drag the orange handle, numbers floating next to your cursor show you how long the clip will be and how many frames you're adding or removing.

To trim more than one second, you can either open the Clip Trimmer window or just click and use the Extendo buttons again. And again. And again.

Tip: You can also *fine*-fine-tune a clip's length with a secret keyboard shortcut. Press Option-left arrow or Option-right arrow. Each press makes the clip one frame shorter or longer. (You're changing either the beginning or the end of the clip, whichever is closest to your cursor.)

Splitting a Clip

The techniques described in the previous section work well when you want to remove some footage from a clip. Sometimes, however, it can be useful to split a clip *without* deleting footage in the process. For example, iMovie can only apply audio changes and video effects to *entire clips*; if you want only *part* of your clip to get special treatment, you'll have to break that portion off into a standalone clip. Don't worry; it still looks like part of the bigger clip on playback.

Tip: If you were thinking of using Split Clip to insert something, maybe a picture, in the middle of a clip, save yourself the trouble and use the "Advanced Drag and Drop" feature discussed on page 88. For example, in a clip of a young snowboarder heading rapidly toward a ramp and then sailing into space, you could insert a quick shot of his parents' horrified faces faster with the drag-and-drop method.

Or you may just want to break off one piece of a clip to use somewhere else in the movie. The Split Clip command is exactly what you need in this case. Just make a selection in any storyboard filmstrip:

- **To chop the clip into two pieces**, select from the desired split point to the end (or beginning) of the clip.

- **To chop the clip into three pieces**, select whatever piece of it that you want to wind up as the *center* piece. The end pieces will wind up as separate clips.

Either way, you can use the Shift-arrow technique described on page 85 to find exactly the right spot. Then choose Edit→Split Clip. The results are shown in Figure 3-14.

Split: Sharp corners

Normal: Rounded corners

Figure 3-14:
After you split a clip, you wind up with two or three pieces. (You can tell where these clips were split by examining the filmstrip corners; they're sharp rather than rounded.)

Tip: If you change your mind immediately, you can always use the Undo command to take back that step. But if you split a clip and change your mind *much later*, after you've done a lot of other editing, iMovie can still accommodate you. Click either part of a split clip and choose Edit→Join Clip; iMovie plays marriage counselor and reunites it with its former soulmate, assuming that it's still adjacent. (If something else is now between them, get it out of the way so iMovie can do its job.)

Cutaways

A *cutaway* is an important, basic editing technique. That's when someone on-camera begins talking…and you hear her *keep* talking, even as the video switches to something different (that illustrates what she's saying, for example). You see cutaways all the time on the nightly news, and in every documentary you've ever seen.

GEM IN THE ROUGH

Split Clip at Playhead

If you grew up editing in previous versions of iMovie, you probably became accustomed to editing with the old "Split Clip at Playhead" command. To get at a good part in the middle of a clip, you'd cut off the front and back parts then delete them. These days, chiseling out the best parts of clips this way is outdated, but it's still useful for other things.

To split a project clip at the playhead, skim to a split-worthy part and Control-click (or right-click) to bring up the shortcut menu. When you do this, iMovie selects the entire clip

with its little yellow borders, but don't let that stop you. Choose Split Clip from the shortcut menu and—presto!—iMovie breaks the clip into two pieces right where your cursor was.

This trick works only with the shortcut menu, *not* with Edit→Split Clip. It also doesn't work if you select just part of a clip. In that case, the Split Clip command behaves normally, and slices up the clip along the yellow selection borders.

Creating cutaways used to be tricky. It involved separating the audio from the person-talking video, cutting out a chunk of that video, trimming the replacement (cutaway) video to just the right length, and then sticking that into the gap in the person-talking video. You might as well be trimming an actual film reel and piecing it back together with tape!

Luckily, iMovie '11 makes cutaways ridiculously easy. Before you start, turn on the Advanced Tools (page 88), if you haven't by now. In the following discussion, you'll work with what the pros call *A-roll* (the beginning video, usually of the person talking) and *B-roll* (the soundless footage that illustrates what she's talking about). Then, to make a cutaway:

1. **Select your B-roll footage from the Event browser.**

   This is whatever footage you want to cut away *to* while the audio of the A-roll plays underneath.

2. **Drag the B-roll selection onto your A-roll filmstrip in the project.**

   When you do, the "Drag and Drop" shortcut menu appears.

3. **Click Cutaway.**

   iMovie now glues the B-roll clip to the top of the A-roll clip (Figure 3-15).

Figure 3-15:
Cutaway shots appear like gray-bordered clips casting a shadow on the main clip underneath. These are great for documentary-style interviews or news programs.

4. **Select your Cutaway clip, and then press Shift-⌘-M to mute it.**

   You've just silenced any audio that came along with the B-roll clip, so it doesn't compete with the sound of the person talking.

Adjusting a Cutaway

To make adjustments to a cutaway clip, double-click it. iMovie's Inspector panel appears—a floating mini-window full of controls that apply only to the clip you clicked. Most of its controls are standard stuff for video clips—video effects (page 154), fast/slow/reverse (page 157), stabilization (page 176). But two of them are especially designed for cutaways, and they're very cool:

- **Fade in/Fade out.** You don't have to cut abruptly to the cutaway video; you can install a graceful crossfade into or out of it. If you click Manual, you can use the slider to specify how *quickly* it fades in and out.

- **Opacity.** Your cutaway video doesn't have to replace the talking-person video completely; it can, if you wish, appear *superimposed* on the talking-person video, as though it's translucent. It's a special effect you won't use often, but it's good to know it's there. Drag the Opacity slider to control *how* see-through the super-imposed video looks.

When you finish making these changes, click Done.

Removing a Cutaway

Just select the cutaway clip in your project and press the Delete key to get rid of it.

The Precision Editor

In editing jargon, a *cut* is the place where one clip ends and another begins—the crossroads where clips meet. A well-designed cut looks very professional, even if it's subtle. For example, you might cut between two birthday parties that happened in the last year. To make the cut really cool, you could move from one birthday to the next using the exact moment when the candles are blown out. One of your kids would lean down to blow out the candles, and the other would stand up smiling. The effect forges a connection between the two birthdays, even though they happened at different points in the year.

The Precision Editor, an innovative tool that debuted in iMovie '09, makes cuts like these—cuts that would involve many steps in a professional editing tool—remarkably simple. Assuming you already have two clips needing a refined cut between them, using the Precision Editor on a cut would go something like this:

1. **Call up the Precision Editor.**

   You can get to the Precision Editor several ways. The easiest is to double-click the space between two clips. But if a clip is already selected, you can also choose Window→Precision Editor or press ⌘-/. You get the same effect by clicking ✿ on the clip itself and choosing Precision Editor.

Note: If you placed a *transition* between two clips (page 127), double-clicking the transition's icon brings up the Inspector for the transition. To get the Precision Editor instead, double-click the empty space just *above or below* the transition icon.

   The Precision Editor drops in, covering up your Event Library. What you see is a layered representation of your cut just like the one shown in Figure 3-16.

Show Extras   Show audio clip

Figure 3-16:
Behold the Precision Editor! The top layer holds the clips leading into a cut. The bottom layer contains the clips trailing the cut. Adjust the cut spot by dragging the vertical blue line. Adjust the clips surrounding the cut by dragging the clips themselves. The icons and faint dots running along the bar between the layers represent the different transitions and cuts in your project.

2. **Adjust the cut point.**

   The blue vertical line with the dot in the middle is the cut line; it represents the cut itself. You can drag it left or right to adjust its timing. Dragging to the right extends the leading clip and shortens the trailing clip. Drag left for the opposite effect.

3. **Adjust the clips surrounding the cut.**

   You may like where the leading clip cuts out, but not where the trailing clip comes in. To adjust the clip itself, drag the clip left or right.

4. **Overlap the audio, if you like.**

   Let's pretend the leading clip has someone describing a fun memory in Grandma's backyard, while the trailing clip shows the next generation running out of Grandma's backdoor to play. Click the Audio Tracks button to see the sound from the two clips, making them available for independent editing.

   If you point to the spot where the blue line crosses the audio track (without clicking), you can sort of snap off that part of the cut line. Dragging the snapped-off part lets you specify where the audio should cut out. This means you can take the audio of the leading clip (memory about Grandma's backyard) and extend it into the video of the trailing clip (kids running out the backdoor to play) for a very nice effect. (Basically, this is another way to do the Cutaway audio trick just explained on page 103.) You can see all this in Figure 3-17.

Note: This trick only works if there's no transition between the clips. Because transitions do their own crossfading between the audio of the two clips, you can't muck about with overlapping soundtracks.

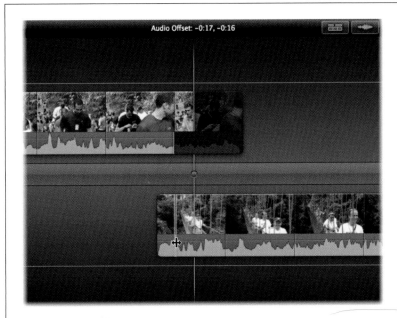

Figure 3-17:
You can change the cut point for audio so that it comes in or leaves independently of the video. This kind of edit connects the two clips in a way that a regular cut can't. You might do this if you shot an interview, but you want the person's voice to start before she actually shows up on screen.

5. **Adjust the "extras."**

   Not everything involved in a cut is video. You may have titles, songs, or photo cutaways in your cut masterpiece. Clicking the Show Extras button, identified in Figure 3-16, displays all the other stuff involved in the edit. You can drag these elements left or right to adjust their timing, just as you do audio or video.

6. **Preview your edit.**

   Previewing in the Precision Editor is just like previewing everywhere else. You can skim and play with all the same commands covered on page 77.

Tip: When skimming in the Precision Editor, be careful where you skim. Skimming over the grey middle bar shows you the cut. Skimming over a clip previews just the clip. Don't skim one of the clips, thinking you're seeing the cut!

---

7. **Go to the next cut, or click Done.**

   Now that you have your cut worthy of an editing Oscar, you can go to other cuts by clicking the right or left arrow buttons, or by clicking the grey dots that run along the middle bar. Each dot represents a different cut.

   If you're finished, just click Done or hit the Esc key.

Video Chunks: Keywords, People, Favorites, and Rejects

In iMovie '11, all the imported footage on all your hard drives sits there, like paints on a palette, to inspire your editorial brilliance. But that blessing is also a curse, because it's such a huge pile of video to manage—and a lot of it's dreck.

Fortunately, iMovie comes with a set of tools—unusual in a video-editing program—specifically designed to help you sort and manage these vast chunks of video. Working in the Event browser, you can:

- Tag pieces of clips as your favorites, to make them easy to find.

- Flag pieces of your clips as rejects—bad footage you'll either *probably* or *definitely* never want to incorporate into an edited project.

  The "probably" stuff you can just hide from view. The "definitely" stuff you can tell iMovie to delete, freeing up space on your hard drive, even if filing it in the "delete" pile means you need to snip off only the bad portions.

- Mark pieces of clips with *keywords* of your choosing—your children's names, adjectives, characterizations like "action" or "moody"—whatever you like. Later, you can summon all matching keywords with a single click.

- Flag pieces of clips that depict people. iMovie does this for you automatically and further distinguishes clips based on the number of people in them. It can even determine whether the clip contains a close-up, medium shot, or wide shot of those people. All of this comes in especially handy when you use the Movie Trailers storyboard described on page 286.

This short chapter explores these clip-flagging tools, and also describes the proper way to get rid of bad shots forever.

Marking Favorites and Rejects: The Two-Step Method

Most people, most of the time, flag a clip, or a piece of one, as a favorite or a reject using this technique:

1. **In the Event browser, select the video you like (or don't like).**

   You can use any of the selection techniques described on page 79. That is, you can select an entire clip, multiple clips, or only part of a clip.

2. **Flag it.**

   To flag the selection as a Favorite, click the black star button (Figure 4-1) or just press the letter F on your keyboard.

Figure 4-1:
Select some video and then click the black star button identified here. iMovie adds a green stripe, which designates a favorite shot.

   To flag it as a reject, either click **✖**, press the letter R key, choose Edit→Reject Selection, or press the Delete key.

Tip: You can also choose Edit→Reject Entire Clip (or press Option-Delete) to flag the *entire* clip as worthless. This saves you a little time, because it means you can select any part of the clip first, rather than highlighting the entire thing.

If you flag something as a Favorite, it sprouts a green line across the top edge (Figure 4-1).

If you mark something as a Reject, it sprouts a *red* line across the top edge—and promptly disappears from view. (If it doesn't disappear, you must have changed the pop-up menu [skip ahead to Figure 4-3 to see the menu] to say "Show: All Clips.")

Marking Favorites and Rejects: The One-Step Method

The usual method of flagging your best and worst footage takes only two steps. But believe it or not, even that's excessive in the eyes of Apple's Faster Editing team.

Hidden in the motley assortment of options known as the iMovie Advanced Tools lies another method, which reduces the favoriting and rejecting process down to *one* step.

To set up this method, turn on "Show advanced tools" as described on page 88.

Now have a look at the horizontal toolbar that divides the iMovie screen. iMovie has added a few additional tools, as shown in Figure 4-2. But you're not interested in the new icons. You're interested in the new behavior of three *original* buttons, the ones near the center— ★ | ☆ | ✕ . They now represent virtual *paintbrushes* that turn anything   you   touch with your cursor into a Favorite or a Reject.

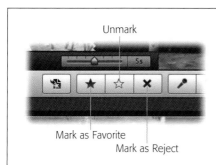

Unmark

Mark as Favorite

Mark as Reject

Figure 4-2:
The three icons identified here let you "paint" portions of your Event browser filmstrips with green highlighting (meaning "favorite") or red highlighting ("reject"). You don't have to select and then click the button.

For example, here's an amazingly fast way to zoom through a freshly imported pile of footage, marking favorite scenes as you go:

1. **Click the Favorite button (★), or press the letter F key.**

    The black star icon darkens to show that you selected it. Your cursor is now loaded with green Favorite paint, so be careful.

    Take a moment to skim (move your cursor over the filmstrip without clicking) and play (tap the space bar) to identify the good parts, and then:

2. **Drag across the filmstrip to indicate the good stuff.**

    The green "favorite" stripe appears instantly. Instead of "select, then flag as Favorite," you managed to select and flag-as-Favorite all in one stroke.

Marking sections as Rejects is just as easy, except that you click the X button in step 1 (or press the letter R key). Now, when you drag across filmstrips in step 2, they instantly become Rejects, which usually means they disappear from view.

Tip: To mark an *entire* clip as a Favorite or a Reject, Option-click it. That's a lot faster than dragging.

For best results, then, you should plow through your footage, riding the F and R keys, painting across good and bad sections of video as you go. Later, this prescreening process makes assembling your movie a heck of a lot easier and faster.

Tip: If you mark something as a Favorite or Reject by mistake, you can unmark it quickly: hold down the ⌘ key. iMovie switches temporarily to the Unmark tool described in the next section, just long enough for you to paint over (or Option-click) the mismarked footage.

Release the ⌘ key to return to the tool you were using.

Unmarking

No matter which method you used to mark Favorites or Rejects, it's easy to change your mind later. Just repeat the original process, but use the hollow star (or the letter U key) as your paintbrush.

- To use the "select, then flag" method, select the piece of filmstrip you want to unmark and then click ☆ (or press the letter U).

- If you prefer the Advanced Tools, "paintbrush" method, turn on Advanced Tools. Then click ☆ (or press the letter U), and begin painting. When you drag your cursor across a piece of filmstrip, you remove *all* colored stripes from it— both the Favorite and the Reject stripes.

Note: Of course, you can't unmark rejected footage unless you can *see* it on the screen. The following section shows you how to bring hidden footage back into view.

Selecting Marked Footage

In time, your Event footage will twinkle with green, red, blue, and even orange bars, corresponding to the various ways you flagged or used your footage.

But these colored stripes aren't just labels, they're also handles. Carefully double-click directly *on* one of the colored stripes, and presto: iMovie neatly selects just the piece of filmstrip that the stripe marks, ready for unmarking, cutting, deleting, placing in your project, and so on.

Hiding and Showing Favorites and Rejects

Flagging clips as Favorites and Rejects wouldn't save you any time if all it did was draw colored stripes on your filmstrips. The real payoff comes when you tell iMovie to *hide* everything except your Favorites or Rejects, making it exceptionally easy to work with a big pool of extraordinary footage, or to review all the lousy footage before you delete it for good.

You can access these various hide/show modes in two places: in the View menu and in the Show pop-up menu on the bottom edge of the iMovie window.

- **Show only Favorites**. Choose Favorites Only, either from the View menu or the Show pop-up menu (Figure 4-3).

Figure 4-3:
When you choose Favorites Only from this pop-up menu, the Event browser hides all your rejects and all footage that you haven't marked at all. This feature should translate into even faster movie-building time, since you're working exclusively with clips you already know you love.

- **Show everything except Rejects**. Choose Favorites and Unmarked, either from the View menu or the Show pop-up menu.

  This is what you see most of the time: iMovie shows you everything you've marked as Favorite *and* everything you haven't marked either way. It hides only the rejects.

Tip: Since this is the view Apple expects you'll use most often, it has a keyboard shortcut all its own: ⌘-L.

- **Show everything**. Choose All Clips, either from the View menu or the Show pop-up menu.

  Now you see everything: Favorites, Rejects, and Unmarked. This can be a handy anti-desperation view when you can't find a certain shot that you're sure you had before. It rules out the possibility that you flagged it as a Favorite or Reject and then hid it.

- **Show only rejects**. Choose Rejected Only, either from the View menu or the Show pop-up menu.

  Now you're seeing *only* the bad stuff. Everything else is hidden.

  You'd summon this view when hunting for a clip you can't seem to find among the good stuff (maybe you rejected it by mistake), or when reviewing your rejected footage before deleting it for good, as described on page 119.

Keywords

In iPhoto, iMovie's sibling in the iLife suite, *keywords* play an important role in helping you manage tens of thousands of photos.

A keyword is a text label that you can slap on a picture, a tag that will help you pluck that photo (and ones like it) out of a haystack later. Some people make keywords for the people in the pictures: "Casey," "Mom," "Robin," and so on; others use them to identify what's going on in the photo: "Vacation," "Home," "Kids." Either way, the point is that if you're consistent in using keywords, you can later round up *all* the photos bearing a certain keyword ("Robin") with one click.

Well, iMovie works with keywords as well, but you wouldn't know it at first. iMovie keywords belong to the handful of miscellaneous efficiency features that Apple calls the Advanced Tools, so most people don't even know they exist. To make them appear, turn on Advanced Tools as described on page 88.

Now, if you look carefully, you'll see that a new button has appeared on iMovie's central toolbar—one that looks like an old-fashioned key. Click it to open the Keywords window (Figure 4-4).

Figure 4-4:
When you turn on Advanced Tools, the Keywords button appears (top). Click it to open the Keywords window (bottom). You can now "paint" a selected keyword, or several, onto a filmstrip, using the Auto-Apply tab. Or, on the Inspector tab, you can select some video on the filmstrip first and then turn on the relevant keyword checkboxes.

You can see that Apple has started you out with several sample keywords: Indoor, Outdoor, Landscape, People, Pets, and so on. There are also keywords related to the people iMovie found in your clips, if you analyzed them (page 118). Notice that the Keywords window has two tabs at the top, Auto-Apply and Inspector. They correspond to the two ways that you can apply keywords to your filmstrips: by "painting" across them, or using the select-then-apply method.

Note: You can apply keywords to your filmstrips either in the storyboard or the Event browser.

Editing the Keyword List

To make up new keywords, click the Auto-Apply tab. Click in the Keyword box (lower-left), type a keyword, and then press Enter. Type the next keyword, and press Enter. Repeat for all your keywords.

To edit a keyword name, double-click it.

Tip: Be careful—keywords are case-sensitive. iMovie treats *kids* and *Kids* as two different keywords.

You can also rearrange the keyword list—to put the most common ones at the top, for example. (The top nine keywords get numeric keyboard shortcuts.) Just drag the keywords themselves up or down the list.

To remove keywords you're not using, click the Auto-Apply tab, click the keyword you want to eliminate (*not* its checkbox) and then click Remove. If that keyword is actually in use—if you've applied it to some footage—iMovie warns you in a confirmation box. Click Yes to proceed with the keyword vaporization.

"Painting" Keywords onto Clips

This method is wicked fast. It's especially good if you want to apply the *same* set of keywords to a slew of different filmstrips. When you get back from your Disney World vacation, for example, chances are good that a lot of your video will fall into the categories "Vacation," "Family," and "Kids." Using this method, you can leave those keyword checkboxes turned on and then whip through the clips, "painting on" the keywords as necessary.

Start by opening the Keywords window and then:

1. **Click the Auto-Apply tab.**

    If you want to add a new keyword to the list, type it into the box at the bottom of the list and then click Add (or press Enter).

2. **Turn on the checkboxes for the relevant keywords.**

    As noted above, you can turn on as many as you like.

Tip: See the little numbers 1, 2, 3, and so on, at the right side of the list? You can press these keys on your keyboard to turn keyword checkboxes on and off, for added speed.

3. **Drag across the filmstrip sections that should have those keywords.**

    As always, you can skim and play to review a clip before you paint the keywords onto it.

    As you drag, a blue line appears at the top of the filmstrip, indicating that you applied keywords to it.

Tip: *Option*-click a filmstrip to apply the selected keywords to the whole thing.

The Select-then-Apply Method

When you have a more motley assortment of video and you'll apply a lot of different keywords as you go, it might make more sense to use this second method. Here, you highlight some video first and *then* turn on the keyword checkboxes.

Start by opening the Keywords window, and then:

1. **Click the Inspector tab.**

    The keyword list appears.

2. **Select some video.**

    You can use any of the techniques described on page 79. Of course, you can skim and play to see what you've got before you apply a keyword.

3. **Turn on the appropriate keyword checkboxes.**

    Click to select the checkboxes—or press the number keys on your keyboard that correspond to the numbers in the keyword list.

    Once again, a blue line appears at the top of the filmstrip, indicating that you applied keywords to it.

    If you see a hyphen (-) in one of the checkboxes, it's because *part* of the selected video has that keyword, and part doesn't. Click that checkbox once to apply the keyword to the *entire* selection, or twice to remove the keyword from the entire selection.

Tip: To apply a keyword that's not yet in the list, type the new keyword into the Keyword text box and then click "Add to Clip" (or press Enter). iMovie simultaneously adds the new keyword to the list *and* applies it to whatever's selected.

Now you can repeat steps 2 and 3, selecting, then applying keywords, and repeating as necessary.

Removing Keywords from Filmstrips

It's easy enough to strip away keywords you've already applied. Just highlight the clip and then, on the Inspector tab, turn off the keywords you don't want. Or, if you don't want *any* keywords on your selected clip, click Remove All.

Note: Any keywords you apply to a clip go with that clip for all your projects. In other words, keywords are not project-specific.

People

If you've ever used iPhoto, you appreciate the awesomeness that is its Faces feature. After identifying and naming some loved ones in a few photos, iPhoto goes to work searching your entire photo library for other pics with those people in them. It's a huge time-saver when you want to find pictures with, for example, Auntie Barb, even though they're scattered throughout your iPhoto library.

The People feature in iMovie is a modest—but useful—step in that direction. iMovie can't identify specific people in your footage; it can't tell Aunti Barb from Uncle Milton. But it *can* tell which clips have people in them at all. It can even distinguish between clips of one, two, or more people, and clips with close-up, medium, and wide shots of the people involved.

"If it can't tell Grandma from Baby Katie, what's the point?" you might ask.

The people finder seems to be tailored for the new Movie Trailers feature (page 283), where iMovie proposes a storyboard for the trailer you're creating. There, you're asked to locate shots of various types—medium shot, two-shot (that is, a shot of two people), group shot, and so on. The People feature, of course, makes that process much simpler.

Video clips with people in them also tend to be the most interesting to friends and family who don't have time to watch your entire summer vacation. In that way, People finder can also help you identify just the good stuff—the people shots.

Analyzing for People

There are two ways to get iMovie to analyze your footage for people:

- **Analyze when importing.** When you copy your footage from your camera into iMovie, the program can take a moment (all right, many moments) to scan all the new stuff for people. This option, described on page 34, works great if you aren't in a hurry to get editing whatever you imported.

- **Analyze in the Event Library.** You can also start the analysis later, applying it to video you've already imported. Select an event, or clips in an event, and choose File→Analyze Video→People. Or right-click the clip(s) and choose Analyze Video→People from the shortcut menu.

Note: You can't people-analyze clips that you've already placed in your Project storyboard. Presumably you already know what's in those shots.

Once you set iMovie to work, it scans your footage. The process takes a while. As a rule of thumb, plan on analyzing for people to take about as long as the clip itself; for example, a 10-minute clip would take 10 minutes to analyze. After iMovie finishes, you can use the Keyword Filter (page 118) to find just the shots you need.

All the clips bearing People keywords have purple stripes (people, purple, get it?) in the same place you'd see blue stripes indicating keyworded footage. Double-clicking a purple stripe selects all the footage under the stripe.

People Keywords

iMovie distinguishes clips by the number of people in a shot and their distance from the camera. Then it assigns keywords to the clips like this:

- **People.** Identifies clips that depict people, no matter the number or closeness of the camera.

- **One Person, Two People.** Identifies how many people are in the shot.

- **Group.** Clips with more than two people in the frame.

- **Closeup.** Clips where the face(s) fill most of the video frame. Directors often use close-ups to convey the emotion of a moment.

- **Medium.** Close enough to see a face clearly, but not close enough to see the person's whole body.

- **Wide.** Long-distance shots where you can see a person's whole body and everything around him or her. Great for showing the scenery, but not for showing facial expressions.

The Keyword/People Filter

The payoff for painstakingly categorizing your footage with keywords and analyzing it for people comes when you need just the right clip, and you don't have time to review the 6 hours of footage you took during your 11-day cruise. You want to see all the footage of museums (or beaches, or fake shipboard Broadway shows), *now*.

That's easy. Choose Window→Show Keyword Filter, or click the magnifying-glass button under the Event browser display. Either way, iMovie opens up a strange little keyword panel, wedged in between the Events list and the Event browser (Figure 4-5).

The minutes:seconds display down the right side is a cumulative tally of all the video in your library that bears each keyword.

Even handier are the red and green pill-shaped things down the *left* side. These traffic lights affect what footage you see in the Event browser. When you click the green light, the browser shows *only* the clips marked by that keyword. The red light, naturally, has the opposite effect, *hiding* all clips with that keyword.

Tip: Clicking the keyword itself acts just like clicking the green light. A bigger target means more efficiency.

Figure 4-5:
As long as you have the master switch turned on ("Filter by Keyword"), the traffic lights hide or show the video with matching keywords. When you turn "Filter by Keyword" off, the Event browser shows everything, regardless of keywords. In this case, the selected keywords filter the clips to show us only medium shots with Sam in them.

At least, that's what it does fresh from the factory. By clicking the buttons below the list, you can manipulate what's hidden and what's visible in several creative ways:

- **Any** means "show me video with *any* of the keywords I selected." If you turn on Vacation and Kids, for example, you see footage that has *either* of those keywords applied.

- **All** means "show me only the video that has *all* of these keywords." If you turn on Vacation and Kids here, you see *only* footage to which you've applied *both* those keywords.

Deleting Footage for Good

When you mark a shot as a Reject, iMovie generally hides it from you, so you can spend less time wading through mountains of video as you build your project.

But marking shots as Rejects has another payoff, too: It's the gateway to iMovie's video *deletion* feature. If a shot is really bad, and you're sure you'll never need it again, you can delete it from your Mac completely, thereby reclaiming a substantial amount of hard drive space.

iMovie '11 can even delete *part* of a clip on the hard drive, leaving the rest for you to work with. Technically speaking, that's quite a trick. (See "Deleting Partial Clips: The Mixed Blessing" on page 121.)

To purge your rejected clips and clip portions, do this:

1. **Choose View→Rejected Only.**

   As shown in Figure 4-6 (top), the Rejected Clips window appears. Skim or play these clips to double-check their worthlessness. The point is to review the rejects to make sure you're not about to nuke anything you'll regret losing.

Note: If you spot an *orange* stripe on any of these clips, then you've actually used that video in a project—you must have marked it as rejected *afterward*—and iMovie won't let you delete it. Remove it from your project first, or unmark it as a Reject.

---

2. **Click "Move Rejected to Trash."**

   You'll find this button in the upper-right corner of the Rejected Clips window. iMovie immediately asks if you're sure (Figure 4-6, bottom).

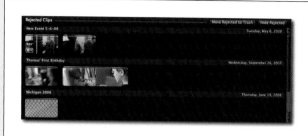

Figure 4-6:
Top: The Rejected Clips window shows you everything you destined for the cutting-room floor. Here's your last chance to look it over before deleting it forever.

Bottom: When you click "Move Rejected to Trash," this confirmation box appears. Click "Move to Trash."

3. **Click "Move to Trash."**

   After a moment of processing, iMovie places all the rejected footage in your *Macintosh* Trash. The filmstrips disappear from the window before you.

Note: At this point, the video isn't yet gone from your hard drive. You have one last, desperate chance to resurrect it. Click 🗑 on your Dock, and then open the iMovie Temporary Items folder within. There you'll find both the deleted clip and the mini filmstrip movie thumbnail that iMovie '11 generated for it.

To rescue some video, drag it out of this Trash folder and back into the appropriate folder in your Movies→iMovie Events folder. (Refresh your memory on how these folders work by flipping back to page 59.) The next time you open iMovie, you'll see it listed in the Event browser.

---

4. **Empty your Macintosh Trash.**

   In other words, switch to the Finder (click ⬛ in your Dock), and choose Finder→Empty Trash. Or, if you can see the Trash icon on your Dock right now, hold down your cursor on it; from the shortcut menu, choose Empty Trash.

Space Saver

Now you know how to permanently vaporize all the footage you flagged as useless. But as it turns out, iMovie offers an additional tool for reclaiming hard drive space—a little something called Space Saver.

It's a bit complicated, thanks to the double-negative wording of its options ("Reject if a clip is *not* this"), but here goes:

Space Saver's function is to mark *all* unused, unfavorited, or unkeyworded video in an Event as Rejects, all in one fell swoop. That way, you can use the steps described above to empty your Rejected Clips window and get a *lot* of hard drive space back.

The most useful application of this powerful command is to purge your Event of leftover footage after you're really, truly finished editing a project. Space Saver can help you throw away *all* the imported video that didn't wind up being used in the project. In essence, you're locking down your project in its current form, removing any chance of expanding the clips you used in it—but you're getting a lot of hard drive space back, too.

Tip: If you have a tape camcorder, and you still have the original tape, this is a no-lose, no-risk proposition. If you're ever desperate to re-edit your movie years from now, you can always reimport the original clips from the tape. In the meantime, you're not filling up your hard drive with a lot of video deadwood.

GEM IN THE ROUGH

Deleting Partial Clips: The Mixed Blessing

iMovie '11's ability to delete *pieces* of clips from your hard drive certainly seems, at first glance, like a refreshing change from previous versions of iMovie.

In iMovie 5 and 6, you'd reclaim hard drive space only if you deleted an *entire* clip. If you incorporated even one second of a clip into your project, iMovie retained the entire clip on your hard drive, even if it was many minutes (and megabytes) long. As a result, even short iMovie projects could occupy many gigabytes of disk space.

Apple's justification for this behavior was, "Well, you might change your mind. You might want to re-edit this movie later and use *more* of that clip in your project." And that was true; it's frequently convenient to tinker with your edit by dragging the outer edges of already-placed clips to bring more of those shots into view. That trick's possible only if you haven't *deleted* the hidden part of a clip.

All of this history is printed here for one purpose: To remind you that partial-clip deletion is a mixed blessing. iMovie '11 can save you an *enormous* amount of hard drive space if you diligently reject, and then delete, the footage you're certain you'll never want anyone to see. But keep in mind that when you do that, you lose the flexibility to change your mind.

To get started, choose File→Space Saver. The dialog box shown in Figure 4-7 appears.

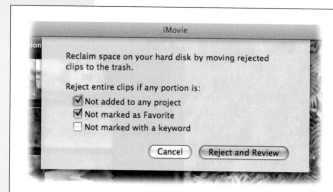

Figure 4-7:
iMovie can save you time and disk space if you let it reject whole categories of clips at a time.

It's offering to mark *everything* as a Reject unless it's:

- **Part of a project**. This is the example described in the box "Deleting Partial Clips: The Mixed Blessing" above. Turn on "Not added to any project" if you want to get rid of all video clips in this Event that you haven't used in any movie project.

- **One of your Favorites**. If you've been using the Favorite feature religiously, and have marked *all* usable video as Favorite, then you can turn on "Not marked as Favorite." Anything you did *not* mark as a Favorite now becomes a Reject (pretty harsh!). The only footage left in this Event will be your Favorites.

- **Categorized with a keyword**. This option is for people who categorize *every-thing* useful with one keyword or another, as described on page 113. Turning on "Not marked with a keyword" marks *everything else* as a Reject, and puts it on the road to deletion.

  There probably aren't very many people who always keyword *everything* that's useful, which is why the factory setting for this checkbox is off.

Once you make your selections, click "Reject and Review." You arrive in the Rejected Clips window (Figure 4-6, top), where you'll see all the clips that Space Saver has marked for termination.

If you're puzzled by what's here and what's not, keep these eccentricities in mind:

- Space Saver marks a clip as a Reject only if *the entire thing* meets the criteria you selected. If you flagged part of it as a Favorite, for example, and you select "Not marked as Favorite," then iMovie won't move any part of the clip to the Rejected Clips window.

- The checkboxes are cumulative. You can turn on as many of the Space Saver checkboxes as you like. But in keeping with Space Saver's double-negative thinking, turning on *more* checkboxes rejects *fewer* clips. That is, if you turn on all three boxes, a clip won't be deleted unless it's unused in a project *and* not a Favorite *and* doesn't have a keyword. This quirk, too, may explain why some clips don't wind up in the Rejected Clips window when you expect them to.

Once you skim or play the filmstrips in the Rejected Clips window and you've assured yourself that they're all expendable, you can delete them just as you'd delete any rejected clip. "Deleting Footage for Good" on page 119 has the full details, but the gist is this: Click "Move Rejected to Trash," click "Move to Trash" in the confirmation box, and then empty the Macintosh Trash.

Transitions, Themes, Travel Maps, and Animatics

Cutting and ordering your clips makes them infinitely more entertaining than the hours of dreck you'd have otherwise. But why stop there? This is *computer* video editing, after all. The next two chapters cover what you can do *between* your clips (this chapter) and what you can do *to* your clips (video effects) to make your whole project more vivid.

Impressively enough, iMovie requires no *rendering time*—no delay while the program computes the effect you're creating—as there is in most other video-editing programs. You see the effect instantly.

About Transitions

What happens when one clip ends and the next one begins? In about 99.99 percent of all movies, music videos, and commercials—and in 100 percent of camcorder movies before the Macintosh era—you get a *cut*. That's the technical term for "nothing special happens at all." One scene ends, and the next one begins immediately.

Professional film and video editors, however, have at their disposal a wide range of *transitions*—special effects that smooth the juncture between one clip and the next. For example, the world's most popular transition is the *crossfade* or *dissolve*, in which the end of one clip gradually fades away as the next one fades in (see Figure 5-1). The crossfade is popular because it's so effective. It gives the transition a feeling of softness and grace, and yet it's so subtle that the viewer might not even be conscious of its presence.

Figure 5-1:
The world's most popular and effective transition effect: what iMovie calls a Cross Dissolve.

Like all video-editing programs, iMovie offers a variety of transitions, of which crossfades are only the beginning. You'll find a catalog of them in "Transitions: The iMovie Catalog" on page 135. iMovie makes adding such effects incredibly easy, and the results look awesomely assured and professional.

When Not to Use Transitions

When the Macintosh debuted in 1984, one of its most exciting features was its *fonts*. Without having to buy those self-adhesive lettering sets from art stores, you could make posters, flyers, and newsletters using any typefaces you wanted. In fact, if you weren't particularly concerned with being tasteful, you could even combine lots of typefaces on the same page—and thousands of first-time desktop publishers did exactly that. They thought it was exciting to harness the world of typography right on their computer screen.

You may even remember the result: a proliferation of homemade graphic design that rated very low on the artistic-taste scale. Instead of making documents look more professional, the wild explosion of mixed typefaces made them look amateurish in a whole new way.

In video, transitions present exactly the same temptation: If you use too many, you risk telegraphing that you're a beginner at work. When you begin to polish your movie by adding transitions, consider these questions:

- **Does it really need a transition?** Sometimes a simple cut is the most effective transition from one shot to the next. Yes, the crossfade lends a feeling of softness and smoothness to the movie, but is that really what you want? If it's a sweet video of your kids growing up over time, absolutely yes. But if it's a hard-hitting issue documentary, then probably not, as those soft edges would dull the impact of your footage.

  Remember, too, that transitions often suggest the *passage of time*. In movies and commercials, consecutive shots in the same scene never include such effects. Plain old cuts tell the viewer that one shot is following the next in real time. But suppose one scene ends with the beleaguered hero saying, "Well, at least I still have my job at the law firm!" and the next shot shows him operating a lemonade stand. (Now *that's* comedy!) In this case, a transition would be especially effective, because it tells the audience we've just jumped ahead a couple of days. Learn taste in transitions. They should be done *for a reason*.

- **Is it consistent?** Once you choose a transition-effect style for your movie, stick to that style for the entire film (unless, as always, you have an artistic reason to do otherwise). Using one consistent style of effect lends unity to your work. That's why interior designers choose only one dominant color for each room.

- **Which effect is most appropriate?** As noted earlier, the crossfade is almost always the least intrusive, most effective, and best-looking transition. But each of the other iMovie transitions can be appropriate in certain situations.

  The catalog on page 135 gives you an example of when each transition might be appropriate. Most of them are useful primarily in music videos and other situations when wild stylistic flights of fancy are more readily accepted by viewers.

Tip: iMovie's Fade Through Black transition is exempt from the stern advice above. Use it at the beginning of *every* movie, if you like, and at the end. Doing so adds a fade in and fade out, lending a professional feeling to your film. But it's so subtle, your audience will notice it only subconsciously, if at all.

Two Ways to "Transish"

You can insert iMovie's transition effects one by one, placing them between scenes only where appropriate, and hand-tailoring each one. That's the way you add transitions in most programs, including the old iMovie.

But lurking one millimeter beneath iMovie's surface at all times is its primary mission: letting you assemble edited video *fast*, automating *everything*. For that reason, iMovie '11 also lets you turn on *automatic, global* transitions (great for slideshows!). The following sections cover both hand-crafted and automatic transitions.

Creating Individual Transition Effects

To see the 20 transitions iMovie offers, click the Transitions button, identified in Figure 5-2. Point to a transition's name (like Cross Dissolve) without clicking to see a small animated preview of it.

Once you find a good effect, drag its icon *out* of the Transitions panel and directly into the storyboard area, in the vertical gap between the two filmstrips that you want transitioned. Figure 5-3 shows the technique.

Tip: Most people think of putting transitions *between* two clips. But if you drag a transition to the *beginning* of your storyboard, the transition works just as well—except that it transitions out of blackness. Fade Through Black and Circle Open work especially well at the start of a movie.

The same happy surprise awaits if you drag a transition to the *end* of a movie. iMovie wipes, fades, or ripples from the final shot into blackness.

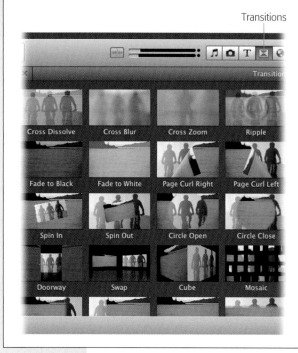

Figure 5-2:
When you point to a transition, you get to see a small preview. Click to pause the tiny playback loop at any point, or double-click to reset the animation to its first frame.

Figure 5-3:
Insert a transition by dragging it out of the Transitions palette and in between two clips (or at either end of your movie). In the storyboard, a transition shows up as a tiny icon. You can even tell what kind of transition it is by the little logo on that icon.

Once you drop a transition into place, you can look over the result easily.

- To watch just the transition itself, click the transition's icon in the storyboard (it sprouts a yellow border to show that it's highlighted) and then press the / key. That's on the bottom row of the keyboard, and it always means "play the selection" in iMovie.

- It's a good idea to watch your transition by "rewinding" a few seconds into the preceding footage, to get a sense of how the effect fits in the context of the existing footage. To watch the transition *and* the clips that it joins together, point to a spot just before the transition, and then hit the space bar. Alternatively, hit the [or] key to preview the 3-second or 6-second video chunk that surrounds the transition.

- If you think the scene seam looked better without the transition, choose Edit→Undo (⌘-Z).

You'll discover that the audio from the clips on either side of a transition still plays—you hear the sounds overlapping for a moment—but iMovie gradually crossfades the two.

Tip: If you want transitions on *most* of your scene seams, turn on the Automatic Transitions feature described on page 133. Then, using the Tip on that page, you can turn all those iMovie-generated transitions into manually editable ones. In other words, you can delete just the transitions you don't want.

Changing or Deleting a Transition

If you like the *idea* of a transition but you just don't like the one you put there, there are two ways to replace it.

- Drag a different one out of the Transitions panel right on top of the old one.

- Double-click the transition; the Inspector window appears. Click the Transition button labeled with the name of your current transition. The Inspector flips around and reveals skimmable previews of all 20 transitions. Select the new one by clicking it, and then click Done.

To get rid of a transition, even months or years later, highlight its icon and then press the Delete key. Your original clips return instantly, exactly as they were before you added the transition.

A Long Discussion of Transition Lengths

In iMovie HD and previous editions, you specified how long each transition effect lasted before you even put it into your movie. iMovie '11 thinks that *that*—choosing a duration each time—is a nuisance. Every transition you insert starts out the same length (which you can specify in the project properties). iMovie isn't a complete tyrant, however; it does let you set individual transition lengths.

There are three ways to adjust the duration of your transitions. Two of these involve a visit to the Project Properties dialog box (see Figure 5-4).

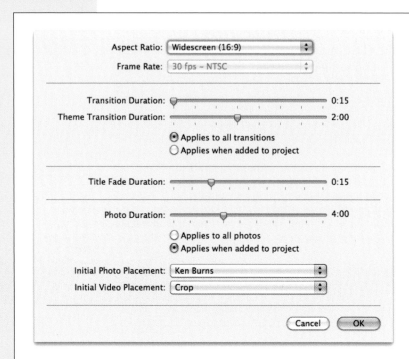

Figure 5-4:
Choose File→Project
Properties. In this dialog
box, drag the slider to in-
dicate how long you want
each transition to last. If
you choose "Applies to all
transitions," then, by golly,
this slider affects all the
transitions in your project
at once.

Here, you'll find a Transition Duration slider (whose settings range from 0.5 seconds to 4 seconds) and several options that affect it:

- **Change all transition durations at once**. If you select "Applies to all transitions," then the Duration slider affects all transitions simultaneously. Taking this road ensures consistency and minimizes the amount of effort you have to expend. For best results, choose something between 1 and 2 seconds.

Note: If you manually set the durations of individual transitions, as described in the following paragraphs, be careful. Using "Applies to all transitions" wipes out all your handwork.

- **Change transition durations from here on**. The weird little option labeled "Applies when added to project" actually means "Whatever duration you choose on the Duration slider applies to the *next* transition you drop into the storyboard—and to all future ones."

So you choose this option, you adjust the Duration slider, and finally you click OK. You've just preserved the durations of all *existing* transitions in your project, but changed the standard timing for all *incoming* transitions. Here again, iMovie is trying to enforce a standard duration, albeit a different one, and trying to remove all necessity for you to manage your durations one by one.

- **Change individual transitions**. Fortunately for control freaks, you can also change transition durations on a one-at-a-time basis. When you double-click a transition icon, the Inspector appears; it offers a Duration box (Figure 5-5). Type in the number of seconds you want the transition to last. You can type in anything using the minutes:seconds:frames format, but iMovie may just ignore you if you type in a number that's too long. See the next section on how a transition can get too long.

Figure 5-5:
Type in the number you want, formatted as minutes:seconds:frames, and then click OK. (This box, as you can see, offers a second way to change the durations of all transitions in your project so far.) Don't be surprised if iMovie ignores you, however, as it did here. Notice how the Inspector says the transition is 30 seconds long, but the little yellow number above the transition itself says that it's one second, 29 frames long.

Why You Don't Always Get What You Want

Even after you master all of the transition-duration permutations described on the previous pages, you may find yourself thwarted by iMovie itself. For example, you may indicate that you want a 2-second transition, but iMovie gives you a half-second one, no matter how many techniques you try. That's because iMovie enforces its own Law of Reasonable Durations, which states that *no transition effect may consume more than half the length of a clip*. Figure 5-6 shows the problem, and the result.

Note: If you can't manually change the durations of *any* transition, it's probably because you've got Automatic Transitions turned on (see page 133).

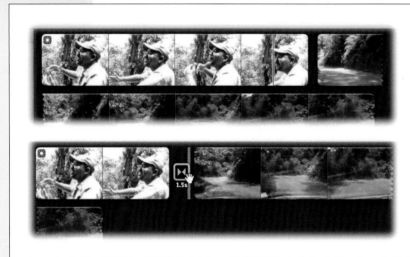

Figure 5-6:
Top: One of the clips in-volved in the transition is only 3 seconds long. You try to add a 2-second transition.

Bottom: iMovie gives you only a 1.5-second transition, because that's half of the clip's 3-second length—and iMovie won't let you add a transition longer than half of a clip's length.

How Transitions Affect the Length of Your Movie

As you can see by the example in Figure 5-7, transitions generally make your movie *shorter*. To superimpose the ends of two adjacent clips, iMovie is forced to slide the right-hand clip to the left, making the overall movie end sooner.

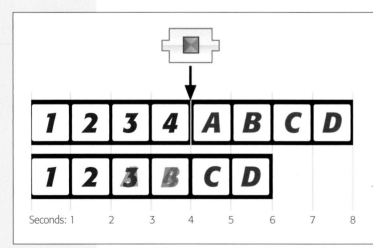

Figure 5-7:
When you insert a 2-second transition (top) between two clips, iMovie pulls the right-hand clip 2 seconds to the left so that it over-laps the end of the left-hand clip. The result (bottom): The entire movie is now 2 seconds shorter.

Under most circumstances, there's nothing wrong with that. After all, that's why, when importing your clips, you wisely avoided trimming off *all* of the excess leader and trailer footage (known as *trim handles*) from the ends of your clips. By leaving trim handles on each clip—which you'll sacrifice to the transition—you'll have some fade-in and fade-out footage to play with.

Sometimes, however, having your overall project shortened is a serious problem, especially when you've been "cutting to sound," or synchronizing your footage to an existing music track. Even if you use the "Snap to Beats" feature covered on page 235, any transitions you add will throw off the timing. (At least iMovie duly warns you of this potential disaster.)

In iMovie '11, there's no good solution to this problem if you opt for manual control over transitions. (The *automatic* transition feature, which puts a transition between every scene in the entire movie, offers a semi-solution; see below.)

Automatic Transitions

If you're really in a hurry to crank out your edited movie, like the now-legendary Apple programmer who wound up writing iMovie '11 so he could whip out highlight reels without hand-tweaking everything, then you're in luck. You don't have to bother placing transitions one at a time. Using the Automatic Transitions feature, you can tell iMovie to put the same, identical, fixed-length transition between *all* clips. Figure 5-8 shows the idea.

Figure 5-8:
The Automatic Transitions feature takes your rough edit (top) and inserts identical transitions everywhere (bottom), masking the divider between every pair of clips.

This feature is OK *if* all of this is true:

- You choose a nontacky transition effect, like the cross-dissolve.
- You set the duration to something short, like 1 second.
- You're creating a highlight reel—a sequence of shots that aren't intended to tell a story.

If you're not careful, these frequent transitions can get annoying or cloying, and they'll lose their impact in a hurry. You should also note that turning on the Automatic Transitions feature *removes* any customizing you did using the individual-transition feature described on the preceding pages; all your duration adjustments get wiped away.

Tip: There is, however, a way to turn all of these automatic transitions into *individual* transitions that you can edit separately; see page 134.

Still interested? Then proceed like this:

1. **Choose File→Project Theme.**

   Alternatively, press Shift-⌘-J. Either way, the Project Theme screen appears.

2. **Turn on "Automatically add." From the pop-up menu, choose the transition you want.**

   This time, you don't get the handy self-illustrating icons that preview the effect. It doesn't matter; the only one you'd ever use without looking amateurish is the Cross Dissolve. (Right?)

3. **Click OK.**

   You return to your project, where the icons for iMovie's automatic transitions now appear in place. Play back the movie to enjoy the effect, keeping in mind that you can't edit, change, or delete them *individually*, only en masse.

Tip: If you add any new clips to your movie, iMovie adds your chosen transition to them automatically.

Adjusting Automatic Transitions

You can change the uniform length or uniform style of *all* those auto-transitions, but you can't edit them individually. Just choose File→Project Properties (⌘-J). In the dialog box (Figure 5-4, page 130), you can change the Duration slider or, using the pop-up menu, the transition style. Any change you make here affects *all* the transitions.

Turning off Automatic Transitions

If you decide that the all-at-once approach is a bit much, you can turn off the Automatic Transitions feature. Choose File→Project Theme (Shift-⌘-J) and just turn off "Add automatically." When you click OK, iMovie has one more bit of business to take care of: what to do about that messy overlapping-ends affair. A message now appears at the bottom of the window asking what you want to do:

- **Remove transitions and extend clip ends**. This option leaves in place the footage the transition uses. For example, if you had an 8-second clip with a 1-second transition at the end, the clip will wind up being about 9 seconds long.

- **Remove transitions and maintain clip durations**. If you spent a lot of energy working out timings, maybe to match a soundtrack, you probably want this choice. Now that 8-second clip will still be 8 seconds long after you remove the transitions. iMovie hides the video the transition *was* using once again.

- **Leave transitions in current locations**. This handy option turns off automatic transitions, but leaves the actual transition icons in place. They've now turned into *individual* transitions, which you can now delete or edit on a one-at-a-time basis.

Tip: This option can be a terrific help when you want transitions on *most* of your clips, but not all. You can turn Automatic Transitions on, and then choose this option as you turn them off again. Now you have a storyboard full of *manual* transition icons. Just delete the ones you don't need.

Transitions: The iMovie Catalog

Here, for your reference, is an explanation of each transition, and what editing circumstances might call for it.

Circle Open, Circle Close

This effect, called *iris close (iris open)* or *iris in (iris out)* in professional editing programs, is a holdover from the silent film era, when, in the days before zoom lenses, directors used the effect to highlight a detail in a scene.

It creates an ever-growing (or opening) porthole, with the first clip inside and the second clip outside (Figure 5-9). It's useful at the beginning or end of a movie, when the subject of the first clip is centered in the frame and the second clip is solid black. In that setup, the movie begins or ends with a picture that grows or shrinks away to a little dot. (If the subject in the center waves goodbye just before being blinked out of view, this trick is especially effective.)

Figure 5-9:
Circle Opening.

Cross Blur

Like an autofocus gone awry, the first clip gets blurry, only to have the focus return with the second clip now on the screen.

Cross Dissolve

The crossfade, or dissolve, is the world's most popular and effective transition. The first clip, superimposed on the beginning of the second clip, gradually disappears, while the second clip gradually fades in. If you must use a transition at all, you can't go wrong with this one.

Tip: You can use a very short cross-dissolve to create what editors call a "soft cut." When the footage would jump too abruptly if you made a regular cut, put in a 10-frame cross-dissolve, which makes the junction of clips *slightly* smoother than just cutting. Soft cuts are common in interviews where the editors have deleted sections from a continuous shot of a person talking.

Cross Zoom

For anyone who's experienced jumping into hyperspace, this transition will look very familiar. The first clip turns into a streaky tunnel, giving the illusion of speeding into the video, only to come out on the other end with the second clip. This transition emphasizes what's at the end of the wormhole.

Doorway

Here's another effect that takes full advantage of the three-dimensional powers built into your Mac. The first clip splits in half, and the two halves swing open like double doors. The second clip charges through the doors, filling the screen.

Fade Through Black, Fade Through White

Use this effect at the beginning and end of every movie, for a handsome, professional fade in/fade out. Or use it at the start of any scene that begins in a new place or time. In that situation, it makes the first scene fade to black momentarily, and then the next one fades in (Figure 5-10).

Fade Through White is the same thing, with one big difference: It fades out to, and then in from, *white* instead of black. Fading in and out to white, an effect first popularized by Infiniti car commercials in the early 1980s, lends a very specific feeling to a movie. It's something ethereal, ghostly, and nostalgic. In today's Hollywood movies (including *The Sixth Sense*), a fade to white often indicates that the character you've been watching has just died.

Figure 5-10:
*Fade Through White/
Black.*

The fade to white is an extremely popular technique in today's TV commercials, when the advertiser wants to show you a series of charming, brightly colored images. By fading out to white between shots, the editor inserts the video equivalent of an ellipsis (…like this…), and keeps the mood happy and bright. (Similar fade-outs to black seem to stop the flow with more finality.)

Tip: If you'd rather fade to black and then *hold* on the black screen for a moment, use the transition between your video and a *black clip*. See page 266 for details on making a black clip.

Mosaic

Like an impatient game of Memory, iMovie breaks your first clip into a bunch of little cards, and then flips them all over to reveal the second clip. The flipped cards blend together to finish the effect.

Page Curl

Here's another slightly tacky transition: the page curl. It makes the upper-right corner of the video frame appear to curl inward and toward you, and then peel down and to the left, as though it's a giant Post-it note being ripped off a pad (Figure 5-11). The clip that follows is revealed underneath.

Figure 5-11:
Page Curl.

Ripple

This effect is gorgeous, poetic, beautiful—and hard to justify. Ripple invokes the "drop of water on the surface of the pond" metaphor (Figure 5-12). As the ripple expands across the screen, it pushes the first clip (the pond surface) off the screen to make way for the incoming new clip (the expanding circular ripple). It's a soothing, beautiful effect but unless you're making mascara commercials, it calls a little too much attention to itself for everyday home movies.

Figure 5-12:
Ripple.

Spin In, Spin Out

Did you see *Superman 3*? That's the one where General Zod and his cronies end up in a space jail that looks like a playing card flipping through space. Now you too can create that visual effect. Amaze your friends!

With Spin In, the second clip looks like a card that zooms forward from the middle of the screen, eventually filling the frame. Spin Out looks similar, but the first clip looks like a card zooming off, while the second one serves as a backdrop. Spin In emphasizes the clip coming in, while Spin Out dwells on the departing clip.

Swap

This transition leaves no doubt that you're changing clips. Again harnessing your Mac's ability to animate in 3D, the first clip slides backward and to the left, as the incoming clip slides in from the right, then comes forward to fill the screen. Several of these in a row would leave the impression of some sort of assembly line.

Wipe Down, Up, Left, Right

In this transition, the incoming clip *covers up* the outgoing one, as though it's being shoved into the frame on a cookie sheet (Figure 5-13). (A cookie sheet with a soft, slightly blurry leading edge, that is; iMovie doesn't *do* hard transition edges.) You could use it to simulate an old-style projector changing slides, or when filming a clever, self-aware documentary in which the host (who first appears in the second clip) pushes his way onto the screen.

Figure 5-13:
Wipe.

Themes

Themes are transitions with graduate degrees. If you have experience with Themes in iMovie HD, you already know what they are: sets of professionally designed and animated transitions and titles that run throughout your movie, usually including an opening-credit sequence, a special transition style, and a closing-credit sequence. Themes in iMovie look and work a lot like the cool animated DVD menus you can make in iDVD (Chapters 17 and 19). But iMovie themes don't require a DVD player; they're built right into your movie with all the same cool artwork and animations.

iMovie has seven themes: Photo Album, Bulletin Board, Comic Book, Scrapbook, Filmstrip, News, and Sports. Each one includes custom transitions and titles. The Sports theme also has some fun customizability up its sleeve.

Choosing a Theme

Any time you create a new project, iMovie gives you the chance to apply a theme to it. The new project dialog box, shown in Figure 5-14, shows you previews of each theme filled with example footage. This way you know what your stuff will look like. (At least, this is what it would look like if you and your friends are all professional models. Still, the iMovie themes can make your footage look pretty great.)

Once you click a theme in this window, iMovie offers to automatically add transitions and titles for you. With the "Automatically add transitions and titles" box turned on, each new clip or picture you add to your storyboard comes along with some sort of added transition or title, either from those specific to the theme or from the standard list of transitions. Whether it's a simple cross-dissolve or an animated photo album, iMovie mixes things up and avoids too many similar transitions in a row.

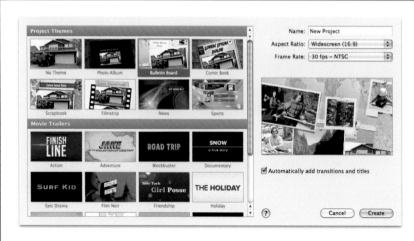

Figure 5-14:
Each of these themes has its own character and style. The preview window gives you an idea of what your themed project will look like. If you want iMovie to automatically insert theme elements as you go, check the box "Automatically add transitions and titles" that appears when you click your chosen theme.

You can always change your mind and add your own transitions, but the moment you do, iMovie warns you that you'll need to turn off automatic transitions to proceed (Figure 5-15).

Figure 5-15:
When it comes to themes and transitions, iMovie insists on being in charge if you accept its help. Once you try to do things your way, iMovie withdraws due to creative differences.

Warning: That is, you can avoid having to insert transitions individually by letting iMovie do the work for you. Once all the transitions are in place, you can change them to your heart's content.

If you turned off automatic transitions and decide that you really were better off with iMovie in charge, go to File→Project Theme, where you can turn automatic transitions back on. Click OK and iMovie promptly scraps your custom transitions and sets them back to its liking.

Custom Theme Transition and Titles

If you choose a project theme, iMovie offers you transitions and titles available only to that theme, as shown in Figure 5-16. If you choose None for your theme, those transitions and titles don't show up in your list of choices.

Figure 5-16:
With a chosen theme assigned to your project, iMovie offers four more transitions and eight more titles than before. If you don't like the theme itself, just click the Set Theme button to change it.

Tip: If you like having options but don't want your movie dominated by a theme, go ahead and pick a theme—but leave the automatic transitions and titles turned off. You can still add them manually.

On the other hand, if you choose a theme, you're locked out from the custom stuff available in the *other* four themes. (Maybe that's for the best. Mixing themes could look pretty ugly anyway.)

Changing a Theme

iMovie is very generous to the wishy-washy. Each theme has title and transition elements that correspond precisely to those in the other themes. When you change to a different theme, iMovie just replaces elements from the old theme with the matching elements from the new one.

To change a theme, choose File→Project Theme and click the new theme you want. Once you click OK, iMovie takes a moment to update all the corresponding elements. Everything else, like timing and the clips in the project, stays the same.

Tip: You can also change a theme by clicking the Set Theme button at the top of either the Titles or Transitions window. Click the new theme you want, and then click OK.

Adjusting Theme Transitions

You can adjust a theme transition's length the same way you adjust a regular transition's length (page 129): Point to the transition and click the ✿ badge on it. From the menu that appears, choose Transition Adjustments. The Inspector pops up; here, you can type in a new duration (in seconds and tenths of seconds). Click Done.

But one of the coolest things about themes is that they incorporate your pictures and video *into* the neat animations that go between clips. The animated photo album, for example (Figure 5-17), displays your video and photos as though they were actual photos in the album.

Figure 5-17:
Your movie looks professionally designed thanks to the way iMovie inserts your photos and videos into theme transitions and titles, like this transition from the Photo Album theme.

iMovie automatically chooses what clips go where in the animation, but you can have some influence on the outcome. (This may be especially useful if iMovie happened to choose the part of a clip where you're shoveling birthday cake into your mouth.) To make a more dignified appearance in theme animations:

1. **Click the animated transition you want to adjust.**

   When you click the theme transition that needs changing, orange numbers hover above various points in your storyboard. The numbers represent different frames in the animation, and iMovie identifies them in the preview window (see Figure 5-18).

Note: If you don't see the orange numbers, one of two things may be going on. First, some transitions just aren't editable. Second, there are often canned *portions* of editable transitions.

Figure 5-18:
You can adjust some theme transitions so that the images in the animation show the part of the project you choose. Dragging the orange numbers around in your project changes the corresponding frame.

2. **Drag the numbers where you want them.**

   As you drag the numbers to different points in your storyboard, iMovie updates the frames, displaying whatever image is under the corresponding number. This is how you change focus from *your* cake-stuffed face to your *brother's* cake-stuffed face.

3. **Preview your changes.**

   As with most editable iMovie elements, such as titles and photos, you can preview your changes by clicking the arrow in the top-right corner of your preview window.

4. **Click Done.**

   iMovie displays the transition with the updated images.

Note: If you used themes in iMovie HD, you know that the old iMovie theme elements could use *any* photos and videos, even if they didn't show up anywhere else in your project. iMovie '11 isn't so generous. Its themes point only to parts of photos or clips that actually appear in your storyboard. Anything that isn't going to be shown full-screen isn't going into the theme transitions, either.

Customizing the Sports Theme

If you're using the Sports theme, you can take it a lot further than just a few neato transitions and titles. Apple devised a slick, professional theme for presenting your team to the world. It works by pulling players' names and stats from a roster you build using the Sports Team Editor. Then, when you want to show a cool graphic highlighting a player during your movie, you just drag a title into your project and choose the player from the roster. Voila! You're making a highlight reel worthy of ESPN.

To build your team and put the Sports theme through its paces, follow these steps:

1. **Open the Sports Team Editor by choosing Window→Sports Team Editor.**

   The handy window that appears contains all the information you need to enter (Figure 5-19).

2. **Create your team.**

   The top third of the Editor window lists all the teams you've created. iMovie already has one there to get you started. You can make changes to that one or create a new one by clicking the + button at the bottom of the list.

Tip: If your assistant coach has created a team roster in her copy of iMovie, she can export it using the Export Teams button under the teams list. This produces a file that she can email to you. Once you have it, import it using the Import Teams button. Now you have everything she's already typed in. That's what you call teamwork.

---

3. **Customize your stats.**

   At the bottom of the Team Editor window, click ▾ next to Sports, and you'll see a list of all the sports already entered into iMovie. Here you can customize the list of sports, as well as the stats you see for each player. Notice that you can set the stat categories to whatever you want, and even specify your players' favorite colors (Figure 5-19).

4. **Add the Sports theme graphics to your project.**

   All your work in the Team Editor pays off when you start adding player graphics to your project. These come in the form of titles, which you can read about in detail on page 199. A customized player graphic/title looks like the one you see in Figure 5-19.

Figure 5-19:
Top: The Sports Team Editor is where you keep track of all of the teams you want to make movies about. You can make team rosters, add player pictures and stats, and even drop in your team's logo.

Bottom: Once you complete your roster, add one of the custom Sports titles to your movie and you can choose from the player list to make a broadcast-worthy graphic highlighting that player.

A movie with these awesome Sports theme graphics will get the other players/parents wondering how much you paid to have it professionally edited. You can just tell them you know a guy at ESPN and they won't have any reason to doubt you.

Removing a Theme

You may come to realize that a particular project is worse off with a theme applied to it. If this happens, you can remove the offending theme. Click File→Project Theme; on the General tab, click None, and then click OK. iMovie sweeps away all the theme-related titles and transitions, leaving you with a decidedly less theme-y project. (Non-theme transitions, like cross dissolves, survive iMovie's sweep.)

Travel Maps

Just in case you didn't get the memo, here's some big news: iMovie loves travel footage. Maybe Apple did some rigorous focus-group research, or maybe the Apple programmer behind iMovie '11 just loves to tour the world. Whatever the reason, if you travel, iMovie has a special place in its heart for you.

Travel Maps are the grandest token of iMovie's travel-love. These are basically animated maps that take viewers from Point A to Point B with a snaking, animated red line across a map or a globe, à la the Indiana Jones movies. They're great for conveying your itinerary in a quick, visually compelling way. Although you might think of them as transitions—after all, they fill the space between things (in this case places), much as transitions do—iMovie doesn't think of them that way. To iMovie, they're specialized video clips.

Adding a Travel Map

In the middle toolbar, click ⊕ to open the "Maps, Backgrounds, and Animatics" pane (see Figure 5-20). You'll see eight animated map options at the top of the list: a globe version and a flat version of four different map styles. You'll also see non-animated versions of each map you can stick in your project as images. Scrolling down, you'll find a bunch of images that look nothing like maps (hence the "Backgrounds and Animatics" part). Backgrounds are just pictures that you can use as backgrounds for titles, for example. Animatics are explained on page 150.

Adding an animated travel map to your project is a matter of dragging one of the eight icons into your project, just as you would a transition or video clip. iMovie generates a specialized video clip you can now customize.

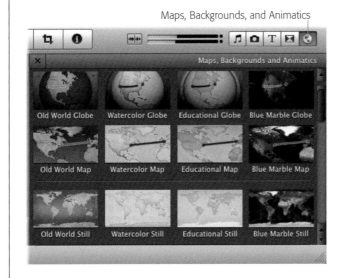

Maps, Backgrounds, and Animatics

Figure 5-20:
At the top of the "Maps, Backgrounds, and Animatics" window are eight animated map options, four globes and four flat maps, to choose from. To add one of these to your project, just drag it in.

Changing Travel Points

As soon as you drag a map icon into your project, the Inspector window appears. (If you don't see it, point to the map clip and click the ✿ badge. From the menu that appears, choose Clip Adjustments.) That's fortunate, because the first order of business is to change the endpoints of your new animated map. After all, showing your dramatic flight from Topeka to Tangiers is why you're putting this thing into your movie to begin with. You can choose your departure and destination points from a list of hundreds of preset locations (Figure 5-21).

To change a location, click the San Francisco button (or whatever it says next to Start Location). The Inspector flips around to reveal a huge list of cities and airports. You can winnow down the list by typing a destination's name into the box at the top of the window. Click to highlight the desired location, and then click OK.

Repeat the process for the End Location, and then click Done.

Tip: If the list doesn't offer the location you want, you can type in the decimal coordinates (for example, *44.768056, –85.622222* points to Traverse City, MI). You can get these coordinates at *www.itouchmap. com/latlong.html*. Then just edit the "Name to display" text at the bottom of the Inspector window.

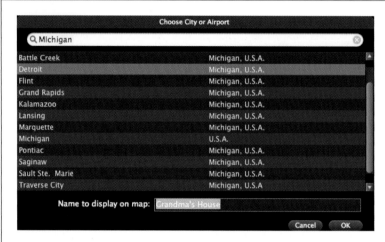

Figure 5-21:
iMovie offers hundreds of potential destinations for your travel map. If you don't see the place you need, you can choose a nearby location, and then change the display name of that spot.

Changing a Map's Style

If you started with a globe map and decide you prefer a flat one, or if you started with the Educational Map and like the Watercolor Map better, you can easily change it. Just drag a new map from the "Maps, Backgrounds, and Animatics" pane onto the map you want to replace. iMovie preserves locations and the length of the animation.

Tip: Because iMovie treats a travel map like a clip, you can apply most video effects to the map as well. You might do this to match a map's style to the rest of your video, for example. If you bring up the Inspector window (select the map and click the ❶ button in the middle toolbar), you see an option for video effects. Click None and iMovie shows you skimmable previews of 20 effects you can apply to your map. Click an effect and then click Done.

If you chose a Globe map, you can find extra options in the Inspector; double-click the map. Here you can zoom in on the globe by checking the box. You can also hide the destination names or the red travel line connecting the points, just by turning off the corresponding checkboxes.

Changing a Map's Timing

If a map's animation is too slow or too fast, you can adjust it using one of three methods.

- **Use the Inspector.** Start by bringing up the Inspector and then click the ❶ button in the middle toolbar). Here, you can type the duration you prefer, in seconds and frames, into the Duration text box. Click Done.

- **Extendo Buttons.** iMovie offers the same Extendo buttons it does for project clips. Click one of the ◄|► icons that appear in either corner when you point to the map clip in your project. An orange handle appears, which you can use to lengthen or shorten the clip by up to 1 second. It doesn't matter which end of the map you use. They both have the same effect on the map.

- **Select a Range and Delete.** This option can only *shorten* a map. Drag across a segment of the map clip's icon, and then press the Delete key. The map animation will still draw a line from Point A to Point B, but faster than before. Beware, though: If you select a middle portion of the map and delete that, iMovie makes *two* maps, each of which draws the line to its destination.

Removing a Map

To remove a map, just select its clip icon in the storyboard and hit the Delete key.

POWER USERS' CLINIC

Adding Locations to iMovie

If your destination isn't in iMovie's permanent list, you can permanently add a location you use a lot, like Grandma's house. You can go into the file that tells iMovie where these places are and add your own. But proceed at your own risk! This trick is pretty advanced, so try it only if you're comfortable mucking about in files Apple didn't intend for amateurs to muck about in.

Find the iMovie icon in the Applications folder. Control-click (or right-click) it and choose Show Package Contents. In the resulting window, open the Contents→Resources folder. Find the file called *WorldLocation.txt*. Make a safety copy of this file, and then double-click the original. Unless you've hacked your Mac's document-to-program relationships, this file opens in TextEdit, revealing a list of map locations.

This is a tab-delimited list. That is, each location is listed something like this: *City TAB State TAB Country TAB Latitude and Longitude.* Feel free to add your custom location to the bottom of the list, following that pattern. For non-US locations, you can replace the State with a region or province.

(Or you can leave it blank. Just press Tab twice to skip that part.) Latitude and Longitude need to be separated by a comma and no spaces. If you need to look up the coordinates for a given location, use Google to help you.

Finally, save the changes to WorldLocations.txt and restart iMovie. The next time you go into your list of locations, the location you added now appears in the list. Adding it to a travel map works just the same as the locations iMovie came with.

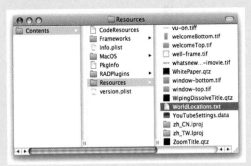

Animatics

When professionals plan the filming of a movie, they typically create a *storyboard*: a shot-by-shot plan of everything in the movie, from the sweeping opening scene down to the shot of the hero tying his shoes. It looks a little bit like a comic strip. If you see it in the movie, it was probably in the storyboard first.

Storyboards are usually hand-drawn depictions of each shot. Each little box gives the director a vivid visualization of the movie's progression. That way, if he comes to realize that what he really needs is a shot of a little dog running in the street, he has one drawn up and plugged into the storyboard. Now he can see what that shot might look like.

The animatics feature in iMovie '11 gives you a set of storyboard scenes so you can do your own version of what the pros do. It's not quite as handy as having a storyboard artist at your beck and call, but it's still pretty cool.

Building a Storyboard with Animatics

To add an animatic to your project, click the "Maps, Backgrounds, and Animatics" button in the middle toolbar of the iMovie window (Figure 5-20). Scroll down past the maps and backgrounds and you'll see 16 black and gray images showing a variety of scenes: with people and without people, medium shots and wide shots, two people and many people, and so on.

Now just drag an animatic into your project like you'd do with a map or video clip. Continue adding animatics until you have the storyboard you want.

Tip: Because a lot of these animatics look the same, use comment markers (page 98) to identify who is who and what is what (Figure 5-22).

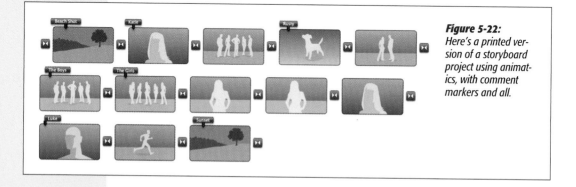

Figure 5-22:
Here's a printed version of a storyboard project using animatics, with comment markers and all.

You can move animatics around by dragging them and delete them by selecting them and pressing Delete.

Print Your Storyboard for Filming

Once you have your storyboard completed, print it out by choosing File→Print. The standard Print window appears, showing you a preview of what you're about to print, comment markers and all (Figure 5-22). Now you can carry this document around, make notes, and even show it to other people for feedback on your plans.

Build Your Movie from Your Storyboard

All that planning and hard work pays off when you start actually building your project. For each animatic, you're supposed to choose a corresponding clip from your Event Library and drop it onto the Animatic. From the menu that appears, choose "Replace from Start" (page 89) if you want to preserve the timing of the animatic in your movie. If you want to use the timing of the clip you selected instead, choose Replace.

Continue through all your animatics. Before you know it, you'll be enjoying the fruits of all your planning: a movie that follows the grandeur of everything you contemplated from the very beginning. Look out, Coppola.

Video Effects

I t's a funny thing that we'll take pristine HD video and make it look old and grainy. On purpose. But video effects, like the popular Aged Film effect, create a mood that you can't really communicate in any other way.

Once upon a time, iMovie '08 came without any built-in video effects. You couldn't even slow clips down or speed them up. To make matters worse, you couldn't install new effects in the form of plug-ins from other companies, as you could with the old iMovie. As a result, a lot of people swore off iMovie '08 altogether.

iMovie '09 brought back all those missing effects, like Slo-Mo, Reverse Motion, and the beloved Aged Film. Apple even added new effects that iMovie never had before, like Picture-in-Picture and Green Screen.

iMovie '11 adds a few more basic video effects for good measure, like Side-by-Side picture, but where Apple really waved its magic wand is in the new One-Step effects. These take selected footage and apply an awesome effect, like Instant Replay, in one step instead of the dozens it would take to create the same effect manually.

Note: Still no plug-ins, though, just in case you've been holding out for them. Don't expect that set of third-party plug-ins you bought for iMovie HD to *ever* work in the new iMovie.

Maybe best of all is that you don't have to wait for iMovie to *render* (process) an effect. Your project immediately reflects any effect you select. iMovie's new state of video effects is pretty compelling, even if it took a detour to get here.

Video Effects

What iMovie calls Video Effects may be better described as video filters. They don't insert lightning bolts or fairy dust, as iMovie effects have done in the past. Instead, iMovie '11's video filters generally change only the color and definition of the underlying video. (The one notable exception is the Flipped effect, which displays a mirror image of your clip.)

The difference between these filters and the Rain and Lens Flare effects of yesteryear isn't just technical—it's stylistic, too. Apple decided, rightly or not, that the old, gimmicky effects didn't do much to make your movies better. (Never mind the fact that you may have had *fun* using them.) The new filters are much more subtle and nuanced.

The Effects

A rundown of iMovie's video effects is in order (Figure 6-1). Some of them will sound familiar if you're a veteran of the original iMovie.

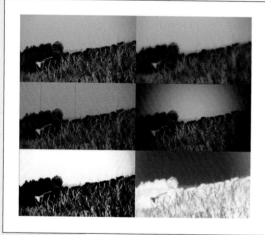

Figure 6-1:
Most video effects in iMovie are really video filters, each of which adds a unique style to your movie. This image demonstrates some of the effects. Clockwise from top left: The original clip, Cartoon, Vignette, X-Ray, Heat Wave, and the much-adored Aged Film.

- **Flipped**. Turns your clip into a mirror image of itself.
- **Raster**. Covers your clip with horizontal scan lines, like you'd see on an old TV.
- **Cartoon**. Smoothes the different colors in your clip to make it look like the clip was taken from a comic book.
- **Aged Film**. One of the most popular effects, Aged Film applies a sepia tone (see below) and film noise to make your clip look like an old, worn-out filmstrip.
- **Film Grain**. Applies a mild sepia tone and adds tiny speckles that look like grainy film.

- **Hard Light**. Overexposes the light colors and darkens the dark colors.

- **Day into Night**. Darkens the whole clip with a bluish hue, as though it were shot at night.

- **Glow**. Overexposes the light colors *without* darkening the dark colors.

- **Dream**. Blurs the clip and washes out its colors, to convey the idea that you're dreaming.

- **Romantic**. Blurs just the edges of the clip, so your focus rests on whatever's in the center (presumably the object of your desire).

- **Vignette**. Instead of blurring the edges, this effect fades the edges to black, not unlike what you'd see in studio photography from the 1980s.

- **Bleach Bypass**. Washes out colors, just like bleach.

- **Old World**. A sepia tone and a glow combined. Yet another way to make that high-tech footage look low-tech.

- **Heat Wave**. This is what your clip would look like under the punishing desert sun, yellow and overexposed.

- **Sci-Fi**. If you've seen the *Matrix* movies, you know exactly what Sci-Fi looks like. It applies a green hue to everything.

- **Black & White**. The old classic.

- **Sepia Tone**. The other old classic. Applies a brownish hue to everything, making it look like ancient photographs or films from the turn of the century (the turn of the *previous* century).

- **Negative**. Inverts all the colors in your clip by replacing them with their color-wheel opposites.

- **X-Ray**. Turns everything into shades of greenish-gray, with lights and darks inverted. Presumably, this is what your movie would look like if you filmed the whole thing with an X-ray machine.

Applying a Video Effect

You can apply video effects to any clip or photo in your project, even cutaways and travel maps. Start by double-clicking the clip (or, if it's already selected, by clicking the ❶ in the middle toolbar) to open the Inspector panel. Click the None button next to the Video Effect label.

The Inspector flips around, revealing a bunch of thumbnails that show what your clip would look like with the video effect applied (Figure 6-2). As you skim across each thumbnail, the preview window demonstrates the effect. To apply an effect, click the thumbnail itself. When the Inspector flips back around, click Done.

Figure 6-2:
iMovie's video effects generally affect the color and clarity of your clips. You can preview them by skimming over the thumbnails.

QuickTime Video Filters

The old iMovie effects haven't all disappeared; some just went into hiding.

In Chapter 15, you'll read about exporting iMovie projects as *QuickTime* movies—digital movie files you write to your hard drive. During that exporting process, you'll have the opportunity to apply the special effects that are still around. These *filters*, as they're called, can process your footage in ways like these:

- **Blur.** Softens the look of the video.
- **Edge Detect.** Creates outlines of the subjects in your footage.
- **Emboss.** Makes your footage look like it was carved into a sheet of metal.
- **Sharpen.** Makes blurry footage sharper (as much as possible, anyway).
- **Color Tint.** Makes your footage turn black-and-white, sepia tone, cobalt, or negative image.

- **Film Noise.** Adds scratches, dust, and rot to otherwise modern footage.
- **Lens Flare.** Adds a cool-looking light flare that progresses across your footage as though caught in the lens of your camera.

Unfortunately, you have to apply these filters at the moment you export your project as a QuickTime movie—and that means the filter applies to your *entire* movie.

So what if you want to apply one of these filters to just *one* scene within a movie? The trick: Create a separate project containing only that one scene. Export the one-clip project using the steps on page 338.

When it's all over, you'll have a QuickTime file on your hard drive that you can bring right back into iMovie using the File→Import Movies command. Once the filtered footage is back in your Event Library, just add it to your main project.

Tip: You can also play the clip (with the effect applied) by tapping the space bar while you preview the video effects. iMovie plays the clip repeatedly while you make up your mind. As your clip plays back, you can point to other effect thumbnails in the preview window (without clicking) to see what *they'd* look like if you applied them to your looping video.

Adjusting a Video Effect

You can't make any adjustments to iMovie's video effects as you could in previous versions of iMovie. If you don't like the way an effect that comes from Apple looks, you're out of luck.

Removing a Video Effect

To remove an effect, pull up the Inspector again, click the button that identifies the current effect, and then click the None thumbnail. The Inspector flips back around. Click Done.

Fast/Slow/Reverse

Whether you're mimicking *Chariots of Fire* or Buddy Hall, you can add a lot to your movie by changing the speed of your footage. Slowing a clip down emphasizes the drama of a moment. Speeding a clip up conveys urgency, depicts the passage of time, or just makes it funny. Throw in a good Reverse effect and you could pretend your protagonist has a remote control that rewinds time.

Changing a Clip's Speed

To make a clip play back faster or slower, double-click it to open the Inspector panel. You'll see one of two things in the middle of the panel:

- **Convert Entire Clip**. Ordinarily, Apple hides ugly technical underpinnings from you. If you want to play with the speed or direction of a clip's playback, however, you come face-to-face with one unfortunate technicality: iMovie can't adjust the speed or direction of a clip unless, as it sits there on your hard drive, it happens to be in a particular file format (the aforementioned Apple Intermediate Codec [page 48], in case you're wondering).

Note: The Convert Entire Clip conversion step isn't necessary if you're editing footage imported from an *AVCHD* camera (page 8). That's because iMovie has *already* converted your footage into the AIC format.

If you see the Convert Entire Clip button, click it (Figure 6-3).

Note: When iMovie says "Convert Entire Clip," it means the *entire* clip. Even if you've used only part of a clip from your Event browser, the conversion process makes a speed-up-able copy of the entire thing.

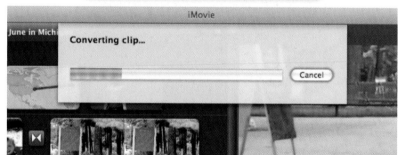

Figure 6-3:
Top: You need to convert this clip before you can change its speed or direction.

Bottom: The conversion process may take a minute or two, depending on the length of your source clip.

- **Speed slider**. If a clip is speed-adjustable (either you've already converted it, or it didn't need conversion in the first place), you see a slider in the middle of the Inspector panel depicting a tortoise and a hare (Figure 6-4). (The hare's winning for the time being, but we can assume it's early in the race.)

Dragging the slider closer to the tortoise slows your clip; dragging it toward the hare speeds it up.

Reversing a Clip's Playback Direction

Playing a clip backward has been a comedic staple since the time film was born. To do it in iMovie, all you need to do is check a box.

Figure 6-4:
Change the speed of your clip by dragging the Speed slider. You can make your clip up to eight times faster or eight times slower. If you want to be really precise, type the percentage change or the desired clip length in the corresponding text boxes next to the slider.

Double-click a clip to open the Inspector window (or click it and then click ❶ on the toolbar). Assuming you converted the clip as described above, a Reverse checkbox appears beneath the Speed slider. Turn it on (Figure 6-5) to make the video play backward. (You'll also notice that the tortoise is now winning the little race, which is as it should be. The two animal icons have flipped themselves around to face the opposite direction. Cute.)

Removing Speed and Direction Changes

If you *just* finished fooling with a clip's speed or playback direction, you can bring it back to normal by choosing File→Undo or pressing ⌘-Z.

If it's too late for that, select the clip, open the Inspector, drag the Speed slider back to the middle position, and turn off Reverse. There: Time and space are back to normal.

Green Screen/Blue Screen

iMovie has opened the door to all kinds of fun with this effect. Why film your kids playing in the backyard, when you can film them playing on the *moon*? Or wherever.

iMovie's Green Screen and Blue Screen effects let you superimpose your subjects on whatever background you can think up, just as they've been doing in Hollywood for decades. With a little preparation, you could film things that would otherwise be impossible to shoot (Figure 6-6).

Figure 6-5:
The Reverse checkbox appears just below the Speed slider. Turn it on to make the video play backward. In this example, you've reversed a clip and slowed it down.

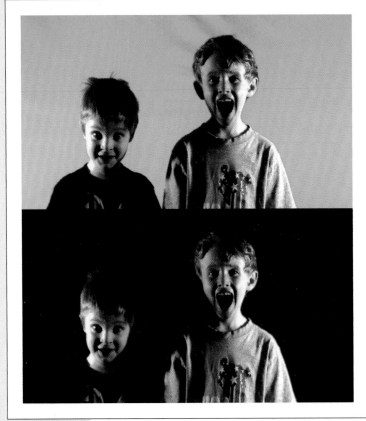

Figure 6-6:
Top: This is what your kids look like in front of a green screen.

Bottom: This is what your kids look like hurtling through space. Pretty cool.

Preparing a Green Screen

Professional green screens can cost hundreds to thousands of dollars, which is *way* too much for something you're editing in iMovie. The brains behind iMovie get this, so they designed the Green Screen effect to work with some pretty common, inexpensive materials.

You can try almost any kind of green background, as long as it's a bright, pure green color (no limes, turquoises, or pines) and isn't too shiny (see below). To get a good idea of the right shade of green, use the color chooser you can find in most applications on your Mac, like TextEdit. (Pressing Shift-⌘-C usually brings it up.) Now click on the crayons tab and choose the Spring crayon. This is the color you need for your background. Fabric stores are a good bet, as are hardware stores that carry broad paint selections. Figure 6-7 shows how you can fake it.

Figure 6-7:
This poor man's green screen cost $20, and was made with four yards of fabric from a fabric store, 24 feet of plastic pipe, and four "L" joints.

Note: The instructions here describe making a green screen, but if you have your heart set on blue, don't let these instructions stop you. Just use the purest blue color you can find, like what you'd see if you used the color chooser in Mac OS X and picked the Blueberry crayon. Then follow the instructions in this section.

Tip: A popular, low-budget approach to green screens is to buy some green fabric and attach it to a frame you make from plastic pipes or wood slats. If you don't glue the pipe joints, you can even make it collapsible. Use green paint only if you have a stiff, smooth surface that you can paint green, like the wall in your basement or garage. Keep in mind that surfaces like this are probably less mobile.

Getting the Shot

Besides having the right color green, here's a short list of other tips that will make a world of difference in your Green Screen shots.

- **Good lighting**. The last thing you want are shadows on your green background, because shadows change the color that your computer sees and ruin the seamless effect. Shadows cast by the actors themselves are particularly frustrating. Your best bet is to light the background and the actor with separate light sources.

- **Lots of space**. Whether or not you have great lighting (but especially if you don't), keep lots of space between your actors and the green background. Four feet is a decent rule of thumb. This reduces the likelihood of shadows messing up the effect your computer will apply.

Tip: Good lighting and lots of space also help you avoid the dreaded halo. When the lighting's poor or the actors are too close to the green screen, green light can reflect off your subjects. The outcome is a strange halo effect that makes it easier to tell that the subject isn't *really* flying through outer space.

UP TO SPEED

How Green Screens Work

Green screen (like its predecessor, *blue screen*) is another term for an editing technique that the Hollywood pros call Chroma Key. The idea is that you tell your computer to replace every pixel of a certain color (like vibrant green) with new footage. In other words, anything that's *not* green (like an actor) gets superimposed onto the background stuff.

This is how Superman flew, how Neo dodged bullets in *The Matrix*, how *The Daily Show* correspondents seem to be in Paris or Iraq or Washington, and how TV actors never seem to hit anyone when they're in driving scenes and paying no attention to the road. The actors performed their scenes with smooth green fabric filling the car windows; later, editors (and their computers) replaced all patches of green

with passing scenery. Watching actors in front of a green screen can be quite funny. They have to pretend they're being chased through the jungle by a dinosaur, when in fact they're sitting in a nondescript studio with its walls painted green, without so much as a vine in sight.

Green replaced blue as the most popular color for this technique because digital cameras are most sensitive to green. (Blue remains the runner-up, which is why it's sometimes used in place of green. iMovie works with either color.) Of course, this also means you can't wear green clothes in the shot, unless you're intentionally going for the floating-disembodied-head thing.

- **No shine**. Some green materials, like poster board, come in the right color but if they're shiny, they reflect white light in addition to green. Green fabric is preferable, because it diffuses light and minimizes reflections. If you use poster board, just make sure you don't see any glare.

- **No bumps or wrinkles**. We're not talking about your actors here. To eliminate shadows, the green surface has to be smooth. Wrinkles and bumps make the computer-added background look wrinkled and bumpy, too.

- **No other greens**. Don't let your actors, or anything else you want in the shot, wear green.

- **Get a key shot**. At the end of your shot, shoot just a few frames of the green background without your subjects in it. You can use the shot later to help iMovie figure out what belongs and what doesn't. Don't stop the camera before you take the shot, however; if you do, iMovie imports this key shot as a separate clip, ruining your chances of putting it to any use. (See page 165.)

Inserting a Green Screen Effect

Now that you've shot your green screen footage and imported it into iMovie, the rest is refreshingly easy. Before you do any of this, in the iMovie Preferences box, turn on Advanced Tools (page 88).

1. **Choose your background footage and add it to your project.**

    You can choose a still image or video footage, but avoid using backgrounds that distract from the subjects in the foreground. Be especially aware of scale; for example, close-up footage of garden flowers will make your actors looks unnaturally small. (Of course, you may be going for that *Honey, I Shrunk the Kids* look on purpose.)

    If you use moving footage as the background, consider two things. First, because you lit your subjects a certain way, try to shoot the background with similar lighting. (Or try to shoot your actors with similar lighting, like daylight for daylight.)

    Second, make sure you filmed *enough* background footage to cover the duration of your actors' scene. Or just repeat the background footage—loop it—by adding it to your project several times over.

2. **Select your green screen footage. Drop it onto your background clip.**

    When you drag it and drop it onto your background, the "Drag and Drop" menu appears (Figure 6-8).

3. **From the shortcut menu, choose Green Screen.**

    iMovie superimposes your green screen clip onto the underlying background. In the storyboard, the green screen clip has a green border and floats on top of the background clip.

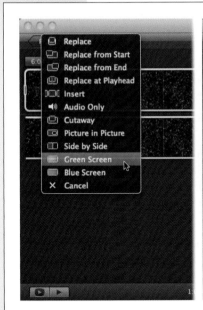 

Figure 6-8:
Left: Adding a Green Screen effect uses the highly touted "Advanced Drag and Drop" feature.

Right: The storyboard displays your green screen clip hovering over the background clip.

4. **Crop your green screen clip.**

   While you have your green screen clip selected, the preview window offers some draggable points. Drag them until they tightly surround your subject. Everything outside the points will show your background, whether it was green or not, so those are areas where you don't have to worry about shadows, lighting, or wrinkles. When you drag the boundaries, be careful not to eliminate an area where your actors will be at some point or they'll wind up losing body parts in a most unnatural way. (To check, play the entire clip by clicking the |►| button in the preview window.)

   Adjust the points accordingly, and then click Done.

5. **Adjust the timing.**

   You can drag the green screen clip (the upper one in the storyboard) left or right to adjust its playback relationship to the background clip. With the green screen clip *deselected*, that is, when it has a turquoise rather than yellow border, you can also drag its ends to move it. To get really specific about the clip's timing, use the Clip Trimmer (page 100).

6. **Adjust the sound.**

   You can use Ducking, the Volume slider, or any of the other volume-adjustment tricks described in Chapter 9.

Adding Effects to a Green Screen Effect

You can stabilize a green screen clip and change its speed or direction. In fact, you can do anything to it that you can do to a regular clip, *except* add a video effect.

That's a shame, really. Imagine how fun it would be to have the green screen actors look like X-rays of themselves while talking to other actors you put in the background shot. Alas, it's not to be.

You can add video effects to the *background*, though. That, at least, has potential.

Removing a Green Screen Effect

To remove a green screen, just select the green screen clip and press the Delete key.

Picture-in-Picture (PiP)

Picture-in-Picture is the effect that lets TV junkies watch two channels at once. The football game fills the big screen, but *60 Minutes* plays in a small inset window in the corner.

In its heyday, PiP was a boon to those who hated commercials. When the ads came on, you could swap to another show, all the while keeping your eye on the channel carrying the game. The moment the commercials ended, click, you were back.

POWER USERS' CLINIC

Using a Key Frame

If iMovie knows *exactly* what your green screen background looks like, shadows and all, it can do a much better job of creating the effect, because it knows exactly what elements to remove.

That's why, when you film your actors in front of a green screen, it's a good idea to include (in the same shot, without stopping the camera) some video of the motionless green background all by itself, with the actors out of the frame.

(Why is it so important to shoot the empty-background video without turning off the camera? Because if you stop the camera, you'll get separate clips in iMovie—and you can't merge Event clips in iMovie. The moving-actors video and the empty-background video must be part of the same clip from the outset.)

Then, once in iMovie, open the Inspector window. Turn on "Subtract last frame."

That doesn't mean iMovie is going to *delete* the last frame. It means, instead, "Subtract the *image* in the last frame when superimposing the green screen video." That is, by comparing the moving-actor footage with the still-background footage, iMovie knows what's background and what's actor. (This background-only portion of the clip doesn't have to appear in your project. As long as it was there at the end of the original, untrimmed clip, iMovie can execute the "Subtract last frame" feature.)

Commercials are obviously not why you'd use the Picture-in-Picture effect in your movie. It's more likely that you'll use it to recreate the effect on the nightly news (or *The Daily Show*), where a magic box floats over the anchorperson's shoulder to display some corny graphic to go along with the story. The PiP box in this case is *supplemental*.

iMovie's PiP effect lets you do the same kinds of things. It might be a family member narrating that great hit from the reunion softball game. It might be a shot of the crowd as your kid takes her bows at a recital. Whatever the reason, the primary footage stays primary, while the PiP box helps it along.

Inserting a PiP

Before the Picture-in-Picture feature can work, you need to turn on Advanced Tools, as described on page 88.

Now drag some Event footage to the storyboard and drop it onto one of your clips. When the shortcut menu appears, choose Picture-in-Picture. iMovie adds a whole new row above your normal project footage and sticks the added clip there (Figure 6-9).

Tip: At a glance, PiP clips in your storyboard may seem indistinguishable from cutaway clips (page 103) or green screen clips, but the color-coding can help you out. PiP clips have turquoise borders, cutaway clips have gray borders, and green/blue screen clips have (what else?) green borders.

Adjusting the PiP Size and Position

On a TV, PiP boxes are relegated to one corner of the screen and usually have a fixed size. If iMovie insisted on such behavior, a PiP box might cover up Aunt Bertie's face the entire time. (Of course, that might not be such a bad thing.) The point is that when it comes to PiP placement, iMovie is much more flexible than your TV.

When you select the PiP clip in your storyboard, look at the preview window to see the effect. Notice the inset picture? You can drag that box anywhere in the frame. You can also resize it by dragging one of the corners inward or outward. In fact, you can, if you want, make the box big enough to cover *all* of Aunt Bertie. (Of course, if you're going to make the PiP box fill the whole screen, it may make more sense to use a Cutaway [page 103].)

Note: Although you can change the size and position of a PiP box, you can't change its *dimensions*. The box will always have the same proportion of height to width—4:3 or 16:9. (See page 62 for a primer on aspect ratios.)

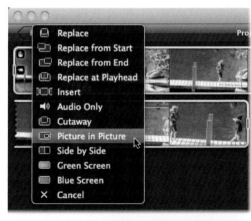

Figure 6-9:
Top: When you add footage on top of a project clip, iMovie offers the Picture-in-Picture feature as an option (assuming you turned on Advanced Tools).

Bottom: PiP clips float over the underlying clip. They're a great way to have a narrator tell a story about what's happening in the main clip.

Changing the PiP Appearance

There's more to a PiP box than just size and position. You can actually change quite a few other aspects of its appearance. Each of these involve a trip to the Inspector panel, which appears when you double-click the PiP clip (Figure 6-10).

- **Change the PiP effect**. Using the PiP Effect pop-up menu, you can control how the smaller, inset video makes its appearance. None means it simply blinks onto the screen. Dissolve makes the inset fade in and out. Zoom makes the PiP box zoom forward to its spot, and then, at the end, zoom back to its original location. Swap makes the two clips trade places, so that the underlying footage becomes the PiP. Adjust the PiP Effect slider to control the speed of these transitions.

- **Change the box border**. The Border Width and Border Color options control the outline that appears around the inset video. Your width options are none, thin, or thick. Choose any color you like for the border color (as long as it's black, gray, or white).

Figure 6-10:
This PiP clip has a thin, white border, a drop shadow, and will fade in and out.

- **Add a drop shadow**. Turn on Drop Shadow to make the inset cast a subtle shadow on the underlying video, as though it's floating just above it.

- **Change it just like a regular clip**. Even though it's a PiP clip, you can still do everything else to it, like stabilize it, add a video effect, or speed it up and slow it down. In fact, you may need to make these adjustments to get the clip to look more like the rest of your project.

Mixing PiP Audio

There are a lot of reasons to use a PiP effect, and *none* of them involve having the audio from both clips on full volume. You want either the underlying clip *or* the PiP clip to be heard.

Fortunately, you can control their relative volume levels just as you would any other clips, using the Volume slider, rubberband editing, or the Ducking feature. You'll find all three described in Chapter 9.

Moving and Trimming a PiP Clip

Odds are, you didn't get your PiP clip into *exactly* the right place you wanted when you dropped it in your storyboard. You can fix its position by grabbing anywhere inside the yellow selection border and dragging it to the correct spot.

Note: If your PiP clip covers a transition, the transition won't work. iMovie creates a clean cut between the clips instead.

You may also have to adjust the *length* of your PiP clip. You don't want too much or too little of the clip to play. While the PiP clip is *deselected* (the border is turquoise, *not* yellow), grab either end of the clip and drag it to make the clip longer or shorter.

Tip: To get *really* precise with the length and content of your PiP clip, use the Clip Trimmer (page 100) instead.

Removing a PiP Clip

Change your mind? Select the PiP clip and hit the Delete key.

Side-by-Side

Now that you've learned all about the Picture-in-Picture effect, you know *almost* everything there is to know about the Side-by-Side effect. Side-by-Side displays your additional clip by filling up half the screen with it. This is a common effect in movies when you want to show two events taking place at the same time, like a house being broken into while the family is having a great time on vacation.

You add Side-by-Side clips to a project the same way you add PiP effects, with a drag-and-drop motion. To work with the clip's audio, positioning and trimming, and removal, see the PiP instructions above.

Note: Make sure you only use this effect with clips that have the subject smack dab in the middle of your shot. When two clips share the screen, the left and right ends of the clips will be cut off. Widescreen footage, in particular, gets severely trimmed on either side. If you're not careful, one of your clips might show a shot of a talking tree instead of the person you filmed.

Changing the Side-by-Side Appearance

There isn't a whole lot to adjust in terms of how the Side-by-Side effect looks on-screen. You can only change its location (left or right) and its departure (sudden or slide). You can make both of these adjustments in the Inspector by double-clicking a Side-by-Side clip (Figure 6-11).

Tip: The slide setting makes your side-by-side clip slip onto the screen with a slick animation. Little touches like this really make your movie look professionally edited.

Figure 6-11:
There are only two appearance settings for a Side-by-Side clip, the Left/Right setting and the Slide setting. Both of them appear in the Inspector when you double-click the clip.

One-Step Effects

Having read this chapter on video effects, your mind is probably cranking away on all the possibilities. For example, you could use the Slo-Mo effect to create an instant replay of your nephew's home run. To do this, you'd: 1) find the footage in your project that you want to replay, 2) select that footage in the Event Library and insert it into the middle of your clip, 3) use the Slo-Mo setting in the Inspector to slow down the replay, and 4) add a title to the replay clip saying "Instant Replay." It might take you 5 minutes to get this all to look right, but now all your relatives can enjoy the crack of the bat replayed like it would be in any Major League game.

Or you could just select your clip and choose Clip→Instant Replay to have iMovie do all the work for you, instantly and automatically.

This example shows you the sheer coolness of iMovie's new One-Step Effects: Select any of the effects in the Clip menu of the menu bar, and iMovie executes all the same steps you'd take to make these effects happen.

Now that you know how One-Step Effects work, all that's left to do is run through the list of what each one does. Choose a clip in your project, and then, in the Clip menu, choose a One-Step Effect to do any of the following:

- **Slow Motion.** Slows your clip down to 50%, 25%, or 10% of normal speed, without you having to fiddle with the Slo-Mo slider in the Inspector.

- **Fast Forward.** Speeds up your clip by 2x, 4x, 8x, or 20x the normal speed, again saving you the minor inconvenience of fiddling with the Inspector.

- **Instant Replay.** This effect does what was described above: it takes the selected part of your clip and creates and inserts a Slo-Mo version right after your selection. It even includes a cool-looking "Instant Replay" title. Once the Slo-Mo clip ends, your movie picks right up where it left off. (Figure 6-12 shows what this looks like.) Choose 50%, 25%, or 10% to choose how slow you want the replay clip to play.

- **Rewind.** Makes a copy of the clip selection and plays it quickly backwards, like it would look if you rewound an old VCR tape for just a moment. It's basically the Instant Replay effect but without the title and a fast rewind instead of a slow replay.

- **Jump Cut at Beat Markers.** This unique effect trims out bits in the middle of your clip to create a jump cut, making your video look like it's skipping along. To enhance the effect, iMovie does this at every beat marker, something you add manually to signify beats in a song. (Read all about beat markers on page 235.) The result looks a lot like something you'd see in a music video.

Note: This effect only works when you have beat markers added to a *background* audio track. (The same goes for the Split/Flip at Beat Markers effects mentioned below.) You can read about background tracks on page 228.

- **Fade to Black and White/Sepia/Dream.** To enhance a particular moment in a clip, this effect takes the part of a clip you select and fades it to the Black and White, Sepia, or Dream filter you read about on page 155.

Note: The Fade to… effect only works if you select *part* of a clip in your project instead of the whole thing

---

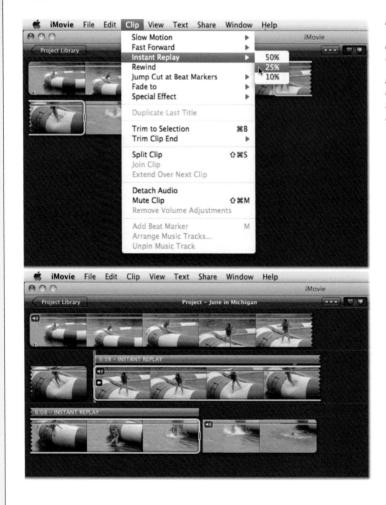

Figure 6-12:
Top: Select a bit of clip and choose Instant Replay from the Clip menu.

Bottom: iMovie automatically creates a Slo-Mo instant replay that comes with a cool title and everything.

- **Flash and Hold Last Frame.** Found in the Special Effects item in the Clip menu, this effect turns the last frame of your selection into a still frame (page 276). There's also a flash-like transition before the frozen frame to make it look like someone just took a photograph.

- **Split at Beat Markers.** Another effect dependent on beat markers, this one simply splits up your clip wherever you have a beat marker. Presumably this is simply for convenience, so you can do other things with your split-up footage, since the video looks the same on playback after you use this effect. You'll find this effect, too, in the Special Effects menu.

- **Flip at Beat Markers.** Also splits up your clip at the beat markers, but flips every other piece into a mirror image of itself. This makes the people in your movie look like they're coming and going in time with the music. It's the third and final effect buried under the Special Effects item in the Clip menu.

Tip: Even if a One-Step Effect doesn't get you exactly where you're going, it might still save you time. You can tweak all these effects to your liking, since they're all fully editable after the fact.

If, after you apply an effect, you don't like the results, just press ⌘-Z to undo the effect.

Stabilization, Color Fixes, Cropping, and Rotating

N ot every piece of video needs fancy effects. In fact, most video is probably better without a Dream filter or a Picture-in-Picture overlay. The unadulterated stuff straight from your camera usually looks best.

If your footage needs any help at all, it's probably in the cameraman department. Don't take this personally. Handheld shots, the most common kind of home video, are notoriously unstable, and that's an instant giveaway that you're an amateur. You can have the hands of a surgeon and still end up with shaky footage. This is true even with all the newfangled image-stabilization technology that comes in the latest cameras.

Don't give up (and don't resort to carrying a tripod everywhere, either). iMovie '11 can stabilize your video *after the fact*, using one of its most amazing features.

And stabilization isn't the only way iMovie can fix your footage, either. The Video Adjustments panel lets you make slight or gigantic changes to the brightness, contrast, white balance, saturation, and other image qualities of any clip.

For example, if a shot looks too dark and murky, you can bring details out of the shadows without blowing out the highlights. If the snow in a skiing shot looks too bluish, you can de-blue it. If the colors don't pop quite enough in the shot of a prize-winning soccer goal, you can boost their saturation levels.

In addition, iMovie '11 offers two features that the old versions of iMovie couldn't even fantasize about:

- **Cropping**. Cropping video means you use only a portion of the frame; it's like an artificial zoom.
- **Rotation**. You can turn the entire video image 90 degrees, or even upside-down.

Coolest of all, iMovie does all of this—picture adjustment, cropping, and rotating—*instantaneously and nondestructively*. That is, you don't have to wait around while iMovie renders (processes) your edits, which makes joyous, real-time experimentation possible. (Stabilization is the major exception to the instantaneous thing, but that doesn't make the results any less impressive.) Furthermore, you're never actually making changes to the original clips—you can restore the original video any time you like.

This chapter introduces you to all of iMovie '11's more subtle video effects.

Video Stabilization

Say what you will about iMovie, one thing's for sure: It has powers that leave other "beginner" video-editing programs panting with envy. It's filled with tools you'd historically find only in professional editing programs. iMovie inherited its stabilization feature, for example, from Apple's $1,000 Final Cut Pro software. Its rolling shutter fix was built for Final Cut, too—but only as a separately sold plugin. (That's right, you're getting a feature that Final Cut users have to *pay* for, for *free*. How's that for a deal?)

Video stabilization works by analyzing every frame in a clip, recognizing the changes in both camera position (movement up, down, left, or right) and camera rotation. Once it figures that bit out, it knows how to slide and rotate your clips to iron out the shakes.

Unfortunately, this sort of analysis takes a *very* long time—roughly 10 minutes for every minute of video (more or less, depending on your Mac's speed).

The results, however, are worth it. The stabilization feature works absolute magic on most jerky, bumpy handheld footage. It works so well, in fact, that it can look positively creepy, as though you were floating along on a magic carpet.

iMovie fixes two kinds of stabilization problems: normal shaky footage and "jellyroll" footage (see page 181). But for iMovie to calm your rollicking video, it first needs to find the shaky bits, and it does that through analysis.

Four Ways to Trigger Stabilization Analysis

Before iMovie can stabilize your video, it has to perform the above-mentioned analysis, which takes a long time. Fortunately, you have a lot of control over when the program does this processing:

- **Stabilize during import**. When you first bring footage into your Mac, iMovie offers to analyze the clips as described on page 34.

- **Stabilize selected clips**. You can analyze certain clips at any time. Select one or a group of them, and then choose File→Analyze Video→Stabilization.

- **Stabilize an entire Event**. In the Event list, click an Event's name and then choose File→Analyze Video→Stabilization. This option is great if the Event in question is someone jumping on a trampoline during an earthquake.

Tip: If you want, you can choose "Stabilization and People," which simultaneously handles the people analysis described on page 117. After all, if you're going to wait for one, you might as well wait for the other.

- **Stabilize a clip in the Event browser**. Double-click a clip to open the Inspector panel. Click Analyze Entire Clip.

Then go knit a sweater while you wait (Figure 7-1).

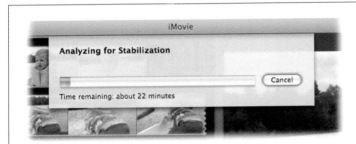

Figure 7-1:
Be prepared to wait when you decide to analyze a clip. Depending on the speed of your computer, it can take between 5 and 12 minutes (or longer for older Macs) for every minute of footage iMovie stabilizes. If you have a lot to analyze, let the Mac do its job overnight while you get some beauty sleep.

Tip: Once iMovie analyzes a clip, it generally applies stabilization only when you add the clip to your project. If you want to preview the stabilization, select the clip in your Event Library, then right-click it and choose "Play with Stabilization Preview." You'll see the stabilized clip play back in the iMovie viewer.

UP TO SPEED

Unstable Stabilization

The iMovie stabilizing feature is impressive, but it isn't magic. In fact, iMovie can't fix a common distortion caused by camera shake, called *motion blur*. iMovie actually makes this distortion look *worse* because it removes the shake that motion blur likes to hide in.

So just what is motion blur? Unless you have a camera that shoots at really high frame rates, it's possible to swing your camera around so fast that the pixels actually become *blurred*. Although iMovie can stabilize the frames relative to each other, it can't sharpen the blurriness of individual

frames. When you play back stabilized footage with blurry frames, it looks like the camera is moving in and out of focus.

When faced with this unfixable shake, it's up to you to decide which looks better: shaky footage or blurry footage. In general, you're probably best off leaving the footage in its natural, unbalanced state rather than fixing it, since people are more accustomed to seeing shaky home footage than weird, blurry footage. The best alternative? Get a better shot.

Fixing Shaky Footage

Once iMovie analyzes your footage, it can stabilize it, usually with remarkable results.

If you've already analyzed your footage, all you need to do is add it to your project. iMovie automatically applies the necessary stabilization to make it look good.

If you need to stabilize an unanalyzed clip that's already in the storyboard, point to the clip, and then, from the ✿ menu, choose Clip Adjustments. On the panel that appears, turn on "Smooth clip motion." This is a great trick when you're looking over a project-in-progress and discover that one particular jerky shot ruins the flow. It can also save you a lot of time, because iMovie stabilizes only the 20 seconds of a clip you actually *use*—plus an additional second on either side of it—rather than processing the whole 15-minute original (see Figure 7-2).

Figure 7-2:
A stabilized clip in your project displays a checkmark in the Stabilization box, plus the Maximum Zoom slider. Turn Stabilization on and off all you like; iMovie only has to analyze a clip but once.

If you later decide to lengthen the clip you stabilized by more than a second, you need to do more analyzing. The once-checked checkbox in the Inspector will require rechecking. Fortunately, iMovie analyzes only the part of the clip you added.

Degrees of stabilization

Once you stabilize some video, you may be delighted and amazed at how professional and smooth it looks. You might ask yourself "Was I wearing a SteadiCam?" (those gyro-mounted camera harnesses the Hollywood pros wear for stability). Or not.

You may be a little alarmed by how fake it looks. You were running down a flight of stairs, for crying out loud—it should look a *little* like you were on foot, not like you were gliding down a sheet of ice.

For that reason, you can *throttle back* the amount of stabilizing that iMovie does. Double-click the stabilized clip to open its Inspector panel, and you see the Maximum Zoom slider (Figure 7-2).

Why does iMovie call it Maximum Zoom? Because the program does its work by shifting the whole picture around in the frame, counteracting your hand shakes pixel by pixel. This means, however, that you would see momentary glimpses of black emptiness between the video and the frame around it, which would be even more distracting than the shaky video. So iMovie conceals those slivers of blackness by enlarging the video just enough to fill the frame and eliminate the exposed black emptiness.

Of course, magnifying a photo (or a video frame) also reduces its resolution, and therefore its quality. It's very unlikely you'll actually notice the degradation, but if you think you do, here's another reason for the Maximum Zoom slider: It can reduce the degree of zooming-in. In other words, Maximum Zoom limits both the stabilizing effect *and* the zooming that goes along with it.

And now some stabilization notes:

- The more shake in your footage, the more zoom iMovie offers.

- As you zoom out, you may see the shaky-hand badge that identifies nervous clips change colors (Figure 7-3). Zooming out on a black-badged clip, for example, may turn the little hand orange.

Hide Shaky Footage

If you're in the habit of analyzing Event footage, you'll probably see swaths of red squiggly lines all over the clips in your browser. Most of the clips are pure dreck—so jerky, they're beyond iMovie's capacity to stabilize them, and unworthy of any project you may create. If you agree, and you're sure you have no use for the footage, you can hide it from view so none of it ever sneaks into your storyboard.

Underneath your Event browser, next to the Favorites filter menu, you'll see a red squiggly button that matches the red squiggly lines branding all your shakiest footage. Click this button to make all of that shaky stuff invisible.

Because shaky footage can sneak into the *middle* of clips, iMovie splits many of your Event clips into smaller pieces, but it's not permanent. Click the squiggly button again, turning the gray line red, to make the shaky footage reappear. Your clips are whole once more.

Note that the button disappears when you use iMovie's keyword filter, as covered in "Deleting Footage for Good" on page 119. In that case, you make shaky footage invisible using the Excessive Shake keyword.

Figure 7-3:
These three clip badges represent different levels of shake in your clip. From top to bottom: The black badge indicates very little to no shake. The orange badge tells you that there's a moderate amount of shake. The red badge means that the clip is very shaky. A red badge with a line through it is the sign that your clip is beyond hope. Clips tagged with the orange and red badges also have red squiggles in them, painted on the parts of your footage that are too shaky to fix.

- If you crop away the shakiest part of a clip, iMovie may do a better job of stabilizing the rest. That's because iMovie figures out exactly how far it needs to zoom in to fix the *shakiest part* of a project clip, and then applies that zoom to the whole clip.

If you see red squiggles painted across the bottom of your clip (see Figure 7-3), those sections are just too shaky for iMovie to fix. No amount of tweaking the zoom, position, or rotation will rescue the video.

Removing stabilization

You may change your mind and decide that a clip looks better without stabilization. It can happen (see "Video Stabilization" on page 117). Just double-click the clip to open the Inspector, and then turn off the box that says "Smooth clip motion." The shake comes back.

And don't worry about having to reanalyze footage if you change your mind yet again. It bears repeating: Once analyzed, always analyzed.

Jellyroll Footage

There's a second type of distortion you should know about, called *jellyroll footage*. It arises when you shoot with a camera that contains a so-called CMOS light-sensor chip. Some still cameras, like the Nikon D90, and many newer AVCHD cameras, contain this sort of chip. The iPhone and iPod Touch cameras use CMOS sensors, too.

Unfortunately, CMOS cameras use a rolling shutter, which means that the sensor records an image starting at the top and working its way down to the bottom, really fast. If the camera moves too much as you film, the subject gradually shifts left or right as the sensor records the image.

The resulting image makes the world look like it's suddenly made of jelly—a source of endless frustration and bewilderment to amateurs and pros alike. "Dang it!" they say. "What's wrong with my camera?"

Unfortunately, iMovie's stabilization feature tends to exaggerate this bizarre jelly effect.

Fortunately, most video cameras—and most still cameras that shoot video—still use CCD sensors rather than CMOS sensors, so you may never see the jelly problem. But if you do have a jellyroll clip, iMovie can help you fix it.

Note: Once you analyze footage for stabilization, iMovie doesn't need to do any further analysis to fix a jellyroll problem.

Rolling Shutter adjustments

To reduce the jellyroll effect, double-click the clip in your project. The Inspector window appears; you'll see a Rolling Shutter checkbox at the bottom. Turn it on (Figure 7-4).

The jelly effect is the product of how fast your camera's rolling shutter works. Slower shutters need the High or Extra High settings in the Amount menu (Figure 7-4). Faster shutters can use the Low or Medium settings.

Less expensive cameras, like the Flip camcorder or the cameras crammed into cell phones, need the High or Extra High setting (they have slower shutters). Midrange cameras, like most consumer camcorders, typically need the Medium setting. Expensive cameras, such as DSLRs, generally get by with the Medium or Low setting because they have very fast shutters.

Figure 7-4:
The Rolling Shutter setting in iMovie helps reduce the jellyroll effect you get in footage shot by certain cameras. Once iMovie analyzes your footage, turn on the rolling shutter fix with a checkbox in the Inspector. Set the level of adjustment ("Amount") to best compensate for your camera.

Tip: Of course, if you want to get precise adjustments, test things out with your own camera. Find a vertical, linear object like a telephone pole. Film it while you pan side to side. (Use a tripod if you want to be really exact.) Pan quickly enough to get the jellyroll effect going. Now just import and analyze the footage, add the clip to your project, and try different Amount settings until you get a nice, straight telephone pole.

Removing shutter adjustments

Uncheck the Rolling Shutter box in the Inspector to turn off adjustment for a clip. You can always turn it back on later. And don't worry about iMovie analyzing your footage again if you do. Once analyzed, always analyzed.

Color Fixes

iMovie can apply some awesome color-correction effects to your video, too. Here's the rundown.

Phase 1: Select the Clip, Find the Frame

iMovie can apply color fixes only to an entire clip at once. You can't make the effect fade in or out, you can't apply it to just a portion of a clip, and you can't apply it to multiple clips at once (although you *can* copy and paste the adjustments you make).

Before you apply an effect, therefore, you may want to start by isolating the piece you want. You can always chop up a clip into smaller pieces (page 102).

Then click the clip that needs help. You can click a filmstrip anywhere:

- **In the Event browser**. If you click a raw source clip here, then the changes you make appear in *every project* that incorporates that clip.

- **In the project storyboard**. If you click a clip you already placed in the storyboard, the changes you make affect that video *in this movie only*. The original, underlying source clip in the Event browser remains unchanged.

(Of course, the truth is, you're never *really* changing anything at all. You can remove all your changes and revert to the original camcorder-captured clip at any time, even months or years from now.)

Once you select a clip, you see a still image of it in the Viewer window.

Phase 2: The Video Adjustments Panel

Now you're ready to open the Video Adjustments panel. Do that by pressing the V key on your keyboard, by clicking the ❶ button followed by the Video tab (Figure 7-5), or by clicking the ✿ on every filmstrip and selecting Video Adjustments from the shortcut menu.

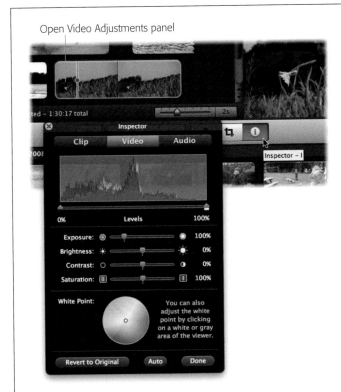

Open Video Adjustments panel

Figure 7-5:
The Video Adjustments panel is part of the Inspector. You can drag it anywhere on the screen, and—here's the part that may not occur to you—you can move on to a different clip without having to close the panel first (click another clip from your filmstrip with the panel still open). Also note that you can drag the tiny red dot to move around in the clip as you work.

If you've ever adjusted the colors of a picture in iPhoto, these controls should look familiar. They affect your video here exactly the same way they affect a digital photo in iPhoto.

Don't overlook the tiny red dot on the filmstrip itself (Figure 7-6). Using this dot, you can move around *within* a clip to find a representative frame as you work. (That's important, because once you open the Video Adjustments panel, you can no longer skim in the usual way.)

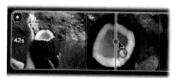

Figure 7-6:
The red dot lets you choose a representative frame you can see in the Viewer. Check a number of frames within each clip to make sure the change you're making looks good all the way through the shot.

Three Channels

As you can see, the histogram actually displays three superimposed graphs at once. These layers—red, green, and blue—represent the three "channels" of color video.

When you make adjustments to a clip's brightness values—for example, when you drag the Exposure slider just below the histogram—you'll see the graphs in all three channels move in unison. Despite changing shape, they essentially stick together. Later, when you make color adjustments using, say, the Saturation slider, you'll see those individual channels move in different directions.

Tip: As you work, don't forget to spot-check your adjustments by moving the tiny red dot on the filmstrip itself (see Figure 7-6).

Exposure

Most of the sliders in the Video Adjustments panel affect the histogram in some way. But where do you begin?

Here's a general suggestion: Make exposure adjustments first. In the simplest terms, the Exposure slider makes your video lighter when you move it to the right and darker when you move it to the left.

Watch the data on the histogram as you move the Exposure slider. Make sure you don't wind up shoving any of the mountain peaks beyond the edges of the Histogram box. If that happens, you're discarding precious image data and you'll see a loss of detail in the darks and lights.

The first step in fine-tuning a clip, then, is to drag the Exposure slider until the middle tones of the footage look acceptable to you. You can't add details that simply aren't there, but brightening a dark, shadowy image, or deepening the contrast on a washed-out shot, can coax out elements that were barely visible in the original.

If the dark and light areas aren't yet perfect, don't worry; you'll improve those areas next with the Levels control.

Adjusting the Levels

After you spend some time working with the middle tones of your clip, you can turn your attention to the endpoints on the histogram, which represent the darkest and lightest areas of the clip.

If the mountains of your graph seem to cover all the territory from left to right, you already have a roughly even distribution of dark and light tones in your picture, so you're probably in good shape. But if the graph comes up short on either the left (darks) or the right (lights) side of the histogram, you may want to make an adjustment.

To do so, drag the right or left pointer on the Levels slider *inward*, toward the base of the mountain. If you're moving the right indicator inward, for example, you'll notice that the whites become brighter, but the dark areas stay pretty much the same. If you drag the left indicator inward, the dark tones change, but the highlights remain steady (Figure 7-7).

Introduction to the Histogram

Learning to use the Video Adjustments panel effectively involves learning about its *histogram*, the colorful little graph at the top of the panel (visible in Figure 7-5).

The histogram is a self-updating visual representation of the dark and light tones that make up your video clip. If you've never encountered a histogram before, this may sound complicated. But the histogram is a terrific tool, and it'll make more sense the more you work with it.

Within each of the superimposed graphs (red, blue, and green), the scheme is the same: The clip's darker shades appear toward the left side of the graph; the lighter tones are graphed on the right side.

Therefore, in a very dark clip—a coalmine at midnight, say—you'll see big mountain peaks at the left side of the graph,

trailing off to nothing toward the right. A shot of a brilliantly sunny snowscape, on the other hand, will show lots of information on the right, and very little on the left.

The best-balanced shots have some data spread across the entire histogram, with a few mountain-shaped peaks here and there. Those peaks and valleys represent the really dark spots and the really bright spots. The mountains are fine, as long as you have some visual information in other parts of the histogram, too.

The histogram for a *bad* shot, on the other hand—a severely under- or overexposed one—has mountains bunched at one end or the other. Rescuing those pictures involves spreading the mountains across the entire spectrum, which is what the Video Adjustments palette is all about.

Figure 7-7:
Left: There's something wrong with the exposure of this clip.

Right: Drag the handles of the histogram inward to brighten the brights and darken the darks. Avoid moving the handles inward beyond the outer edges of the mountains—you'll throw away data outside the handles, which degrades the image quality.

Brightness and Contrast Sliders

Once you massage a clip's Exposure and Levels controls, the footage's overall exposure usually looks pretty good. In effect, you've created a clip with a full range of tones, from dark to light.

So why, then, does Apple include Brightness and Contrast sliders, which govern similar aspects of the video's appearance? Because they're not quite the same as Exposure and Levels.

- **Brightness**. When you move the Brightness slider, you make the *entire* image lighter or darker. You're literally moving the entire histogram to the left or right without changing its shape. (Remember that the Exposure and Levels controls affect the midtones, highlights, and shadows independently.)

  In other words, if the shot's contrast is already exactly as you want it, but the whole clip could use darkening or lightening, Brightness should be your tool of choice.

- **Contrast**. The Contrast slider, on the other hand, *does* change the shape of the histogram. Contrast is the difference between the darkest and lightest tones in your clip. If you increase the contrast, you stretch out the shape of the histogram, creating darker blacks and brighter whites. When you decrease the contrast, you scrunch the shape of the histogram inward, shortening the distance between the dark and light endpoints. Since the image data now resides in the middle area of the graph, the overall tones in the video are duller. Video pros might call this look "flat" or "muddy." (See Figure 7-8.)

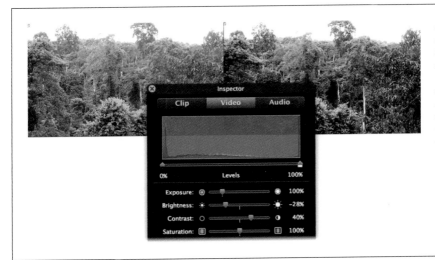

Figure 7-8:
Here's another way to fiddle with the darks and lights in your video—use the Brightness and Contrast sliders manually. The somewhat washed-out vista at left looks a lot better with the contrast goosed and the brightness toned down a tad.

Automatic Correction

Dragging the Exposure, Levels, and Brightness sliders by hand is one way to address color imbalances in a clip. But there's an easier way: iMovie can adjust all three sliders *automatically*.

Just click the Auto button at the bottom of the Video Adjustments palette. Watch the results in the Viewer.

Amazing, isn't it? You'll be stunned at how much better your camcorder video can look with this one-click trick (Figure 7-9).

Figure 7-9:
The before (left) and after shots of a clip that needed help. The only difference between the two is one click on the Auto button. (It affects only the brightness, contrast, and exposure; it doesn't attempt to fix color problems.)

Tip: To compare the before and after looks of your clip, press ⌘-Z and then Shift-⌘-Z, which correspond to the Undo and Redo commands. For added fun, go back and forth a few times.

Color Balance

Camcorders don't always capture color very accurately. You may encounter scenes with a slightly bluish or greenish tinge, dull colors, lower contrast, or sickly-looking skin tones. And you may wish you could fix it.

Or maybe you just want to take color adjustment into your own hands, not only to get the colors right, but to create a specific mood for an image, too. Maybe you want a snowy landscape to look icy blue, so friends back home realize just how freakin' cold it was.

The Video Adjustments panel offers three controls that wield power over this sort of thing: Saturation, White Balance, and individual sliders that control the intensity of the primary colors red, green, and blue.

- **White Balance**. Different kinds of light—fluorescent lighting, overcast skies, and so on—lend different color casts to video footage. Use the white balance setting to eliminate or adjust the color cast according to the lighting.

  If you find a clip with such a color cast, it's easy to fix. Move your cursor into the Viewer window and find a spot that's *supposed* to be pure white or gray. (It might help to press ⌘-9 or ⌘-0 to enlarge the frame first.) The instant you click that white point, iMovie suddenly understands exactly what the nature of the color cast is—and adjusts *all* the colors accordingly. Often, that one click does the trick and fixes the entire clip (Figure 7-10).

Figure 7-10:
In the Viewer, the cursor appears as a tiny eyedropper. (When you click a spot that's supposed to be white, the whole scene's color tint changes. You'll also see the tiny circle in the White Point color wheel shift to a new location, indicating its new understanding of the frame's color cast.)

Other times, you have to click around a few more times until you find a spot that makes the color cast go away.

As a last resort, you can try clicking inside the White Point color wheel *manually*, watching the results in the Viewer as you go.

- **Saturation**. Once you're happy with the color tones, you can increase or decrease their intensity with the Saturation slider. Move it to the right to increase the intensity and to the left for less saturation.

When you increase the saturation of a clip's colors, you make them more vivid; essentially, you make them "pop" more. You can also improve clips that have harsh, garish colors by dialing *down* the saturation, so that the colors end up looking a little less intense than they appeared in the original footage. That's a useful trick in shots whose composition is so strong that the colors are almost distracting.

Individual Channel Sliders

It's hard to imagine that any iMovie aficionado would need any more control over the colors in a shot than what the White Point and Saturation controls provide—especially in a program that's so simple and limited in so many other ways.

But believe it or not, iMovie can also offer you three individual sliders to control the amount of red, green, and blue in a clip. You can use these sliders to correct color-tint problems manually, or you can use them to create crazy special effects, like "Kids on Mars" or "I'm Feeling Really, Really Blue."

Tip: You may be tempted to use the channel sliders to turn a clip from color to black-and-white. Save yourself the trouble. iMovie offers a Black & White video effect, which you can read about on page 155.

So how come you don't see these sliders? Because they're hidden—they don't appear unless you turn on Advanced Tools, as described on page 88.

As you know from Chapter 3, the advanced tools are a motley assortment of hidden editing features. What the dialog box *doesn't* tell you is that it makes these three sliders magically appear in the Inspector's Video Adjustments panel: Red Gain, Green Gain, and Blue Gain (Figure 7-11).

Use these sliders to adjust the color mix of a clip. For example, if a scene is too bluish (because you shot it under fluorescent lighting, for example), you can nudge the Blue Gain slider a bit to the left.

Move the Red Gain slider to the right to warm up the tones, making them more orange-ish—a particularly handy technique for breathing life back into skin tones that have been bleached white with a spotlight or flashlight.

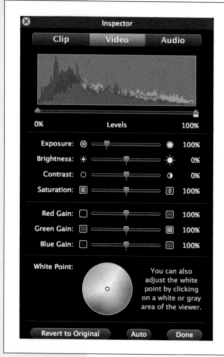

Figure 7-11:
In iMovie→Preferences, you can turn on the secret on/off switch for the three color Gain sliders. These new, bonus sliders control the amount of each color present in a clip. (Compare that with the standard Adjustments panel, shown in Figure 7-5.)

Removing or Adjusting Adjustments

Note: Whenever you unleash the awesome powers of the Video Adjustments panel on a clip, you leave that clip branded—with a tiny sun icon in the upper-left corner of its filmstrip. That's to remind you, "Hey, I didn't always look like this."

None of the changes you make in the Video Adjustments panel are permanent. You can return at any time—minutes, days, or years later—and adjust them or remove them entirely.

- **Adjusting changes**. Click a clip, open the Video Adjustments panel, and make any changes you like.

- **Removing changes**. If you click a clip and then click "Revert to Original" (at the bottom of the Video Adjustments panel), you're saying, "Throw away *all* the changes I made. Bring back my unmodified clip." iMovie instantly reinstates the original clip.

Copying and Pasting Adjustments

All of the fun you might be having in the Video Adjustments panel comes to a crashing halt the minute you realize one massive bummer in iMovie '11: You can adjust color on only one clip at a time. You might have just spent 15 minutes tweaking the color of your opening ski-school clip into submission, but what about the other 25 skiing shots in your montage? Are you condemned to repeating all that handwork 25 times over?

Fortunately, no. While you can't edit multiple clips at once, you *can* copy and paste *just* the video adjustments. Once you get the blue cast worked out of the first skiing shot, for example, you can wipe it out of each additional shot with a single command. Figure 7-12 shows the drill.

Figure 7-12:
Click the clip that you've already got looking good. Then choose Edit→Copy (⌘-C). Now click the next clip that needs the same touch-up and choose Edit→Paste Adjustments→Video (or press Option-⌘-I). Proceed through all the clips that you filmed under the same lighting conditions: Paste, paste, paste. You've just saved a heck of a lot of time.

Tip: If you're the kind of person who plans ahead, consider this: If you intend to excerpt several clips from a single, long, master clip in the Event browser, you'll save time by fixing *the original clip* before you start adding clips to your storyboard.

The reason: If you make color adjustments to the master clip *before* you grab chunks of it, the pieces inherit the fixes. If you adjust the master clip *after* you add some pieces of it to the storyboard, the pieces themselves won't change. (You can always use the Paste Adjustments command at that point, of course, but that's still more steps.)

Cropping Video

The Video Adjustments panel is only one example of the incredibly sophisticated, pro-level features that you stumble across in this supposedly simple, idiot-proof program. Another example is the Cropping tool, which was previously relegated to the stratosphere of professional, $1,000 video-editing programs like Final Cut Pro.

This tool lets you crop a video clip the same way you crop a photo; that is, you chop off the edges of the video frame. Figure 7-13 gives you the idea.

Figure 7-13:
Top: Suppose you were too far away from your subject, or your zoom wasn't powerful enough to catch it.

Middle: Adjust the green rectangle so that it encloses the portion of the video you want to keep. The rectangle is either squarish or wide, depending on your project's aspect ratio, whether that's the standard 4:3 ratio or widescreen format (16:9). (See page 62 for details on aspect ratios.)

Bottom: After you crop, the smaller portion of the frame expands to fill the entire frame. You lose some resolution in the process, of course, but you won't notice any graininess unless you crop out a lot of the original image.

Cropping isn't something you'll do every day, but it can be handy in situations like these:

- **You add a clip that's got the wrong aspect ratio to a project** (page 63). For example, say you're creating a regular, squarish, standard-definition movie, but you want to place a widescreen clip into it. The Cropping tool lets you lop off the sides of the widescreen clip so it fits perfectly into the squarish frame without using any black bars.

- **There's something at the margins of the picture that you want to get rid of.** Maybe your finger was on the lens. Maybe there's some ugly pipe or wire that you didn't notice. Maybe a telephone pole appears to be sticking out of your interviewee's head. Or maybe you just want to crop out the bonehead who kept trying to get on camera.

- **The scene is off-center.** Maybe the camera was on a tripod, self-running, when you and a buddy did your comedy schtick, but you didn't frame the scene right. By cropping away the empty part of the frame, you can recenter the whole thing.

- **The subject of the shot isn't prominent enough.** This happens often with accidental footage: That is, you were filming Uncle Ned reminiscing about his days working for the National Guard when, *bam!*, there's a three-car collision in the intersection behind him. By cropping away Uncle Ned, you can isolate the car-crash portion of the frame. It now fills the screen; in effect, you created an artificial zoom.

Whenever you crop video, you leave fewer pixels behind. You therefore lose resolution and create a less-sharp picture. If you crop away a *huge* amount of video info—more than half of the frame—you may wind up with noticeable pixelation and graininess.

If that happens, you can either live with it or use Undo.

In any case, here's how you crop a shot in iMovie:

1. **Select the clip you want to edit, and then select the frame within the clip.**

   If the clip is in the Event browser, your crop applies to this clip every time you use it in a project, from now on. If the clip's already in the storyboard, then you're cropping it only there.

   Find a good representative frame of the clip to work with in the Viewer. Do that by dragging the red dot across the filmstrip itself (Figure 7-6). Remember, you're working with video here, so things do tend to move around on the screen, but the iMovie cropping area *doesn't* move. You don't want to crop the clip in a way that centers your subject nicely in frame 50, but cuts it out completely in frame 100.

Tip: You'll find this action a lot easier if you magnify the image. Choose Window→ Viewer→Large, or press ⌘-0.

---

2. **Press the letter C key on your keyboard, or click the Crop button on the toolbar, or double-click the faint crop *badge* that sometimes appears when you point to a clip (Figure 7-14).**

   Now the Viewer window sprouts a few new controls at the top, like Fit and Crop. You'll see the Crop button already selected.

Figure 7-14:
Top: To crop a clip, click ⊡, or press the letter C, or click the tiny Crop badge.

Bottom: Once you crop a clip, a little icon appears on the filmstrip to show that you cropped it.

Crop, Rotate and Ken Burns – C

Crop badge

Note: The crop badge always appears on photos in your project, but appears on video clips only if you cropped them once before.

3. **Drag across the Viewer window to select what you want to keep.**

   As you drag, you create a green rectangle. iMovie throws away everything outside that rectangle when you click the Crop button (or press the letter C or click the Crop badge).

   As you work, you can drag inside the rectangle to move it around the frame. And you can drag any of the four corners to make the rectangle bigger or smaller. (You can't crop away more than half of the video area, however.)

   Don't forget to move that little red dot on the filmstrip itself to spot-check the video, to make sure you don't crop out anything important somewhere else in the clip. Or just click the Play button (or press your space bar) to play the clip from the beginning.

4. **Press Enter (or click Done).**

   You completed the crop.

Adjusting or Removing a Crop

Cropping, like any iMovie edit, is nondestructive. That is, you haven't done anything permanent to the source video on your hard drive, and you can adjust or remove the cropping any time you like.

To do that, just click the Crop badge on the clip (Figure 7-14), or select the clip and then click the Crop tool (or press the letter C), and redo the cropping in the Viewer. For example, you can adjust the green boundary rectangle.

To remove the cropping altogether, click the Fit button in the Viewer. Then press Enter (or click Done).

Rotating Video

If there's any iMovie feature you'll use even less often than cropping, it's rotating. But sure enough, iMovie lets you rotate a clip by 90 degrees, or even upside-down.

When would you use this? OK, the answer is "almost never," but here are a couple of remote possibilities:

The Ken Burns Effect, Now for Video!

If you've ever filmed a sporting event, like a kid's football game, the biggest problem is framing the action just right. If you zoom in too close, you're sure to miss something. But if you're too far away, there's no amazing detail to enjoy because you're basically watching ants. And even if you are zoomed out, there's no guarantee that the amazing play will happen in the middle of the screen, where it belongs.

Since you don't have the Monday Night Football crew at your disposal, you might be excited to know that you can dynamically zoom and pan on your video with the once-limited-to-photos Ken Burns Effect. Read more about it on page 273. Once you know how it works, applying the effect is pretty easy.

Choose a video clip in your project and press the letter C key, as though you were going to crop it. Click the Ken Burns button in the Preview window and you'll see the exact same interface you get for using Ken Burns on photos. You control the effect the same way. The speed of the pan and zoom depends on the length of your clip.

Just as with photos, the effect only pans and zooms in one direction for each clip, so if you want to zoom in, hang for a few moments, and then zoom back out, you need to split your clip into corresponding pieces, applying the correct Ken Burns Effect for each one. (Read page 102 for instructions on splitting clips.)

There's one caveat. When you zoom in on a photo, it's usually of high enough quality that you won't notice any graininess (unless you zoom in *a lot*). Not so with video, even HD video. There simply aren't as many pixels to go around, so you'll notice some quality degradation if you use the Ken Burns Effect to zoom in on your clips.

Knowing you have this tool at your fingertips means you don't have to chase the action all the time. Instead, you can keep everything in frame and then come back later to make the good stuff fill the screen.

- Somebody actually filmed the scene with the camera turned 90 degrees. (This sometimes happens when people record video with a digital *still* camera, which they're used to turning 90 degrees for capturing tall subjects. Sometimes people forget that they can't rotate the camera that way when they shoot *video*.)

- You shot a kid crawling along the rocks and want to make it look like he's mountain-climbing, vertically, straight up a cliff.

- You're making some strange, avant-garde film, and you're hoping to intentionally disorient your audience.

Anyway, if you're reading this, you must have your reasons, so here's how you rotate video:

1. **Select the clip you want to edit, and the frame within that clip.**

   As usual, if the clip is in the Event browser, the rotation applies to this clip every time you use it in a project from now on. If the clip is already in the storyboard, you're rotating it only there.

   You can also move the red dot in the filmstrip itself (Figure 7-5) to find a good representative frame of the clip to watch in the Viewer.

2. **Press the letter C key on your keyboard, or click ⬚.**

   So far, this is exactly like the cropping procedure.

3. **Click one of the Rotate buttons at the top of the Viewer (Figure 7-15).**

   With each click, the entire video image rotates by 90 degrees in the corresponding direction. If you click twice, you flip the whole picture upside-down.

Figure 7-15:
With each click of the rotation arrows, you rotate the image 90 degrees. Use for special effects, or just for fun.

If you rotate the image only 90 degrees, of course, the video no longer fits in the frame and black bars appear on either side. At this point, you have two options: You can either leave it as-is, or you can crop it so that it fills the frame.

To do the latter, click the Crop button in the Viewer, and then drag the green rectangle exactly as described in the previous section.

4. **Press Enter (or click Done).**

   You finished rotating the image.

The little Crop icon appears in the upper-left corner of the clip's filmstrip (Figure 7-14). OK, you haven't necessarily *cropped* the video, but in iMovie's head, rotation is close enough to cropping for icon purposes.

Adjusting or Removing the Rotation

When you rotate your video, you're not changing the underlying footage. You can adjust or remove the rotation any time.

Just click the clip, click the Crop tool (or press the letter C key), and then click those rotation arrow buttons again until the video looks the way you want it. Then press Enter (or click Done).

Titles, Subtitles, and Credits

Text superimposed over film footage is incredibly common in the film and video worlds. You'd be hard-pressed to find a single movie, TV show, or commercial that doesn't have titles, captions, or credits. In fact, one telltale sign that you're watching an amateur video is the *absence* of superimposed text.

In iMovie, the term *title* refers to any kind of text: titles, credits, subtitles, copyright notices, and so on. You don't need to be nearly as economical in your use of titles as you are with, say, transitions. Transitional effects interfere with something that stands perfectly well on its own—your footage. When you superimpose text on video, on the other hand, the audience is much more likely to accept your intrusion. You're introducing this new element for their benefit, to convey information you couldn't transmit otherwise.

Moreover, as you'll see, most of iMovie's text effects are far more focused in purpose than its transition selections, so you'll have little trouble choosing the optimum text effect for a particular editing situation. For example, the Scrolling Credits effect rolls a list of names slowly up the screen—an obvious candidate for the close of your movie.

Setting Up a Title

Adding text to your movie requires several setup steps:

1. Choose a title style (centered, scrolling credits, or whatever).

2. Drag the title into position in the storyboard.

3. Type the text.

4. Choose a font, color, and type size.

Here are these steps in more detail.

Choose a Title Style

Start by choosing Window→Titles (⌘-3), or clicking the T button just below the Viewer. The Titles panel appears (Figure 8-1).

Figure 8-1:
The icons here represent iMovie '11's various title styles. Apple has added quite a few new styles over previous versions.

Figuring out what each title style is for isn't rocket science, but here's a quick run-down:

- **Centered**. The Centered title style may be the most useful of all iMovie text effects. It produces a single line of text (or two lines, if you take advantage of the subtitle option), fading in, staying onscreen for a moment, and then fading out, making this style ideal for the title of your movie. This is a tasteful, professional, and powerful effect.

Tip: You can always string together several consecutive Centered titles to imitate the way a movie's major stars' names appear at the beginning of a typical Hollywood movie.

- **Lower Third**. This title name comes from the TV business—it refers to the lower third of a TV screen—but most people know it as a *subtitle*. On TV, a lower-third title usually identifies a talking head ("Harold P. Higgenbottom,

GrooviTunes CEO"). You can use it that way, too, or use it to identify the location of a scene, or to translate what a person or baby is saying.

- **Lower**. This title hovers in the bottom-right corner of the screen, as in an MTV music video, but on the wrong side (see the tip below, though).

- **Upper**. This one gives you Lower's exact opposite: The text appears in the upper-left corner.

Tip: You can make these Lower and Upper titles appear in opposite corners by changing the justification of the text. Press Shift-⌘-[to move the Lower title to the left corner. Press Shift-⌘-] to put the Upper title in the right corner.

- **Echo**. This unusual style features a title, a subtitle, and an *echo* of the main title. An enormous, semitransparent, all-caps version of the main title appears *behind* your text, almost as a graphic element.

- **Overlap**. Two bits of text, one red and one white, meet briefly in the middle at the bottom of the frame, and then keep going their merry way. If you place several Overlap titles consecutively, they alternate colors.

- **Four Corners**. A very colorful series of titles, where the text swoops in from different sides to meet in the middle before swooping out again. Each time you add one of these titles, the entry points and colors of the text change, with up to four variations.

- **Scrolling Credits**. This effect produces a line of text with two columns, for credits like *Director...Steven Spielberg* and *Writer...Robert Towne*, or *character name...actor name* (Figure 8-2).

  Be careful when you use this effect, for two reasons. First, iMovie automatically adjusts the speed of scroll so that it displays all the names you specify in the duration you specify. If you make the title effect too short, the credits will scroll by too fast for anyone to read.

Tip: Setting up this title style requires special instructions, which appear on page 209.

Second, the type is fairly small, which could be a problem if you intend to save your movie as a QuickTime file, which measures 3 inches square.

- **Drifting, Sideways Drift, Vertical Drift**. These are three variations on the same basic idea: The text zooms onto the screen, decelerates as it gets to the middle, and then speeds up to leave the frame, never really coming to a full stop. If your clip were a stop sign, these titles would probably get a ticket.

Figure 8-2:
Top: You control the speed of Scrolling Credits by controlling the length of the title strip in your storyboard.

Bottom: These subtitle variations all include an opaque or semi-opaque background to make your text stand out against the video. You can change the color of that background bar by simply clicking it.

- **Zoom**. Like a centered title, but subtly grows (slightly) bigger over time.

- **Horizontal Blur**. This effect simulates your two eyes coming into focus to see the title, then going out of focus again.

- **Soft Edge**. Another very subtle effect. The text drifts slightly right; a magic eraser wipes it into existence, and then promptly erases it again.

- **Lens Flare, Boogie Lights, Pixie Dust**. These titles all use something shiny to announce themselves to the world (Figure 8-3). Definitely useful when you want something flashy.

- **Pull Focus**. If you play around much with the manual focus on a camera, this one will look familiar. As the text comes into focus, the background goes blurry. At the end of the title, the background comes back into focus, only to have the title get blurry and disappear.

- **Organic Main and Organic Lower**. These are both very elegant titles, the kind you'd love to have in a wedding video. Both involve delicate, viney animated plants that grow along with the title before fading away.

- **Ticker**. You know how cable-news channels run breaking news headlines across the bottom of the screen? In the same way, the Ticker title runs text, right to left, across the bottom. It's much more plain, however, than what you see on CNN.

Figure 8-3:
The Boogie Lights title exempli-fies the cool, animated titles in iMovie '11.

- **Date/Time**. The only entirely uneditable title. When you select it, the preview window denies you access. It just sits there, impervious to clicking. This title's only job is to display the date and time of the underlying clip, something you generally want done automatically. The title can come in handy if you want to remind viewers when an event took place. You'll see the Date/Time title in the bottom-left corner of the screen.

Tip: OK, this style isn't *totally* uneditable. You can change the date and time of your footage, as described on page 68.

- **Clouds**. This is a whimsical, animated, lower-third title. Two clouds, one blue and one pink, bounce up into the frame, carrying some equally whimsical text.
- **Far Far Away**. For all the budding George Lucases out there, this title displays text in the iconic, scrolling *Star Wars* style.

Tip: For added fun, you can display this title on top of the starscape image that comes with iMovie '11. See the next section for details.

- **Gradient, Soft Bar, Formal, Torn Edge, Paper**. These are all variations on the Lower Third style. The only difference is what's *behind* the text. You have a choice of semi-opaque backgrounds to make the text more readable and to make it stand out more from the video playing behind it.

Tip: In these styles, the background behind the text–the transparent bar, the torn-edged paper, and so on–starts out black, white, or tan. You can, however, choose *any* color for this background bar (Figure 8-2). When you edit the text, click anywhere *on* that background bar to open the Color Picker. (The Color Picker is described on page 218.)

Theme-based titles

If you added a theme to your project (page 139), iMovie lists eight additional title styles at the top of the Titles pane (Figure 8-4). Four of them are heavily animated, embedding your clip into a shot of a photo album, for example. The other four titles are simpler, but stylistically designed to match your theme.

Figure 8-4:
These titles appear only if you apply a theme to your project (page 139). Each is designed around the theme's style. In this case, the style is like that of a comic book.

You can use theme titles only if you've applied a theme to your project. This also means you can't use titles from multiple themes in a single project.

Tip: Want a particular theme title, but not the entire theme itself? Just make sure that when you add a theme (page 139), you *turn off* the box that tells iMovie to automatically add transitions and titles. That way, your movie uses only the theme elements *you* choose, even if you end up using just one theme-based title in your entire project.

Drag the Title into Position

Once you choose a title style, drag its icon directly into the storyboard. As you do, iMovie highlights the filmstrip you hover over in blue (see Figure 8-5). That's iMovie's way of helping you pinpoint where the text will *first appear*.

As you'll soon see, knowing when to release the mouse button is extremely important. As you helicopter over a clip, you'll find that you can drop the title into any of four places; at each one, iMovie snaps the title into the appropriate position:

- **At the beginning of the clip**. As the blue highlighting in Figure 8-5 illustrates, iMovie proposes covering the *first 4 seconds* of the filmstrip with the title. Placeholder text appears with moving video behind it.

- **Over the middle of the clip**. If your cursor winds up here, the title covers *the entire clip*, beginning to end.

- **At the end of the clip**. If your cursor falls here, the title stretches over the *final 4 seconds* of the clip.

Note: If your clip is fewer than 12 seconds long, iMovie titles just the first third or last third of the clip.

- **Between clips**. Under normal circumstances, iMovie text gets superimposed over video. But you may want a different background, particularly for opening or closing credits. You might, for example, want the title to appear on a nice, static background, such as black, for a striking and professional-looking effect.

In those cases, drag the title to the gap *between* filmstrips. iMovie surprises you (the first time, anyway) by displaying a palette of background images for your title.

These are the same background images available in the "Maps and Backgrounds" panel, discussed on page 146. They let you place the text against a solid color, a photograph of red velvet curtains, or another attractive backdrop.

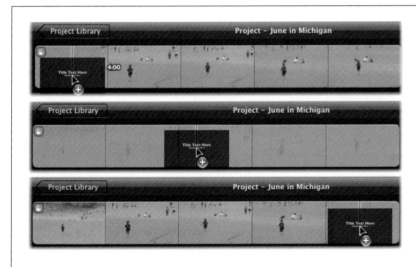

Figure 8-5:
As you drag a title onto a clip, the blue highlighting shows how long the title will stay onscreen. It snaps into three positions relative to the clip, shown in these three examples.

Top: If you drag toward the beginning of the clip, the title covers the first 4 seconds of it.

Middle: If you drag over the middle, the title covers the entire clip.

Bottom: if you drag toward the end of the clip, the title covers the final 4 seconds of it. Of course, you can adjust any of this later.

Note: There's no longer a checkbox for "Over black," as in previous iMovie versions; you must simply drag the title between two clips, or to the very beginning or end of the storyboard. See Figure 8-6.

Figure 8-6:
Top: If you drag a title between two filmstrips, iMovie asks you to pick a background image (bottom left), even if you want basic black.

Bottom right: You can adjust the title's time onscreen by dragging the ends of its blue stripe. You can adjust the background clip's timing by double-clicking it and typing a new length into the text box in the Inspector.

In professional movie editing, a black background is by far the most common. More often than not, this is the one you want to choose, for three reasons. First, it looks extremely professional. Second, the high contrast of white against black makes the text very legible. Third, the audience will *read* it, instead of being distracted by the video behind it.

Note: When you create a title over a background, you *add* to the total length of your movie. You force the clips to the right of your title to slide further rightward to accommodate the credit you just inserted. That's just a reminder in case you're editing a video in sync with music. (When you insert text over video, by contrast, you don't change the overall length of your movie.)

Adjust the Timing

Once you drop a title into place, it turns into a blue stripe over the filmstrip. (This, as it turns out, will become a familiar element in iMovie. iMovie represents audio, such as background music, with draggable stripes, too.)

The stripe indicates how long the text appears on the screen. As you can see in Figure 8-7, this stripe can straddle part of a clip, a whole clip, or many clips, which gives you a huge amount of flexibility.

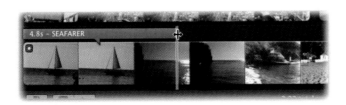

Figure 8-7:
When your cursor approaches either end of a title stripe, it changes to a double-headed arrow. That's your cue that it's OK to start dragging the stripe's endpoint horizontally to make it longer or shorter.

Note: iMovie doesn't let you overlap titles. You can, however, have more than one title in the same clip. Drag one onto the front third and another onto the back third of the clip, for example. Then move those away from the ends and add even more titles, always using the ends of the clip as landing spots. The only rule is that titles can't overlap.

You can adjust this stripe in three ways:

- **Adjust the starting point** by dragging the *left* end of the stripe.
- **Adjust the ending point** by dragging the *right* end of the stripe.

Tip: Adjusting either end of the stripe also changes its duration.

- **Move the entire title in time** by dragging horizontally *anywhere else* on it.

As you make adjustments, take into account your viewers' reading speed. There's only one thing more frustrating than titles that fly by too quickly to read, and that's titles that sit there onscreen forever, boring the audience silly. Many video editors use this guideline: Leave the words onscreen long enough for somebody to read them aloud twice.

Also consider the location of your title carefully. If you superimpose it on a solid-color background or a still image, no problem. But if you plan to superimpose it on moving video, choose a scene that's relatively still, so the video doesn't distract the audience from the words onscreen.

Be particularly careful not to superimpose your titles on an unsteady shot; the contrast between the jiggling picture and the rock-steady lettering will make your audience uncomfortable.

Note: The beauty of titles in iMovie '11 is that there's no rendering (computing) time. They appear instantly, so you can freely adjust the placement and timing of your titles as often as you like.

Type the Text

Unless the name of your movie is, in fact, "Title Text Here," you probably want to edit the dummy text of your newly born title.

To do so, click the blue stripe in the storyboard to select it. In the Viewer, text boxes appear, ready for an edit.

Tip: Enlarge the Viewer (Window→Viewer→Large, or ⌘-0) for easier access to these text boxes.

In most styles, you actually see *two* text boxes: a main title, and a subtitle. Just click inside one of the boxes to edit the dummy text.

Note: You don't have to type text into both of these boxes. The subtitle box is there solely for your convenience, for those occasions when you need a second, smaller line of type underneath the larger credit. If you don't need text there, just delete the placeholder text.

All of the usual Mac OS X text-editing tricks apply in the text boxes. For example:

- Double-click a word to highlight it.
- Triple-click inside the text box to select the entire title; at this point, you can begin typing to replace the placeholder text.
- Press Option-arrow key (left or right) to jump one word at a time.
- Press Control-arrow key to jump to the beginning or end of the text box.
- Add Shift to those keystrokes to jump *and* select the intervening text simultaneously. For example, Shift-Option-right arrow highlights the word to the right of your insertion point.
- Cut, Copy, and Paste work just as you'd expect.
- Press Tab to jump between text boxes.

When you finish editing (and formatting, as described next), click Done in the Viewer.

Special Notes on Scrolling Credits

When you click the blue stripe representing a Scrolling Credits title, you see place-holder text snippets like the one shown in Figure 8-8.

Figure 8-8:
Press Tab between names to create one big scrolling list of credits. Press Enter after a row to create a left-justified heading. After you type the heading, press either Tab (to list another name on the same row) or Enter, and then Tab (to leave the heading on a row by itself).

To replace the dummy text with the actual names of your actors and characters, heed these notes:

- First, double-click where it says "Starring." Now you can type something new in its place, like "Featuring" or "Cast."

- When you see a dotted red underline, iMovie is warning you of a misspelling. Control-click (or right-click) the word to see spelling alternatives.

- Next, drag diagonally through the scrolling list of placeholder names. Once you highlight them, you can begin typing your own cast list: type in the character name ("Raymond," for example), then press Tab, and then type the actor's name ("Dustin Hoffman," for example). Press Tab to go to the next row. Type the next character name, press Tab, and then add that actor's name. And so on.

- As you go, you can create headings like the ones shown in Figure 8-8 by pressing the Enter key at the end of a row. iMovie places the insertion point at the *left* side of the frame, so you can type the heading (like "CREW" or "SECOND UNIT").

- You can create a blank line in the credits by pressing Enter, Enter, and then Tab.

Tip: Using the Font panel, you can control the spacing between the lines of credits. See the tip on page 209.

If you have too many names to fit on one screen, don't worry; the list scrolls auto-matically when you reach the bottom of the frame. You can keep typing until you credit every last gaffer, best boy, and caterer. (You can scroll back up again by holding down the up arrow key.)

Font, Size, and Style

iMovie's creators are rather fond of Gill Sans; that's a typeface, not a renowned video editor. iMovie uses Gill Sans in most of its title styles. It looks great, but it also looks like everyone *else's* iMovie '11 videos.

Note: Unfortunately, some titles are impervious to font changes, thanks to the way iMovie animates them. There's an easy way to tell if you can change a title's font, though: If you see a Show Fonts button in the top-left corner of the preview window (Figure 8-8), you're good to go. If there's no Show Fonts button, your title is a one-font pony.

Fortunately, you have a surprising amount of typographical flexibility with most titles. That may come as a surprise, considering that you can't see *any* font, size, style, or justification controls when you create a title.

The most basic style options are available in the Text menu.

Start by highlighting the text you want to change. That is, click the blue stripe of a title you've already placed. Then drag through some of the text in the text boxes in the Viewer.

Tip: For most titles, iMovie '11 doesn't limit you to a single font and size. You can use different fonts within a single text block, if you must. You can even use a different font for *every letter*, if you so desire (or if you're making a ransom-note video).

Now you can choose a style from the Text menu. Your options include:

- **Bold, Italic, Underline, Outline**. Avoid Underline; it looks cheesy. In a doc-ument, Outline usually looks cheesy, too. But in iMovie, it's a terrific help. It means that each letter has a fine hairline around it, to help set it off against the video background. If the lettering is white, for example, it would otherwise dis-appear against white parts of the background.

- **Bigger, Smaller**. Here's a quick way to enlarge or shrink the highlighted text.

- **Align**. This submenu refers to the horizontal alignment of the text within its text block. You can choose Left (against the left side), Center (centered), or Right (against the right side). (The final choice, Justified, does nothing in iMovie.)

- **Kern**. *Kerning* is the typographic process of squishing characters closer together. Sometimes doing that makes a title more readable, more artistic, or just a better fit in a small space. The commands in this submenu let you either tighten or loosen the spacing a tiny bit at a time.

- **Ligature**. *Ligatures* are character pairs, usually beginning with the lowercase *f*, that are artistically fused into a single unit. For example, the word "figure," with ligatures turned on, becomes *figure*. To turn ligatures on, highlight the text that contains the ligature-able pair (fl, fi, oe, or ae) and then choose Text→Ligature→Use All. To turn ligatures off, highlight the text and choose Text→Ligature→Use None.

- **Baseline**. The *baseline* is the invisible horizontal line on which text sits. Using this control, you can raise or lower some text, like this, or even create superscript (2^2) or subscript ($H_2 0$) characters. (The Use Default command restores the text to the original baseline.)

- **Justification**. Press Shift-⌘-[to align the text with the left side of the text box, Shift-⌘-] for the right side, or Shift-⌘-\ to center it.

Figure 8-9 shows examples of many of these styles in use at once in a single, truly hideous opening credit.

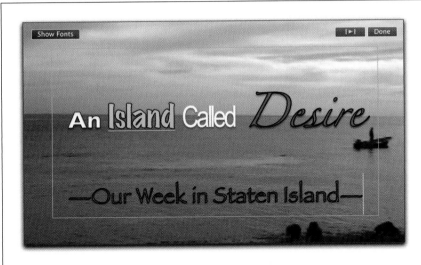

Figure 8-9:
You would never use all of iMovie's typography variations in a single title. But you could.

Tip: Most of the Text menu's commands have easy-to-remember keyboard shortcuts. It's always Shift, ⌘, and the first letter: B for bold, I for italic, + for bigger, – for smaller, and so on.

The iMovie Font Panel

The iMovie Font Panel is new in iMovie '11. It's a creative and simplified approach to changing your title's style. (This window is different from the System Font Panel described below.) The idea is to put the most common fonts and colors at your fingertips.

Select a title in your storyboard, and then click Show Fonts in the preview window.

An Inspector-like window appears, but you can tell at first glance that it has a unique purpose. The window contains a big grid with three distinct columns. The first contains a list of title fonts. The second column offers an array of colors. And the last shows type-size numbers, 1 through 9. Take a look at Figure 8-10 to see it in action.

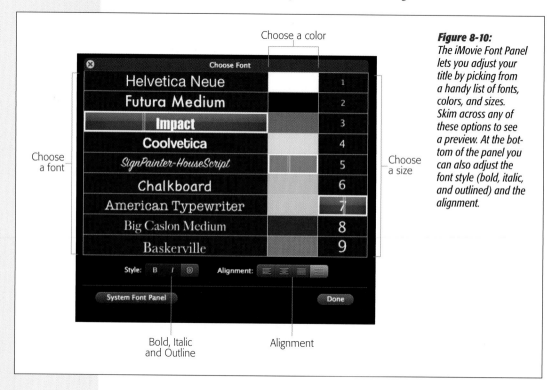

Choose a color

Choose a font

Choose a size

Bold, Italic and Outline

Alignment

Figure 8-10:
The iMovie Font Panel lets you adjust your title by picking from a handy list of fonts, colors, and sizes. Skim across any of these options to see a preview. At the bottom of the panel you can also adjust the font style (bold, italic, and outlined) and the alignment.

As you run your mouse over the grid, the font, color, or type size of your title changes immediately, even without clicking. When you see a style you like, click to lock in that font, color, or size.

You can also turn certain font styles (bold, italic, and outline) on or off by clicking the buttons at the bottom. You can adjust the title's paragraph alignment (left-justified, centered, right-justified, fully justified) by clicking the little icons (Figure 8-10).

Click Done when your title looks just right.

The System Font Panel

Handy as the iMovie Font Panel may be, it offers only a tiny slate of options. Nine typefaces, nine colors. What is this, graphic-designer preschool?

Fortunately for control freaks, iMovie also gives you full access to the System Fonts Panel, a standard Mac OS X feature that puts all typographic controls in a single place.

Suppose you just highlighted a title block, and now you want to choose an appropriate typeface. If the iMovie Fonts Panel is open, click the button in the bottom-left that says System Font Panel. If not, choose Text→Show Fonts (⌘-T).

Here's what you'll find there (Figure 8-11):

- **Collections**. The first column lists your *collections*, which are canned sets of fonts. Apple starts you off with collections called things like "PDF" (a set of standard fonts used in PDF files) and "Web" (fonts you're safe using on web pages—that is, fonts likely installed on the Macs or Windows PCs of your web visitors).

Tip: You can create your own collections called, for example, Headline or Sans Serif, organized by font type. Then you can switch these groups of fonts on or off at will, just as though you'd bought a program like Suitcase. You use Mac OS X's Font Book program for this purpose.

POWER USERS' CLINIC

Choose Favorite Fonts and Colors

As naturally stylish as Apple employees are, you may disagree with their default font and color choices in the iMovie Font Panel. Hot Pink, for example, may never make it into the titles of any of your movies. Luckily, you don't have to go through life with Hot Pink wasting space on the panel.

To customize the default fonts and colors that appear in the Font Panel, choose iMovie→Preferences, and click the Fonts tab. It lists all the fonts and colors that currently appear in the panel.

To change a font, click the tiny arrows next to it, and then choose from the very large Font menu that appears. You just replaced that standard font in the Font Panel.

To change a color, click the color you want to replace, and the Color Picker panel (page 218) appears. Choose a color,

and keep choosing until you find the one you like. When you do, close the Color Picker.

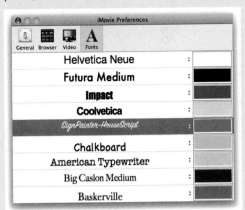

- **Family, Typeface**. The second column shows the names of the actual fonts in your system. The third, Typeface, shows the different style variations—Bold, Italic, Condensed, and so on—available in that type family. (Oblique and Italic are roughly the same thing; Bold, Black, and Ultra are varying degrees of bold-face.) Just click the font you want to use in your iMovie title.

- **Size**. The last column lists a sampling of point sizes. You can use the size slider, choose from the point-size pop-up menu, or type any number into the box at the top of the Size list.

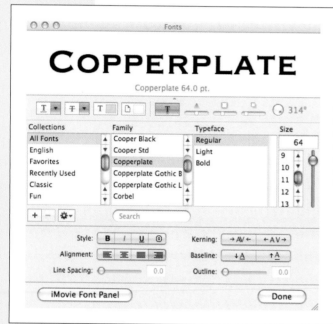

Figure 8-11:
The Fonts panel, available from many Mac OS X programs, offers elaborate controls over text color, shadow, and underline styles. It also contains some of the genetic material of old-style programs, like Suitcase and Font Juggler. See the handy font sample shown here above the font lists? To get it, choose Show Preview from the Action (✿) pop-up menu at the bottom of the panel. Or use the mousy way: Place your cursor just above the headings (Collections, Family, and so on) and drag downward.

Underline, strikethrough, color, shadow

You'll see five rectangular buttons at the top of the Font Panel. Each is a pop-up menu that gives you an even more ridiculous amount of typography control:

- **Underline**. You can choose how you want iMovie to underline the selected text: with one underline, two, or none. If you choose Color, then the Mac OS X Color Picker appears (Figure 8-12), so you can specify what *color* you want the underlines to be.

- **Strikethrough**. This option draws a line through your text, as though you crossed it out. These days, there's really only one situation when you might find it useful: the way bloggers indicate a correction, either a real one or a fake one done for humorous purposes. You know: "Cellphone Companies Are ~~Greedy Slimebags~~ Profitable."

Figure 8-12:
Some of the typographic options can get ridiculous. When you request a different color for an underline or strikethrough, you get the Mac OS X Color Picker dialog box, which gives you a million different ways to dial up a precise shade.

- **Text color**. The third pop-up rectangle opens the Color Picker dialog box. Here, you can specify the *color* of the highlighted text. (See the box on page 218.) The important thing is to choose a color that *contrasts* with the footage behind the lettering. Use white against black, black against white, yellow against blue, and so on.

Tip: iMovie doesn't limit you to TV-safe colors. But be careful. If colors are too bright (saturated), the edges of the letters can smear and tear when played back on a TV.

- **Document color**. The next pop-up rectangle is supposed to let you choose a background color for your text, but it doesn't work in iMovie.
- **Drop shadow**. The rightmost pop-up button is responsible for the shadow that iMovie adds to your titles to help them stand out from the background (Figure 8-13).

Secondary controls

The bottom of the Fonts Panel offers controls for Bold, Italic, Underline, and Outline; Alignment; Kerning; and Baseline height. All of these duplicate the equivalent commands in the Text menu.

Figure 8-13:
The four tiny controls to the right of the Shadow button control the shadow itself: its opacity, degree of "spread," distance from the main characters (controls how far away the "page" looks from the text), and the angle of the light that's casting the shadow.

There are, however, two controls *not* in the Text menu, and you may sometimes find them very useful:

- **Line Spacing**. In a word processor, this slider would affect the distance between lines of text in a single paragraph. iMovie doesn't let you create paragraphs, of course—each text block contains only a single line of type—but you can still find this slider helpful—it governs the distance between the main title and its *subtitle*, so you can add some space between the two.

Tip: In the Scrolling Credits title style, this control lets you adjust the amount of vertical space between the rows of credits. Cool!

- **Outline**. This slider governs the thickness of the outline (when you're using the Outline font style). Make it thick enough, and you can create some truly, er, *unforgettable* effects.

Tip: Once you get a piece of text formatted just the way you like it, you're not condemned to repeating all that work to format the *next* title. Instead, highlight some of the text that already looks good. Choose Text→Copy Style (Option-⌘-C). Then highlight the text that you want to match, and choose Text→Paste Style (Option-⌘-V). The second title now changes to match the formatting of the first one.

General Guidelines

As you choose fonts and type effects for the various credits in your movie, consider these guidelines:

- **Be consistent**. Using the same typeface for all the titles in your movie lends consistency and professionalism to the project.

- **Remember the QuickTime effect**. If you plan to distribute your finished movie as a QuickTime file—an electronic movie file that you can distribute by email, network, CD, disk, or web page—use the biggest, boldest, cleanest fonts you have. Avoid spindly, delicate fonts or script fonts. When QuickTime compresses your movie down to a 3-inch square, what looks terrific in your Viewer will be so small it may become illegible.

Come to think of it, you might want to choose big, bold, clean fonts even if you're going to play the finished movie on a TV with a resolution far lower than that of your computer screen. Be especially careful if you use one of the text effects that includes a subtitle, as iMovie subtitles often use an even smaller typeface than the one for the primary title, and you may lose legibility if the font has too much filigree.

Finally, favor *sans serif* fonts—typefaces that don't have the tiny *serifs*, or "hats and feet," at the end of the character strokes. The typeface you're reading now is a serif font, one that's less likely to remain legible in a QuickTime movie. The typeface used in the tip below is a sans serif font.

Tip: Some of the standard Mac fonts that look especially good as iMovie fonts are Arial Black, Capitals, Charcoal, Chicago, Gadget, Helvetica, Impact, Sand, Techno, and Textile.

Some of the fonts whose delicate nature may be harder to read are Monaco, Courier, Old English, Swing, Trebuchet, Times, Palatino, and Verdana.

The beauty of iMovie's titling feature is that the fonts you choose become embedded in the actual digital picture. In other words, when you distribute your movie as a Quick-Time file, you don't have to worry that your recipients may not have the same fonts you used to create the file. They'll see on their screens exactly what you see on yours.

Tip: Don't forget that you can superimpose text on a *still* image too (Chapter 10)—such as a photo or some gradient fill you created in, say, Photoshop Elements.

Add Your Own Custom Title

The Titles feature isn't the only way to create text effects. Using a graphics program like Photoshop or Photoshop Elements, you can create text "slides" with far more flexibility than you can find in the Titles feature. You're free to use any text color and any font size you want, and you can import the resulting file into iMovie as a title card. You can even dress up such titles with clip art, 3-D effects, and whatever other features your graphics software offers. Figure 8-14 (bottom) shows the idea.

Creating a title like this involves creating an *alpha-channel PNG* file. A little Photoshop experience is helpful, but here's the gist:

Use the text tool to type and format the text in Photoshop. In the Layers palette, ⌘-click the text layer's thumbnail to select it. Then, at the bottom of the Channels palette, click the "Save Selection as Channel" button. Finally, choose File→Save As.

Choose PNG as the format, and Photoshop makes you save the file as a copy. (Don't worry, the transparency should be preserved.) Name the title and save it to your desktop.

Now just drag the title graphic off your desktop and onto a title, as shown in Figure 8-14 (top). iMovie prompts you with the "Drag and Drop" menu, just as it does when you drag and drop a photo (page 267). Choose Cutaway; your PNG graphic will now look like a title to anyone who watches your movie.

The Color Picker

Here and there—not just in iMovie, but also in System Preferences, TextEdit, Microsoft Office, and many other programs—Mac OS X offers you the opportunity to choose a *color* for some element, like your desktop background, a window, and so on.

The Colors dialog box (Figure 8-12) offers a miniature color lab that lets you dial in any color in the Mac's rainbow. *Several* color labs, actually, arrayed across the top, are each designed to make color-choosing easier in certain circumstances:

Color Wheel. Drag the scroll bar vertically to adjust the brightness, and then drag your cursor around the ball to pick the shade.

Color Sliders. From the pop-up menu, choose the color-mixing method you prefer. *CMYK* stands for Cyan, Magenta, Yellow, and Black. People in the printing industry will feel immediately at home, because these four colors are the component inks for color printing. (These people may also be able to explain why *K* stands for *black*.)

RGB and HSV. *RGB* is how a TV or computer monitor thinks of colors: as proportions of red, green, and blue. *HSV* stands for Hue, Saturation, and Value—a favorite color-specifying scheme in scientific circles. In each case, just drag the sliders to mix up the color you want, or type in the percentages of each component.

Color Palettes. These palettes present canned sets of color swatches. They're primarily for programmers who want quick access to the standard colors in Mac OS X.

Image Palettes. Image palettes offer the visible rainbow arrayed yet another way—as cloudy, color-arranged streaks.

Crayons. Now *this* is a handy tool. You can click each crayon to see its color name: Mocha, Cayenne, Fern, and so on. (Some interior decorator in Cupertino had a field day naming these crayons.)

In any of these color pickers, you can also "sample" a color that's *outside* the dialog box—a color in the video shot, for example, or one that you found on a web page. Just click Q and then move your cursor around the screen. You'll see the sliders and numbers automatically change inside the dialog box when you click.

Finally, note that you can store frequently used (or frequently admired) colors in the mini-palette squares at the bottom. To do that, drag the big rectangular color swatch (next to the magnifying glass) directly down into one of the little squares, where it will stay fresh for weeks.

Note: You won't see the Cutaway option unless you turned on Advanced Tools (page 88).

Figure 8-14:
Top: Drag your alpha-channel PNG title graphic right off the desktop and onto a filmstrip, and then choose Cutaway from the "Drag and Drop" menu that appears.

Bottom: iMovie treats the graphic like a cutaway to a photo, and superimposes it on your video. To the rest of the world, though, it looks like a snazzy title.

Checking the Result

As you edit a title, you can see how it looks in context by clicking the |▶| button in the upper-right corner of the Viewer. Or, once you finish your title, point to a spot in the storyboard just before the title and then press the space bar to view the title in the context of the movie. You can also simply move your cursor back and forth across the title without clicking to see how it looks.

If the title isn't quite what you wanted—if it's the wrong length, style, or font, or if there's a typo, for example—you can change its settings as described in the next section. If the title wasn't *at all* what you wanted—if it's the wrong title style, for example—you can undo the entire process by highlighting the blue title stripe and pressing the Delete key (or choosing Edit→Undo, if you added the title recently).

Editing or Deleting a Title

If you don't like the title style you chose, just drag another one from the Titles pane and drop it right on top of the one you want to replace. iMovie updates the title instantly to reflect the change.

Of course, you may be a window-shopper, someone who likes to see *all* your choices before committing. If that's you, double-click the title's icon in your storyboard to bring up the Inspector. In the window that appears, click the button to the right of the Title label, labeled "Lower" (or whatever style the title has now).

The Inspector flips around to reveal skimmable previews of all the title styles, incorporating your own title text. You see exactly what you'll get from each style. When you find the one you like, click it, and then click Done.

Making other changes to a title is easy:

- **Change the start or end points** by dragging the endpoints of the blue stripe in the storyboard.

- **Move the entire title earlier or later** by dragging its stripe left or right in the storyboard.

- **Edit the text or its typography** by clicking the title's blue stripe in the storyboard. The text boxes appear immediately in the Viewer. Press ⌘-T to open the Font panel if you need to change the color, font, or other typographical niceties.

- **Delete a title** by clicking its blue stripe and then pressing the Delete key.

Title Fade-In/Fade-Out Timing

There's an important question regarding titles that doesn't always come to mind: How long does it take my title to fade in and out? This doesn't occur to you until you want, for example, a title that cuts in suddenly for dramatic effect. A fading title just won't do.

Every iMovie project has a global setting for title fades, which you can set in File→Project Properties under the Timing tab. The Title Fade Duration slider controls how long every title takes to fade in and out.

If you want one title to pop and another to plod, you can override the global fade setting in the Inspector. To open the Inspector for a title, double-click ❶ in the storyboard. Next to the Fade In/Out label, turn on Manual, and adjust the duration slider.

You can also just type a duration into the text box. Even though the slider goes up to only 2 seconds (and down to zero), you can actually type in a ridiculously long fade duration here. Want the title to take 20 minutes to fade in? Type *20.0.0* (for minutes.seconds.frames).

Because you're setting the *fade out* timing as well, you'd have to make your title at least 40 minutes long to accom-modate this setting: 20 minutes for the fade in, and 20 minutes for the fade out.

You would also be insane.

Unfortunately, you can't set the fade out time independently. Whatever timing you set for your title fade affects the fades on both ends.

Also, don't bother trying to set the fade time for some titles, usually the ones that do something other than fade in and out. You can't.

Narration, Music, and Sound

I f you're lucky, you may someday get a chance to watch a movie whose soundtrack isn't yet finished. You'll be scanning channels and stumble across a special about how movies are made, or you'll see a tribute to a film composer, or you'll rent a movie DVD that includes a "making of" documentary. These TV shows and DVDs sometimes include a couple of minutes of the finished movie as it looked *before* the musical soundtrack and sound effects were added.

At that moment, your understanding of the film medium will take an enormous leap forward. "Jeez," you'll say, "without music and sound effects, this $100 million Hollywood film has no more emotional impact than…my home movies!"

And you'll be right. It's true that the *visual* component of film is the most, well, visible. Movie stars and directors become household names, but not the sound editors, composers, *foley* (sound effects) artists, and others who devote their careers to the audio experience of film.

But without music, sound effects (called SFX for short), and sound editing, even the best Hollywood movie will leave you cold and unimpressed.

Three Kinds of Audio

In iMovie '11, Apple finally heard the cries of iMovie users everywhere. With this version, you can finally edit the audio in clips with a traditional rubber-band/timeline tool. This tool shows you the waveforms of the clips, where you can make all the volume changes you want.

iMovie's designers have also designated two additional kinds of audio clips, which are (supposedly) focused on the way people actually use audio in home movies:

- **Background music** is a solid block of music that sits "behind" the clips in your project, playing through everything, no matter how you shuffle the video clips around. You can even line up a playlist of several songs; they play consecutively, with a nice crossfade between them.

- **Sound effects**. When you add a sound effect, you attach an audio file to a specific spot in your video. As you rearrange your clips during the editing process, the effect goes along for the ride.

Now, the following gets confusing, so read it slowly: There's no difference between the *kinds* of audio you can use in these two additional ways. *Any* audio, including sound effects, can be background audio; and *any* audio, including songs, can behave like a sound effect. You'll learn the details later in this chapter.

Audio Sources

Much like traditional film cameras, iMovie stores a movie's audio and video on separate tracks, which you can view and edit independently. In iMovie, audio shows up as a colored stripe in, under, or behind your filmstrips.

In addition to the audio built into every video clip, you can *add* sound to a project from any of these sources:

- **Camcorder audio**. You can extract the audio from a camcorder video clip to use as an independent sound clip, for use somewhere else in your movie.

- **iTunes tracks**. Adding background music to your flick is as easy as can be. As described later in this chapter, iMovie displays your complete iTunes music collection, playlists and all. This, of course, is an example of what makes iLife a *suite* and not just a handful of separate programs: iMovie's integration with the other Apple programs.

- **Narration**. This can be anything you record with your microphone.

- **Sound effects**. Choose these effects (gunshots, glass breaking, applause, and so on) from iMovie's Audio palette.

- **MP3, WAV, AIFF, and AAC files**. iMovie can directly import files in these popular music formats. You can drag them in from the Finder or bring them in from iTunes.

This chapter covers all these sound varieties.

Importing Music from a CD

For several versions of iMovie, you could import songs from a CD directly into iMovie. You could just insert your favorite music CD (Carly Simon, The Rolling Stones, the Cleveland Orchestra, or whatever), choose the track you wanted to swipe, and the deed was done.

That feature mysteriously disappeared starting in iMovie 6. Now you're supposed to switch into iTunes, import the CD into your music collection there, and then return to iMovie to import it.

Adding Audio to the Storyboard

Nothing adds emotional impact to a piece of video like music. Slow, romantic music makes the difference between a sad story and one that actually makes viewers cry. Fast, hard-driving music makes viewers' hearts beat faster—scientists have proven it. Music is so integral to movies these days that, as you walk out of a theater, you may not even be aware that a movie *had* music, but virtually every movie does—and it emotionally manipulates the audience.

Home movies are no exception. Music adds a new dimension to your movie, so much so that some iMovie fans *edit to music*. They choose a song, lay it down in the audio track, and then cut the video footage to fit the beats, words, or sections of the music.

Tip: Even if you don't synchronize your video to music this way, you may still want to experiment with a music-only soundtrack. That is, set the volume for your camcorder clips to zero (page 246), so your movie is silent except for the music. The effect is powerful and you often find it used in Hollywood montage sequences.

The Music and Sound Effects Browser

Here's how you go about choosing a piece of music or a sound effect for your movie:

1. **Choose Window→Music and Sound Effects (or press ⌘-1).**

   Alternatively, click ♫ just beneath the Viewer. Either way, iMovie displays the "Music and Sound Effects" browser in the lower-right corner (Figure 9-1).

2. **Find just the right song or sound. iMovie fills the browser with useful folders to help you find the right sound. Its listings include:**

   iMovie Sound Effects. This folder includes about 100 handy sound effects, like doors closing, trains passing, and animal sounds.

   iLife Sound Effects. This list represents another enormous collection of sound effects, organized into subfolders. Don't miss the Jingles folder in particular; it contains 200 pieces of terrific, professionally recorded, *royalty-free* background music in every style.

   GarageBand. Here's a nice perk of having an integrated suite of programs like iLife: You can share the output of each program and touch it up in the others. For example, any musical compositions you work up in GarageBand show up here.

Tip: Actually, you see in this list only the compositions you saved with what Apple calls an iLife preview. To make sure your musical opus includes this preview, open GarageBand→Preferences, click General, and then turn on "Render an audio preview when saving," This increases the time it takes to save your GarageBand song, but it's necessary if you want your musical masterpieces to show up in iMovie.

Figure 9-1:
*Welcome to the "Music and Sound Effects"
browser, which reveals your iTunes music
collection, your GarageBand masterpieces,
and several hundred stock sound effects. (If
you don't see the category you want, click
the corresponding flippy triangle at the top
of the list.)*

iTunes. If you keep your music collection in the free iTunes software, you're in
luck; the entire assortment shows up right here, in the iTunes category of the
"Music and Sound Effects" browser. And if you organized your iTunes music
into *playlists* (subsets), you'll see those listed here, too. You can also use the
Search box at the bottom of the list, as shown in Figure 9-2.

To listen to a piece of audio in *any* of these categories (GarageBand, iTunes, and
so on), click its name, and then click the ▶ button beneath the list (to the left
of the search box; see Figure 9-2). Or, if you think life is too short already, just
double-click a song name. (To interrupt playback, either double-click a different
song, double-click the same song, or click the ▶ button again.)

You can sort the list alphabetically by song name, artist name, or song length
by clicking the appropriate heading above the list. (Ordinarily, you wouldn't
think that it would be very useful to sort a list by track length, but remember
that in the context of video editing, finding a song that's exactly the right length
for your video could wind up being more important than which band plays it.)

Tip: *The "Music and Sound Effects" playback controls work independently of the playback controls in the
Monitor window. You may find it useful, therefore, to manually play back your movie* as *you listen to the
different songs, so you can preview the impact of the two together. The easiest way to do that is to click
▶ in the "Music and Sound Effects" browser at precisely the same instant that you press the space bar to
begin movie playback.*

Figure 9-2:
Choose any of your playlists to navigate your massive music collection. You can also click in the Search box. As you type a song or performer's name, iMovie hides all the songs that don't match your search term. (To delete your search term and restore the entire list, click ⊗ at the right end of the Search box.)

3. **Drag the music into your storyboard.**

Using the song's name as a handle, drag it directly out of the list and into the storyboard. Release the mouse when the song looks like it's in the right place.

And what, you may ask, is "the right place" for a song? It turns out that *where* you drop a song is extremely important. If you release the mouse when the background of the *entire* storyboard has turned from its normal black to green (Figure 9-3), you create what iMovie calls background music (see the next page for details).

Tip: If your intention is to add background music, you can drag *more than one* song from the "Music and Sound Effects" browser simultaneously. To select more than one, click the first one, and then ⌘-click each additional one. iMovie adds each song to the soundtrack in the same order in which you selected them.

This presumes, of course, that you have enough video to cover all the songs. If your video comes up short, iMovie won't play all the tunes. You need to either add more video or photos, or cut your songs using the Clip Trimmer (page 232).

If you release the mouse when the pointer is on a filmstrip, you create what iMovie calls a sound effect; page 234 has more information.

Adding Audio from the Finder

The "Music and Sound Effects" browser is a great way to find music and effects for your movie—*if* they're listed there. You may very well have folders full of audio files that *didn't* come from iTunes, GarageBand, or Apple.

Figure 9-3:
Background music turns into a huge green bubble behind your filmstrips. Try skimming/playing the movie after you place the music. If it doesn't have quite the effect you thought, press ⌘-Z (Edit→Undo) and try another song.

Fortunately, you can incorporate them easily; see Figure 9-4. Just keep in mind that *how* you drag files in from the desktop determines whether they become background audio (big green bubble) or sound-effects audio (horizontal stripes), just exactly as described above.

Background Music

If you drag a piece of music into the *background well* of your storyboard—basically, anywhere *except* onto a clip—the background of the entire storyboard area turns into broad green bubble. That's your clue that you just added a piece of what Apple calls background music.

Understanding what, exactly, Apple means by this term—and figuring out how it's different from *sound effects*-style music—isn't especially easy. This much, though, is clear:

- **Background music appears in the storyboard**. The music appears as a huge green background bubble behind your filmstrips (or purple if you "pin" the tune to the video; see "Pinning and Unpinning Background Music" below). Sound-effects audio, on the other hand, appears as a skinny horizontal stripe under the filmstrip.

- **The music ends at the end of your video, even if the song isn't over**. If the song is *longer* than your movie, a special vertical indicator bar appears after the last filmstrip to let you know. (It's a vertical dotted line with two musical notes.) If you then add *more* video to the project, the background music auto-expands to include it. It's stretchy that way.

Figure 9-4:
If you have audio files not listed in the iMovie audio browser, make the iMovie window smaller (drag its lower-right corner inward) so you can see the desktop behind it. Open the desktop window that contains your audio clips, and then drag them into your storyboard.

- **Background music generally plays from the beginning of your movie.** You can drag it into a different spot, however, as described below.

- **If you place two pieces of background music one after the other, iMovie plays them consecutively, with a crossfade in between.** You can add the second piece the same way you added the first one: by dragging its name from the "Music and Sound Effects" browser. (Two pieces of background music can never overlap, though.)

Pinning and Unpinning Background Music

When you drag music into the background of your storyboard, it starts out being *unpinned*, meaning that it's not locked to your video scenes. You can add or delete chunks of video, but that good ol' music stays right where it is, unaffected. It's a steady stream of music that starts at the beginning of your movie. iMovie depicts unpinned background music with a green bubble.

There are times, however, when unpinned music can be a real pain. You might want to line up a certain video moment (like Bill-Gates-getting-hit-with-a-pie footage) with a particular audio moment (like a cymbal crash). You'll find that when you insert or delete video footage *after* you line up audio with specific video, everything goes out of alignment. This syndrome can rear its ugly head in many video-editing programs.

You may wind up playing a frustrating game of find-the-frame, over and over again, all the way through the movie, as you try to redo all your careful audio/video alignments.

The solution is to *pin* the audio. Click carefully on the *name* of the background audio bubble, and drag it horizontally (Figure 9-5).

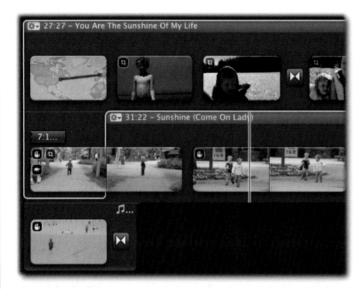

Figure 9-5:
Top: These two consecutive green background songs are unpinned. They're free of any link to your footage, completely unaffected by any video editing you do.

Bottom: If you drag one of the bubbles to the right, you pin it to a particular video frame—which you'll know because of the purple coloring and the pushpin. You can add new video clips or take some away, but this audio will always begin playing at this spot in the video.

When you release the mouse, iMovie turns the background audio bubble purple and adds a tiny pushpin, indicating that it's locked the audio to the video at that frame (Figure 9-5, bottom). Even if the video later gets moved around in its track, or even if you later trim away some footage from the beginning of the video clip, the music will still begin at that point in the video.

Once you lock an audio clip to its video, you no longer have to worry that it might lose sync with the video when you edit your clips.

By the way, pinning an audio clip doesn't prevent *you* from shifting it. Dragging the audio clip does *not* drag the attached video clip along with it. You're still welcome to slide the audio clip left or right in its track, independent of any other clips. Doing so simply makes iMovie realign the clip with a new video frame, lining up the pushpin accordingly. (If you *cut* the video clip, the background audio disappears entirely.)

Tip: You can overlap pinned background tracks if you want. Simply drag one background track over another.

POWER USERS' CLINIC

Adding or Removing Sound Effects

The list of sound effects in the "Music and Sound Effects" panel isn't magical. It's simply a listing of the sound files that come with iMovie. If you know the secret, you can delete, move, or rename your sound effects—or even install new ones. Here's how:

First, quit iMovie. In the Finder, open your Applications folder. Control-click (or right-click) iMovie's icon; from the shortcut menu, choose Show Package Contents.

The iMovie *package window* appears. You've just discovered, if you didn't already know, that many Mac OS X program icons are, in fact, thinly disguised folders (which Apple calls *packages*) that contain dozens or hundreds of support files. You just opened up iMovie for inspection.

Open the Contents→Resources folder. Welcome to the belly of the beast. Before you sit hundreds of files, most of them the little graphics that make up the various iMovie buttons, controls, and so on. (If you're really feeling ambitious, you can actually open up these graphics and edit them, completely changing the look of iMovie.)

The icon you want is the folder called iMovie '08 Sound Effects. (Yes, the folder still bears the '08 name, even though you paid for iMovie '11.) It's full of individual sound files—in MP3 format—that make up the list you see in the "Music and Sound Effects" pane (Figure 9-2).

Feel free to reorganize these files. For example, you can throw away the ones you never use, or rename the ones you do. You can add new MP3 files to this list. You can even make new folders to categorize the selection. Later, you'll see them show up as subfolders of the iMovie '08 Sound Effect heading in the "Music and Sound Effects" browser.

(Looking for even more sound effects? The Internet is filled with downloadable MP3 files you can use in your iMovie projects. Start your favorite search engine and type *free sound effects* into the search box. Many effects already exist in MP3 format; many others are in AIFF format, which you can convert to iMovie-friendly MP3 files using iTunes.)

Close all the windows. When you return to iMovie, you'll see, under the iMovie Sound Effects heading, the updated list of MP3 sound-effects files.

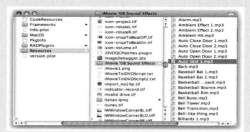

To *unpin* an audio clip, restoring it to its free-floating status, click it, and then choose Clip→Unpin Music Track. The audio bubble turns green again, and slams against the left side of the storyboard area (or against whatever background audio bubble is to its left). It's no longer attached to the video.

Rearranging Unpinned Background Music

If you understand the concept of unpinned, free-floating background audio (and you're forgiven if you don't), then you realize that, unless you drag and pin the songs, they stack up beside each other, left to right in your storyboard, and play sequentially, with a 1-second crossfade between them.

Now suppose you want to rearrange them. How are you supposed to do that? If you drag them, you'll wind up pinning them, which changes their whole function. Fortunately, iMovie offers another way, a way that keeps them unpinned.

POWER USERS' CLINIC

The Clip Trimmer

Most people treat background music in iMovie as a set-it-and-forget-it affair. You drop it into the storyboard, it plays as long as necessary to cover your video, and end of story.

Truth is, though, you have a little more control than that. Exhibit A: You can start playing any piece of music from someplace *other* than its beginning (and stop it before its end). If you have an iTunes track that begins with an annoying 35-second drum solo, for example, you can lop it out, so that the music (and your movie) begins with the actual hook of the song—the main part.

To edit background audio, click anywhere on the green background bubble to select it (a yellow outline appears on it). Now click the ✿ button in the upper-left corner of the background audio bubble. From the shortcut menu, choose Clip Trimmer.

Suddenly, the Event browser filmstrips disappear, replaced by the Clip Trimmer window, which you read about back on page 100.

You see the soundwaves representing the background music. The 'waves you'll actually hear are light green. If the music is longer than the video, the soundwaves you *won't* hear (because they would play after the video is over) are black.

Your job here is to adjust the position of the yellow vertical end handles. Drag the first one to the right if you want the music to begin at a point that's later in the song; drag the final one to the left if you want the music to end before the official end of the song. You can skim or play to hear where you are in the piece.

Click Done when you finish.

Incidentally, this trick also works on sound-effects audio (page 234), narration, and so on. In those situations, begin with one click on the same ✿ icon at the beginning of the sound effect.

The trick is to choose Clip→Arrange Music Tracks. The weird little dialog box shown in Figure 9-6 appears.

It's a master list of all the background audio clips you added. Two master lists, actually, helpfully color-coded to match the background audio bubbles in the storyboard:

- **Pinned Music Tracks (purple)**. This is a list of all the audio you pinned to specific moments in the storyboard, complete with their durations.

  You can't do anything in this upper list *except* to click a song, and then click the Unpin Track button. Doing so makes the song leave the purple list and jump down to the green list, Floating Music Tracks. (Meanwhile, back in the storyboard, that bit of audio turns green and slams against the next available piece of green, floating background audio.)

Fun with Copyright Law

Don't I break some kind of law when I copy music from a commercial CD, or use iTunes Store music in one of my movies?

Exactly what constitutes stealing music is a hot-button issue that has tied millions of people (and recording executives) in knots. That's why some iMovie fans hesitate to distribute their films in places where lawyers might see them—like the Internet.

Frankly, though, record company lawyers have bigger fish to fry than small-time amateur operators like you. You're perfectly safe showing your movies to family and friends, your user group, and other limited circles of viewers. In fact, Apple *encourages* you to use iTunes Music Store purchases in your movies. After all, Apple is the one who made them available right in iMovie.

You'll risk trouble only if you go commercial, making money from movies that incorporate copyrighted music.

Still, if your conscience nags you, you can always use one of your GarageBand compositions. And even if you're not especially musical, the world is filled with royalty-free music—music that artists compose and record expressly for the purpose of letting filmmakers add music to their work without having to pay a licensing fee every time they do so. Some of it's even free. You'll find 200 free musical pieces in the Jingles folder of your "Music and Sound Effects" browser, for example, ready to use.

Or check out *www.freeplaymusic.com*, a website filled with prerecorded music in every conceivable style. You're welcome to use it in your movies at no charge for noncommercial use.

If that's not enough for you, visit a search page like Google (*www.google.com*), search for *music library* or *royalty-free music*, and start clicking your way to the hundreds of sites that offer information about (and audio samples of) music that you can buy and use without fear.

Tip: In all, there are three ways to unpin a piece of music. You can use the Unpin Track button described here; you can use the Clip→Unpin Music Track command; or you can Control-click (right-click) a piece of pinned, purple music, and, from the shortcut menu, choose Unpin Music Track.

- **Floating Music Tracks (green).** Here are all the background audio pieces that you *haven't* pinned to your video. They "float" from the left side of your storyboard, playing sequentially, without any connection to the video.

  And here's the main idea behind this dialog box: You can drag the names of the floating tracks up or down in this list to rearrange them. (Music at the *top* of this list appears at the *beginning* of your project.)

When you finish, click OK.

Deleting Background Audio

To remove a piece of background audio from your project, click its green or purple bubble once. When the yellow border appears, press the Delete key.

Sound Effects (Pinned Music)

As you now know, iMovie has two kinds of audio. It represents background music with a big green bubble *behind* your filmstrips. That music plays continuously in the

---

background, regardless of the video that's playing. (Yes, yes, it's true, you *can* pin this type of audio to a specific video frame, but for the sake of clarity, let's ignore that.)

iMovie calls the other type of audio *sound effects*, and iMovie expects you to attach, or pin, it directly to a particular frame of a particular clip. If that clip gets pushed around in the storyboard during editing, the audio goes along for the ride.

There are three interesting things about sound-effects audio (Figure 9-7). First, iMovie represents it as a green horizontal stripe below the filmstrip. Second, you can attach more than one of these stripes, stacking them up as high as necessary. Basically, you're overlapping them. And finally, you can move, shorten, or delete the sound-effect stripes with a simple drag motion.

Figure 9-7:
You can attach multiple sound effects to a single clip and they all move when the video clip moves. To delete a sound effect, click its stripe, and then press the Delete key. To move it, drag the stripe horizontally. And to shorten the clip, drag either end inward.

Tip: Actually, there are two ways to adjust the length of a sound-effect stripe. You can drag its right end with your mouse, which is quick and direct. You can also click the ✿ button at the front of the stripe and, from the shortcut menu, choose Clip Trimmer. For details on using the Clip Trimmer window, see the box on page 232.

Editing to the Beat

If you've ever made a music video, you know how easy it is to pull your hair out trying to match a transition with a beat in the background. To make sure you don't go bald, iMovie offers a subtle, but very powerful, tool called a *beat marker*.

Beat markers aren't the same thing as chapter markers (page 380) or comment markers (page 98). They're specially designed indicators that correspond to particular musical moments in your background track. Video clips that you add to your project automatically snap against these beats, even resizing themselves if necessary. Later, adjustments you make in the Precision Editor (page 105) will also snap to line up with the beats you mark.

Note: Beat markers are also necessary for some of iMovie '11's One-Step Effects to work (page 170).

The truth is, beat markers are one of the coolest iMovie features that no one talks about. They're not even listed in Apple Marketing's short list of cool new features. What beat markers lack in publicity, they make up for in power. They'll save you huge swaths of time editing a movie to the beat of a song.

Before you do anything, go to View→"Snap to Beats" and make sure you have "Snap to Beats" enabled.

Phase 1: Add Your Background Music

Start with a new project. Drop a background music track into your project, as described on page 228.

Now, at this point, you may protest, "Wait a minute! You told me songs won't play unless I have video clips in place!" You have learned well, Grasshopper. And your concern is justified. Your song appears like a lonely green blob in your timeline, and the movie won't play.

But your song *is* there. You can still edit the song itself with things like audio adjustments (page 246) and the Clip Trimmer (page 232). Besides, you have a great reason for putting the song in first: All of your added video and photos will automatically resize to match the beats you're about to mark.

Tip: You can add beat markers to projects you've already created, but they won't have any effect on the existing clips (like resizing them to fit the beats). You can still exploit beat markers in an existing project, however. The Precision Editor, described below, lets you drag video clips by hand into alignment with beat markers.

Phase 2a: Insert Beat Markers

Click the ✿ button on your lonely song's bubble. From the shortcut menu, choose Clip Trimmer. (The Clip Trimmer's power over music is described on page 232. This time, you're using it for a different purpose.)

In the Clip Trimmer, you can skim and play your music (by tapping the space bar). But notice the note among the buttons at the top of the Clip Trimmer. This little musical-note icon is a draggable beat marker, which you can grab and drop onto any point in your music track (Figure 9-8). The supply is unlimited, so drag as many as you want into your song.

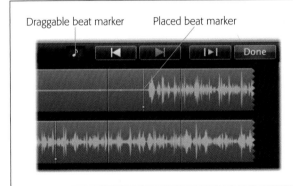

Draggable beat marker   Placed beat marker

Figure 9-8:
Using the note icon in the top-right corner of the Clip Trimmer, you can drag beat markers down into your song. The beat markers appear as thin, vertical, white lines with a dot in them. You can move beat markers after you place them by dragging them around. Delete them by dragging them past the bottom or the top of the Clip Trimmer.

Tip: You can mark beats in *any* kind of audio track: pinned, unpinned, sound effect, or even a voiceover. However, some beat-marker features, like One-Step Effects, work only when the beat markers are in a background track.

Mark any spot that needs special attention in your editing. Most of the time, these will be the beats to the music where you want one clip to cut to the next. But there could be some big musical swells or a key bit in the lyrics that also merit a mark.

The actual markers appear as thin, vertical, white lines with a dot in them (Figure 9-8).

Tip: The audio waveforms give you visual cues about what's going on with the music, and can guide you to the right beat spots in a song.

Phase 2b: Tapping Out Beats

Dragging is great and all, but you'll find it a lot simpler to just hit the letter M key on the keyboard to add beat markers. (Alternatively, you can right-click [or Control-click] the spot you want to mark, and, from the shortcut menu, choose Add Beat Marker.)

Using your expertise with the M key, start the audio track playing from the beginning. As the song plays, tap the M key on every musical beat where you want the video to cut to a new shot. It's OK to boogie in your chair while you tap out the beats to the entire song; no one is watching.

Once you tap out the whole song, take a moment to fix your mistakes. Beat markers are draggable, even after you place them. You can remove a marker entirely by dragging it off of the top or bottom of the Clip Trimmer window. If you want to start over, just right-click (or Control-click) any point along your music track and, from the shortcut menu, choose Remove All Beat Markers.

Tip: Usually, if you cut right on the beat, the cut will appear to be late. If you practice tapping the M key just barely *before* the beats, your cuts will look just right.

Also, don't group your beat markers too closely together unless you're trying to get a very fast-paced effect. If the video cuts happen *too* fast, your viewers won't be able to absorb them.

Once you're happy with all the beat placements, click Done in the top-right corner of the Clip Trimmer.

Phase 3: Add Your Video Clips

You should be back in your Event browser now, having a basically blank project awaiting some footage. Grab a video chunk from the browser and add it to your project.

Voilà: There it is. iMovie added your chunk to the project, but resized it to match the next-closest beat marker. Try it with a photo now (page 267). Isn't that cool? (If you don't see any auto-resizing, make sure you have View→"Snap to Beats" turned on.)

After very little work, your project will look something like Figure 9-9.

Figure 9-9:
A project edited to the beat of music. Each clip cuts out right in front of the next beat marker—with one exception. See how the beginning clip doesn't touch any beat markers and has the background audio pinned to it? You do this by pinning the background audio after you place your first clip, in spite of iMovie's warning (page 240).

Notice how the beat markers show up in your project to remind you why the cuts are taking place there. Seeing them in your project lets you keep them in mind should you want to edit around them, or want something in the middle of a clip to happen at the beat.

Snap to Beats in Your Project

With "Snap to Beats" turned on, your beat markers in place, and your footage added, you can start plugging in things like titles and sound effects. As you drag these other elements around, they, too, snap into position against beat markers, as though magnetically attracted. You can adjust their timing too, so they also match the beats in your project.

Warning: You can add all kinds of other project elements, but *transitions* will disrupt your timings, as described below.

Beat Markers in the Precision Editor

What if the video isn't showing exactly what you want when the cut takes place? What if you added your beat markers *after* putting in all your footage? Not a problem. The Precision Editor knows all about beat markers.

To use the Precision Editor, double-click any empty space between two project clips. Page 105 covers the basics of the Precision Editor, but it offers some handy extras when you work with beat markers.

First, make sure you can see the background song. Click the Show Extras button, identified in Figure 9-10, to do that. (The Show Extras button changes from gray to blue when you turn it on.)

Show Extras

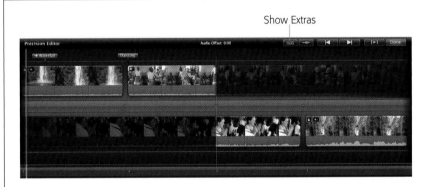

Figure 9-10:
With beat markers plugged into your song and "Snap to Beats" turned on, the Precision Editor takes on a new twist. As the cut line nears a beat marker, it snaps to line right up with the beat, turning yellow to let you know what happened.

Your song appears at the bottom of the window, with all the beat markers standing at attention (Figure 9-10).

Drag the video cut line around. Each time it approaches a beat marker in the background song, the cut line turns yellow and snaps against the marker.

Here's a rundown of how you could use beat markers in the Precision Editor:

- You can go back through cuts you made before you added beat markers, lining them up to look good with your background song.

- You can ignore the snapping effect and line up a video moment in the *middle* of a clip, like at the crack of a bat, with a meaningful moment in the music.

- You can line up other things, like a title, to match a beat.

The Beat Warning

With all of this work done, you may want to go back and tweak some things to your liking, such as throwing a transition into a few places or inserting a video clip between two others. As long as you have "Snap to Beats" turned on in the View menu, iMovie plays the vigilant guard dog, yapping at you every time you attempt a change that will throw off the beat alignment (Figure 9-11).

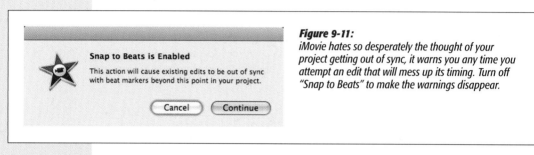

Snap to Beats is Enabled

This action will cause existing edits to be out of sync with beat markers beyond this point in your project.

Cancel   Continue

Figure 9-11:
iMovie hates so desperately the thought of your project getting out of sync, it warns you any time you attempt an edit that will mess up its timing. Turn off "Snap to Beats" to make the warnings disappear.

You can dismiss every single warning individually or, to put a permanent muzzle on iMovie, turn off "Snap to Beats" by choosing View→"Snap to Beats" (⌘-U).

Recording Narration

If anyone ever belittles iMovie for being underpowered, point out an iMovie feature that isn't even available in most expensive video-editing programs: the ability to record narration while you watch your movie play. If your Mac has a microphone, you can easily create any of these effects:

WORD TO THE WISE

Beats and Transitions

Since you can save so much time using beat markers, you may decide to speed things up even more with automatic transitions, as described on page 133. If so, here's some timely advice.

A simple cut almost always looks good to a beat, because it's just as quick as the beat itself. They match up perfectly. But transitions, like cross dissolves (page 136), generally last longer than the beat. The musical beat won't line up as precisely as a regular old cut does.

You'll encounter this problem no matter which transition you use; iMovie can't read your mind to figure out where in the transition you want the beat to take place. As a rule, iMovie puts the beat in the middle of the transition.

Knowing all this, if you still want to use automatic transitions with beat markers, all the same rules about automatic transitions apply, including the way they change the length of your clips.

There's one more oddity (probably a bug): Ordinarily—when you're not using automatic transitions—iMovie shortens each piece of footage so that it ends on the next beat. In other words, iMovie might cut down a 10-second selection to 2 seconds. If you turn automatic transitions on, though, iMovie may skip over beat markers entirely. (A 10-second video clip might skip three beat markers, ending with the beat marker closest to the end of the clip.) You'll have to cut your clips down to approximate size before you add them to your project.

- **Create a reminiscence**. As the footage shows children playing, we hear you saying, "It was the year 2009. It was a time of innocence. Of sunlight. Of children at play. In the years before the Great Asteroid, nobody imagined that one 6-year-old child would become a goddess to her people. This, then, is her story."

- **Voiceover**. The technique of superimposing an unseen narrator's voice over video is called a *voiceover*. It's incredibly popular in TV, commercials, and movies (such as *Saving Private Ryan, Sin City*, and of course, the *Look Who's Talking* movies).

- **Identify the scene**. Even if your movie isn't one with a story line, iMovie's narration feature offers an extremely convenient method of identifying your home movies. Think about it: When you get photos back from the drugstore, the date is stamped across the back of each photo. In years to come, you'll know when you took the photos.

Video cameras offer an optional date-stamp feature, too—a crude, ugly, digital readout that permanently mars your footage. But otherwise, as they view their deteriorating VHS cassettes in 2025, most of the world's camcorder owners will never know where, why, or when they shot their footage. Few people are compulsive enough to film, before each new shot, somebody saying, "It's Halloween 2007, and little Chrissie is going out for her very first trick-or-treating. Mommy made the costume out of some fishnet stockings and a melon," or whatever.

Using iMovie, though, it's easy to add a few words of shot-identification narration over your establishing shot. (To find out the time and date when you shot the footage, just double-click the clip.)

FREQUENTLY ASKED QUESTION

Music Beyond the Video

How the heck do I make the music start before the video, or play on for a few seconds past the end of the video?

You're on to something here. There is no way to drag audio, of any type, to the *left* of the first filmstrip in your storyboard. And there's no way to make one extend to the *right* of the last one. Therefore, there doesn't seem to be any way to make the music begin before the movie, or play past the end of it. Ah, but that's what workarounds are for.

The solution, in this case, is simple: Insert a *black background* at the beginning or end of your movie. Fill the screen with nothingness. Your music will play happily, since it *thinks* that it's playing under video, but your audience will see a black screen as the music plays.

Details on background images appear on page 266.

- **Provide new information**. For professional work, the narration feature is an excellent way to add another continuous information stream to whatever videos or still pictures appear onscreen. Doctors use iMovie to create narrated slideshows, having created a storyboard filled with still images of scanned slides (see Chapter 10). Real estate agents feature camcorder footage of houses under consideration, while narrating the key features that can't be seen. ("Built in 1869, this house was extensively renovated in 1880...".) And it doesn't take much imagination to see how *lawyers* can exploit iMovie.

To create a *voiceover* (a narration), follow these steps.

1. **Click the Voiceover button (Figure 9-12, top), or press the letter O key.**

   The Voiceover window appears (Figure 9-12, bottom).

2. **Choose a sound source, like your Mac's microphone.**

   Your Mac's microphone takes one of two forms: built-in, or external. The built-in mic, a tiny hole in the facade of the iMac, eMac, or MacBook, couldn't be more convenient. It's always with you, and always turned on.

   If your Mac doesn't have a built-in microphone, you can plug in an external USB microphone, an old external iSight camera, or a standard microphone with an adapter (like the iMic, *www.griffintechnology.com*).

   The Record From pop-up menu lists all the audio sources the Mac knows about—Built-in Microphone, Built-in Input (meaning the audio-input jack on the back or the side), USB Microphone, or whatever you've got connected.

   Note: The selection you make here is independent of the input currently selected in System Preferences. That's a welcome change from older versions of iMovie.

   ---

3. **Set the input level.**

   That is, move close to the microphone and practice your spiel. If the level meter bars dance, but only partway across the graph (Figure 9-12), your narration isn't loud enough. On playback, it'll probably be drowned out by the camcorder audio track.

   If the meters hit the right end of the graph, on the other hand, those bars turn bright red to get your attention. In that case, the sound source is too loud, and the recording will have an ugly, "overdriven" distortion.

   To increase the recording volume, drag the Input Volume slider to the right. (You can learn tricks for boosting the volume of audio tracks later in this chapter, but it's much better to get the level right the first time.)

Figure 9-12:
Click the Voiceover button (top) to open the Voiceover window (bottom), where you set up the voice recording to come. Test your setup by speaking into the microphone. If the live VU meter twitches in response, and has a decent level, you're ready to record. When it's all over, you'll see a purple stripe below the filmstrip (top). It behaves just like the green stripes of other sound-effects audio.

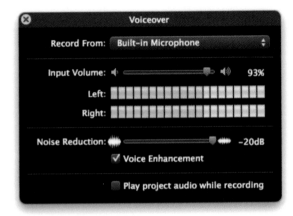

4. **Adjust the Noise Reduction and Voice Enhancement controls, if you like.**

   The Voice Enhancement checkbox is supposed to electronically alter your voice to sound more smooth. The Noise Reduction slider is supposed to screen out ambient background noise. Neither one produces an earth-shaking effect, but you can experiment with them to see how you like the result.

5. **Turn the "Play project audio" checkbox on or off.**

   The question you're answering here is: Do you want to hear the audio from your movie playing back while you record? Usually, the answer is "Yes." That way, you can avoid talking over somebody's on-camera conversation, and you can time your own utterances to perfection. The problem is, your microphone *hears* the movie playback coming out of your Mac's speakers and records a second copy of it, or even triggers squealing feedback.

Therefore, turn on "Play project audio" only if you're wearing headphones to monitor the playback.

6. **Find the spot where you want the narration to begin.**

   You can use all the usual techniques to navigate your clips: skim (point without clicking), press the space bar to play the movie, and so on. Don't click the mouse; just skim and play.

7. **When you find the right spot, click the mouse.**

   Big red letters in the Viewer say, "Get ready...," and a big 3-2-1 countdown timer appears, accompanied by attention-getting countdown beeps. You even see preroll—the Viewer shows the three seconds of video that *lead up* to the point you clicked. All of this is intended to help you get ready to speak at the spot you clicked.

8. **When the Viewer says Recording, start talking. Press the space bar (or click anywhere) to stop.**

   Now a new, purple stripe appears below your filmstrip, already highlighted, bearing the name Voiceover Recording 1 (or 2, or 3), as shown in Figure 9-12. Point to a spot just before the beginning of the new recording, and then press the space bar to listen to your voiceover.

9. **Close the Narration window.**

   If the narration wasn't everything you hoped for, it's easy enough to record another take. Just hit ⌘-Z (Undo) or click the purple stripe, and then press Delete. Then repeat the process above.

   You can record as many overlapping narration takes as you like. The purple stripes just pile up and they behave exactly like the sound-effects stripes described in "Deleting Background Audio" on page 234. That is, you can:

   - **Delete a stripe** by clicking it and then pressing the Delete key.

   - **Shorten a stripe** by dragging its endpoints (or by clicking the purple stripe, and then using the Clip Trimmer as described on page 232).

   - **Move a stripe** by dragging it to a new spot, using the middle of it as the handle.

When you finish, click the Voiceover button again, or hit the letter O again, to return to normal editing.

Extracting Audio from Video

iMovie is perfectly capable of stripping the audio portion of your footage apart from the video. The recorded audio suddenly shows up as an independent audio clip. Its pushpins indicate that it's locked to whatever spot on the video you've selected. Figure 9-13 shows the process.

Figure 9-13:
Top: Highlight part of a filmstrip in your Event browser, and then drag the selection into your storyboard. When you let go, the "Drag and Drop" menu appears. Click Audio Only.

Bottom: The camcorder audio appears as an independent clip, which you can manipulate just like any other audio clip: delete it, shorten it, trim it, move it, and so on. You can create a reverb or echo effect by overlaying the same extracted audio several times.

The Audio Only command unleashes all kinds of useful new tricks that are impossible to achieve any other way:

- **Make an echo**. This is a cool one. Park the extracted audio clip a few frames to the right of the original, as shown at the bottom of Figure 9-13. Use the volume controls (page 246) to make it slightly quieter than the original. Repeat a few more times, until you've got a realistic echo or reverb sound.

Tip: If you're not picky about fine-tuning the echo effect you're going for, consider using the Echo or Cathedral audio effects, covered on page 253.

- **Reuse the sound**. You can put the extracted audio elsewhere in the movie. You've probably seen this technique used in dozens of Hollywood movies: About 15 minutes before the end of the movie, the main character, lying beaten and defeated in an alley, suddenly pieces together the solution to the central plot mystery, as snippets of dialog we've already heard in the movie float through his brain, finally adding up.

Tip: You may be tempted to extract audio to create a *cutaway*, something like you see in documentaries. An interviewee starts on camera, but historic pictures soon replace the video while the interviewee's voice forges on excitedly about the history of dirt.

But don't. Cutaways like these are much easier to make using the dedicated Cutaway feature, covered on page 103.

- **Grab some ambient sound**. In real movie-editing studios, it happens all the time: A perfect take is ruined by the sound of a passing bus during a tender kiss and you don't discover it until you're in the editing room, long after the actors and crew have moved on to other projects.

  You can eliminate the final seconds of sound from a scene by cropping or splitting the clip, of course. But that won't result in a satisfying solution, and you'll have three seconds of *silence* during the kiss. The real world isn't truly silent, even when there's no talking. The air is always filled with *ambient sound*, such as breezes, distant traffic, the hum of fluorescent lights, and so on.

  Even inside, in a perfectly still room, there's *room tone*. When you want to replace a portion of the audio track with silence, what you usually want, in fact, is to replace it with ambient sound.

  Professionals always record about 30 seconds of room tone or ambient sound just so they'll have material to use in case of an emergency. You may not need to go to that extreme; you may well be able to grab some sound from a different part of the same shot. The point is that by extracting the audio from another part of the scene (when nobody was talking), you've got yourself a useful piece of ambient-sound footage you can use to patch over unwanted portions of the originally recorded audio.

- **Add narration**. The technique described on page 240 is ideal for narration that you record at one sitting, in a quiet room. But you can add narration via camcorder, too. Just record yourself speaking, import the footage into iMovie, extract the audio, and then throw away the video. You may want to do this if you're editing on a mic-less Mac, or if you want the new narration to better match the camcorder's original sound.

It's important to note that iMovie never *removes* the audio from the original video clip. You'll never be placed into the frantic situation of wishing that you'd never done the extraction at all, unable to sync the audio and video together again (which sometimes happens in "more powerful" video-editing programs).

Instead, iMovie places a *copy* of the audio into the storyboard. The original video clip retains its original audio. As a result, you can extract audio from the same clip over and over again, if you like. iMovie simply spins out another copy of the audio each time.

Volume Adjustments

Ah, yes: volume adjustments…one of the most controversial aspects of iMovie '08 and '09. What caused the uproar was the absence of "rubber-banding" in iMovie, the little graph that represents the way a clip's volume rises and falls over its length.

Without it, there was no way to make the music get softer at a point you select. Tempers flared, people shook their heads in dismay.

You can finally put Apple back on your Christmas card list. Not only does iMovie '11 have the rubber band to control audio, but it's nicer looking and easier to use than ever before. Plus, iMovie kept all the old tools, like the ducking feature. This section covers all the different ways that you can adjust the volume in your movie.

The Rubber Band: A Re-Introduction

If "rubber-banding" makes you think of office supplies instead of volume levels, then meet a little iMovie tool that's super useful. (Audio editors call volume adjustments "rubber-banding" because the volume graph seems to stretch tight against the "start fade" and "end fade" points.)

Finding the rubber band

To see the rubber-band tool, you need to click the Show Audio Waveforms button below either your event footage or your project storyboard (Figure 9-14). It's right next to the thumbnail slider you read about on page 76.

Figure 9-14:
Behold the previously mourned rubber band, waveforms and all! To see the waveforms and to bring this handy little audio tool back from the dead, click the Show/Hide Audio Waveforms button identified here.

Rubber-band tool

Show/hide audio waveforms

As promised, a new set of horizontal tracks appear, representing the audio waveforms for everything in your project that produces sound. An identical-looking button appears under the Event Library; it opens a similar set of waveform tracks for the clips there.

As you may have read on page 231, waveforms represent the volume levels of the audio.

A single, thin line runs horizontally across your waveforms, looking as though it wants to chop off their tips (Figure 9-14). That little line is the rubber-band tool.

Using the rubber band

The height of the rubber band determines the volume of your clip. The higher the line, the louder the clip. The starting position, about a third of the way down from the top, is the standard, 100% volume. If you drag the line higher or lower, iMovie provides a little floating window to show you how much you're changing the volume (Figure 9-15).

If all you could do was change the height of the line for the entire clip, there wouldn't be much point to this whole new feature. The beauty of the tool comes in when you stretch it up or down on parts of your clips. You can, for example, soften the background music when Grandma Alice tells her (very) softly spoken story. Alternatively, you could just goose Grandma Alice (her audio, that is).

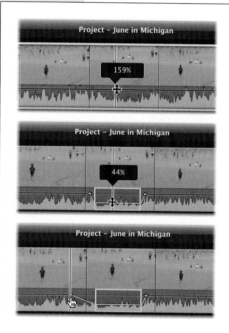

Figure 9-15:

Top: If you drag the entire rubber band up or down, you see the volume for the whole clip change, and iMovie shows you the percentage change with a floating window.

Middle: To adjust the volume for just part of a clip, drag horizontally across the waveform to select a range of audio. The yellow box shows you what you selected. Now drag the rubber-band line inside the yellow; you're changing the volume only for the selected region.

Bottom: To adjust the fade for volume changes, making them gradual or abrupt, grab the little yellow bubbles on either side of a volume change. Drag them outward for a gradual fade and in for an abrupt one.

To move just part of the rubber band, see Figure 9-15, bottom. The key is to drag horizontally first to select the region you want to affect, and then to drag the rubber-band line within the selected area. You can see the line stretch up or down as you drag it.

Note: Any whole or partial volume adjustments you make in your project are project-specific. That is, other projects using those same clips don't see (or hear) the changes. That's not true, however, for volume changes you make to clips in the Event Library. Any volume changes to Event footage affect every project that uses that footage.

The stretched parts of the rubber band show you the pattern of fading in or out for the volume. If you want to change the length of the fade, to make it gradual or abrupt, grab the little yellow bubbles on either end of the volume adjustment and drag them horizontally (Figure 9-15). Dragging them outward makes the volume change more gradually. Dragging them inward makes the volume change more suddenly, which you might do, for example, if you want the music to pop back in really loudly.

Note: You might have noticed that some of the waveform waves go above the rubber-band line, while most stay below it. That's because the rubber band just sets the base volume for your clip. Every movie still has loud parts and quiet parts, no matter where you set the volume. The high peaks in your waveforms are the loud parts.

Using the Other Volume Tools

Although the basics of the rubber band allow for all kinds of specific and intricate volume adjustments, iMovie carries a whole host of other volume setting tools, many of them holdovers from the time when there was no rubber band tool. The following discussion covers volume adjustments using these tools.

Adjusting Overall Clip Volume

You may want to make an *entire* song or clip louder or softer, raising or lowering all of its peaks and valleys simultaneously. You already read how to do that with the rubber-band tool. But you can also do it through the Inspector.

First, double-click the clip. You can edit any kind of audio: a background audio bubble, a purple narration stripe, or a green sound-effect stripe. In fact, you can even click a *video* clip, with the understanding that you're about to adjust the camcorder audio's volume.

Tip: You can edit a clip that's still in your Event browser, too, even before you place it in a project. In that case, the audio changes you're about to make will affect that video selection in *every* project from now on.

The Inspector window appears. Click the Audio button (shown in Figure 9-16), or just press the letter A once you select the clip. The Audio Adjustments dialog box appears immediately.

Warning: Whenever you adjust the volume of a video clip, a tiny, faint ◀) logo appears in the top-left corner to remind you that you fooled around with the audio. You can double-click it to open the Audio Adjustments panel, too.

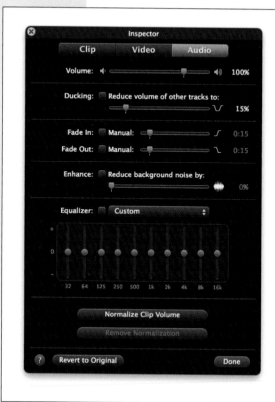

Figure 9-16:
Click the ❶ button to open the Inspector, and then select the Audio tab to make all kinds of audio adjustments.

You'll find four items of interest here:

- **Volume slider.** By dragging the Volume slider, you can adjust the overall volume of the selected clip. You can mute it entirely (drag the slider all the way to the left), or make it five times as loud (all the way to the right).

  At this point, you *can't* skim your filmstrips to hear the changes you're making. To spot-check your work, click the filmstrip corresponding to the audio change you're making. Drag the little red dot handle to position the playhead before your edit, and then press the space bar to start playback.

- **Ducking.** Apple's original response to, "Hey, you took away manual audio controls!" was, "You don't need them. We'll do your mixing *for* you!" And that's the purpose of this intriguing checkbox. When you turn it on, you're saying, "The selected audio clip is the most important audio. I want to hear it above any other audio that's going on." This checkbox, in other words, makes all other simultaneous audio clips play more softly. Using the slider, you can specify just how *much* softer they get. Even though you have the rubber band at your disposal, this checkbox still comes in handy, because it can save you multiple steps.

In the film business, lowering the music volume so you can hear spoken dialog is called *ducking*. What Apple offers here is *automatic* ducking. For example, suppose you clutter up your storyboard with so many background songs, crowd noises, and sound effects that you can no longer hear the dialogue in the original video. You can apply this option to the *video itself* (not to one of the colored audio stripes or bubbles) to bring out the original filmed dialog.

Note: You can't use this checkbox to boost the volume of background audio; it's dimmed and unavailable for background tracks. If you want to duck everything *but* the background track, you have to do it the old-fashioned way: Use the rubber band or volume sliders to lower the volume on *other* tracks, and/or to raise the volume on the background audio track.

- **Fade In, Fade Out**. Ordinarily, you hear the audio for a sound or video clip immediately. But if you click Manual, you can create a graceful audio *fade-in* or *fade-out* for the selected clip—even if it's a *video* clip from your camcorder. Use the slider to indicate how long you want that fading to take, in seconds (up to 5 seconds).

Tip: At the start and end of every clip, sitting on the top of the blue waveform strip, you'll find gray fade handles. Drag these away from the start or end of the clip to change the time it takes for the audio to fade in or out. You can make the fade last longer than 5 seconds, in fact, using this technique—you can even make it last as long as the entire clip.

- **Normalize Clip Volume**. You may not have much call for this button, but it can be handy now and then. It's designed for situations when you recorded the clips in your project at different volume levels, resulting in some jarring unevenness during playback.

  iMovie can *normalize* the clips, so that all of them have roughly the same volume. Just click the clips containing volume that's out of whack, and then click Normalize Clip Volume. (For tips on selecting multiple clips, see page 82.)

  iMovie takes a moment to compute the clip's new audio level. And then, just as a reminder that you've messed around with that clip, iMovie displays a tiny speaker icon (◀) near the beginning of it (Figure 9-17, bottom).

When you finish fiddling, click Done. The dialog box goes away, and you return to the movie.

Figure 9-17:
Top: In the iMovie scheme, the ✿ badge gives quick access to audio adjustments.

Bottom: The upper clip's audio has been made louder or softer (the badge is now permanent, and shows round sound waves). The lower clip's audio has been normalized (straight sound waves). It may sound truly abnormal, but at least its audio levels are roughly even with the rest of the movie.

Volume has been adjusted

Volume has been normalized

Multiple Clip Adjustments

Say you've got an interview with a 100-year-old man, interspersed with footage of the old town where he grew up, and his audio needs boosting *every single time* he's on camera. You may suppose that you're in for a bit of work. You'll have to click those clips, one at a time, and fix their audio. Right?

Thankfully, no. There are two ways out of this predicament.

First, you can select all the clips in your project that need a boost, and then press A to bring up the audio inspector. Once there, the audio adjustments you make will affect all the clips you selected. Click Done when you finish.

But what if you've made several audio adjustments to one of the clips, including some equalizer fine-tuning (page 256)? You don't want to have to go to each clip, one by one, and set all the sliders by hand. Fortunately, you can make the changes once, and then *copy and paste* those changes to all the other clips.

First you need to find and click a clip that has the audio just right. Choose Edit→Copy (or press ⌘-C).

At this point, you can select all the other clips you want to change (see page 82 for multi-clip selection tips), and then choose Edit→Paste Adjustments→Audio (or just press Option-⌘-A). The appearance of the little icons shown in Figure 9-17 (above) lets you know that all those other clips have now taken on the audio adjustments of the first.

Or you can plow through your storyboard, clicking and hitting Option-⌘-A, to apply the same settings to each additional clip. Either way, you can breathe a sigh of relief that at least you don't have to work through the Audio Adjustments dialog box to edit each clip.

Removing Audio Adjustments

As with all iMovie editing tools, the changes you make in the Audio Adjustments dialog box are nondestructive, meaning that you never actually changed the underlying clips. You can undo or adjust your changes at any time, even years later.

Just click the clip you edited and then double-click the clip and select the Audio tab (or press the letter A, or double-click the tiny ◀ badge), and then click "Revert to Original." The clip now has its original audio levels back. Finally, click Done.

Audio Effects, Enhancements, and Equalizers

The rubber band track in iMovie '11 was a big birthday cake to the world's disgruntled iMovie fans. But Apple, in its typical fashion, asked, "What's cake without some frosting?"

Along with what may be the best rubber-band audio implementation ever, Apple crammed all kinds of fun and useful enhancements into iMovie '11, like audio effects, audio enhancement, and an equalizer tool.

Audio Effects

iMovie's new audio effects are really cool and a ton of fun to play with. Want your dad to sound like a mouse? Piece of cake. Want your baby to sound like a robot? Easy-peasy. Want to be able to sing like T-Pain, the rapper who made autotuning famous? You get the idea.

Applying an audio effect

Applying an audio effect to a clip, song, sound effect, or voiceover is easy.

1. **Select the clip, song, sound effect, or voiceover track, then open the Inspector.**

   To open the Inspector for a selected clip, press I on the keyboard, or just double-click the clip. You can also select clips in your Event Library, but remember that audio you change in Event footage will affect every project that uses that footage.

Tip: You can't apply an audio effect to part of a clip or song. You have to split the clip or song in question first. To do so, put the playhead right where you want the effect to start or end, then right-click (or Control-click) that spot and choose Split Clip from the shortcut menu. (You might need to repeat this step if you cut out a piece from the middle of something.) Once you have the bit you need separated from the rest, proceed with the steps that follow.

2. **In the Clip pane of the Inspector, click Audio Effects.**

   Doing this reveals a skimmable grid of effects (Figure 9-18), not unlike the one for video effects (page 154). But this time, when you skim, iMovie plays a preview of the audio effect instead of a video effect. Pause for a moment to enjoy the fact that this takes zero rendering time.

Figure 9-18:
iMovie offers you a range of audio effects, from muffled to cosmic and from mannish to mousy. Note the cute little figures illustrating what each effect does.

3. **Skim through the effects, and then click the one you want.**

   Once you choose an audio effect, iMovie applies it to your entire clip or song. If it's a clip, iMovie also attaches the same little audio badge you saw in Figure 9-17 when you normalized the clip's volume.

   If you later change your mind and want the clip's audio back to normal, bring up the Inspector again. On the Audio tab, click "Revert to Normal."

The audio effects catalog

Although you've got the adorable little stick figures doing interpretive performances of each effect (Figure 9-18), you might still like a rundown of each effect and what it accomplishes:

- **Muffled.** This makes people sound like they're talking through a pillow.

- **Robot.** If you're making a throwback B-movie about robots attacking earth, this will overlay your actors' voices with a monotone, buzzing noise that sounds, well, robotic.

- **Cosmic.** Imagine taking an FM radio dial and turning it from bottom to top to bottom. The Cosmic effect makes your voice sound as though it were coming from a radio. (It also adds a monotone effect to enhance the cosmicness.)

- **Echo.** Although iMovie calls this effect Echo, it sounds a lot more like reverb, because the "echo" is fast and doesn't fade the way an echo would in a large space.

- **Telephone.** This option slightly muffles the sound to match what you'd hear over the phone. A great way to simulate a phone conversation if your actor's on the phone and you can hear the audio track of the other person on the line.

- **Shortwave Radio.** A lot like the Cosmic effect, just tamed down.

- **Multitune.** You've heard this effect before, even if you don't know it. The rest of the world calls it Autotune; it was popularized by rapper T-Pain, Autotune the News, and others. It tunes your voice (or any sound) to the nearest musical tone, rounding off the pitch to the nearest piano-key note. Autotone is applied gently to just about every pop singer's recording to fix the pitch, but turned up all the way, it creates a distinctive mechanical, clicky edginess to the singing. Normal speaking doesn't really show off this effect, but singing, or drawn-out vocal sounds, make it sound really cool. Play around with this effect just for the fun of it.

- **Small/Medium/Large Room.** These three options create the same level of echo you'd encounter in a correspondingly sized room.

- **Cathedral.** Like the Small/Medium/Large room effects, but in a *really* big room. This is a nice alternative to the Echo effect.

- **Pitch Down/Up.** These effects all lower or raise a person's voice by an amount that you can control. Here you can make your 5-year-old daughter sound like a man—or your bowling buddy sound like your 5-year-old daughter.

Enhance Audio

Other than shaky video (page 176), the surest sign of amateur video is bad audio. Most people pay so much attention to what they're filming, they tune out the sound they're recording. So without your even noticing it, your camera's microphone can pick up the hum of fluorescent lights, the drone of the clothes dryer, or even the whir of its own zoom lens. Professionals know all this, and that's why they're famous for shouting, "Quiet on the set!" They know that you can point a camera lens right where you want it, but microphones aren't so discriminating.

So if you're at the beach and just got a great little shot of your 4-year-old singing "Bob the Builder" over his sand castle, you want to hear the singing and not the wind or waves. For this sort of thing, iMovie offers you the Audio Enhance tool. It's remarkably effective. Think of it as shake correction (page 178) for audio.

To enhance your clip's audio (that is, to de-emphasize the bad parts of it), select your clip and press A on the keyboard to open the Audio tab of the Inspector (pictured in Figure 9-16, previously). Turn on Enhance, then drag its slider to reduce the background noise to an acceptable level. To spot-check your adjustment, click the clip and press the Spacebar to play it. Click Done when everything sounds good.

Note: While this tool can reduce even a roaring waterfall to a low hum, it can't entirely eliminate many background noises. In fact, if you ratchet the effect too high, it makes your clip sound like it's playing from a set of broken speakers.

The Equalizer

An equalizer is a set of sliders that lets you increase or reduce the low, medium, and high tones in a track of audio. They've been around for years, but most people don't ever use them.

That's because most people don't need them. Usually they show up only in music-playback software like iTunes. If you have decent speakers and the song was recorded professionally, there's little point to messing around with audio levels. The balancing work has been done for you.

Your camcorder's audio, on the other hand, hasn't been professionally adjusted. As a result, you might find that the bass guitar at the concert you're (legally) recording sticks out like a sore thumb. This is where the equalizer comes in handy. You can reduce the low-end sounds to make everything balance out.

Figure 9-16 shows you what the iMovie equalizer looks like. You get to it by selecting a clip and then pressing A on the keyboard. The sliders on the left control the volume for the low tones in your audio track, the ones in the middle control the mid tones, and the ones on the right control the high tones.

If you're still not sure what to do with these, try some of the preset equalizer settings. If you choose Bass Reduce, for example, the sliders on the left jump down a bit. You can preview the result by clicking on a spot then pressing the spacebar. (Make sure you turned on the Equalizer checkbox, or the adjustments won't matter.) Click Done to get back to your project.

Note: The equalizer doesn't change anything permanently. You can always undo any changes by clicking the "Revert to Original" button pictured in Figure 9-16. Just this once, you can make an omelet *without* breaking any eggs.

Editing Audio in GarageBand

What if you *really* want to dig into your movie's audio? iMovie's audio tools are great and all, but they could leave you wanting. What you need is an audio-editing program. Perhaps one like the application that comes on *the same DVD as iMovie!*

That would be a reference to GarageBand, the music composition program included with iLife. It offers all kinds of audio-specific tools not found in iMovie, the most prominent of which are the composition tools you can use to create your own movie scores.

Fortunately, you can export your movie into GarageBand to edit the soundtrack with its much more powerful tools. Don't read any further, however, until you absorb these two warnings:

- Your movie arrives in GarageBand with only a single, boiled-down audio track. You can't adjust the camcorder audio and the iMovie music independently. (That's a good argument for avoiding adding *any* music in iMovie. Wait until you're in GarageBand to add all music and sound effects.)

- The iMovie→GarageBand train goes only one way. Once you work with a movie in GarageBand, you can no longer return to iMovie for further edits. You *can* return to iMovie, edit the video, and re-export the thing, but of course then you lose all the audio work you did in GarageBand the first time.

GarageBand Basics

GarageBand is a music composition program containing dozens of powerful tools. It lets you combine multiple of audio tracks, giving you fine control over each track's sound effects, volume, and even stereo panning.

But if you're like most people, you've never even set foot in GarageBand. (Apple says that GarageBand is the second least-used iLife program, just behind iWeb.) Here's a crash course:

1. **Export your movie from iMovie.**

   Either send it to the Media browser (page 404) or save it as a QuickTime movie (page 338) in your Home→Movies folder. (GarageBand can import from either of these locations without any digging around on your part.)

2. **Open GarageBand.**

   GarageBand's icon looks like an electric guitar— ; it's in your Applications folder.

3. **Create a new project.**

   If this is your first time in GarageBand, a welcome screen greets you with a list of choices. If you *have* worked in GarageBand before, it opens the last project you worked on. Choose File→New.

In either case, select New Project from the list on the left, and then double-click the icon labeled "Movie" (Figure 9-19).

iMovie asks you to name your project and save it *before* you start editing. Then click Create.

Figure 9-19:
GarageBand appears to be designed for either the short-sighted or for those with really bad mouse-aim. Either way, double-click the icon labeled "Movie" to create a new movie project.

4. **Add your movie from the Media browser.**

   The Media browser now appears. (If it isn't showing for some reason, choose Control→Show Media Browser.) Find your movie on the Movies tab, under either the iMovie or Movies heading. Drag the movie into the GarageBand timeline, right into the movie track. (You can also drag in a movie file from the Finder.)

Note: You may have noticed that the Media browser also gives you full access to everything in your Event Library. Theoretically, you can build your whole movie right here in GarageBand. Who needs iMovie? (Well, everyone who wants titles, transitions, clip trimming…but you get the idea.)

   GarageBand creates its own thumbnails to represent your movie.

5. **Edit your movie's audio track.**

   Once GarageBand imports your movie, you'll see an audio track directly under the video track. This is the audio from your exported movie. It contains *all* your movie's audio, merged into one track. Now that it's in GarageBand, you can manipulate the audio in a multitude of ways. At the left edge of the window, under the words "Movie Sound," tiny icons let you mute, isolate, lock, and pan the audio (shift the stereo sound right or left). You can also make the volume rise and fall at particular points, as shown in Figure 9-20.

Figure 9-20:
To call up the rubber-band tool, click the button marked (A) to expand the volume graph (B). Drag any point on the graph to make the volume rise or fall. Using the pop-up menu (C), you can also plot a graph for the panning. Use the Add Automation menu item to add other sophisticated audio effects.

6. **Add audio tracks.**

Add additional tracks, if you like, by choosing Track→New Track (Option-⌘-N), or by clicking the + button on the toolbar. You might use these new tracks to create a custom score (read on). In GarageBand, you can create as many parallel audio tracks as you like, although a huge number slow your Mac to a crawl.

You can also drag songs from the Media browser right into a blank area of the GarageBand window. GarageBand automatically creates a new track and places the song in it.

Note: Copy-protected songs you bought from the iTunes Store (back when Apple sold protected music) won't work. GarageBand isn't on the guest list for protected songs (unlike iMovie, which has an all-access pass). In fact, protected songs won't even show up in the iTunes list in GarageBand.

---

7. **Export your movie.**

Once you finish the audio editing, send the movie out into the world using the commands in the Share menu. For example, you can send the movie directly to iWeb, iTunes, or iDVD.

Or, if you choose Share→"Export to Disk," you can create a standalone QuickTime movie on your hard drive. In theory, you can actually import *that* movie *back* into iMovie, although the shuttling back and forth might be getting a little ridiculous at that point.

Scoring in GarageBand

Because GarageBand is a music program, its greatest strength is its ability to help you create a custom musical score for your movie. You can actually record or compose music crafted to run in perfect harmony with your video, turning you into a regular John Williams. (Actual musical ability may vary.) GarageBand shows the movie in the timeline, frame by frame, so you know exactly where to add a cymbal crash or guitar riff.

Here's a supercondensed review of the different tools for scoring:

- **Use prerecorded loops**. Click ⬤ to see all the different categories of prerecorded *loops* (musical building blocks) you can drag directly upward into new tracks beneath your video. Once you add it, you can drag the upper-right corner of a loop to make it repeat over and over, for as long as you drag to the right. (This works well with drum parts.)

- **Record a MIDI instrument**. If you have a MIDI instrument connected to your Mac (usually a musical keyboard or synthesizer), choose Track→New Track, click Software Instrument, and then click Create. Now you can choose an instrument sound from the list that appears at the lower right, and then click the round red Record button to begin recording as you play. You can even use the Tempo control (hold your mouse down on the digits) to make the movie play back more slowly, so that you have a better chance at a perfect performance. After you finish playing, you can crank the tempo back up to its original speed.

- **Record a live instrument or voice**. GarageBand can record live sounds, like your own singing or saxophone playing. Choose Track→New Track, click Real Instrument, and then click Create. Next, choose a reverb preset from the list at the lower-right (like Female Basic or Male Rock Vocals). Click the round red Record button to begin recording.

When you finish the soundtrack, export the results using the methods described on the previous page. With enough practice, you might eventually wind up on Steven Spielberg's speed dial.

Photos

Y ou may think that iMovie's primary purpose is working with video. But the truth is, it's quite handy with still photos, too. You can bring in still images from iPhoto or your hard drive for use in slideshows. You can also turn individual frames of your movie *into* still images, for use as freeze-frames. And, if you know the secret, you can even *export* individual frames as graphics files to your hard drive, suitable for emailing or Web posting.

This chapter tells all there is to tell.

Importing Still Images

You may want to import a graphics file into iMovie for any number of reasons. For example:

- You can use a graphic, digital photo, or other still image as a backdrop for iMovie's titling feature (Chapter 8). A still image behind your text is less distracting than moving footage.

- You can use a graphics file *instead* of using the iMovie titling feature. As noted in Chapter 8, iMovie's titling feature offers a number of powerful features, but it also has a number of serious limitations. For example, you have only rudimentary control over the title's placement in the frame (see Figure 10-1).

Figure 10-1:
Preparing your "title cards" in a graphics program gives you far more typographical and design flexibility than iMovie's own titling feature. Using graphics software, for example, you can enhance your titles with drop shadows, a 3-D look, or clip art.

Preparing your own title "slides" in, say, Photoshop Elements or Photoshop gives you a lot of flexibility that the iMovie titling feature lacks. You get complete control over the type size, color, and placement, and you can also add graphic touches to your text or to the "slide" on which it appears.

- One of the most compelling uses of video is the *video photo album*: a smoothly integrated succession of photos (from your scanner or digital camera), joined by crossfades, enhanced by titles, and accompanied by music. Thanks to iMovie's ability to import photos directly—either from your iPhoto collection or your hard drive—creating this kind of video slideshow is a piece of cake.

Note: Of course, *iPhoto* can create video photo albums, too. And in iPhoto, you can opt to loop a slideshow (which iMovie doesn't offer); rearranging and regrouping your photos is much easier than in iMovie, too.

But building them in a movie has several advantages. First of all, your audio options are much greater; you can record narration as you watch the slideshow, for example. You have a full arsenal of tools for creating titles, credits, and special effects, too.

As your life with iMovie proceeds, you may encounter other uses for its picture-importing feature. Maybe, when editing a home movie of your kids tussling in the living room, you decide it would be hilarious to insert some *Batman*-style fight-sound title cards ("BAM!") into the footage. Maybe you need an establishing shot of, say, a storefront or apartment building, and realize that you could save production money by inserting a still photo that passes for live video in which there's nothing moving. And maybe you want to end your movie with a fade-out—not to black, but to maroon (an effect described later in this chapter).

You have a delicious choice of two methods for bringing still photos into a project. The first and most convenient is to choose the photo from among those you've organized in iPhoto, using iMovie's window into your picture collection. If you're not using iPhoto to organize your digital photos, you can use the older method of importing pictures directly from your hard drive.

The Photo Browser

The more you work with iMovie and iDVD, the more you appreciate the way Apple has linked them to the other i-programs, like iTunes and iPhoto. Here's a classic case:

When you open the Photos browser (Figure 10-2), or choose Window→Photos, or press ⌘-2, you see what amounts to iPhoto Lite: a scrolling panel of thumbnail images reflecting the contents of your iPhoto Library. Using the navigation panel just above the thumbnails, you can browse your photos by event, album, folder, or according to the other iPhoto presets (like flagged photos or photos added in your last import). You can filter your photos based on Faces or Places you identified in iPhoto. You can also view your MobileMe, Facebook, and Flickr albums. If you use Aperture, Apple's pro photo-organization program, its library shows up here, too. Even the photos you take with Photo Booth, Apple's little iSight camera application, make the cut.

iPhoto albums, events, and groups   Photos browser

Figure 10-2:
The Photos browser shows all the pictures you imported into iPhoto (or Aperture, if you have it). Use the navigation menu to limit the photos display to those in a certain album or folder. (The white lettering at the lower right tells you how many events or photos you're currently viewing.) Note the Search box. As you type into it, iMovie smoothly hides all photos except those whose names or keywords contain matching text. It's an amazingly quick way to pinpoint one photo out of several thousand. To clear the search box and return to viewing all photos, click the ⊗ at the right end of the box.

Thumbnail size

Tip: Events in iPhoto are a lot like Events in iMovie. That is, iPhoto groups all the photos taken on the same day into an Event.

Albums are the category containers that you can create in iPhoto by choosing File→New Album (or by clicking the + button in the lower-left corner). You can drag a single picture into as many of these albums as you like. Folders are simply structures that let you group albums. Complete details are in *iPhoto '11: The Missing Manual.*

Here are more handy Photos browser tips:

- iMovie starts out showing you rows of photo thumbnails. You can control their size by dragging the slider below the browser.

- iMovie offers an alternative—and very useful—way to view your photos. Control-click (or right-click) anywhere in the Photos browser. From the shortcut menu, choose "Display as List." iMovie changes the Photos browser's display into columns, as shown in Figure 10-3. (This tip doesn't work when you view your photos as Events.)

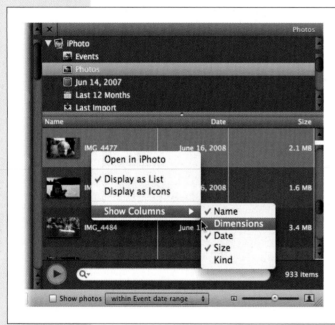

Figure 10-3:
The List view shows each photo, the day it was taken, and its size. An additional right-click lets you add even more columns that show the photo dimensions and file type. To return to icon view, right-click (Control-click) again and choose "Display as Icons."

- When you click a photo to select it, iMovie displays the photo in your preview window, giving you a chance to review it.

- If you want to edit a photo before adding it to your movie, you don't have to fire up iPhoto manually. Just Control-click (or right-click) the photo, and from the shortcut menu, choose "Open in iPhoto" (Figure 10-3). iPhoto opens and takes you directly to the photo you clicked. Once you make the necessary changes, iMovie returns and uses the updated version of your photo.

- In addition to the preview window, you can double-click a thumbnail to make the photo fill the *entire* Photos browser for a much closer look. Then press the left and right arrow keys to walk through the adjacent photos at this larger size. Click a photo once to return to the thumbnails.

- If you want to save space in your Photos browser, use your mouse to grab the line separating your photos and the list of albums, and drag that line up until iMovie replaces your list of albums with a handy menu.

Photos from the Finder

If you haven't added the image you need to your iPhoto library, you can still add it to your movie project. All you have to do is locate it in the Finder and drag it into your project window.

Tip: iMovie can import graphics in any format that QuickTime can understand, which includes PICT, JPEG, GIF, PNG, Photoshop files, and even PDF files (for when an IRS form is exactly what you want to illustrate in your movie). Avoid the GIF format for photos, which limits the number of colors available to the image; otherwise, just about any format is good still-image material.

POWER USERS' CLINIC

Match Event Dates

It doesn't take long to get a full iPhoto library. A few soccer games, a couple of birthdays, a trip to Disney, and suddenly you feel like you're storing the Library of Congress on your computer. And then you have to scroll through thousands of pictures, represented as tiny icons, in iMovie.

You can drill down through iMovie Events to find the photos you want, or you can show some discipline and put those photos into albums. But you don't want to, so what now?

iMovie '11 kicks in this little freebie: You can tell it to match photos from iPhoto with the Event you're currently browsing in iMovie. This little stroke of genius makes a lot of sense, since both programs rely on the Event dates of your stuff (and since you probably took both stills and videos during that same big day).

To turn on Event date matching, turn on the tiny Show Photos checkbox below your Photos browser. Using the tiny menu to the right of it, you can limit the photos you see to those shot the same day as your iMovie Event, or those shot within a day, week, or a month of your footage.

This is a great trick, mainly because a lot of special events involve footage *and* photos. This feature makes finding the right photos a piece of cake.

Once you add a photo to iMovie, you don't have to keep track of the original. Behind the scenes. iMovie actually creates a movie version of all the images you import. Even if you delete a photo file from iPhoto or the Finder, iMovie can still use the image in your project. (Just don't try this with video clips or music files, as iMovie treats them very differently!)

iMovie Backgrounds

Generations of iMovie fans have dressed up their opening credits and chapter titles by creating custom backgrounds, so that text appears in front of red curtains or a Hollywood opening-night spotlight instead of plain black. To save you that hassle, iMovie now comes with a handsome set of premade background images (Figure 10-4). Some are even animated; for example, the Underwater background shows shimmering rays of sunlight filtering through the water.

Figure 10-4:
Behold the reason this is called the "Map, Background, and Animatic" browser. If you count the maps, that's 24 high-quality image backgrounds you can use to jazz up your project.

Tip: You can use these images and animations as backgrounds for your green screen work, too (page 159). That is, instead of revealing your newscaster skit to have been shot in your pathetic basement, you can insert one of these much more handsome backgrounds.

Even though these backgrounds are basically image files, there are a few key differences:

- **iMovie knows these are backgrounds**. If you double-click one after you place it in your project, the Inspector appears, identifying it as such.

Tip: In the Inspector, you can also click the Background button to get a skimmable palette of all the backgrounds. That's how you can swap one background image for another without having to re-place it in your project.

- **Backgrounds go between clips only**. This means you can't use backgrounds for cutaways, discussed on page 103.
- **Backgrounds are immune to video effects**. You can't adjust their colors or apply video filters. (But you *can* crop or rotate backgrounds. You can even animate them with a Ken Burns effect.)

To use a background, drag it out of the "Maps and Backgrounds" browser and into any empty area of your project (for example, between two clips, or following your clips). It appears as a 4-second clip; double-click it to change its duration or style.

Two Ways to Add Photos

Adding photos to your project is a lot like adding music, in that there are two ways to go about it. If you use photos from your iPhoto library or the Finder, you add them the same way you add titles, as described in Chapter 8. That is, there are two places to drag photos: between clips, or onto them. The results are quite different.

Photo Filmstrips

If you drag a photo *between* two filmstrips in your storyboard, you create a new *photo filmstrip* (Figure 10-5, top).

POWER USERS' CLINIC

Add Folders to the Photos Browser

Not everyone uses iPhoto. There are plenty of other good programs for organizing pictures. Many people just store photos in folders in the Finder, and don't use any fancy photo-shoebox program at all.

Fortunately, you can still access them from within iMovie. You can add a folder—any folder—to your Photos browser.

To do this, switch into the Finder. Find the folder that you want to add to your Photos browser. Drag it directly into the list in the browser (where it now says "iPhoto").

Now you have an additional item in your list called Folders. Click its flippy triangle to see what's in it—the folder you just dragged. You can add as many more photo folders as you like.

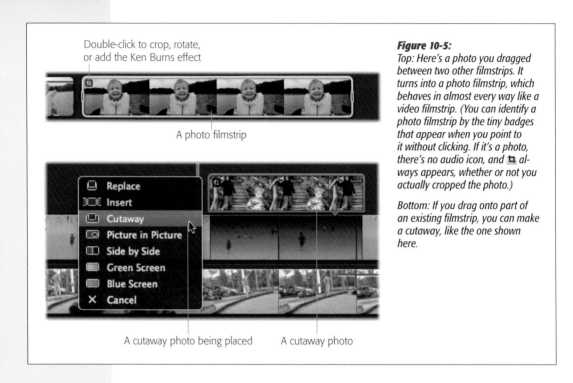

Double-click to crop, rotate, or add the Ken Burns effect

A photo filmstrip

Replace
Insert
Cutaway
Picture in Picture
Side by Side
Green Screen
Blue Screen
✕ Cancel

A cutaway photo being placed   A cutaway photo

Figure 10-5:
Top: Here's a photo you dragged between two other filmstrips. It turns into a photo filmstrip, which behaves in almost every way like a video filmstrip. (You can identify a photo filmstrip by the tiny badges that appear when you point to it without clicking. If it's a photo, there's no audio icon, and ⧉ always appears, whether or not you actually cropped the photo.)

Bottom: If you drag onto part of an existing filmstrip, you can make a cutaway, like the one shown here.

Tip: You can add more than one photo at a time this way—a handy trick if you're creating a slideshow. Select multiple photos in the iPhoto browser just as you'd select multiple icons in the Finder. For example, you can click the first one, then Shift-click the last to select a group, or ⌘-click individual thumbnails. You can even just drag an entire album or event from the album list.

In most regards, the photo now behaves exactly like a video filmstrip. You can crop it, rotate it, and make color adjustments to it, for example, exactly as described in Chapter 7. You can apply the snazzier video effects described in Chapter 6. You can superimpose titles and credits on it, just as described in Chapter 8. You can even use the Split or Trim commands on a photo.

Key differences: You can't adjust a photo's timing by dragging the clip ends or by using the Fine Tuning controls (page 93). Instead, you have to use the Inspector, described on page 271. You also can't make any audio adjustments because, well, you can't adjust what ain't there.

Photo Cutaways

Alternatively, you can drag a photo *on top of* a video clip (or photo filmstrip). At that point, the "Drag and Drop" menu appears (Figure 10-5).

If you aren't inserting the photo or replacing something else with it, the most common and useful command in this menu is Cutaway. This is the documentary style effect discussed on page 103. When you use a photo as a cutaway, iMovie sticks it right on top of the underlying clip in the timeline. (It even casts a shadow on the clip below it.)

Note: Photo cutaways get close to full iMovie citizenship. You can crop, rotate, and apply effects to adjust colors of all photo cutaways. What you *can't* do is adjust audio or crop/trim a photo. Those two actions don't fit the concept of a photo cutaway.

Of course, it also covers up the video in the movie itself. So if the photo blocks the video, what good is it? Why not just create a photo filmstrip?

Actually, a photo cutaway has four advantages over a photo filmstrip:

- **Cutaways are much easier to adjust**. You can slide a cutaway left or right, earlier or later in the movie, with the touch of the mouse. And you can shorten or lengthen it by just dragging its ends. (Oddly, this last trick works only when the clip is *not* selected.)

- **You can make cutaways transparent**. Because iMovie lets you adjust the transparency of a photo cutaway, you can dial it back, turning the photo into a translucent layer. You might take a photo of clouds, dial back the opacity, and—bam!—you have fog covering the clip underneath. To adjust the transparency of a photo you place in your project, double-click the photo to open the Inspector, and then drag the Opacity slider (Figure 10-6).

Figure 10-6:
By dialing back the opacity of a photo cutaway, you can add cool effects, like the fog covering this clip. (Compare the top and bottom images.) The effect was created with a cutaway picture of clouds, set at half transparency. You can use this trick for your "Scooby Doo and the Haunted Forest" remake.

- **Cutaways are incredibly useful**. You've seen it a million times on TV. Someone starts talking; as the narration continues, the camera *cuts away* to a photo or another video clip; and then we return to the original person speaking.

  It's actually pretty remarkable how easy iMovie makes this. Instead of having to extract audio from your video clip and then create a still clip to plug in the middle, you just drop a photo over the video and choose Cutaway. The result is a cutaway (with a cross dissolve, if you like) that looks like it took a lot more work than it actually did.

- **You can poke holes in it**. This tip is for Photoshop (or Photoshop Elements) mavens, but it's wicked cool. It lets you create see-through *pieces* of a photo—and the video behind it plays through the holes. (It's not the same as the whole-photo transparency setting described above.) The steps for creating this fantastic effect appear in Figure 10-7.

Figure 10-7:
This effect pops up often in opening credits for TV shows (at least ones from the 1970s) and the occasionally cheesy movie. Make a graphic in Photoshop that contains cutouts. Select the pieces that you don't want to be transparent; ⌘-click the "Save selection as channel" button on the Channels palette, and save the result as a PNG graphic with an alpha channel. Drag the resulting file right off the desktop onto any filmstrip in iMovie. (Page 268 shows the effect.) Once it becomes a photo cutaway in iMovie, the underlying video plays through the holes!

This trick opens up a host of effects that iMovie can't do with its built-in tools. You could make a black image with two holes. They'll show up in iMovie as though you're peering through a pair of binoculars. (A great way to pump up your 10-year-old's spy movie!)

Use this trick to put a pair of nose glasses or a funny hat on someone. Or create text titles, like *Batman*-style "BAM!"s and "KAPOW!"s superimposed on your footage. As long as you use the PNG image format (which recognizes transparency), then a little creativity can lead to all kinds of cool effects. (iMovie '11 does *not* support transparency in TIFF files.)

Timing Changes

The way you change the duration and position of a photo depends on what kind it is.

Photo filmstrips

A still image doesn't naturally have a *duration*, as a movie clip might. (Asking "How many seconds long is a photograph?" is like asking, "What is the sound of one hand clapping?")

Still, it's working like a clip, so iMovie has to assign it *some* duration. iMovie turns every filmstrip photo into a 4-second clip. If you prefer a different default timing, choose File→Project Properties (⌘-J) and then adjust the Photo Duration slider. You can change the default timing to as little as 1 second or as long as 10 seconds.

Actually, there are *three* ways to adjust filmstrip photos' durations:

- **Change all photo durations at once**. If, in the Project Properties dialog box, you select "Applies to all photos," then the Duration slider affects all photos simultaneously.

- **Change photo durations from here on**. The weird little option labeled "Applies when added to project" actually means "Whatever duration you choose on the Duration slider applies to the *next* photo you drop into the storyboard—and all future ones." It preserves the durations of all *existing* photos in your project, but changes the standard timing for all *incoming* photos.

- **Change individual photo durations**. You can also change photo durations on a one-at-a-time basis. Double-click the photo and the Inspector appears.

Warning: When you use the Inspector to change photo durations, pay very close attention to the checkbox that says "Applies to all stills." When you turn on that box, *all* photos in your project will get the duration you type in. The last thing you want is to reset a bunch of custom timings you painstakingly entered for each photo. (Hint: If you accidentally did this, Edit→Undo [⌘[-Z] is your friend.)

In the Duration text box, type in the number of seconds you want for the photo. You can make your photo appear on the screen for as little as a quarter of a second (a favorite of subliminal advertisers) or as long as 10 minutes (a favorite of all other advertisers).

Note: When you get right down to it, 10 minutes is just way too long for looking at one particular photo, no matter how good it is. Still, if for some bizarre reason you need it to last longer–perhaps because you're using it as a background for a long series of titles–you can always overcome the 10-minute limit by placing the same photo into your project over and over again, side by side.

Photo Cutaways

As noted earlier, changing the duration of a superimposed photo cutaway is much easier. Just drag the ends of the cutaway clip to make it longer or shorter. (You can even span more than one filmstrip.)

Tip: You've probably noticed that cutaway photos cut in and out at a set speed, that is, without a quick fade. If you prefer a cutaway to fade in slowly (or pop in dramatically), double-click it to open the Inspector.

Next to the Cutaway Fade label, turn on Manual and drag the slider to change the fade's duration (shown in the Inspector in Figure 10-6). (You can also just type the timing into the text box next to the fade slider. In fact, you can have it last ridiculously long, but never longer than your photo's actual duration.)

The Dimensions of an iMovie Photo

If you're designing a custom image for your movie, you generally want it to have the same dimensions as your video. Otherwise, iMovie crops the photo or inserts black bars to make it fit.

iMovie offers two aspect ratios for your videos: Standard (4:3) and Widescreen (16:9). (See page 62 for a complete discussion.) For now, here's how big to make your photos so that they fit these movie frames:

- **Standard 4:3**. Make your image 640 pixels wide and 480 pixels tall. Be aware that the outer edges may get chopped off on standard-definition TVs, as explained in "The title-safe area" on page 376.

- **Widescreen 16:9**. Your imported photo should be at least 960 pixels wide and 540 pixels tall. (True high definition is more than that—1920 pixels wide and 1080 pixels tall—but Apple doesn't think you'll see much difference. Still, feel free to make your photo that big if you want the higher quality in your project.)

If you have an image that wasn't born with the right dimensions, don't worry. The powerful Crop tool and the Ken Burns effect can help you compensate.

Crop, Fit, Rotate

One of iMovie's greatest virtues is its resolution agnosticism. You can combine widescreen footage from your new HD camcorder with standard-def footage from your old DV camera in the same movie; iMovie gracefully handles their different dimensions.

This adaptability extends to photos. Chapter 7 contains a detailed discussion of cropping *video* to fit the frame (or to draw emphasis to a certain part of the picture) by adding letterbox bars and even rotating it.

Well, surprise, surprise: iMovie makes *exactly* the same features available for photo filmstrips. See the write-ups beginning on page 191 for the full discussion.

Tip: You can crop, fit, and rotate both photo *filmstrips* and photo *cutaways*. The process is exactly the same.

The Ken Burns Effect

The only problem with using still photos in a movie is that they're *still*. They just sit there without motion or sound, wasting much of the dynamic potential of video.

For years, professionals have addressed the problem using special sliding camera rigs that produce gradual zooming, panning, or both, to bring photographs to life.

But this smooth motion isn't just about adding animation to photos for its own sake. It also lets you draw the viewer's attention where you want it, *when* you want it. For example: "Little Harry graduated from junior high school in 1963"—slow pan to someone else in the school photo, a little girl with a ribbon in her hair—"little suspecting that the woman who would one day become his tormentor was standing only a few feet away."

Among the most famous practitioners of this art is Ken Burns, the creator of PBS documentaries like *The Civil War* and *Baseball*, which is why Apple named the feature after him.

Tip: In iMovie '11, you can also apply the Ken Burns effect to video. You can create very smooth pans and zooms in footage where the camera didn't actually move an inch. Powerful feature! (Familiarize yourself with the Ken Burns tools, then see page 195 for more info.)

UP TO SPEED

Avoiding Pixelated Images

You may have tried adding an image to iMovie and found that it looked pretty rotten. Blurry, pixelated, or jagged images are ugly and quite jarring when they appear in a movie surrounded by pristine video footage.

Sloppy-looking images like these usually result from using a photo file whose resolution is too low to begin with. For example, you might have taken a hilarious little shot with your cameraphone—emphasis on little. Images downloaded from the Web often have very low resolution, too.

iMovie, thinking it's doing you a favor, stretches that photo larger than its original size to make it fit the movie frame, and ugly-looking coarseness results.

If you absolutely must use a small image, consider framing your picture inside a larger image of the proper dimensions. iMovie shows the small picture with the frame surrounding it, preventing the jagged, blurry resizing you'd otherwise see.

Applying the Ken Burns Effect

iMovie '11's Ken Burns controls are totally different from what was in the iMovie of yore. Here's how you use them:

1. **Click a photo filmstrip or cutaway.**

   A yellow border appears.

2. **Press the letter C key, or click ⬚ on the toolbar, or click the tiny Crop badge that appears when you've already cropped a photo.**

   All three of these techniques open up the Crop/Fit/Rotate/Ken Burns window in the upper-right corner of the iMovie window.

3. **Click the Ken Burns button.**

   Now you see the outlines of two rectangles over your photo, one green and one red. They represent the framing of your photo during its short moment in the sun: the way it will first appear (the green box), and the way it will conclude (red). Basically, you're setting up the start frame and the end frame. iMovie automatically produces the animation required to smoothly pan and/or zoom between them.

4. **Set up the photo's starting point.**

   That is, select the green box by clicking it. Drag its corners to resize the box and drag in the middle to move it.

Tip: Getting your hands on those boxes isn't always easy, since they're hugging the outer edges of the Viewer. Here's a tip: Try clicking the *word* Start or End. Then drag inside the frame, anywhere, to pull the box boundaries into view. Now you can drag the corners to make the box smaller.

You're setting up the green box so it frames the photo as you want it to *start out*—the part that your viewers will see first. For example, if you want to zoom in on the photo, make the green box big. (Drag its corners to resize it.) If you want to pull back from the photo, make the green box small. See Figure 10-8.

Note: In previous versions of iMovie, you could adjust your start or end points so that the picture slid into or out of the frame. Unfortunately, you can't do that in iMovie '11; a photo *must* begin and end in the frame.

---

5. **Adjust your end point (the red box).**

   Click the red box, or the word End, to select it. Move and resize it just as you did with the green box.

   If you want your shot to move but not to zoom, make sure the red box is the same size as the green one. Line them up, match their sizes, and then move each where you want it. With the start and end points the same size, iMovie simply pans from one perspective to the other.

Drag corners to resize

Figure 10-8:
Top: In this somewhat confusing display, you adjust the green box and then the red one, to show iMovie how you want to pan and zoom across the photo. A yellow arrow shows the current direction of iMovie's pan, from the green box to the red one, to help you visualize the motion of the shot.

Bottom: This three-frame sample shows a representation of the pan and zoom that the settings above will produce.

Click Start/End to edit start/stop points   Click to swap start/stop frames

6. **Preview your effect and make adjustments.**

   Click the |▶| button to preview your Ken Burns effect. If you don't like what you see, adjust your green and red boxes accordingly.

   If you decide that you want to *reverse* what you've set up—you want to zoom out instead of in, or pan left instead of right—click the very tiny Swap button identified in Figure 10-8. That turns your green box into the red one, and vice versa.

7. **Click Done.**

   You can always adjust the Ken Burns effect by selecting the photo filmstrip and pressing the letter C again.

Note: If you drag a group of photos into your project all at once, iMovie creates automatic, *varied* Ken Burns effects, subtly panning and zooming in different directions for each one. Add a sweet little crossfade to all of them simultaneously (page 136), and you've got a gorgeous slideshow. (If you're a killjoy, you can always turn off the automatic Ken Burns feature. Choose File→Project Properties and use the Initial Photo Placement pop-up menu.)

Creating Still Images from Footage

iMovie doesn't just accept still photos; it also *creates* them for its own purposes. To do this, iMovie can pluck a frame out of any footage, whether it's in the storyboard or the Event browser.

And why would you want to create a still from your video? Let us count some ways:

- **Create cool titles.** One of the best reasons to get to know iMovie's still-image feature is to supplement iMovie's built-in titling feature. Using still images as titles gives you the freedom to use any colors, type sizes, and positions you want.

  Since you know about Ken Burns, you can even animate still images now that you know about alpha channels (Figure 10-7), and even make video play behind them (if they're cutaways).

- **The freeze-frame effect.** One of the most obvious uses of a still frame is the *freeze-frame* effect, in which the movie holds on the final frame of a shot. It's a terrifically effective way to end a movie, particularly if the final shot depicts the shy, unpopular hero in a moment of triumph, arms in the air, hoisted onto the shoulders of the crowd. (Fade to black; bring up the music; roll credits.)

Tip: If you like the look of the automatically created One-Step Effect called "Flash and Hold Last Frame" (page 172), then don't bother doing the work on your own. Let iMovie '11 do it for you!

POWER USERS' CLINIC

The Fade-to-Black (or Fade-to-Puce) Secret

As noted in Chapter 5, it's easy to create a professional-looking fade-out at the end of your movie. But unlike professional movies, which fade to black and then hold for a moment, iMovie fades to black at the end of the movie and then stops playing, sending your viewers back to iMovie, your desktop, the football game, or whatever was on the computer or TV screen before you played the movie.

The solution is very simple, and well worth making a part of your regular iMovie repertoire. Here's the drill:

- Insert a black background just after the final fade-out (page 266 has the instructions).

- Use the Cross Dissolve transition so that iMovie fades smoothly from the final footage of the clip into your black frame—and holds.

- Use the Inspector to make your black frame last as long as you desire.

Don't be content with fading to black. In fact, you can cross-dissolve to whatever color you want—white, blue, gray, anything. Instead of adding a black background, insert any other iMovie background or use a solid-colored image of your own creation.

- **Credits sequences**. If you were a fan of 1970s action shows like *Emergency!*, you may remember how the opening credits looked. You'd be watching one of the starring characters frantically at work in some lifesaving situation. As she looked up from her work, just for a moment, the picture would freeze, catching her by lucky happenstance at her most flattering angle. At that instant, you'd see her credit flashed onto the screen: "JULIE LONDON as Dixie McCall, RN."

  That's an easy one to simulate. Just create a freeze-frame as described in the next section, and then add a superimposed title image.

- **The layered effect**. In many cases, the most creative use of still-image titles comes from using *several* of them, each building on the last. For example, you can make the main title appear, hold for a moment, and then transition into a second still graphic on which a subtitle appears.

  If you have more time on your hands, you can use this trick to create simple animations. Suppose you were to create 10 different title cards, all superimposed on the same background, but each with the words in a different size or position. If you were to place each title card on the screen for only half a second (15 frames), joined by very fast crossfades, you'd create a striking visual effect. Similarly, you might consider making the *color* of the lettering shift over time. To do that, create two or three different title cards, each with the text in a different color. Insert them into your movie, join them with slow crossfades, and you've got a striking, color-shifting title sequence.

Creating a Still Frame

Here's how you go about extracting a still frame from your video.

1. **Position the playhead on the frame you want frozen.**

   You can choose from any filmstrip in the Event browser.

2. **Right-click (or Control-click) the filmstrip at the spot from which you want to extract the still. From the shortcut menu, choose "Add Still Frame to Project." (See Figure 10-9.)**

   This command directs iMovie to place a new photo clip at the end of the storyboard.

3. **Drag the still clip into the right place in your storyboard.**

   iMovie sticks the still frame at the end of your project. Drag it to the right spot, if the end isn't where you want it.

4. **Adjust the still's duration, cropping, color, and so on.**

   Your still frame behaves like any other photo. You can use the Ken Burns effect, for example, to zoom in on a meaningful part of the shot. (Ever seen a suspense movie, where the director zooms in on the once-vanquished villain watching the hero from the middle of a crowd? Works every time.)

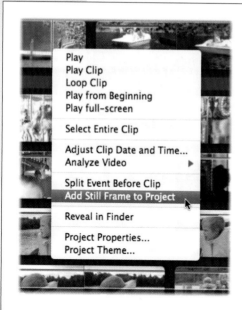

Figure 10-9:
"Add Still Frame to Project" is one of the very few iMovie commands that's available only in the shortcut menu—not in any of the main menus. Note that if you generate a still image from a filmstrip in your Event browser, iMovie applies a subtle Ken Burns effect to it. If you captured the still from your storyboard, however, iMovie assumes that you wanted a freeze-frame effect. It keeps the still image still (unanimated).

Creating a Freeze Frame

A freeze frame is basically a still frame, but one that gets automatically inserted into the spot from which you took it. Confused? Why would you put a photo in the exact place you were taking it from?

Well, just imagine that moment when Baby Tommy *finally* smiles into the camera. You could freeze on that spot for a second or two, and then have your video keep going. The smile has 10 times the impact if you can dwell on it just a little.

To make a freeze frame, follow the steps described above for creating a still frame—but use a *project* clip as the source material rather than an Event clip. (The shortcut menu command, in this case, says "Add Freeze Frame.") iMovie inserts your photo on the spot, rather than shoving it in at the end.

Note: The inserted photo splits the clip surrounding it. If you delete the photo, your clip remains split in two. If you don't like the effect of the freeze-frame, choose Edit→Undo (⌘-Z) to keep your clip together.

Once you have the freeze frame in place, you can apply color adjustments, crop it, changes its duration, and so on.

Tip: If you want to create a still from the first or last frame of a clip, point to a spot near that end of the filmstrip, and then hit the left or right arrow key. The playhead jumps to the first or last frame of the clip.

Figuring out how to handle the *audio* in such situations is up to you, since a still frame has no sound. That's a good argument for starting your closing-credits music *during* the final clip, and making it build to a crescendo for the final freeze-frame.

Exporting a Still Frame

The still-frame feature is primarily designed for adding still shots of your footage within iMovie. But you may sometimes find it useful to export a frame to your hard drive as a graphics file—for emailing to friends, installing on your desktop as a background picture, posting on a web page, and so on. An exported frame also makes a neat piece of "album art" that you can print out and slip into the plastic case of a homemade DVD.

The Resolution Problem

It's worth noting, however, that the maximum *resolution* for a standard-definition digital video frame—the number of dots that compose the image—is 640 across and 480 down. As digital photos go, that's pretty pathetic, on a par with the photos taken by some cameraphones. One-third of a megapixel is a pretty puny number compared with the shots from today's 5-, 8-, and 10-megapixel cameras. High-def video produces better stills, but it's nothing like what you'd get from a digital camera.

The low resolution of the video frame is only half the reason your captured pictures look so bad. Most camcorders capture images the same way television displays images: as hundreds of fine horizontal stripes, or *scan lines*. You don't actually see all of the scan lines at any one instant; you see odd-numbered lines in one frame, and even-numbered lines in the next. Because the frames flash by your eyes so quickly, your brain smoothes the lines together so that you perceive one continuous image.

This system of *interlacing* may work fine for moving images, but it presents an unpleasant problem when you capture just one frame of video. Capturing a still image from this footage gives you, in essence, only half of the scan lines that compose the image. QuickTime does what it can to fill in the missing information, but as shown in Figure 10-10, the horizontal scan lines still cause jaggedness.

Figure 10-10:
Digital still frames you export from your DV footage suffer from two disadvantages. First, the resolution is comparatively low. Second, the horizontal scan lines of the original video may sometimes create subtle stair-stepped, jagged edges in the still.

Note: If you're not sure if your HD camera records interlaced video, then look for an "i" in the recording settings on your camera. For example, "1080i" footage is interlaced.

Now that your expectations have been duly lowered, here's how you export a frame in iMovie. There's really only one, long way to do it, but it offers you lots of control.

The Long Way

Although there's no short way to export a still frame, the long way offers just about every option you could want (except for a *fast* option).

1. **Create a new project.**

   You'll be exporting to QuickTime for this task, and iMovie can export only an *entire project* at a time. So you have to isolate the frame you want in a new, separate project.

Tip: Rather than create another project every time you want to export a frame, consider creating a single project called Image Export. Use this project every time you want to export a still frame.

2. **Add the video frames you want to export.**

   Here's where you get to practice your frame-accurate editing skills. In the Event browser, select only the frame—yes, you can select a single frame—that you want to export as a still image. (See page 83 for details.) Actually, you can select a *several*-frame stretch of footage; you'll wind up with each frame as a separate graphic.

   Add the selection to your new project by dragging it there or hitting the E key on your keyboard.

3. **Choose Share→Export Using QuickTime.**

   The QuickTime export window appears, letting you adjust the myriad settings that come with a QuickTime export (Chapter 15).

   As iMovie creates your pile of stills, it uses as its naming scheme whatever you type into the Save As box (Movie Frame 1, Movie Frame 2, and so on).

4. **From the Export pop-up menu, choose "Movie to Image Sequence."**

   This setting tells iMovie to save a separate image for every frame. You might want to save these in a special folder. If you're exporting a lot of frames, they'll clutter your desktop pretty quickly.

5. **Click Options. In the next dialog box, click Settings.**

   You now arrive at the mighty Export Image Sequence Settings box (Figure 10-11).

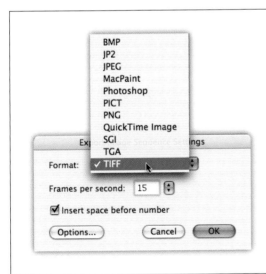

Figure 10-11:
Use this handy dialog box to specify the still-image format you want, and how many frames you want per second.

6. **From the Format pop-up menu, choose the graphics format you want for the exported frames.**

    All the usual suspects are here: JPEG (great for web posting and email), TIFF (higher quality, larger files, better for printing), and so on.

    Also choose how *many* stills you want iMovie to pull from each second of video. For the greatest freedom in choosing just the right expression, you'll want to extract *every single frame* of the video. In that case, type *29.97* (to match standard North American video), *30* (for high-def video), or *25* (European video).

7. **Click OK, and then click Save.**

    Head over to your destination folder, where you'll find all the images you exported, named and ready for use in other applications.

Tip: If you plunked down the $30 for QuickTime Player Pro (Chapter 15), you can export a still with much greater efficiency. Find the source footage in the Finder. (Right-click or Control-click a clip and from the shortcut menu, choose "Reveal in Finder.")

Double-click it to open it in QuickTime Player Pro. Set the playhead on the frame of video you want, and choose File→Export. The resulting dialog box looks much the same as in the exercise above, but the Export pop-up menu offers a "Movie to Picture" option. You'll wind up exporting only the one frame you wanted.

Movie Trailers

From iMovie's beginning, its *raison d'etre* has been to take your otherwise boring home videos and make them shine with excitement and professionalism. Features like themes, titles, transitions, video effects, editing to a beat, and the Ken Burns effect give your movies a sleek veneer with very little effort on your part; if you attempted the same tasks manually in high-end editing software, it would take a lot more time and effort.

iMovie's new movie-trailers feature is another gigantic leap forward in letting you create awesome videos with just a little extra work. In fact, iMovie's trailers capability represents a merger of all the things that iMovie has done well for a long time: It combines titles, music, transitions, and artwork to give you a professional-looking trailer made from all your own footage. And iMovie does all the hard work for you!

What exactly is a movie trailer? It's simply a preview, like the "Coming Attractions" commercial you see before a feature film, or the ad on TV that touts "Transformers 5: Hybrids Gone Mad." In about 2 minutes, a trailer tells you enough about the movie so that you want to watch the whole thing. Trailers have become a form of entertainment all their own. For almost a decade, Apple, Yahoo, and other Internet bigwigs have dedicated entire websites to trailers for upcoming movies. Major studios even shoot footage just for a movie's trailer. Pretty much every Pixar trailer, for example, contains funny, entertaining scenes not found in the movie itself.

iMovie's trailers are one- or two-minute long videos that look exactly like Hollywood movie previews, complete with swelling, majestic music; animated, flying title credits; and fast intercuts of scenes from the actual movie—only this time, they're your footage from your life. The results can be absolutely hilarious, because your viewers will recognize the format instantly—or actually tantalizing. If anything can make your casual acquaintances want to see your home movies, this is it.

Note: Apple put a ton of work into making these trailers look and sound great. The background music scores, for example, were custom-composed for this feature and recorded by the London Symphony Orchestra. Not bad for a home movie.

Trailers Basics

Trailers aren't your typical iMovie project. With a typical video project, you start with a clean slate, and your movie is what you make of it—literally. Trailers, on the other hand, are highly structured. You don't have much control over basic things like shot length, title styles, or other elements you usually dictate.

Once you start playing with iMovie's trailers feature, you'll quickly realize that you have rules to follow. For that reason, it's good to get to know the basic trailer elements.

Starting a Trailer Project

To start a trailer project, choose File→New Project (⌘-N) or click the + button in the bottom-right corner of your project list. You've seen this New Project window before, back on page 58. Here, though, you want to choose one of the trailer projects on the left. Scroll down to see all of them (Figure 11-1).

Figure 11-1:
To make a new trailer, click File→New Project (⌘-N) and choose one of the trailer projects you find on the left. If you click one of them, iMovie shows you a full preview in the window on the right so you know what you're getting before you go through the trouble of clicking Create.

You can read about iMovie's trailer styles in "The Trailers Catalog" on page 287. Once you pick a style, click the Create button to get started.

You'll immediately notice that you don't have a project palette. Instead, you have a notebook with three tabs: Outline, Storyboard, and Shot List. You use these tabs to build your trailer.

Tip: It's easy to spot the trailers you've created in iMovie's Projects list; their icons look like movie tickets instead of the document icons used for regular projects.

The Outline

The Outline tab in your trailers project records all the basic information about your trailer (Figure 11-2). For example, you'll type in the name of your movie, the starring actor(s), and the production credits.

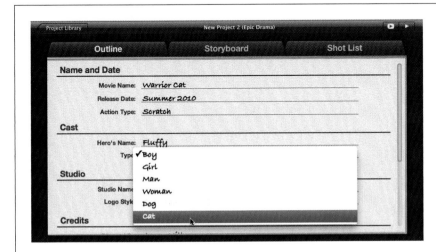

Figure 11-2:
This is the outline tab of your trailer project. You type in your movie's name, the cast name(s), the studio name and logo, and the production credits (not that people actually read those). Each trailer has custom fields; here, the Epic Drama trailer lets you change the hero's identity from "Boy" to "Cat".

You also name your "studio" in the Outline tab, and choose from six logos (Glowing Pyramid, Sun Rays Through Clouds, and so on) to represent your fledgling empire. iMovie models a few of the logos after some of the more famous studio logos (check out Snowy Mountain Peak, for example). You can change your choice at any point.

Note: If you select the Snowy Mountain Peak logo and name your studio "Paramount," or if you type in "Universal" with the Spinning Earth in Space image, iMovie displays "---" instead. These styles look so much like real movie studios' logos that Apple's lawyers block you from duplicating them exactly. (These names work fine with the other logo styles, though.)

When you move your cursor over each of the title sections in the Outline tab—Name and Date, Cast, Studio, and Credits—the pane on the right previews how the title will appear with the stuff you type in. It's a nice way to examine your changes as you make them.

The Storyboard

The trailer's Storyboard tab is where you do most of the work building your preview. It's the closest thing to the regular project palette you'll see in the trailer-builder. For example, as you move your cursor across the different clips in the Storyboard, iMovie skims through them just as it does with project and event footage.

The Storyboard gives you pre-made slots into which you drop footage (Figure 11-3). You can also select the text of a scene header (like "And Dared to Scratch" and "A Cat" in Figure 11-3) and replace it with whatever you want.

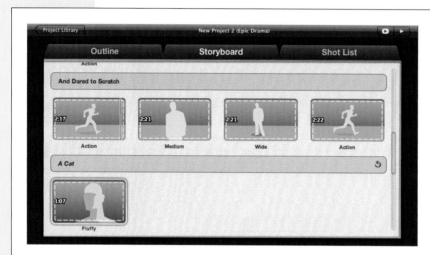

Figure 11-3:
You'll do most of your trailer-building in the Storyboard tab, pictured here. All you have to do is drop clips from your Event Library into each of the premade slots. You can also type in your own text for each of the headers. To undo a title change, click the circle-arrow button next to the title.

The Shot List

Here in the Shot List tab, you see all the shots that go into your trailer. They're grouped by kind of shot ("Action," "Landscape," and so on) instead of trailer sequence (Figure 11-4). Organizing your shots this way helps you know how many shots of a certain kind you'll need.

As you look over the shot list, it might occur to you that this could be a great planning tool, too. In fact, you can print the Shot List (File→Print or ⌘) and then take it with you as you shoot your footage. (You can actually print any of the three tabs in your movie trailer project.) The shots even show the length in seconds:frames format, so you know how long to make each shot.

Tip: The gender of the little silhouettes in each shot changes based on the gender you enter for the cast member(s) in the Outline tab. This helps you make sense of which actor you need for which shot.

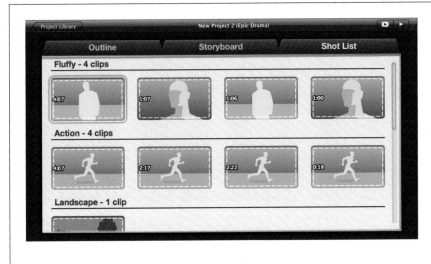

Figure 11-4:
The Shot List, the last tab in your movie trailer project, shows you all the shots in your trailer grouped by subject. This helps you better plan the kind of shots you need, which is especially useful if you use the trailer-builder before you shoot your footage. (Notice that when you have the actor's name set to "Fluffy," iMovie updates the Shot List, showing you the shots you need of Fluffy.) You can even print the Shot List and use it "on set."

The Trailers Catalog

Apple was generous with its trailer styles—you get 15 templates to choose from. Each one includes a unique set of titles, transitions, and music. The following catalog gives you a rundown of your choices.

Tip: Remember, you can click on a trailer in the New Project window (Figure 11-1), and iMovie shows you a preview—in other words, you get a trailer for a trailer.

- **Action**. *Similar movie*: *The Fast and the Furious*. *Cast members*: 2. *Duration*: 44:24 (seconds:frames).

  Vacation footage never looked this thrilling. Marked by fast-paced techno music and white-on-red titles, the Action trailer is what your vacation would be like if you spent it running from international drug cartels.

Note: Fun fact: The guy featured in this trailer preview is Randy Ubillos, the original designer of the new iMovie. He's apparently an avid traveler, which you can tell from this cool footage of his trip to New Zealand.

- **Adventure**. *Similar movie: Indiana Jones and the Raiders of the Lost Ark. Cast members*: 1. *Duration*: 54:02.

  We all love movie heroes, and this trailer turns you into one. It focuses on a single person and his quest to do something heroic. Feel free to use this trailer ironically if you filmed your husband finally taking out the garbage.

- **Blockbuster**. *Similar movie: Jurassic Park. Cast members*: 2-6. *Duration*: 55:05.

  If you've been to a remote, exotic location facing dangers never before encountered by human beings, or if you just had a blast at the local water park, this is the trailer for you. It features ominous music that swells to a magnificent climax.

- **Documentary**. *Similar movie: Deep Blue. Cast members*: 2. *Duration*: 1:08:23.

  Clean lines and Philip Glass-esque music just scream sophistication. If that's what you're going for, choose the Documentary trailer. It makes even the backyard swing set look pivotal for humanity's future.

- **Epic Drama**. *Similar movie: Gladiator. Cast members*: 1. *Duration*: 1:06:15.

  If you've ever seen the movie *Gladiator*, then you've seen this trailer. The triumphant music is absolutely spot-on. Feel free to use it even if you didn't conquer insurmountable odds.

- **Film Noir**. *Similar movie: The Maltese Falcon. Cast members*: 2. *Duration*: 1:19:20.

  Real movie trailers looked like this for about three decades. From *The Maltese Falcon* all the way to *North by Northwest*, this classic trailer pays tribute to the dark, brooding films that defined the noir genre.

- **Friendship**. *Similar movie: The Sisterhood of the Traveling Pants. Cast members*: 2–6. *Duration*: 54:25.

  Sometimes feel-good movies are just what the doctor ordered, and the Friendship trailer has feel-good all over it. You don't even have to come of age or form lifelong bonds to use this cheerful preview.

- **Holiday**. *Similar movie: Deck the Halls. Cast members*: 1. *Duration*: 1:18:23.

  Sleigh bells. Red-and-white titles. It's a great trailer, even if your Christmas miracle was just surviving the family ski trip.

- **Love Story**. *Similar movie: The Notebook. Cast members*: 2. *Duration*: 1:30:15.

  In the movie world, true love is hard to find and easy to lose. You can pay tribute to *real* true love with this trailer. Imagine taking old photos and home movies of your parents and putting this trailer together for their anniversary.

- **Pets**. *Similar movie: My Dog Skip. Cast members*: 1. *Duration*: 1:07:10.

  If a member of your family is furry (and not because he needs to shave), the Pets trailer is a great way to pay tribute to your four-footed friend. The music is cheerful and meaningful. The paw prints in the titles add a great touch.

Tip: At the outset, you see a dog's paw prints in this trailer. But on the Outline tab you can change them to a cat's paw prints or even a dinosaur's footprints.

- **Romantic Comedy**. *Similar movie*: Any of dozens of romantic comedies. *Cast members*: 2. *Duration*: 44:24.

  Romantic comedies are a clichéd genre, but that doesn't stop people from enjoying them. This trailer nails the motif, especially with the quirky, lighthearted music that suddenly turns meaningful, just like every romance in these movies.

- **Sports**. *Similar movie*: *Miracle*. *Cast members*: Any. *Duration*: 48:21.

  Put your kid's soccer game into the annals of sports history with this trailer. It showcases dramatic action shots, cheering crowd noises, flashbulb titles, and inspiring fanfare, all essential elements of a great sports movie.

- **Spy**. *Similar movie*: Any James Bond Movie. *Cast members*: 1. *Duration*: 1:15:29.

  Every little (and big) kid dreams about being a spy like James Bond. This is your chance. Imagine how much fun you your kids will have starring in this beat-heavy, fast-moving preview.

- **Supernatural**. *Similar movie*: *The Da Vinci Code*. *Cast members*: Any. *Duration*: 1:27:16.

  If you recently filmed something mysterious or arcane, like how your baby got out of her crib *again*, this trailer fits the mood nicely, with ominous music and ethereal titles.

- **Travel**. *Similar movie*: *Mr. Bean's Holiday*. *Cast members*: 2. *Duration*: 1:20:28.

  iMovie calls this one a "fast-paced screwball comedy." Here's hoping that not all of your vacations fit this description, but if they do, here's your trailer of choice. It features big, brassy music and bright titles.

Building Your Trailer

Follow these steps to build your trailer:

1. **Choose File→New Project (⌘), click a trailer style, and click Create.**

   Unlike themes (page 139), you can't change a trailer's style later if you change your mind.

2. **Fill out the Outline tab.**

   This is where you name your movie, cast, studio, and production staff.

3. **Click the Shot List tab to review the kind and number of shots you'll need.**

   Everything you learned about favorites and keywords (page 133) and all the work you did analyzing your footage for people (page 117) pays off here, big time. Use the people keywords to find shots matching your needs, and use the Keywords or Favorites tools to mark the shots you want to use.

At this point, you can plug your footage into each shot, but your shots may not appear in the right order (remember, the Shot List organizes your shots by subject, not by the order in which they appear in your preview). You might want to wait until you switch over to the Storyboard tab.

4. **Click the Storyboard tab and add your shots.**

As you add each shot to each placeholder, iMovie automatically trims the clip to fit the allotted time.

If iMovie doesn't frame a shot quite right—say it starts and stops at the wrong times—click the little blue box in the bottom-left corner of the clip. That brings up the Clip Trimmer (page 100), where you can choose a different section of the clip. You can't, however, change the length of the clip; iMovie locks in each clip's timing so that the cuts sync up with the trailer's music and titles.

5. **Fill out the trailer titles.**

Each trailer uses custom titles that you can fill in with your own story. If your trailer portrays a boy with special powers embarking on an adventure of a lifetime, for example, the titles are a great place to tell that story.

Click on a band of text in the Storyboard tab to change the title. You might notice that some titles are separated into more than one text box (Figure 11-5). That's because the trailer uses multiple font styles and sizes, and the boxes' formatting is predetermined.

6. **Preview your trailer.**

Click either the full-screen or regular preview buttons in the top-right corner of the Storyboard tab, and you'll see your trailer in all its glory. At this point, you can customize things using the instructions below.

7. **Share your trailer.**

You share trailers just like you do regular projects, so turn to Chapters 13 and 14 for ways to distribute your preview.

Customizing Your Trailer

Your editing options in the Storyboard tab are limited. You can't change the length of any of the clips, for example. However, you *can* make some changes in both the Storyboard and Shots List tabs:

- **Change a clip's color settings.**

As described on page 182, you can adjust a clip's color tone. For example, if the snow in your shot looks a little blue, iMovie's automatic white balance will fix it with just one click.

- **Make audio adjustments to the clip.**

The trailer style you choose probably automatically mutes the clips you add, so that the majesty of the musical score shines through. To unmute them, click the clip's ◀ and make the audio adjustments (page 246).

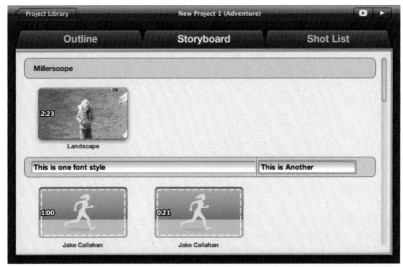

Figure 11-5:
Some trailer titles use multiple font styles and sizes. iMovie separates them into different text boxes in the storyboard (top), so they appear in their proper styles in the title itself (bottom).

- **Apply a video and/or audio effect.**

  Any of the really cool video effects, like Aged Film or Hard Light (page 154), or audio effects like Cosmic or Telephone (page 253), work in the trailers editing screens. Just double-click the clip to bring up the Inspector. From there, you can apply whatever effect you want.

Note: You can apply audio effects until you're blue in the face, but most trailer templates mute your clips, so you won't hear them unless you manually unmute them as described above.

- **Apply stabilization.**

    If, after building your trailer, you realize that your clips are just way too shaky, you can fix them by applying video stabilization, covered on page 178.

Converting to a Project

If you feel constrained by the limited editing available in the trailer-building section, iMovie gives you a way to cut the apron strings and set out on your own. You can convert your trailer into a regular iMovie project to get all the control you want.

To make the conversion, open the trailer and choose File→"Convert to Project." Now your trailer looks and works like a normal video project (Figure 11-6). The only minor difference: you can't edit the stock titles that begin the trailer. (However, since you're in regular project mode, you can *delete* the trailer titles and replace them with those of your own design.) You'll also notice that when you use the Inspector for trailer titles, you can't adjust the titles using the tricks described on page 210.

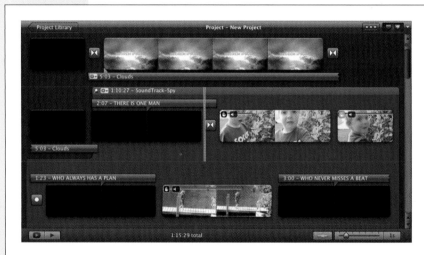

Figure 11-6:
This looks like a normal project now, but it used to be a trailer. All you need to do to convert a trailer to a project is choose File→"Convert to Project." Be careful, though, because once you convert a trailer to a project, there's no going back.

Tip: Although the Inspector is useless for editing trailer titles, you can manipulate them in all kinds of other ways, including dragging them around, lengthening or shortening them, and changing the font styles. Of course, you can still type in new title text, too.

What you *can* do is pretty much everything else. You can change the music, the length of clips, transitions, title backgrounds, and so on.

For example, one big missing feature in the trailer-editing screen is the ability to do voiceovers (page 240). This is a strange thing to disable, since half of all Hollywood trailers have a professional voiceover narrating. But if you convert your trailer to a project, you can be your very own Don LaFontaine. (Mr. LaFontaine was, perhaps, the most famous voiceover actor ever, narrating the trailers for almost 5,000 movies.)

A word of warning, however: Once you convert a trailer to a project, the result is permanent. There's no way to take your project and turn it back into a trailer. Because this is a one-way street, be sure to do all you need to do in the trailer-editing screen before you head back to the familiar neighborhood of the project storyboard.

Tip: If you just want to try something out in the project storyboard but you're not sure you want to leave the trailer editor behind, go to your Projects list, select your trailer, and then choose File→Duplicate Project. This creates a copy of your trailer that you can convert to a project, ready for experimentation.

Advanced Editing

S tumble around long enough in iMovie '11, and you'll be able to figure out most of its workings. But in this chapter, you'll read about another level of capability, another realm of power and professionalism, that would never oc- cur to most people.

This chapter covers two advanced topics:

- **Advanced editing theory**. Where the preceding chapters covered the *technical* aspects of editing video in iMovie—what keys to press, where to click, and so on— the first part of this chapter is about the *artistic* aspects of video editing. It covers when to cut, what to cut to, and how to create the emotional impact you want.

- **Back and forth with iMovie 6**. It's a fact of life: iMovie '11 is at best a distant cousin of iMovie 6. They're two different programs, designed for different pur- poses, with different audiences in mind. Each offers features that aren't found in the other.

    There's no reason you can't use *both* programs, swinging deftly back and forth, using each for what it's good for. In this chapter, you'll find out why and how.

The Power of Editing

The editing process is crucial to any kind of movie, from home videos to Hollywood thrillers. Clever editing can turn a troubled movie into a successful one, or a boring home movie into one that, for the first time, family members don't interrupt every 3 minutes by lapsing into conversation.

You, the editor, are free to jump from camera to camera, angle to angle, to cut from one location or time to another, and so on. Today's audiences accept that you're telling a story. They don't stomp out in confusion because one minute James Bond is in his London office, but shows up in Venice a split second later.

You can also compress time, which is one of editing's most common duties. (That's fortunate, because most movies tell stories that, in real life, would take days, weeks, or years to unfold.) You can also *expand* time, making 10 seconds stretch out to 6 minutes—a technique familiar to anyone who's ever watched a bomb's digital timer tick down the seconds to blast-off as the hero races to defuse it.

Editing boils down to choosing which shots you want to include, how long each shot lasts, and in what order they should play.

Modern Film Theory

If you're creating a rock video or an experimental film, you can safely chuck all the advice in this chapter—and in this book. But if you aspire to make good "normal" movies, designed to engage or delight your viewers rather than shock or mystify them, then you should become familiar with the fundamental principles of film editing that have shaped virtually every Hollywood movie (and even most student and independent films) over the last 75 years. For example:

Tell the story chronologically

Most movies tell a story from beginning to end. This part is probably instinct, even if you're making home movies. Arrange your clips roughly in chronological order, except when you want to represent your characters' flashbacks and memories, or when you deliberately want to play a chronology game, as in *Pulp Fiction*.

Try to be invisible

These days, an expertly edited movie is one where the audience isn't even aware of the editing. This principle has wide-ranging ramifications. For example, the simple cut is by far the most common joint between film clips because it's so unobtrusive. Using, say, the Circle Open transition between alternate lines of the vows at somebody's wedding would hardly qualify as invisible editing.

Within a single scene, use simple cuts and not transitions. Try to create the effect of seamless real time, making the audience feel as though it's witnessing the scene in its entirety, from beginning to end. This kind of editing is more likely to make your viewers less aware that they're watching a movie.

Develop a shot rhythm

Every movie has an editing *rhythm* that's established by the lengths of its shots. The prevailing rhythm of *Dances with Wolves*, for example, is extremely different from that of *Natural Born Killers*. Every *scene* in a movie has its own rhythm, too.

As a general rule, linger less on closeup shots, but give more time to establishing wide shots. (After all, in an establishing shot, there are many more elements for the audience to study and notice.) Similarly, change the pacing of the shots according to the nature of the scene. Most action scenes feature very short clips and fast edits. Most love scenes include longer clips and fewer changes of camera angle.

Maintaining Continuity

As a corollary to the notion that the audience should feel that they're part of the story, professional editors strive to maintain *continuity* during the editing process. This continuity business applies mostly to scripted films, not home movies. Still, knowing what the pros worry about makes you a better editor, no matter what kind of footage you work with.

Continuity refers to consistency in:

- **The picture**. Suppose we watch a guy with wet hair say, "I'm going to have to break up with you." We cut to his girlfriend's horrified reaction, but when we cut back to the guy, his hair is dry. That's a continuity error, a frequent by-product of having spliced together footage that was filmed at different times. Every Hollywood movie, in fact, has a person whose sole job is to watch out for errors like this during the editing process.

- **Direction of travel**. To make edits as seamless as possible, film editors and directors try to maintain continuity of direction from shot to shot. That is, if the hero sets out crawling across the Sahara from right to left to be with his true love, you better believe that when we see him next, hours later, he'll still be crawling from right to left. This general rule even applies to much less dramatic circumstances, such as car chases, plane flights, and even people walking to the corner store. If you see a character walk out of the frame from left to right in Shot A, you'll see her approach the corner store's doorway from left to right in Shot B.

- **The sound**. In an establishing shot, suppose we see hundreds of men in a battlefield trench, huddled for safety as bullets fly and bombs explode all around them. Now we cut to a closeup of two of these men talking, but the sounds of the explosions are missing. That's a sound continuity error. The audience is certain to notice that hundreds of soldiers were issued a cease-fire just as these two guys started talking.

- **The camera setup**. In scenes of conversations between two people, it would look really bizarre to show one person speaking only in closeup, and his conversation partner filmed in a medium shot. (Unless, of course, the first person were filmed in *extreme* closeup—just the lips filling the screen—because the filmmaker is trying to protect his identity.)

- **Gesture and motion**. If one shot begins with a character reaching down to pick up the newspaper from her doorstep, the next shot—a closeup of her hand closing around the rolled-up paper, for example—should pick up from the exact moment where the previous shot ended. And as the rolled-up paper leaves our closeup field of view, the following shot should show her straightening into an upright position. Unless you've made the deliberate editing decision to skip over some time from one shot to the next (which should be clear to the audience), the action should seem continuous from one shot to the next.

Tip: When filming scripted movies, directors always instruct their actors to begin each new scene's action with the same gesture or motion that *ended* the last shot. Having two copies of this gesture, action, or motion—one on each end of each take—gives the editor a lot of flexibility when it comes to piece the movie together.

This principle explains why you'll find it extremely rare for an editor to cut from one shot of two people to another shot of the *same* two people (without inserting some other shot between them, such as a reaction shot or a closeup of one person or the other). The odds are small that, as the new shot begins, both actors will be in precisely the same body positions they were in when the previous shot ended.

When to Cut

Some Hollywood directors may tell their editors to make cuts just for the sake of making the cuts come faster, in an effort to pick up the movie's pace. More seasoned directors and editors, however, usually adopt a more classical view of editing: Cut to a different shot when it's *motivated*. That is, cut when you *need* to cut, so that you can convey new visual information by taking advantage of a different camera angle, switching to a different character, providing a reaction shot, and so on.

Editors look for a motivating event that suggests *where* they should make the cut, too, such as a movement, a look, the end of the sentence, or the intrusion of an off-camera sound that makes us *want* to look somewhere else in the scene.

Choosing the Next Shot

As you read elsewhere in this book, the final piece of advice when it comes to choosing when and how to make a cut is this: Cut to a *different* shot. If you've been filming the husband, cut to the wife; if you've been in a closeup, cut to a medium or wide shot; if you've been showing someone looking off-camera, cut to what she's looking at.

Avoid cutting from one shot of somebody to a similar shot of the same person. Doing so creates a *jump cut*, a disturbing and seemingly unmotivated splice between shots of the same subject from the same angle.

Video editors sometimes have to swallow hard and perform jump cuts for the sake of compressing a long interview into a much shorter sound bite. Customer testimonials on TV commercials frequently illustrate this point. You'll see a woman saying, "Wonderglove changed…[cut] our lives, it really did…[cut] My husband used to be a drunk and a slob…[cut] but now we have Wonderglove." (Often, directors apply a fast cross dissolve to the cuts in a futile attempt to make them less noticeable.)

However, as you can probably attest if you've ever seen such an ad, that kind of editing is rarely convincing. As you watch it, you can't help wondering exactly *what* was cut and why. (The editors of *60 Minutes* and other documentary-style shows edit the comments of their interview subjects just as heavily, but conceal it better by cutting away to reaction shots—of the interviewer, for example—between edited shots.)

Popular Editing Techniques

Variety and pacing play a role in every decision a video editor makes. The following sections explain some common tricks of professional editors that you can use in iMovie.

Tight Editing

One of the first tasks you'll encounter when editing your footage is choosing how to trim and chop up your clips, as described in Chapter 3. Even when you edit home movies, consider the Hollywood guideline for tight editing: Begin every scene as *late* as possible, and end it as *soon* as possible.

In other words, suppose the audience sees the heroine receiving the call that her husband has been in an accident, and then hanging up the phone in shock. We don't really need to see her putting on her coat, opening the apartment door, locking it behind her, taking the elevator to the ground floor, hailing a cab, driving frantically through the city, screeching to a stop in front of the hospital, and finally leaping out of the cab. In a tightly edited movie, she would hang up the phone and then we'd see her leaping out of the cab (or even walking into her husband's hospital room).

Keep this principle in mind even when editing your own, slice-of-life videos. For example, a very engaging account of your ski trip could begin with only three shots: an establishing shot of the airport; a shot of the kids piling into the plane; and then the tumultuous, noisy, trying-on-ski-boots shot the next morning. You get less reality with this kind of tight editing, but much more watchability.

Variety of Shots

Variety is important in every aspect of filmmaking—variety of shots, locations, angles, and so on. Consider the lengths of your shots, too. In action sequences, you may prefer quick cutting, where each clip in your Movie Track is only a second or two long. In softer, more peaceful scenes, longer shots may set the mood more effectively.

Establishing shots

Almost every scene of every movie and every TV show—even the nightly news—begins with an *establishing shot*: a long-range, zoomed-out shot that shows the audience where the action is about to take place.

Now that you know something about film theory, you'll begin to notice how often TV and movie scenes begin with an establishing shot. It gives the audience a feeling of being there, and helps them understand the context for the medium shots or closeups that follow. Furthermore, after a long series of closeups, consider showing *another* wide shot, to remind the audience of where the characters are and what the world around them looks like.

As with every film-editing guideline, this one is occasionally worth violating. For example, in comedies, a new scene may begin with a closeup instead of an establishing shot, so that the camera can then pull back to *make* the establishing shot the joke. (For example, closeup on main character looking uncomfortable; camera pulls back to reveal that we were looking at him upside down as he hangs, tied by his feet, over a pit of alligators.) In general, however, setting up any new scene with an establishing shot is the smart—and polite—thing to do for your audience's benefit.

Cutaways and cut-ins

Cutaways and *cut-ins* are extremely common and effective editing techniques. Not only do they add some variety to a movie, but they let you conceal enormous editing shenanigans. By the time your movie resumes after the cutaway shot, you can have deleted enormous amounts of material, switched to a different take of the same scene, and so on. Figure 12-1 shows the idea.

The *cut-in* is similar, but instead of showing a different person or a reaction shot, it usually features a closeup of what the speaker is holding or talking about—a very common technique in training tapes and cooking shows.

Reaction shots

One of the most common sequences in Hollywood history is a three-shot sequence that goes like this: First, we see the character looking offscreen; then we see what he's looking at (a cutaway shot); and finally, we see him again so that we can read his reaction. This sequence is repeated so frequently in commercial movies that you can feel it coming the moment the performer looks off the screen.

From the editor's standpoint, of course, the beauty of the three-shot reaction is that the middle shot can be anything from anywhere. That is, it can be footage shot on another day in another part of the world, or even from a different movie entirely. The ritual of character/action/reaction is so ingrained in our brains that the audience believes the actor was looking at the action, no matter what it is.

In home-movie footage, you may have been creating reaction shots without even knowing it. But you've probably been capturing them by panning from your kid's beaming face to the petting-zoo sheep and then back to the face. You can make this sequence look great in iMovie by just snipping out the pans, leaving you with crisp, professional-looking cuts.

Figure 12-1:
Top: You've got a shot of your main character in action.

Middle: We cut away to a shot of what he's looking at or reacting to.

Bottom: When you cut back to the main character, you could use a different take on a different day, or dialog from a much later part of the scene (due to some cuts suggested by the editor). The audience will never know that the action wasn't continuous. The cutaway masks the fact that there was a discontinuity between the first and third shots.

Parallel cutting

When you make a movie that tells a story, it's sometimes fun to use *parallel editing* or *intercutting*. That's when you show two trains of action simultaneously and you keep cutting back and forth to show the parallel simultaneous action. In *Fatal Attraction*, for example, the intercut climax shows main character Dan Gallagher (Michael Douglas) downstairs in the kitchen, trying to figure out why the ceiling is dripping, even as his psychotic mistress Alex (Glenn Close) is upstairs attempting to murder his wife in the bathtub. If you're making movies that tell a story, you'll find this technique an exciting one when you're trying to build suspense.

Back and Forth to iMovie 6

Owning a copy of the new iMovie used to mean that you got a free copy of iMovie 6. It was Apple's way of saying, "OK, look, we know that the new iMovie ('08) is, ahem, a work in progress. To tide you over, here's a link to download the old version."

That link, and that offer, are gone now. Clearly, Apple feels that iMovie '11 has restored all the necessary missing features (like fast/slow/reverse, special effects, and the audio rubber band).

The following pages, therefore, are only for people who already have a copy of iMovie HD (or iMovie 6, as it's also known), sitting there in the Applications→iMovie [Previous Version] folder—or for people who know how to find a copy kicking around online.

So why do you care about iMovie 6? Because even though iMovie '11 brought back many iMovie 6 features, not all of them made the trip. The following left-behind iMovie 6 features may tempt you to continue using the older version:

- **Video special effects**. iMovie '11 matches iMovie 6 in many ways, such as offering video filters and slow motion, fast motion, and reverse motion effects.

    iMovie 6, on the other hand, still beats the new iMovie with the *flashier* video effects, like Lens Flare, Mirror, Crystallize, Glass Distortion, Water Color, and Rain. So there's no reason you can't do most of your editing in iMovie '11, and then send the whole thing back to iMovie 6 to apply these effects.

- **Export to tape**. This one's *huge*. When you're finished with an iMovie '11 project, you can export it to the Web, burn it to a DVD, or export it as a QuickTime movie. Unfortunately, *all* of those options involve some degradation of video quality. (Yes, even a DVD compresses the video somewhat.)

    In iMovie 6, there's an easy solution. You can preserve the really important videos, the ones you want to save forever with 100 percent of the original quality, on tape. iMovie 6 can play your finished masterpiece directly into a DV camcorder at full original quality—a great way to archive your masterpiece so that not even a hard drive crash can obliterate it.

    By exporting your movie from iMovie '11 into iMovie 6, you grant yourself the freedom to back up your best work onto tape.

- **Plug-ins**. iMovie 6 can also accommodate *add-on* effects and transitions from other companies. (iMovie '11 can't.) If you invested a lot in plug-ins, they can still do the job you paid for. You could edit most of your movie in iMovie '11 and then ship it over to iMovie 6. Alternatively, you could use the plug-ins you need on just the clips that need them, then send those clips over to iMovie '11.

Transferring Your Project, iMovie '11→iMovie 6

In all the examples described above, it usually makes sense to begin your project in iMovie '11, and then to finish it up in iMovie 6.

Here's how you go about it. (For more explanation of what you're doing here, see Chapter 15, which goes into more detail about exporting iMovie projects as QuickTime movies.)

1. **When you've gone as far as you can go in iMovie '11, choose Share→"Export using QuickTime."**

   The "Save exported file as" dialog box appears. Type a name for the intermediate transfer file you're going to create. In this example, suppose you call it *Transfer Movie*.

   Choose a location for the exported movie, as shown in Figure 12-2, top.

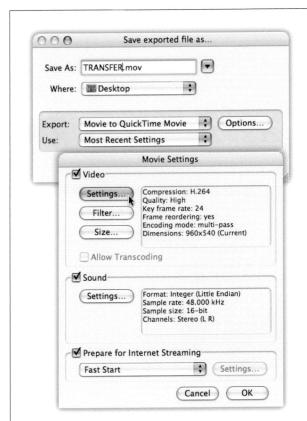

Figure 12-2:
Top: In this first dialog box, your job is to type a name for the exported movie. It doesn't really matter what you call it. Choose your desktop as the save location, but don't click Save yet.

Bottom: Here's where you specify a format for your exported QuickTime movie. Click Settings. Incidentally, you can also pass your iMovie '11 projects off to Final Cut Pro or Final Cut Express (page 470 has the details). That way, you can use iMovie for what it's good at (importing video from tapeless camcorders, and quickly choosing the best shots)—and then use Final Cut for what it's good at (everything else).

2. **Make sure the Export pop-up menu says "Movie to QuickTime Movie." Then click Options.**

   Now the Movie Settings dialog box appears (Figure 12-2, bottom).

3. **Click the top Settings button.**

   The Video Compression Settings dialog box appears.

4. **From the Compression Type pop-up menu, choose Apple Intermediate Codec.**

   You can read more about this important format on page 48. In essence, it's a file format that's understood by all of Apple's video-editing programs, past and present, and retains 100 percent of the video quality of the original.

5. **Click OK, and then click OK in the next dialog box. Click Save.**

   iMovie takes a few moments to export the video.

   You now have on your desktop a QuickTime movie version of your project, named "Transfer Movie" (or whatever you called it in step 1).

6. **Open iMovie 6.**

   It's probably in your Applications→iMovie [Previous Version] folder. Oh, and it's probably called iMovie HD. (And yes, it's perfectly OK to have iMovie '11 and iMovie 6 open at the same time.)

Note: Apple is schizophrenic in its naming scheme. The icons for both iMovie 5 and iMovie 6 were named "iMovie HD."

---

7. **In iMovie 6, create a new, empty project. Name and save it. Choose File→ Import (Shift-⌘-I). In the Open dialog box, find and double-click the exported movie file you created in step 5 ("Transfer Movie" in this example).**

   The project shows up in iMovie 6 on the Clips shelf, as shown in Figure 12-3.

8. **Drag the Transfer Movie icon down to the Timeline at the bottom of the window.**

   You're ready to edit it!

Tip: iMovie 6, of course, is an entirely different ball of wax. Not to be totally mercenary here, but the best way to learn it is to read *iMovie 6 and iDVD: The Missing Manual*.

Transferring Your Project, iMovie 6→iMovie '11

As noted above, most people will probably go from iMovie '11→iMovie 6. But you may very well want to go in the other direction. Maybe you want to begin in iMovie 6, and then finish up in iMovie '11, because:

Figure 12-3:
*Your partially
finished iMovie
'11 movie is now
safely ensconced
in iMovie 6. It's
represented by a
single icon on the
Clips shelf. Drag
it down to the
Timeline and start
editing.*

- **You want to send the finished movie to YouTube.** Only iMovie '11 has that feature built right in.

- **You want to use the newest video and audio effects.** With video stabilization, green screen, picture-in-picture, travel maps, cutaways, pitch up/down, audio enhance, and multitune features, iMovie '11 is clearly the superior tool for these functions.

- **You want to use iMovie '11's titles.** The newer version offers better-looking text over video, not to mention far greater typographical control. (For example, only iMovie '11 lets you create different fonts, sizes, and colors *within* a single title.)

Actually, the process of transferring an iMovie 6 project to its successor is almost the same as going the other way. Here's what you do:

1. **When you're ready to export your iMovie 6 project, choose Share→QuickTime.**

   The Share dialog box appears.

2. **From the pop-up menu, choose Expert Settings. Click Share.**

   You arrive at the dialog box shown in Figure 12-2 (bottom).

3. **Follow steps 2 through 5 in "Transferring Your Project, iMovie '11→iMovie 6."**

   Creating the transfer movie is exactly the same, no matter in which direction you go.

4. **Open iMovie '11. Choose File→Import→Movies.**

   The Open dialog box appears (Figure 12-4).

Note: Remember that importing a QuickTime version of your iMovie 6 project is different from importing the project itself through iMovie '11's File→Import→iMovie HD Project command. The steps described here preserve all the transitions, titles, effects, and audio in your movie (albeit in an unchangeable form). Importing the iMovie HD project itself strips these things away.

---

5. **Locate and open your transfer movie.**

   The former iMovie 6 movie is now safely ensconced in iMovie '11, in the Event you specified. You can add it to a project and begin your final surgery on it.

Tip: There's no reason you can't go back and forth between the two iMovies, repeating the process as necessary. You're not losing any video quality with each trip.

Figure 12-4:
Before you find and open your transfer movie, specify whether you want it to become part of an existing Event or a new one. (See page 34 for details on this process.)

Part Two: Finding Your Audience

Chapter 13: Exporting to iPod, iPhone, iPad, Apple TV, or Front Row

Chapter 14: Exporting to YouTube and the Web

Chapter 15: From iMovie to QuickTime

Chapter 16: QuickTime Player

2

Exporting to iPod, iPhone, iPad, Apple TV, or Front Row

I f you hadn't noticed, Apple thinks that the traditional destinations for your home movies—like sending your movie to a DVD or recording it back to tape—are ancient history. What Apple *really* wants you to do with your video is post it on the Web (see Chapter 14) or transfer it to another Apple machine, like an iPod, iPhone, iPad, Apple TV, or Front Row (to play on your Mac from across the room).

That's what this chapter is all about: sending your finished masterpiece to another fine piece of Apple merchandise.

Exporting the Movie to iTunes

As it turns out, the steps for exporting a movie to Apple's five video-playing machines (iPod, iPhone, iPad, AppleTV, and Front Row) are nearly identical. All of them involve exporting the movie to iTunes, which is the loading dock for your gadgets and Front Row. The only difference is the size of the movie you create.

So, for the sake of saving the Brazilian rainforest, the instructions appear here only once, with the necessary variations pointed out along the way:

1. **When your project is ready for prime time, choose Share→iTunes.**

   The "Publish your project to iTunes" dialog box appears (Figure 13-1). You've probably never seen a dialog box quite like this one.

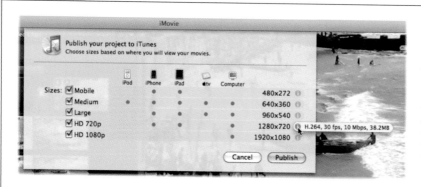

Figure 13-1:
This unusual-looking dialog box is just Apple's way of offering you some ready-made compression settings for typical playback gadgets. Point to the ❶ button to see some techy details.

In essence, iMovie offers to export your movie at various screen sizes, each one geared to a particular device. The little blue dots indicate which screen sizes are appropriate for which gadgets.

For example, the iPhone 4's screen measures 960 × 640 pixels, so you'd select the Large option to send your movie to iPhone-owning friends. A standard-definition TV set has 640 × 480 pixels, which is why the chart offers Medium as an option for Apple TV playback. And because you can connect an iPod to a TV for playback, you see the Medium option listed there, too.

2. **Turn on the checkboxes that correspond to the sizes you want to export.**

   You can actually turn on *more than one* of these checkboxes (as in Figure 13-1). If you do that, you'll wind up with *several* copies of your video.

Tip: If you point to the ❶ button without clicking, a tooltip appears. As shown in Figure 13-1, it gives you details about the exported movie file you're about to create. For example, you'll see the file format (H.264); the number of frames per second (fps); the Internet speed required to watch the video from the Web (in megabits per second—for comparison, a typical cable-modem connection is 2 megabits per second); and the file size (in megabytes).

---

3. **Click Publish.**

   Now the time-consuming exporting and compression process begins. Feel free to switch to other programs—check your email or surf the Web, for example—while iMovie crunches away in the background. A progress bar lets you know how much farther iMovie has to go.

When it's all over, iTunes opens by itself. If you click the Movies folder, you'll see the newly exported movies nestled there (Figure 13-2). iMovie names them after the project and the screen size at which you exported them. For example, you might see "Birthday Party–Mobile" and "Birthday Party–Medium."

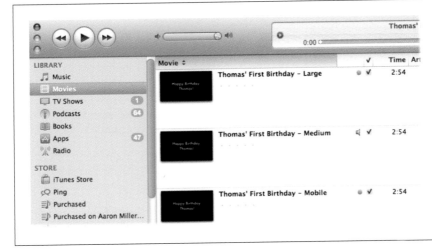

Figure 13-2:
*Here, tucked in
among your other
movies, are your
exported iMovie
videos. To watch one,
double-click it;
it starts playing in the
lower-left corner of
the screen. Click that
playback window
once to make the
movie play bigger in
a window of its own.*

From iTunes to iPod, iPhone, and So On

Once you have your movies in iTunes, getting them onto your iPod, iPhone, Apple TV, or copy of Front Row works just like it always does:

- **iPod, iPhone, iPad.** Connect the gadget to your Mac. Its icon shows up in the column at the left side of iTunes, under Devices. Click the Movies tab and select the movies you want iTunes to copy over to your i-gadget when you next sync them (Figure 13-3).

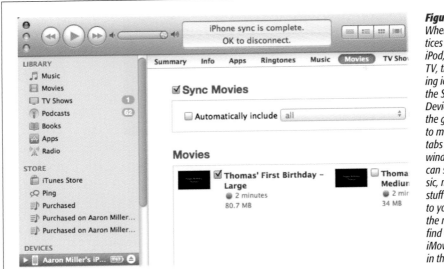

Figure 13-3:
*When iTunes no-
tices that you have an
iPod, iPhone, or Apple
TV, the correspond-
ing icon appears in
the Source list under
Devices (left). Click
the gadget's name
to make the media
tabs appear (main
window), where you
can specify what mu-
sic, movies, and other
stuff you want to copy
to your i-gadget at
the next sync. You'll
find all of your
iMovie '11 exports
in the Movies tab.*

- **Apple TV**. Same deal here. The Apple TV's name and icon show up in the left-side column of iTunes. Click it, and then click the Movies tab and turn on the movies you want synced to the Apple TV, so you can enjoy your iMovie productions on the big screen.

- **Front Row**. Front Row is the movie/music/DVD player built into every current Mac model (except the Mac Pro). Apple designed the program so you can operate it (and enjoy the entertainment) from a couch across the room—that's why all of Front Row's fonts and menus appear in huge, razor-sharp text, and why all Front Row computers come with a tiny white remote control.

Tip: If you lose the remote, you can open Front Row by pressing ⌘-Esc or, on some Mac models, F1.

The movies and music that Front Row lists simply reflect whatever you've got in iTunes. All you have to do to see the videos you just exported, therefore, is to use the remote to choose Videos from Front Row's menu. Your exported iMovie masterworks appear right there, ready to watch (Figure 13-4).

Figure 13-4:
Here's the Front Row listing of your videos. Lo and behold, here are all the movies you exported from iMovie, ready to enjoy!

Exporting to YouTube and the Web

If you ask Apple, the DVD has had its day in the sun. The format is more than 14 years old. *Nobody* puts movies on DVD anymore. Plastic shiny discs that have to be—ugh—*mailed*? That's such an old-fashioned, clumsy, *physical* way to share video.

The real action is on the Internet, that billion-seat megaplex where unknown independent filmmakers get noticed, and where it doesn't cost you a penny to distribute your work to a vast, worldwide audience.

It's all about YouTube, baby. One hundred million videos watched per day. It costs nothing to sign up and post your videos there.

You can put your videos up on your MobileMe account, too. MobileMe costs $100 per year ($66 if you buy from Amazon.com), but man do videos look fantastic against the black background of your MobileMe Gallery. Visitors can choose from multiple frame sizes to accommodate Internet connections of different speeds, too. Your fans can even skim your iMovie '11 movies using your mouse pointer, just like you can on your Mac.

Facebook is no slouch, either. Although its video-sharing tools aren't as beautiful as MobileMe's, Facebook has over 500 million members. That's a lot of people you can impress.

For projects that need a certain sophistication, try the classy YouTube alternative, Vimeo. Vimeo even plays back your movies in glorious hi-def.

Fancy yourself a witness to history? Do some citizen reporting and post your movies to CNN's iReport website, where one of the CNN networks might even pick it up and broadcast it to the world.

Or what the heck: Post videos on your own website.

This chapter covers all these ways of making your opus viewable on the Web.

iMovie to YouTube

By far the easiest way to post your movies on the Internet is to use iMovie '11's You-Tube command.

YouTube, of course, is the insanely popular video-sharing website, filled to the brim with hundreds of millions of funny home videos, TV excerpts, amateur short films, memorable bloopers—and now your iMovie projects. Once you post your movie there, other people can find it in many ways: by typing in its web address, by searching for your name, by searching for keywords (often called *tags*) you list in the video's description, and so on.

You can't post to YouTube from iMovie, however, unless you have a YouTube account. To get one (it's free), visit *www.youtube.com/signup* and fill in the blanks. After you do that, YouTube sends an email to the address you specified. (Not always immediately, however. The path to YouTubeness is not always instant.) The email, when it finally arrives, contains a link that says "Confirm your email address." What it really means is, "Click me to confirm that you're a real person with a real email account and not one of those annoying software robots that tries to set up thousands of bogus You-Tube accounts in hopes of spreading spam."

Posting to YouTube (The First Time)

Suppose your movie is now ready for the masses. Here's what you do:

1. **Choose Share→YouTube.**

   A *sheet* (a dialog box attached to the window) appears. Since you're a YouTube virgin, it probably looks something like Figure 14-1, bottom—except that it's empty.

2. **If your YouTube account name doesn't already appear in the pop-up menu, click Add.**

   A strikingly plain window prompts you for your YouTube account name. Enter it and click Done.

3. **Enter your password.**

   Don't worry—iMovie won't use your YouTube password to post that embarrassing footage you forgot to delete. If you can't trust iMovie, who can you trust?

4. **Fill in the name, description, and tags (keywords) for your movie (see Figure 14-1).**

   The name and description appear right beside your movie.

5. **Specify what size you want the movie to be.**

   YouTube can play back movies in any of five sizes: Mobile, Medium, Large, HD 720p, or HD 1080p (assuming your source video even has that much resolution). For details on this table-like dialog box, see page 310; for now, it's enough to know that YouTube supports a range of movie sizes. Be aware that going all-HD can be fraught with peril (see "HD YouTube Videos" on page 316). Whatever you do, if you think your audience will be using cellphones or dial-up modems, choose the Mobile option.

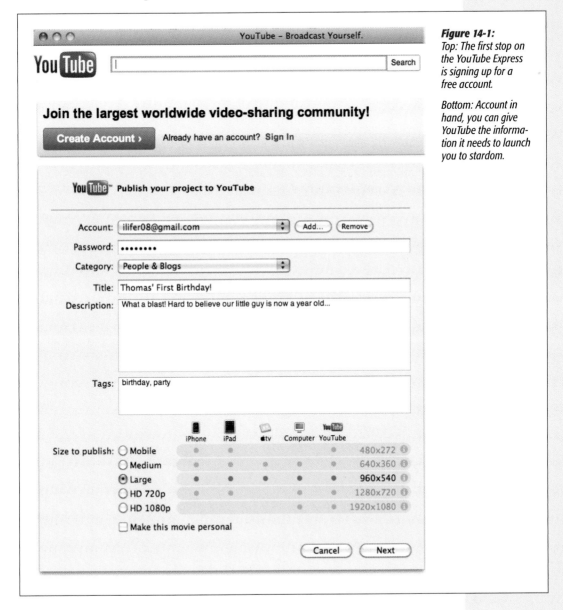

Figure 14-1:
Top: The first stop on the YouTube Express is signing up for a free account.

Bottom: Account in hand, you can give YouTube the information it needs to launch you to stardom.

6. **Turn off "Make this movie personal," if you like.**

   Most YouTube movies are available to the entire universe of people on the Internet. iMovie's factory setting is to keep your movie private. *Nobody* will see it unless you specifically invite them to, by sending them the movie's web address (which YouTube gives you). If you don't care who sees your video and you want to invite the whole world to the party, therefore, you have to uncheck the box.

7. **Click Next.**

   A dialog box appears reminding you that it's naughty to upload TV shows, movies, or anything else that you don't own the copyright for.

8. **Click Publish.**

   iMovie springs into action, compressing and uploading your video. This part can take a while. Feel free to check your email while iMovie crunches away.

   When the upload is finally complete, you see the message shown in Figure 14-2.

9. **Tell a friend, view the movie, or just return to iMovie.**

   If you click "Tell a Friend," your Mac thoughtfully opens your email program with a new, outgoing message with "My Great iMovie!" in the Subject line, and it fills in the body with a message that alerts your fans to the presence—and the web address—of your new video.

POWER USERS' CLINIC

HD YouTube Videos

For years, YouTube earned a reputation as an all-you-can-eat buffet of grainy, pixelated webcam rants. But it's fighting back. YouTube has now opened its doors to the elite snobs of Internet video by offering videos in high definition format (720p and 1080p HD).

"Hey!" you say, "I'm editing in HD! Let's make the most of this YouTube thingy." Before you dive in, here are some good things to know about how it really works.

First, YouTube's upload and conversion process for HD movies takes longer than it does for lower-res movies. Not only do you have to wait for iMovie to convert your project, but after you upload that huge file, YouTube's computers have to do their own round of file-crunching. In other words, don't expect your hi-def YouTube video to be available within minutes of uploading it.

Once your video is viewable on YouTube, some of your loved ones may have a choppy ride when they try to watch it. If they have an older computer or a slow Internet connection, the movie simply won't play smoothly for them. Luckily, they can turn off the HD option by clicking the tiny HD button just underneath your video.

If you don't mind these niggling issues, then go all the way. HD YouTube videos are worth it.

Note: The "Tell a Friend" feature isn't perfect. If you use Apple's own Mail program, the outgoing message includes the correct clickable address for your movie (such as *www.youtube.com/watch?v=tdcark_siiU*). But if you use another program, like Microsoft Entourage or Outlook, the address includes only *www.youtube.com/watch*, which doesn't take your fans *directly* to your movie. This seems to be a bug.

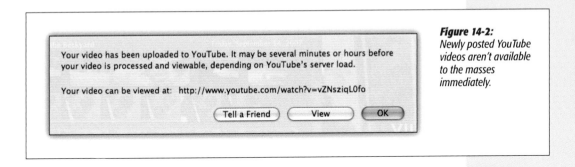

Figure 14-2:
Newly posted YouTube videos aren't available to the masses immediately.

Your video has been uploaded to YouTube. It may be several minutes or hours before your video is processed and viewable, depending on YouTube's server load.

Your video can be viewed at: http://www.youtube.com/watch?v=vZNsziqL0fo

Tell a Friend   View   OK

Posting to YouTube (After the First Time)

Once you do all that account setting-up, the posting-to-YouTube process is much simpler. With a finished project open on your screen, choose Share→YouTube. The dialog box you saw in Figure 14-1 appears again, but filled out with your YouTube account information. Then follow the preceding instructions from step 4.

Tip: If you upload a movie that's *exactly* the same length as one you uploaded earlier, YouTube may reject the new video, claiming that it's a duplicate. The solution is to humor YouTube. Make your new video a fraction of a second longer or shorter.

After the YouTube Movie Is Up

Once you successfully post a video to YouTube, you won't forget it, thanks to the new icons and labels you see in iMovie's Projects list (Figure 14-3).

At this point, you have several movie-management options. They appear when you double-click the project name, and then click the YouTube button above the storyboard:

- **Tell another friend about the movie**. This generates an email embedded with your movie's YouTube link.

- **Watch the YouTube video yourself**. Choosing Visit takes you to the video in your browser.

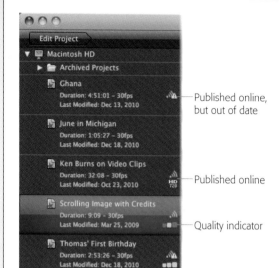

Figure 14-3:
After you publish a project to YouTube, iTunes, MobileMe, or anywhere else, the Projects list reminds you—and lets you know which of iMovie's standard export sizes you used. If you see ⬛, *beware! Your desktop (or laptop) version of the project no longer matches what you shared online or in iTunes!*

Published online, but out of date

Published online

Quality indicator

- **Edit the movie and republish it**. As soon as you start making changes to the published project, all hell breaks loose. A yellow exclamation-point icon (⚠) appears at the top of the storyboard, along with the notation "out of date." And just in case you didn't get the point, a warning box appears, too.

  Click OK to dismiss the warning box. Finish making your changes, and then choose "Publish to YouTube" from the YouTube button above the storyboard. Repeat the publishing process starting from step 4 on page 314.

Note: Actually, this process doesn't *update* or even *replace* the original version of the video; it just uploads another copy of it.

  If you update your movie this way, you have to delete the original manually—you can't use iMovie's "Remove from YouTube" command to do that. You have to go to YouTube, sign into your account, and delete the old file.

- **Delete the movie from YouTube**. Once you feel that a movie has outlived its usefulness (or become embarrassing), you can remove it from YouTube. Click the YouTube button and choose "Remove from YouTube." (You can also use a menu command: choose Share→"Remove from"→YouTube.) iMovie tells you that you have to manually remove the video from your My Videos page on YouTube (*http://www.youtube.com/my_videos*). Once you do that, come back to iMovie and click Done. The YouTube button disappears from your project.

Note: You read that right. iMovie won't remove your YouTube video for you. You have to do it on your own through YouTube's web page. The Remove option here really just means, "Tell iMovie that you removed the video, so it doesn't think the video is still on YouTube."

iMovie to MobileMe

YouTube certainly is the people's video-sharing service. It's got the most videos and the most eyeballs watching them, and it offers buttons that let your audience leave fan mail (or hate mail) in the comments section and rate your work on a five-star scale.

YouTube does not, however, offer the best environment for playback. The page displaying your movie is cluttered and ugly. And unless you post a high-definition file to YouTube (page 316), your videos look grainy and small.

If you publish your masterwork to a MobileMe account, though, it's a whole different world. The presentation is classy and glamorous—in high definition, even—and the movie itself is nice and big (see Figure 14-4).

MobileMe is Apple's suite of Internet services and conveniences: It synchronizes calendars, address books, and web bookmarks among the different Macs in your life, provides a backup program, lets you check your email online, and offers iWeb publishing, which lets you create your own web pages.

Here's how you get your movie into your MobileMe Gallery:

1. **With your project on the screen before you, choose Share→MobileMe Gallery.**

   The dialog box shown in Figure 14-5 appears.

2. **Fill in the title and a description for your movie. Then choose the movie's frame size: Mobile, Medium, or whatever.**

   Medium is a great size if your viewers have high-speed Internet connections (like cable modems or DSLs). If they're using dial-up or slow DSL, choose Mobile instead.

UP TO SPEED

Getting a MobileMe Account

MobileMe, Apple's subscription online service, provides everything you need to put a collection of your movies online. A MobileMe membership will set you back $100 per year—much less if you buy from Amazon.com.

Mac OS X makes it easy to sign up for an account, and a two-month trial account is free. If you don't already have an account, start by choosing →System Preferences.

Click , and then click Sign Up. Your web browser opens up to the MobileMe sign-up screen; simply follow the steps.

When you return to System Preferences, you'll see that the Mac has filled in your account name and password automatically. You're now ready to use your MobileMe account—and to post iMovie masterworks to it.

Figure 14-4:
Movies you post to MobileMe look quite a bit better than they do on YouTube. The background is dark and classy, the scroll bar and volume controls are easy to figure out, and the top-left button takes you back to the full "table of contents" for the movies and iPhoto slideshows on your site.

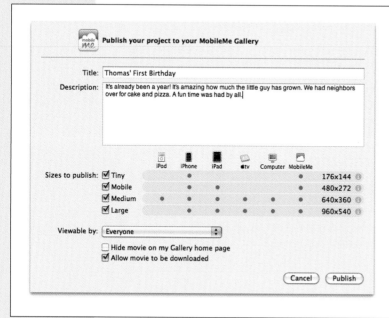

Figure 14-5:
If you've ever published a video on YouTube, this dialog box should look distinctly familiar. Here you can specify a title, description, and frame size for your web movie.

Tip: You can choose *more* than one size, if you like. See page 310 for details on the size options. (Incidentally, iMovie keeps track of which sizes of each project you export to your MobileMe Gallery. If you see some of the size checkboxes dimmed, it's because you *already* posted versions of this project in those sizes.)

3. **Turn on "Allow movie to be downloaded," if you like.**

   Do you want to let people watch your movie *online only*—to stream it, in other words? If so, leave this checkbox turned off.

   Or do you want to permit them to download the movie as a file to their hard drives? That means they can play it even when they're not online. It also means they could edit your movie, incorporate it into their own presentations, and so on, if they were so inclined. If that's OK with you, turn on this checkbox.

4. **Hide the video from the unwashed masses by turning on "Hide Movie on my Gallery home page," if you like.**

   If you do that, nobody will see the movie's icon on your MobileMe Gallery home page. The only way they'll be able to watch your movie is through a personal invitation from you—one that includes the movie's web address. So turn on this checkbox for movies that you don't want the whole world to see.

5. **Click Publish.**

   iMovie begins the time-consuming process of compressing and uploading your movie. When it's done, you see a message much like the one in Figure 14-2 (page 317).

6. **Click the "Tell a Friend," View, or OK button.**

   The first button opens a new, outgoing email message, ready to address and send to your adoring public. The second takes *you* to the MobileMe Gallery to enjoy the online version of your flick. And clicking OK just takes you back to iMovie.

After Your MobileMe Movie Is Up

Once you successfully hang a new movie in your MobileMe Gallery, the project takes on new icons and labels in iMovie (Figure 14-3, page 318).

As with YouTube, you can now manage your online movie in several ways:

- **Tell another friend about the movie**. Click the project's name, then the MobileMe button above the storyboard, and then click "Tell a Friend."

- **Watch the video yourself**. Click the MobileMe button above the storyboard, and then click Visit to watch the movie in your browser.

- **Edit the movie and republish it**. Once you edit the project, iMovie makes it very clear that the online version no longer matches the master version by displaying a yellow exclamation-point icon, the words "out of date," and a warning dialog box. Click OK to dismiss the warning box. Finish making your changes, and then choose Share→"Re-publish to MobileMe Gallery" (or choose the same after clicking the MobileMe button). Then repeat from step 2 of the previous instructions.

Note: When you republish to MobileMe, iMovie actually *does* replace the original published movie. You don't wind up with two versions, as you do with YouTube.

- **Delete the movie from your web gallery.** To take down a movie—perhaps because of rampant picketing from special-interest groups who declare your film offensive despite never having seen it—click the MobileMe button and choose "Remove from MobileMe Gallery." (There's an equivalent option under Share→"Remove from"→MobileMe Gallery.)

iMovie to Facebook

500 million people is a lot. With that many Facebook members, the odds are pretty good that someone (everyone) you know has a Facebook account—probably one that's checked frequently. For this reason, Facebook is a no-brainer when you're looking for a place to share videos with your friends and family. It even plays 720p HD videos, so your work can look its best.

Posting to Facebook

When you choose Share→Facebook for your project, you see the Facebook publishing screen (Figure 14-6). The steps for uploading to all these services are basically the same for Facebook as for YouTube and the other sites: You enter your account information in the same way, type in movie titles and descriptions in the same way, and choose your video quality in the same way.

The notable difference with Facebook is that you have different choices about who you share your video with (Figure 14-6). You can make it an entirely private affair (click Only Me). Alternatively, you can share it with Friends, Friend of Friends, or the whole world (Everyone). Choose wisely. Of course, you can change your mind later by visiting the video on Facebook and changing the sharing settings that appear when you click Edit This Video.

Facebook takes a few minutes to process your video before you can view it. As you're probably well aware, Facebook offers plenty of other ways to spend your time while you wait.

After the Facebook Movie Is Up

A nice little Facebook button appears atop your project. Clicking it reveals the same choices you saw with YouTube videos (page 315). You can view your movie, email a link to friends, publish it to Facebook again, or remove it.

As with YouTube, publishing your video again only creates a second version of the movie in your Facebook account. And, again as with YouTube, choosing to remove the video in iMovie is really just a way to tell iMovie that you've deleted it manually from Facebook. To delete the movie from Facebook for real, you have to go to Facebook's video page and click Delete Video.

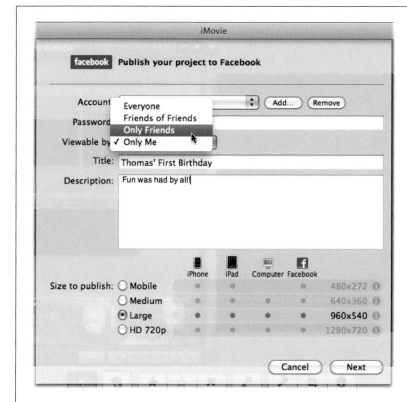

Figure 14-6:
Publishing your video to Facebook basically works the same as publishing to YouTube or MobileMe. The biggest difference is the privacy settings you have available. You can keep your movie to yourself or share it with friends, friends of friends, or all 500 million Facebook users.

iMovie to Vimeo

If YouTube is the McDonald's of online video—ubiquitous but full of "fast-food" movies—then Vimeo is the Whole Foods version, directed at those with a more refined palate. Fundamentally, it's still a video-sharing website, but the kind of videos posted there tend to have higher quality. The site also shies away from the cluttered look you find on YouTube. For this reason, people who are picky about how their videos look online tend to turn to Vimeo.

If you're the Vimeo type, you can create an account at *http://vimeo.com/join*. You can even sign up for a Plus account, which, for $10 a month, gives you a bunch of additional benefits, like higher upload limits and more control over how your videos appear to your viewers.

Uploading to Vimeo

Choose Share→Vimeo to upload your video. The Vimeo publishing screen (Figure 14-7) has the same account and password fields you saw on the YouTube and MobileMe screens. There's also a way to limit who sees your video. (You can change this setting later by going to the video page while logged in and clicking Settings in the top-right corner.) The quality controls let you upload different size movies, all the way up to 1080p. As usual, be sure to enter a good description and tags so people searching the Internet will have more luck finding your video.

When you finish filling out the form, click Next to get the same copyright warning/scolding that you see when you upload to YouTube. iMovie processes and uploads your video, displaying a confirmation message when it's done.

After the Vimeo Movie Is Up

Once you publish your movie to Vimeo, you get the usual badge/button at the top of your iMovie project. Clicking it lets you visit the video in a browser, email the link to a friend, publish the video again, or remove it.

Once again, if you share the video to Vimeo once and then share it again, you'll post two versions of it on the Vimeo website.

And once again, when you ask iMovie to remove your video, it tells you to delete it from Vimeo yourself and then click Done to let iMovie know you removed it. The Vimeo badge/button disappears.

Tip: To delete a Vimeo video, visit the video's page while logged in, and then click the big Delete button at the top right corner of the page.

---

iMovie to CNN iReport

Now that almost everyone carries around a camera, laptop, or phone, the big news agencies are starting to wise up to the power of citizen journalism. These days, the first video you see of a natural or celebrity disaster usually comes from the Man on the Street™.

If the idea of citizen reporting excites you, make sure to take advantage of the convenience iMovie offers in sending your reports straight to CNN's iReport website (*http://ireport.cnn.com/*).

iReport is CNN's system of publishing video news reports from ordinary people like you. (Some of the photos and videos even make it onto CNN's TV broadcasts.) The first time you visit, CNN's site give you a brief explanation of how it all works (Figure 14-8). Follow the link in the top-right corner to create your account and get started.

Figure 14-7:
Uploading to Vimeo works almost identically to uploading to YouTube. If you don't have a Vimeo account, you can create one at http://vimeo.com/join.

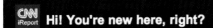

Figure 14-8:
*Your first visit to CNN's iReport website (*http://ireport. cnn.com/*) greets you with this message. Basically, they'll love to take the great stuff you create, but won't take the blame for the bad stuff.*

Tip: Once you create your account, you'll notice that CNN regularly sends out "assignments" to you, the citizen reporter. Obviously, if your goal is to be seen on TV, your chances of success go up if you file reports meeting these assignments.

Uploading to iReport

When you have your Pulitzer-worthy report ready to go, choose Share→CNN iReport. The upload screen (Figure 14-9) offers various resolution options, including a 720p HD version. Enter your iReport account vitals (email and password) using the process described in steps 2 and 3 on page 314. Also, be sure to take the time to enter a thorough description and tags to make sure CNN pays attention to what you upload.

The major difference when you upload a video to iReport is that there's no opportunity to limit who sees it. That's because everything you upload is public, viewable by *anyone*. (iReport is for public reporting, after all, not private video-sharing among friends.)

Once you upload your report, you have the chance to view it online and tell a friend about it. If you try to watch your report right away, you might see a message telling you that CNN's servers are still processing the video.

Figure 14-9:
The publish screen for CNN's iReport service has most of the common options, except for the one to keep it private. This is news, people! (Your 1-year-old's birthday doesn't happen every day, right?) Be sure that what you upload is exactly how you want it, because there's no simple way to remove or update an iReport.

After the iReport Is Up

When you click the CNN iReport button at the top of your iMovie project, you see the options to visit the video, tell a friend, publish to CNN, or "remove" the video from iReport.

Warning: Although iMovie contains an option to remove an iReport video, you should know that there's no easy way to do so, short of contacting CNN and asking them to take it down. (When you choose to remove an iReport, the next iMovie window tells you as much.)

This menu option doesn't really offer you a way to remove the video, it's just giving you a way to tell iMovie that you've removed it. In the case of an iReport, removing a video is much easier said than done, so be sure that you know exactly what you're uploading.

Custom Web Pages: Two Roads

What's amazing about the MobileMe Gallery is that it's so perfectly tailored for presenting movies. The black background, the high-tech scroll bar, the absence of text…it's just awesome.

Unless, of course, you *want* to control the background, the look, and the text on the page. Why can't you embed a movie into a *normal* web page, just like any ordinary person?

Actually, you can, in two ways:

- **The iWeb way**. Use iWeb, which is one of the other iLife '11 programs. It's a website-design program that requires zero hand-coding, so you don't need to know HTML (the language of the Web). You just pick a page design, type in new text, slap in some pictures or movies, and you're done. iMovie can hand off a movie to iWeb with only a couple of mouse clicks; from there, you can incorporate them into the web pages you design.

Tip: Once you design a website in iWeb, you can post it on your MobileMe account (if you're paid up) *or* post it using the space provided by, for example, your Internet provider. In other words, you don't *have* to post it to a MobileMe page.

- **The freehand way**. Suppose you're a savvy, webmastery kind of person, and you design your own web pages and post them on the Internet without any help from sissy templates like iWeb. In that case, you can embed *any* movie into *any* of your web pages—without paying Apple *any* money every year.

The rest of this chapter covers both of these methods for creating your own web pages with movies in them.

iMovie to iWeb

This isn't a book about iWeb, of course, but here's enough information to get your movie onto a web page via the program—and hang the whole thing on the Internet for the masses to see:

UP TO SPEED

Meet the Media Browser

The *Media Browser* is a common, central multimedia library for your Mac that's designed to facilitate sharing photos, music, and movies among Apple programs. You can open the Media Browser in programs like Keynote, Pages, Numbers, iDVD, GarageBand, iWeb, and iMovie. (The Media Browser looks slightly different in every iApp; Figure 14-10 shows what it looks like in iWeb.)

And here's what you'll see in the Browser: music from iTunes (complete with your playlists) and GarageBand; photos from iPhoto (complete with your albums) and Pho-toBooth; and movies from iMovie, iPhoto, iTunes, and the Movies folder in your Home folder.

The Media Browser is especially important to iMovie be-cause it provides by far the easiest way for you to hand off

your videos to iWeb, Keynote, or any other program that speaks Media Browser-ese.

In fact, iMovie even uses the Media Browser when you up-load videos to YouTube or your MobileMe Gallery. If you watch the progress bars closely, you'll see that these are actu-ally two-step procedures. First, iMovie creates a compressed QuickTime version of your movie and puts it *in the Media Browser*; then it uploads a copy of that movie to the Web. The original movie, however, *remains* in the Media Browser. That's how iMovie always seems to know which size ver-sions of each project you've sent to the Web (Figure 14-3)—because they're still sitting right there on your hard drive!

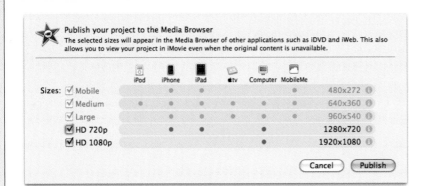

Figure 14-10:
The Media Browser (see the box below) is your one-stop shop-ping center for all the music, photos, and movies on your com-puter. You're about to load it up with even more movies to share with your other Apple programs.

---

1. **With the finished iMovie project open, choose Share→Media Browser.**

   The dialog box shown in Figure 14-10 appears (see page 310 for a description of its options).

2. **Choose the size(s) you want for the movie on your web page.**

   You can choose multiple sizes to send to the Media Browser, if you like, although the more sizes you choose, the more hard drive space you use. (Word to the wise: In general, choose Tiny or Mobile. Use Medium only if all of your fans use high-speed Internet connections.)

3. **Click Publish.**

   iMovie cranks away, compressing your project to an exported QuickTime movie file at the size you specified.

Note: iMovie keeps track of which sizes of each project you export to the Media Browser. If you see some of the size checkboxes dimmed, it's because the Media Browser *already* has versions of this project in those sizes.

---

4. **Open iWeb (Figure 14-11). Open the page you want to edit, or choose File→New Page to create a new one. Click the Media button at the bottom of the screen (or choose View→Show Media Browser).**

   Clicking the Media button opens—what else?—the Media Browser.

Figure 14-11:
Welcome to iWeb, a what-you-see-is-what-your-website-will-look-like editing world for websites. The left column lists the web pages you've created so far; the links at the top connect to them. The small Inspector palette (here labeled QuickTime) lets you tweak your movie's characteristics.

5. **Find the movie you exported in step 3 and drag it wherever you want it on the page.**

   If you drag it on top of one of the sample photos, it snaps nicely into alignment. Finish editing your page as usual in iWeb.

6. **Edit the page title, subtitle, and description text.**

   Don't be concerned by the presence of all the Latin ("Lorem ipsum dolor amet…"); that's just placeholder text. Simply drag your cursor through it and type new stuff to replace it.

7. **Edit the design of the page, if you like.**

   Choose View→Show Inspector. The Inspector window's eighth tab, labeled QuickTime, is a palette of movie-frame options. (First, click the movie itself.) You can control its start and end points, choose the poster frame (a movie still the page displays when your movie *isn't* playing), and whether or not the clip autostarts, loops, and shows its playback controls.

8. **In the lower-left corner of iWeb, click Publish Site. In the confirmation box, click OK.**

   This is the big moment: iWeb connects to your MobileMe website and transfers the video and its page to the server. This magic requires, of course, that you already have a MobileMe account (page 319). It can also take a *very* long time. When the upload is complete, a dialog box appears containing three buttons: Announce (email the site's address to your friends), Visit Site Now, and OK.

   Congratulations—you've just published your own website with a movie in it.

Tip: You don't need a MobileMe account to use iWeb. If you maintain your own website, for example, click your site's name in the left column of the iWeb window and you see a list of options for the site. Click the "Publish to" menu and choose either FTP Server or Local Folder.

If you know your web server's FTP (file-transfer protocol) settings—usually an address and a password—you can enter that information directly into iWeb, which makes publishing your iWeb site a piece of cake. If you upload files to your server some other way, choose Local Folder. You wind up with a folder of correctly linked HTML documents and folders on your hard drive. All you have to do is manually upload them to your site.

What you get when you're done

When you see what you've created with iWeb, you'll be impressed: It's a professional-looking, stylishly titled web page with your movie plugged right in. Click the ▶ button under your movie to start playback.

Note: In the web addresses of your MobileMe websites, capitalization counts. If your friends type one of these addresses into a browser with incorrect capitalization, they may get only a "missing page" message. It might work better to send your friends a much shorter, easier-to-remember address. You can convert long URLs into shorter ones using a free URL-redirection service. At *www.tinyurl.com*, for example, you can turn that long address into something as short as *http://tinyurl.com/bus4*.

Editing or deleting the web page

To update your movie, launch iWeb and make your changes, and then click the Publish button at the bottom of the screen. iWeb sets about updating the movie page online.

To delete a page, click its name in iWeb's left-side panel (the Site Organizer) and press the Delete key. Then click Publish at the bottom of the window to tell iWeb, "OK, make the online version of my site match what's in iWeb." Deleting a movie page like this also deletes all the online movie files, which frees up space on your iDisk.

Posting a Movie on Your Site

Maybe you prefer the control and freedom of putting movies on your *own* web page, designed the way you like it, without any hand-holding from Apple's templates or having to sign up for a MobileMe account.

If you already have a website, you can export a QuickTime version of your flick from iMovie (see Chapter 15) and upload it to your site, no matter what the hosting service. (Most Internet accounts, including those provided by your cable-modem or DSL company, like Comcast or AT&T, come with free space for pages uploaded in this way.)

This is the most labor-intensive route, but it offers much more flexibility if you know how to work with HTML to create more sophisticated pages. It's also the route you should take if you hope to incorporate the resulting movie into an existing site (that is, one where movies aren't the only attraction).

This isn't really a book about web design, but to get you started, a free PDF appendix to this chapter, called "Movies on Custom Websites," awaits you on this book's Missing CD page at *http://tinyurl.com/33blf68*. It provides the HTML code you need to post a movie on your web page, make it pop up in a window or play embedded in the page, look into QuickTime Streaming Server, and other advanced topics.

From iMovie to QuickTime

To give your audience the best and most cinematic movie-viewing experience, play your finished iMovie production on a TV (from a DVD, on tape, or streamed to an Apple TV); or show it at high resolution on a big computer screen. That way, your public gets to see the full-sized picture that your camcorder captured. (iMovie '11 can't play a movie from tape or export your finished project to tape for archiving and viewing—but iMovie 6 can. See Chapter 12 for details.)

But when you want to *distribute* your movies, you should convert them to Quick-Time files. Both Mac and Windows machines can play QuickTime movies with little more than a double-click, and your options for creating QuickTime files are far greater than those when you save movies to videocassette or DVD. You can email a QuickTime file to somebody or post it on the Web for all the world to see (Chapter 14). You can put bigger QuickTime files onto a disk, like a recordable CD, DVD, external hard drive, or an iPod, to transport them. And you can export only the audio portion of your movie—or only the video portion.

This chapter covers all these techniques, step by step.

Understanding QuickTime

When a computer plays back video, it displays hundreds or thousands of still images in rapid succession. If you've ever worked with color images, you know how storage-hungry they are. A full-screen photograph might occupy 5 MB or 10 MB of space on your hard drive, for example, and take several seconds to open.

Most computers today are fast enough to open and flash 30 full-screen, photographic-quality pictures per second. Problem is, movies of that size and quality consume hundreds of megabytes of disk space, and take many hours to download from the Web or as an email attachment—a guaranteed way to annoy citizens of the Internet and your friends, and doom your moviemaking career to obscurity.

That's why most QuickTime movies *aren't* full-screen, photographic-quality films. In fact, most of them are much smaller files, slimmed down in three ways:

- **The playback window is much smaller**. It's rare to see a QuickTime movie fill a computer screen. Instead, most movie masters create QuickTime movies that play back in a much smaller window (Figure 15-1), therefore requiring far less data and resulting in far smaller files.

Figure 15-1:
Here's the same movie in two playback sizes. High-definition movies are, at a minimum, 1,280 pixels wide and 720 pixels tall (1280 × 720). Cut each dimension in half (640 × 360), and the resulting video is one-quarter the size of the original. That makes a big difference in the size of the files on your hard drive (and in the smoothness of Internet playback). Using the same video compression settings, this 28-second clip weighs in at 32 MB in high definition, and only 7 MB at the smaller size.

- **The frame rate is lower**. Instead of showing the standard 30 frames per second, many QuickTime movies have far lower frame rates; even 15 frames per second produces smooth motion. On the Web, especially during live QuickTime broadcasts, still lower frame rates, like five or ten frames per second, are common. The resulting broadcast is noticeably jerky, but requires so little data that even people with telephone-line modems can watch live events.

- **The video is *compressed*.** This is the big one—the technical aspect of QuickTime movies that gives you the most control over the resulting quality of your video. In short, when QuickTime compresses your video, it discards some of the information that describes each frame. True, the picture deteriorates as a consequence, but the resulting QuickTime file is a tiny fraction of its original size. The following section describes this compression business in much greater detail.

The bottom line is that by combining these three techniques, iMovie can turn a 10-gigabyte digital movie into a *3-megabyte* file that's small enough to email or post on your web page. The resulting movie won't play as smoothly, fill as much of the screen, or look as good as the original footage, but your viewers won't care. They'll be delighted to be able to watch your movie at all, and grateful that the file didn't take hours to download. (And besides, anyone already familiar with QuickTime movies knows what to expect from them.)

Tip: The newer the QuickTime version on your Mac, the better and faster the movie-exporting process. Mac OS X's Software Update feature is supposed to alert you every time a new version becomes available (if you have it turned on in System Preferences).

A Crash Course in Video Compression

The following discussion explores some of the technical underpinnings of Quick-Time technology. It may take you a few minutes to complete this behind-the-scenes tour of how a computer stores video, but without understanding the basics, iMovie's QuickTime-exporting options will seem utterly impenetrable.

Spatial compression

Suppose you overhear a fellow Mac fan telling her husband, "Would you mind running to the grocery store? We need an eight-ounce box of Cajun Style Rice-A-Roni, and an eight-ounce box of Cajun Style Rice-A-Roni, and also an eight-ounce box of Cajun Style Rice-A-Roni."

You'd probably assume that she's enjoyed a little too much of that new-computer smell. Why didn't she just tell him to pick up three boxes of it?

When it comes to storing video on a hard drive, your Macintosh faces the same issue. When it stores a picture file, it has to "write down" the precise color of *each pixel* in each frame. It could, of course, store the information like this:

- *Top row, pixel 1*: Beige
- *Top row, pixel 2*: Beige
- *Top row, pixel 3*: Beige

…and so on. Clearly, this much information would take up a lot of storage space and take a long time to download.

Fortunately, when Apple engineers designed QuickTime in the 1980s, they realized that the individual dots in solid-colored areas of a picture don't need to be described individually. That top row of pixels could be represented much more efficiently, and take up a lot less disk space, if the Mac were simply to write down:

- *Top row*: 60 consecutive pixels of beige

This simplified example shows the power of *compression software*, whose job it is to make graphics files smaller by recording their pixel colors more efficiently. Compression explains why a JPEG file always takes up far less space on your hard drive (and less time to download) than, for example, the Photoshop document that created it; when you create a JPEG file, you automatically compress it as part of the file-saving process.

This form of file-size reduction is called *spatial* or *intraframe* compression. iMovie analyzes the picture in each frame of a movie and reduces the amount of information needed to describe it.

Temporal compression

But there's another way to reduce the size of a QuickTime file. Not only is there a lot of redundant color information from pixel to pixel in a single frame, there's also a lot of repetition from *frame to frame*.

Suppose, for example, you captured footage of a man sitting behind a desk, talking about roofing materials. Picture the first pixel of the back wall in that piece of footage. Chances are good that this pixel's color remains absolutely consistent, frame after frame, for several seconds at least, especially if you shot the footage using a tripod. Same thing with the rug, the color of the desk, the fern in the pot, and so on. These elements of the picture don't change at all from one frame to the next.

Here again, if it were your job to record what's on each frame, you could choose the slow and laborious method:

- *Frame 1*: The upper-left pixel is beige.
- *Frame 2*: The upper-left pixel is still beige.
- *Frame 3*: The upper-left pixel is *still* beige.

…and so on. In this case, a clever QuickTime movie would record the details of only the *first frame*. "The upper-left pixel on the first frame is beige," it might begin. In filmmaker terminology, that first, completely memorized image is called the *key frame*.

Thereafter, rather than memorizing the status of every pixel on the second frame, the third frame, and so on, the Mac might just say, "For the next 60 frames, pixel #1 is exactly the same color as it was in the first frame." That more efficient description just made the resulting QuickTime file a *lot* smaller, as shown in Figure 15-2. (Geeks often call the subsequent, shorthand-recorded frames *delta frames*.)

This kind of shorthand is called *temporal* or *interframe* compression, because it refers to the way pixels change over time, from one frame to the next.

Figure 15-2:
When iMovie saves a QuickTime movie, it doesn't bother writing down the description of every pixel on every frame. If a lot of areas remain identical from frame to frame, the QuickTime movie doesn't remember anything more than, "Same as the previous frame." In this example, the faded portions of the picture are the areas that the QuickTime movie data doesn't describe—because they're the same as the first (key) frame. (At last you understand why using a tripod for your footage doesn't just give your movies a more professional look; by ensuring that most of the picture stays exactly the same from frame to frame, a tripod-shot video helps produce smaller QuickTime files, too.)

About Codecs

When you save your movie in QuickTime format, iMovie asks you which of several schemes you want to use to compress your footage. In technical terms, it asks you to choose a *codec* from a long list of possibilities. Codec is short for "compressor/decompressor," the software module that translates the pixel-by-pixel description of your footage into the more compact QuickTime format, and then *un*translates it during playback.

Each QuickTime codec works differently. Some provide spatial compression, some temporal, some both. Some are ideal for animations, others for live action. Some work well on slower computers, others on faster ones. Some try to maintain excellent picture quality, but produce very large QuickTime files, and others make the opposite tradeoff. Later in this chapter, you'll read about each of these codecs and when to use them.

In the meantime, all this background information should help explain a few phenomena pertaining to converting your movies into QuickTime files:

- **Saving a QuickTime movie takes a long time**. It's nothing like saving, say, a word-processing document. Comparing every pixel on every frame with every pixel on the next frame involves massive amounts of number-crunching, which takes time. (Some codecs take longer than others, however.)

- **QuickTime movies usually don't look as good as the original video**. Now you know why: In the act of shrinking your movie down to a file size that's reasonable for emailing, copying to a CD-ROM, and so on, a codec's job is to *throw away* some of the data that makes a movie look vivid and clear.

- **QuickTime is an exercise in compromise**. By choosing the appropriate codec and changing its settings appropriately, you can create a QuickTime movie with excellent picture and sound. Unfortunately, it will consume a lot of disk space. If you want a small file *and* excellent picture and sound quality, you can make the QuickTime movie play in a smaller window—320 × 240 pixels, for example, instead of 640 × 480 or something larger—or at a slower frame rate. The guidelines in this chapter, some experimentation, and the nature of the movie you're making all contribute to helping you make a codec decision.

The Export Pop-up Menu

After you finish editing your iMovie production, the first step in exporting it as a QuickTime movie is to choose Share→"Export using QuickTime."

The "Save exported file as" dialog box appears (Figure 15-3). Here, you'll eventually type a name and choose a folder location for the file you're about to save. But for now, resist the temptation.

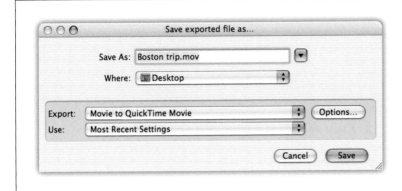

The real power of this little box lies in its buttons and pop-up menus. For starters, the Export pop-up menu (visible in Figure 15-3) gives you a wealth of conversion options. This is your opportunity to save your film as:

- **An AVI file to give to your Windows PC-using friends**. Choose "Movie to AVI."

- **A huge folder full of still images, one per frame of your movie**. Choose "Movie to Image Sequence." Click the Options button to specify the file format—like JPEG or Photoshop—and how many stills per second you want.

- **A soundtrack**. Here's a great opportunity to convert your movie's audio tracks into standalone sound files. Choose "Sound to AIFF," "Sound to Wave," or whatever format you want (see page 347 for the differences among audio codecs).

  You'll find this feature very handy every now and then. For example, certain troubleshooting situations, usually involving an out-of-place noise, call for exporting and reimporting your finished soundtrack—in essence, temporarily splitting it apart from the video. (You can even edit the soundtrack file in GarageBand or another program along the way, if you're so inclined. That's one way to get rid of the occasional pop or crackle.)

- **A movie that's formatted for the iPod, iPhone, or Apple TV**. Of course, there are easier ways to go about these tasks; see Chapter 13.

But most of the time, you'll ignore the Export pop-up menu. Usually, you'll want to leave it set to "Movie to QuickTime Movie," and then click the Options button to make some settings changes.

The Options button opens a very important dialog box: the Movie Settings box (Figure 15-4). Here's where you can export your finished product with *exactly* the size-smoothness-speed compromise you want.

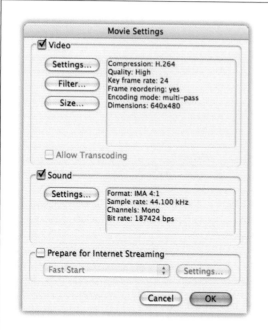

Figure 15-4:
*When you click Options, you get the Movie Settings box.
It's just a summary screen for the dialog boxes that hide
behind it: Settings, Filter, Size, and so on.*

You'll notice that this box has three buttons for video: Settings, Filter, and Size. Below that, you get one Settings button for sound, and at the bottom of the box, you get options for *Internet streaming*. You'll learn about all these settings in the next few pages.

The Video Settings Button

The Settings button for video takes you to the powerful Standard Video Compression Settings dialog box (Figure 15-5), the heart of the entire Options software suite.

Here's what the controls do:

Compression Type pop-up menu

The Compression Type pop-up menu at the top lets you choose one of several dozen codecs—or None, which means that iMovie won't compress your project at all. Each codec compresses your footage using a scheme that entails different compromises. See page 337 for details. For now, note that for live video you can play back on today's computers, the H.264 codec almost always produces the highest quality at reasonably small file sizes.

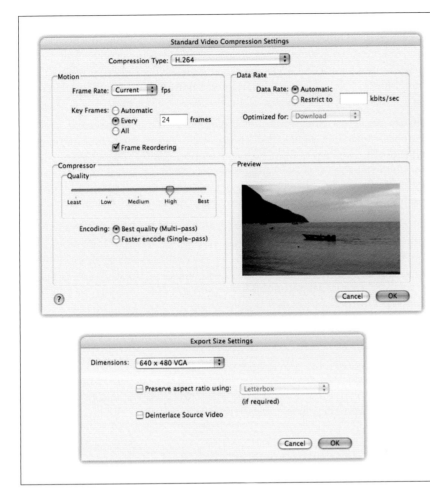

Figure 15-5:
Top: This dialog box gives you point-by-point control over the look, size, and quality of the QuickTime movie you export. Not all these controls are available for all codecs. Furthermore, only some of the codecs have an Options button in the middle of the dialog box.

Bottom: Here's where you can specify the dimensions of the movie you're saving, in pixels. (This box appears when you click the Size button shown in Figure 15-4.)

Frames per second

The number you specify in the Frame Rate box makes an enormous difference in the smoothness of the movie's playback. As always, however, it's a tradeoff—the higher the number, the larger the QuickTime file, and the more difficult it is to email, store, or transfer. You can type any number between 1 and 60 in the Frame Rate box (click Custom in the pop-up menu to call it up), or choose a preset from the pop-up menu itself.

Here's what you can expect from these settings:

- **8, 10**. These movies are very compact, and make good candidates to send over the Internet. They're also very jerky on playback.

- **12, 15**. These are the most common frame rates for the QuickTime movies you find on the Internet. By playing only half as many frames as you'd see on a TV show, the QuickTime movie requires less data, resulting in a smaller file size and, most likely, smoother playback over slower connections. And yet this many frames per second tricks the eye into perceiving satisfying, smooth motion. Most people can sense that they aren't quite seeing the motion they'd see on a TV, but they don't miss the other 15 frames each second.

- **24, 25**. An actual Hollywood movie plays at 24 frames per second, and the European television signal (PAL) plays at 25. You can use these settings, in other words, when you want excellent motion quality without going all the way to the maximum of 29.97 frames per second of the American TV standard (NTSC). You save a little bit of disk space while still showing as many frames as people are accustomed to seeing in motion pictures.

- **29.97**. If you're wondering how this oddball number got into the pop-up menu, you're not alone. As it turns out, every source that refers to television broadcasts as having 30 frames per second (including other chapters in this book) is rounding off the number for convenience. In fact, a true television broadcast plays *29.97* frames per second. iMovie can reproduce that rate for you, if it's important to do so. In fact, this is iMovie's top frame rate.

- **30**. This is the proper setting for full-quality high-definition footage.

Tip: If you're not working with hi-def video, ignore 30 in the Frame Rate pop-up menu; it's for suckers. *Standard*-definition video, at least in North America, is itself 29.97 frames per second. So asking iMovie to save a QuickTime movie with an even *higher* rate is like thinking you'll be wealthier if you exchange your dollar bills for quarters. If you *do* try choosing 30 from the Frame Rate pop-up menu, when you click OK, iMovie will scold you, tell you you're out of line, and then return you to the dialog box to make another choice.

---

30 fps Drop-Frame

OK, I'll bite. Why on earth did the USA, which is supposed to be so technically advanced, settle on a TV standard that plays at such an oddball frame rate? Why is it 29.97? Why wasn't it rounded off to 30?

The 29.97 frame rate, known in the TV business as 30 fps drop-frame, dates back to the dawn of color TV. As studios prepared to launch color TV broadcasts in January 1954, network engineers wanted to make sure that the expensive black-and-white TV sets of the day could receive the color shows, too. (Talk about backward-compatible software!)

Trouble was, when they tried to broadcast a color signal at the then-standard 30 frames per second, the extra color information wound up distorting the audio signal. Eventually, they hit upon a discovery: If they slowed down the frame rate just a hair, the distortion disappeared. The video, meanwhile, looked just as good at 29.97 frames per second as it did at 30.

A standard was born.

You don't have to export your movie in its entirety just to see the effects of different frame-rate settings. Create a dummy project that contains only a few seconds of a movie, and try exporting it at each frame rate. Then play back these short Quick-Time movies. You'll get a self-taught course in the effects of different frames-per-second settings.

Key frame every _ frames

You read about *key frames* earlier in this chapter—they're the full frames that get memorized in your QuickTime movie, so that QuickTime can store less data for subsequent frames. (See Figure 15-2, page 337.)

Oddly Shaped Movies

I'm doing a project where I need my movie to be perfectly square, not in a 4:3 width-to-height ratio. But every time I try to specify these dimensions in the QuickTime Settings dialog box, I get a distorted, squished iMovie movie. What can I do?

What you're really asking is how to crop your movie.

iMovie '11, of course, is capable of cropping your video—but only in the standard 4:3 or 16:9 aspect ratios (see page 62).

Unfortunately, neither iMovie nor QuickTime Player Pro (Chapter 16) have a simple way to crop the picture for any other aspect ratio.

Apple's professional video-editing programs, Final Cut Pro and Final Cut Express, can freely crop video, but they're expensive. Unfortunately, not many cheap options exist for this dilemma. Purchase either of these and you at least get an all-around powerful editing tool.

But if you have more expertise than cash, the freeware program ffmpegX can crop video, too. You have to do it by typing in coordinates (rather than adjusting a visual cropping frame), but it works. (You can download ffmpegX from this book's Missing CD page at *http://tinyurl.com/33blf68*.)

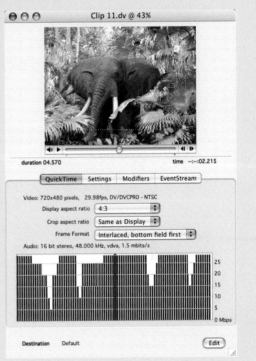

In most cases, one key frame per second is about right. For movies you'll play back from beginning to end without rewinding to review footage, you don't need as many key frames, so it's safe to increase the number in this box. This makes key frames less frequent and reduces the size of your movie file.

Quality slider

This control offers another tradeoff between file size and video quality. In general, the value iMovie proposes (usually Medium or High) gives you the best balance between size and quality. But on important projects, by all means experiment. Export a representative sample of your movie several times, moving the slider each time, so you can compare the results.

Limit data rate

Whether you distribute your movie by CD-ROM, cable modem, 56 K modem, or some other means, each medium delivers information at a different rate. If you want to ensure that your movie doesn't skip any frames or jerk around on playback, go to the Data Rate section of the dialog box. There, turn on the checkbox next to "Restrict to," and then type a number into the box.

The precise number you type depends on the way you distribute your movie. Here are some guidelines:

If the movie will be delivered by a:	Use this maximum data rate:
56 K modem	5 K/second
T1 or cable modem	20 K/second
CD-ROM	100 K/second
Hard drive	250 K/second

iMovie automatically adjusts the picture quality as necessary, on a moment-by-moment basis, so that the QuickTime movie never exceeds this rate.

The Filter Button

As noted in Chapter 6, iMovie '11 doesn't offer all the special effects found in iMovie 6; it's missing the flashy ones like Lens Flare and Rain, for example. But unbeknownst to nine out of 10 iMovie fans, you can still tap into an enormous range of visual effects, which you can apply to your movie on its way *out* of iMovie. Simply click the Filter button in the Movie Settings dialog box (shown in Figure 15-4).

When you do, the dialog box shown in Figure 15-6 appears. By opening the various flippy triangles, you'll find a lot of favorite effects that were in the old iMovie (color balance, brightness and contrast, lens flare, fake old-film grain)—and a few that weren't (blur or sharpen, emboss).

The list of effects appears at the top left of the box; you can preview the results at the lower left. Use the controls on the right side of the box to change the settings for each effect.

As you work, remember that QuickTime applies whatever filter you select here to your *entire movie*. Given that, you might be inclined to pooh-pooh this whole feature—really, when would you ever want to apply the same degree of blur to an entire movie?

But with a little forethought, you can still apply an effect to just one clip. The trick is to create a new iMovie project containing *only that clip*. Export it using the Apple Intermediate Codec (page 48) to make sure that you retain the footage's digital-video size and quality—and apply the filter you want in the process. Save this exported chunk somewhere easy to find—on your desktop, for example.

When it's all over, you can reimport your exported, processed clip into the original iMovie project.

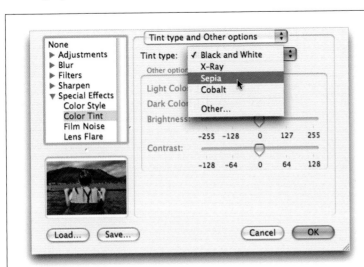

Figure 15-6:
The Filter dialog box has special effects that let you adjust the color, brightness, or contrast of the footage; sharpen or blur it; add a phony lens flare; or even add fake film "noise," like scratches and dust. Using both the Load and Save buttons, you can even save an effects configuration to your hard drive, so you can apply exactly the same settings to another clip at another time. (Unfortunately, you can apply only one effect at a time.)

Warning: iMovie preserves your Options settings from export to export, even if weeks or months elapse in between. That's an especially treacherous feature when it comes to these filters. Next time you sit through a 45-minute export you may find that the resulting movie is all embossed and color-shifted because you used those settings last time. The only way to escape this nightmare is to reopen the Filter dialog box, and then choose None.

The Size Button

And now, back to your tour of the Movie Settings dialog box shown in Figure 15-4.

The Size button on the Movie Settings dialog box summons the dialog box shown at the bottom of Figure 15-5, where—after clicking "Use custom size"—you can specify the dimensions for your QuickTime movie's playback window. Of course, the larger the window, the bigger the resulting file, the longer it will take to save, and the slower it will travel over the Internet.

Keeping the dimensions you specify here in a width-to-height aspect ratio of 4:3 (for standard video) or 16:9 (for high-def video) is important. The QuickTime software plays back your movie most smoothly if you retain these relative proportions. Furthermore, if the width and height you specify *aren't* in one of those ratios, iMovie has to squish the picture accordingly, which may distort your movie like a funhouse mirror.

Most QuickTime movies play in one of several standard sizes, like 320 × 240 or 640 × 480—both examples of the 4:3 aspect ratio. Still, there are dozens of other possible sizes that maintain the correct proportions.

Audio Settings

You'll find a *second* Settings button in the Movie Settings dialog box (see Figure 15-4) under Audio. It lets you specify how—and by how much—QuickTime compresses your *soundtrack* (Figure 15-7).

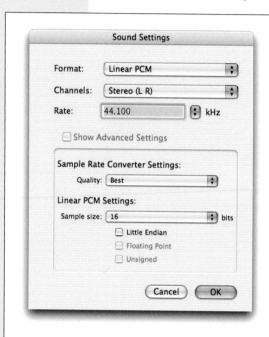

Figure 15-7:
It probably goes without saying that the better the audio quality you specify, the larger your QuickTime movie file will be. In any case, this is the dialog box where you make such decisions. Audio isn't nearly as data-greedy as video, so compressing it isn't quite as urgent an issue (unless you want your movie to play over the Internet).

Format

When most people think of codecs—those who've even *heard* of codecs, that is—they think of *video* compression. But iMovie gives you a choice of audio codecs, too. The Format pop-up menu lets you specify the one you want to use.

Many of the audio codecs aren't, in fact, appropriate for movie soundtracks. Remember that QuickTime provides these codecs, not iMovie, and that QuickTime is designed to be an all-purpose multimedia format. It's supposed to be just as good at creating pictureless sound files as it is at creating movies. It's also supposed to recognize every format that ever trudged through the music industry—including plenty that nobody uses anymore. The ones you might conceivably care about are these:

- **AAC**. If you choose this audio codec, you'll save your soundtrack in AAC format—the same one that songs you buy from the iTunes music store use. The sound quality is superb, although you can degrade it if you're stingy with the settings you choose when you click Options. (For best results, choose at least 128 Kbits/second from the Bit Rate pop-up menu to match the quality of iTunes songs.) The file size, meanwhile, is only a fraction of the original. It's a welcome and useful choice for movies not intended for Internet playback.

- **AMR Narrowband**. AMR stands for Adaptive Multi-Rate, and it's intended for movies in the 3GPP format (a standard developed for cellphones). Use it if you have a 3GPP-compatible phone. For other phones, use the Qualcomm PureVoice codec (described below), click Options, and then turn on the Half Rate option.

- **Apple Lossless**. This option gives you truly *lossless* audio compression. Lossless means that although this codec cuts the audio track's file size in half, it doesn't lose *any* of the sound quality in the process. The resulting files are too big for the Web or email, but Apple Lossless is a great audio codec when you save a movie for best-quality playback from a hard drive.

- **IMA 4:1**. This codec was one of the first QuickTime audio compressors. It provides excellent audio quality—you *can't* change it to a sample size less than 16-bit—and plays back equally well on Macintosh and Windows computers. It's great for movies you'll play from a hard drive or CD, or over a fast Internet connection.

- **QDesign Music 2**. This aging codec is still useful for movies you distribute online or via email. It maintains terrific audio quality, but compresses the sound a great deal, producing files small enough to deliver over dial-up modems. Apple's favorite example: One minute of music from an audio CD requires 11 MB of disk space, but after this codec compresses it, it consumes only 150 KB and sounds almost as good.

Rate, Size

A computer captures and plays back sound by recording thousands of individual slices, or snapshots, of sound per second. As though describing somebody at a wine tasting, computer nerds call this process *sampling* the sound.

The two controls here let you specify *how many samples* you want the Mac to take per second (the sampling rate) and *how much data* it's allowed to use to describe each sample (the sampling size).

Even if that technical explanation means nothing to you, the principle is easy enough to absorb: The higher the Rate and Size settings (see Figure 15-7), the better the audio quality and the larger the QuickTime file. The following are a few examples of the kind of file-size increases you can expect for each of several popular rate and size settings. (Note that the information here is *per channel*. If you're going for stereo, double the kilobyte ratings shown here.)

- **11 kHz, 8 bits**. Sounds like you're hearing the audio track over a bad telephone connection. Tinny. Use it only for speech. 662 KB per minute.

- **11 kHz, 16 bits**. Sounds a lot better. Roughly the sound quality you get from the built-in Mac speaker. 1.3 MB per minute.

- **22 kHz, 16 bits**. Starting to sound very good. Suitable for playing on a computer equipped with external speakers. 2.6 MB per minute.

- **44.1 kHz, 16 bits**. This is the real thing, the ultimate audio experience. CD-quality audio. Suitable for headphone listening. It's the ultimate storage and transmission headache, too—this much data requires 5.3 MB per minute, mono. But of course, you'd never go this far without also including the stereo experience, so make that 10.6 MB per minute in stereo.

Channels: Mono/Stereo

These radio buttons let you specify whether or not your movie's soundtrack is in stereo.

Exporting your QuickTime movie in stereo format is often a waste of data. Many computers, including Power Macs, Mac Pros, and Mac Minis, don't *have* stereo speakers.

Furthermore, even though most camcorders include a stereo microphone, there's virtually no separation between the right and left channels, thanks to the fact that manufacturers mount the microphone directly onto the tiny camcorder. Nor does iMovie let you edit the right and left audio channels independently. Even if people are listening to your movie with stereo speakers, they'll hear essentially the same thing out of each.

Therefore, consider using the Mono setting as you try to minimize the amount of data required to play back the soundtrack.

The Video Codecs: A Catalog

When you decide to export your iMovie production as a QuickTime movie, you can exert a great deal of control over how the Mac produces the resulting movie file by clicking Options in the dialog box shown in Figure 15-3 (page 339), and then clicking Settings (Figure 15-4, page 340). You get access to a long list of video codecs. Few of them are very useful for everyday use. Many of them are intended for:

- **Saving still frames (not movies)**. Examples: BMP, PNG, Photo-JPEG, JPEG 2000, TGA, TIFF, Planar RGB.

- **Keeping around for old times' sake, despite having been technologically surpassed**. Examples: Cinepak, Component Video, Sorenson.

- **Professional cameras and high-end production firms**. Examples: Apple Pixlet Video, Apple ProRes, MPEG IMX, HDCAM.

Most of the time, the compressor called H.264 will make you and your audience the happiest.

Tip: The list of codecs in your dialog boxes may not match what you see here. Your codecs reflect the version of QuickTime you have, which may be older or newer than version 7.6, described here.

Here are some of the codecs that *aren't* totally useless:

- **Animation**. This codec is significant because, at its Best quality setting, it maintains *all* the original picture quality while managing to create smaller files with no compression at all. (As its name implies, this codec was originally designed to process video composed of large blocks of solid colors—that is, cartoons.) The resulting file is huge when compared with the other codecs described here, but not as huge as it would be if you chose None in this pop-up menu.

- **Apple Intermediate Codec**. You can read all about this clever, sneaky codec on page 48. It's how Apple makes it possible for iMovie to handle high-definition video and AVCHD video at standard-video speeds: by first *converting* it into this intermediate format for use on the Mac. Your primary interest in this codec is for transferring videos back and forth between different versions of iMovie.

- **DV/DVCPRO-NTSC**. Suppose you just completed a masterful movie, and the thought of compressing it to a much smaller, image-degraded QuickTime movie breaks your heart. You can use this codec to turn your finished, effect-enhanced, fully edited iMovie production into a new, raw DV clip, exactly like the DV clips that iMovie captures when it imports footage from a tape camcorder.

  You might do this if, for example, you want to send a full-quality DV clip to somebody electronically, or as an alternative to the Apple Intermediate Codec for moving video between editing programs. (*DV*, of course, means digital video; NTSC is the format used in the Western Hemisphere and Japan. DVCPRO50 is a high-end variation used in professional TV cameras.)

- **DV-PAL, DVCPRO-PAL**. These options let you export your iMovie masterpiece in the European video format (PAL), while retaining full size and frame rate. (DVCPRO and DVCPRO50 are slight variants of the DV format, intended for use with expensive professional broadcast TV video gear.) Unfortunately, the quality of the video suffers when you make this kind of conversion, especially in action scenes.

- **H.264**. This is it—Apple's favorite video codec. It's also the format used by satellite TV, high-definition DVDs, iPod and iPhone videos, MobileMe Web gallery videos, newer YouTube videos, and other quality-dependent videos. Technically speaking, it's a flavor of *MPEG-4*, described below. It looks spectacular, compresses relatively well, and scales beautifully from cellphone screens all the way up to high-definition TVs. It's not, however, the fastest codec on earth. (If you have a client standing beside you, tapping his foot, the MPEG-4 Video codec takes less time to export.)

- **Photo - JPEG**. This codec (also called Motion JPEG) doesn't perform any temporal (frame-to-frame) compression. It saves each movie frame as an individual, full-sized color picture. The disadvantage is, of course, that the resulting files are extremely large.

So what good is it? Motion JPEG is the format that many professional DV-editing machines (like those from Avid, Accom, and Discreet) use. Because there's no key-frame business going on, editors can make cuts at any frame. (Doing so isn't always possible in a file created by a codec that stores only the *difference* between one frame and the next. A particular frame might contain data that describes only new information.)

Note: Motion JPEG is *not* the same thing as MPEG, which is the format used to store movies on the DVD discs you rent from Netflix. Despite the similarity of names, the differences are enormous. For example, MPEG uses temporal compression and requires special software to create it.

- **MPEG-4 Video**. MPEG-4 is an older version of the H.264 codec described above. (By the way, AAC, the audio format of the iTunes music store, is an audio version of MPEG-4.) It compresses your movie much more quickly, although the files aren't as small and the quality isn't as good as H.264.

- **None**. If quality is everything to you and you don't have to worry about disk space or Internetability, you can use this option, which (like the DV codecs) doesn't compress your video at all. The resulting QuickTime file may contain so much data that your computer can't even play it back smoothly. You can, however, put it in a cryogenic tank in anticipation of the day when superfast computers come your way.

Saving a QuickTime Movie

All right—having read all of that theory of QuickTime and compression, you're ready to do the actual exporting.

1. **Choose Share→"Export using QuickTime."**

   The "Save exported file as" dialog box appears (Figure 15-3).

2. **Type a name for your movie.**

   Unless, of course, you want to name your movie whatever the current project is called, as iMovie suggests.

   Don't remove the letters *.mov* from the end of the file name, especially if you might play it back on a Windows computer. That suffix identifies movie files for machines that aren't savvy enough to know one when they see it.

3. **Navigate to the folder where you want to store the resulting QuickTime file.**

   You can simply press ⌘-D if you want to save your QuickTime Movie to the desktop, where it'll be easy to find.

4. **Make sure the Export pop-up menu says "Movie to QuickTime Movie." Click Options, and then click Settings at the top of the next dialog box.**

   The dialog box shown in Figure 15-5 (top) appears.

---

5. **Choose your compression options, and then click OK.**

   You return to the "Save exported file as" dialog box.

6. **Click Save.**

   Now the time-consuming compression process begins. Compression can take a long time to complete—from a minute or two to an hour or more, depending on the settings you selected, the length of your movie, and the speed of your Mac.

   Feel free to switch to other programs—check your email or surf the Web, for example—while iMovie crunches away in the background.

   A progress bar lets you know how much farther iMovie has to go.

Exporting High-Def Video for the Web

High-definition video on the Web is coming of age. And not the learning-how-to-walk coming of age, either—the real deal, the can-I-borrow-the-car coming of age. Major online video-sharing sites like YouTube and Vimeo offer an HD option, as you read in Chapter 14, so getting HD movies *out* of iMovie has become pretty important.

HD on the Web is generally in the format called 720p. It's a video image created when your TV paints 720 lines down the screen, really fast. It's not quite as sharp as *1080p*, for obvious reasons, but it's still really great-looking.

YouTube and Vimeo can play the higher-quality 1080p HD video, too, and you can use iMovie to publish directly to these sites, as explained on page 314 and page 323, respectively.

In computer terms, 720p video has dimensions of 1280 × 720 pixels or greater. (Don't attempt to convert *standard*-definition footage, like that from a DV tape, into hi-def format. The results will look terrible.)

iMovie does offer a simple, HD-quality export option, saving you the need to muck about in QuickTime. Choose Share→Export Movie and choose one of the HD options available there. Name the file accordingly and choose where to save it, and you have an HD movie file ready to go once iMovie finishes the export.

Exports like this will be suitable for uploading to YouTube, Vimeo, or some other HD video-sharing site manually, should the need arise.

Now, if you need the fine-tuning you get with a QuickTime export but want an HD version of your movie, use the following settings:

- **Size: 1280 × 720**. These dimensions are the smallest a video can be and still qualify as HD. Any smaller, and sites like YouTube, for example, won't label or play it as a hi-def video.

- **Deinterlaced**. When you choose the size for your movie, you can also turn on Deinterlace Source Video. (It deinterlaces video that would otherwise be displayed by rapidly alternating two interleaved sets of horizontal scan lines—created, for example, by a so-called 1080i hi-def camcorder.)

- **Compression Type: H.264**. This compression scheme looks fantastic, and online video sites accept it.

- **Frame Rate: original (but no greater than 30 frames per second)**. The frame rate controls the smoothness of the video; it tells QuickTime how many images per second to flash by when your movie plays. If you somehow ended up with a frame rate slower than 30 frames per second in your iMovie project, don't bother trying to make the frame rate *higher*. It won't make the video look any better, and may make it look a lot worse.

- **Audio: AAC (256 kbps or higher)**. AAC is a great compression format. The major video sharing sites think so, too.

When iMovie finishes the export, the progress bar disappears. Switch to the Finder, where you'll find a new QuickTime movie icon (Figure 15-8). Double-click it to see the results.

Tip: You can click Stop during the export process, but you'll wind up with no exported movie at all.

Figure 15-8:
When you double-click the QuickTime icon on your hard drive (left), it opens your copy of QuickTime Player, the movie-playing program described in Chapter 16. Press the space bar or click the play arrow to start playback (right).

QuickTime Player

If iMovie is the video playback program that's the master of *DV* and *HD* files, its sibling software, the corresponding master of traditional *QuickTime* movies, is QuickTime Player, a small, free program that comes with every Macintosh (it's in your Applications folder). QuickTime Player does three things very well: shows pictures, plays movies, and plays sounds. If you have the latest version of the program, QuickTime Player X, you can also trim your movies, upload them to YouTube or MobileMe, and even record what's on your Mac's screen (or record yourself using the iSight camera).

If you're willing to pay $30, you can get QuickTime Player Pro. Doing so grants you a long list of additional features, most notably the ability to *export* your QuickTime movies into just about any format you want.

There are two reasons QuickTime Player is worth knowing about. First, if you turn your iMovie projects into QuickTime movies (Chapter 15), you'll probably use QuickTime Player as the playback program on your Mac. Second, the Pro version acts as an accessory toolkit for iMovie, offering you the chance to execute several tricky editing maneuvers that you couldn't do with iMovie alone.

This chapter covers both versions of the program, using QuickTime Player version 10.0 and QuickTime Pro version 7.6 for illustration purposes.

Note: You read that right. The Pro version of QuickTime is behind the regular player. In fact, Apple has basically said that they're not planning to continue updating the Pro version. That said, it's still a perfectly serviceable piece of software.

QuickTime Player X

The free QuickTime Player offers quite a few handy features. It exports your Quick-Time movies to commonly used formats. (It even publishes them to iTunes or You-Tube for you.) It trims your movie's length quickly and easily, and even lets you record a new movie from your built-in iSight camera or record what's on your screen.

You can open a movie file by double-clicking it, by dragging it onto 🔍 , or by opening QuickTime Player and then choosing File→Open.

Tip: If your movie file ends in .M4V, then it might open in iTunes if you double-click it. Use one of the other methods mentioned here to open the movie in QuickTime Player.

Once you open the movie file, you see the streamlined, black player window that debuted with QuickTime Player X (Figure 16-1). This minimalist design works great when all you want to see is your movie. In fact, if you move your mouse away while the movie is playing, the title bar and controls fade away, leaving nothing but your movie. When you move your mouse cursor back over the movie, the controls reappear. (You'll find all the controls explained in Figure 16-1.)

Sharing with QuickTime Player X

You can share any movie file that QuickTime Player X can play. It offers you three options, all of which you can see by clicking the share/trim button pictured in Figure 16-1 or by choosing Share from the menu.

- **iTunes.** When you choose Share→iTunes, QuickTime shows you a screen like the one pictured in Figure 16-2. You can, for example, choose the iPhone option if that's where you'll watch your movie. Then click Share; QuickTime creates a perfectly-sized movie and adds it to your iTunes library .

Tip: If you want more than one size of your movie in iTunes, say one for your iPhone and the other for your Apple TV, export the movie again, once for each size you want.

- **MobileMe.** If you use QuickTime Player X to share to MobileMe, you'll see a screen that's almost identical to the one you saw back in Figure 14-5. The principal difference is that you can't choose what size movie you send to MobileMe. QuickTime exports all MobileMe videos in the tiny, small, and medium sizes shown in Figure 14-5, even if your movie is of higher quality than that. Once QuickTime finishes the export, the little export progress window (press Option-⌘-P if it disappeared) shows you the link to your movie.

Figure 16-1:
QuickTime Player X has some cool tricks up its sleeve. In this screen, you see the typical play/pause, fast-forward, and rewind buttons. A volume slider lets you control the loudness of your movie. You can also drag the playhead to a specific part of your movie. The share/trim button lists your sharing options and lets you launch the trimmer window (Figure 16-2). Finally, click the full-screen button to see only your movie (and nothing else) on your screen.

Playhead
Volume slider

Full-screen view
Share/Trim

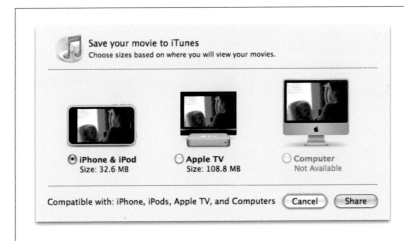

Figure 16-2:
If you share a movie from QuickTime Player X to iTunes, you only have one simple decision to make: what size you want. Choose the one that best fits the ultimate destination for the movie (for example, choose iPhone if that's where you'll eventually watch your movie).

- **YouTube.** Publishing to YouTube from QuickTime Player X is very similar to publishing to YouTube from iMovie (page 314). The key difference is that after you enter your account information, you can't select the size of the movie to upload to YouTube's servers. QuickTime will publish the highest quality your source video is capable of, up to 720p HD.

Tip: Unlike iMovie, QuickTime Player X can share to multiple services at once. It does all of the exporting and uploading in the background, allowing you to do other things in the meantime.

If you want to remove any of your shared movies, you need to delete them manually, rather than relying on QuickTime Player X to do it for you. See page 318 for more on deleting manually from YouTube and page 322 for deleting from MobileMe.

Tip: If you'd rather export your movie with a little more control, you can always use the File→Save As command in the menu bar. Here you can choose the name, location, and format for your movie. Click the Format menu to choose from a list of device-specific and HD formats.

The File→"Save for Web" command exports multiple versions of your movie, and creates a Quick-Time reference file (page 366) that serves up the best size movie for the destination device. All the files end up together in one folder, along with an HTML file for referencing the movie. If you build your own websites, you can use this HTML file to plug your movie into your pages. The file even contains handy instructions.

Trimming Your Movies

If you just need to make a quick trim to a movie file, you'll save loads of time by using QuickTime Player X instead of iMovie. The latter requires you to add your movie to the Event Library, add it to a project, and then export the result. QuickTime X lets you trim the movie on the spot.

To do so, open your movie in QuickTime Player X, click the share/trim button pictured in Figure 16-1, and then choose Trim. (Alternatively, choose Edit→Trim or press ⌘-T.) When you do, QuickTime replaces the movie controls with a trim editor (see Figure 16-3). The yellow border with handles on either end should look familiar. It behaves just like the equivalent selection tool in iMovie '11 (page 80).

Figure 16-3:
Trimming in QuickTime Player X couldn't be easier. Just drag the yellow handles so that everything you want to keep sits inside the yellow border, and then click Trim to cut your movie down to size.

To trim your movie, drag the handles on either end of the yellow border until everything you want to keep lies inside the yellow box. (Make sure everything you *don't* want is on the outside of the yellow border, too.) As you drag the handles, the playback window shows you exactly where you'll be cutting. You'll notice also that you can't do multiple selections, trimming out different bits. You can only trim from each end of your movie; you end up with one continuous piece of footage.

Once you isolate the part of the movie you want to keep, click the yellow Trim button. All the unwanted video disappears.

All that remains is to save the shorter version of your movie. You can't save over the movie file you're editing. Instead, when you click File→Save As, you see a Save window that gives you a chance to choose a file name and location for your new movie file.

Recording in QuickTime Player X

If you ever need to record what's on your screen (to show a colleague how to use a program, for example), or just record a quick webcam video wishing your mom a happy birthday, QuickTime Player X makes the process incredibly easy.

Under the File menu, you see three record options:

- **New Movie Recording** (Option-⌘-N). This records a movie using your built-in iSight camera.

- **New Audio Recording** (Option-⌘-N). This records an audio "movie" using the sound input source you select from the little arrow button in the record window (Figure 16-4).

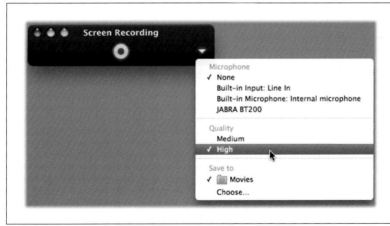

Figure 16-4:
Recording a movie in Quick-Time Player X is super easy. To change the sound source, the quality of the recording, or the save location for your movie, click ▼ in the Recording window.

- **New Screen Recording** (Option-⌘-N). This records everything on your screen, applications, mouse cursor, and all. It also records audio from the sound source you choose by clicking the little arrow button in the record window.

Tip: If you ever need to teach someone how to do something on a computer, like instructions for Grandma on how to run Software Update, QuickTime Player X's screen-recording feature is an awesome way to *show* rather than simply tell. Just record the steps, narrating as you go, then export an email-sized version of your movie and send it on.

To start and stop recording, click the big red button in the Recording window. (If you're recording your screen, the Stop button is up in the menu bar.) Once you stop, QuickTime X automatically saves your movie as "[Movie/Audio/Screen] Re-cording.mov" in the Movies folder. You can change the location by clicking ▼in the Recording window before you start recording.

Once that's done, your movie file is ready to go. Use one of the sharing options listed on page 354 to send it off to the world.

QuickTime Player 7 (Free Version)

Having two versions of QuickTime around is confusing enough. But since you can download and install the free version of QuickTime 7 without ever activating the Pro features, Apple is really shipping out *three* versions of QuickTime Player. You can always recognize QuickTime Player 7 by its brushed metal look. To see if you have just the free version, check the menus and look for grayed-out menu items with the Pro label on them. If the Pro features are locked, you still have the free version.

Note: If you don't have QuickTime Player 7 on your Mac *at all*, go to *http://support.apple.com/kb/DL923* to download and install it.

Because QuickTime files ordinarily open in QuickTime Player X, you have to open a movie in QuickTime Player 7 by dragging it onto Player 7's icon, or by opening QuickTime Player 7 and then choosing File→Open. As shown in Figure 16-5, the QuickTime Player 7 window looks noticeably different from that of QuickTime Player X.

A number of controls help you govern movie playback:

- **Audio level meters**. This tiny graph dances to indicate the relative strength of various audio frequencies in the soundtrack; it's like the VU meters on a stereo. If you don't see any dancing going on, then you've opened a movie that doesn't have a soundtrack.

- **Resize handle**. Drag diagonally to make the window bigger or smaller.

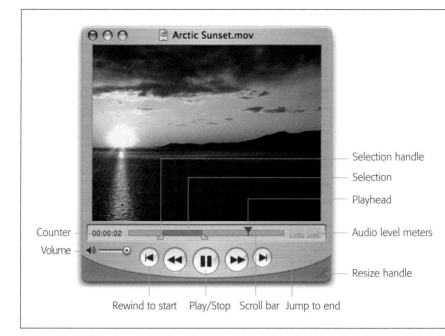

Figure 16-5:
When QuickTime Player's "stainless steel" look debuted in version 4, it inspired a firestorm of criticism on the Internet. Among other design limitations, its title bar didn't have a collapse box, zoom box, or stripes that told you when a window was active. The newer QuickTime Player 7.6, shown here, addresses all those concerns and dispensed with many confusing controls.

Selection handle

Selection

Playhead

Audio level meters

Resize handle

Counter

Volume

Rewind to start   Play/Stop   Scroll bar   Jump to end

Tip: When you drag the resize handle, QuickTime Player strives to maintain the same *aspect ratio* (relative dimensions) as the original movie, so that you don't accidentally squish it. If you want to squish it, however (perhaps for the special effect of seeing your loved ones as they would look with different sets of horizontal and vertical genes), press Shift as you drag.

If you press Option while dragging, meanwhile, you'll discover that the movie frame suddenly grows or shrinks by factors of two—twice as big, four times as big, and so on. On slower Macs, keeping a movie at an even multiple of its original size ensures smoother playback.

- **Scroll bar.** Drag the diamond (or, in the Pro version, the black triangle) to jump to a different spot in the movie.

Tip: You can also press the right and left arrow keys to step through the movie one frame at a time. If you press *Option*-right or -left arrow, you jump to the beginning or end of the movie. In the Pro version, Option-arrow also jumps to the beginning or ending of a selected stretch of the movie.

- **Play/Stop button.** Click once to start, and again to stop. You can also press the space bar, Return key, or ⌘-right arrow for this purpose. (Or avoid the buttons altogether and double-click the movie itself to start or stop playback.)

Tip: You can make any movie play automatically when you open it so you can avoid the Play button altogether. To do so, choose QuickTime Player→Preferences→Player Preferences, and turn on "Automatically play movies when opened."

- **Selection handles**. These tiny black triangles appear only in the $30 Pro version of QuickTime. You use them to select, or highlight, stretches of footage.

- **Volume**. If you like, you can make the soundtrack louder or softer by dragging this slider with your mouse or clicking in its "track." You may find it easier, however, to press the up or down arrow keys.

Tip: To mute the sound, click ◀ᵈ), or press Option-down arrow. Press Option-up arrow to make the volume slider jump to full-blast position.

- **Counter**. This display shows, in hours:minutes:seconds format, how far into the movie your diamond cursor has moved. If you have QuickTime Pro, the counter reveals the position of the selection handle you most recently clicked (if any).

- **Rewind, Fast-Forward**. By clicking one of these buttons and keeping the mouse button pressed, you get to speed through your movie backward or forward, complete with sound. This is a terrific way to navigate your movie quickly, regardless of whether you use QuickTime Player or QuickTime Player Pro.

- **Jump to Start, Jump to End**. These buttons do exactly what they say: scroll to the beginning or end of your movie. In the Pro version, they can also jump to the beginning and end of a selected portion of a movie (if any). All of this, in other words, is exactly the same as pressing the Option-left or -right arrow keys.

Tip: Try minimizing a QuickTime Player window while a movie plays. It shrinks to the Dock—and *keeps on playing*. Do this enough times, and you'll know what it's like to be Steve Jobs on stage.

Hidden Controls

Don't miss the Window→Show A/V Controls command. As shown in Figure 16-6, this is where you can fine-tune the video and audio you're experiencing.

Fancy Playback Tricks

Nobody knows for sure what Apple was thinking when it created some of Quick-Time's additional features—exactly how often do you want your movie to play backward?—but here they are. Some of these features are available only in the unlocked, Pro version of QuickTime Player, as indicated below:

- **Change the screen size**. Using the View menu commands, such as Double Size and Full Screen, you can enlarge or reduce the "movie screen" window.

  Making the window larger also makes the movie coarser, because QuickTime Player simply doubles the size of every dot present in the original. Still, when you want to show a movie to a group of people more than a few feet away from the screen, these larger sizes are perfectly effective.

- **Play more than one movie**. You can open several movies at once and then run them simultaneously. (Of course, the more movies you try to play at once, the jerkier the playback gets.)

  As a sanity preserver, QuickTime Player plays only one soundtrack—that of the movie you most currently clicked. If you really want to hear the cacophony of all the soundtracks being played simultaneously, choose QuickTime Player→Preferences, and turn off "Play sound in front most player only." (The related checkbox here, "Play sound when application is in background," controls what happens when you switch out of QuickTime Player and into another program.)

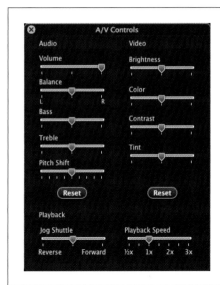

Figure 16-6:
Here, you can adjust a QuickTime movie as though it's a TV set. Boost the brightness, turn up the treble, correct the color, and so on. Oddly enough, the two Playback sliders at the bottom aren't settings at all. Rather, they're real-time controls. Dragging the Jog Shuttle handle, for example, actually triggers forward or reverse playback at high speed, and dragging the Playback Speed handle makes playback proceed at the indicated multiple of real time. (Be careful, though. This one is also a setting. If you leave the slider at 3X and close the window, your movie will always play back at 3X and you probably won't know why.)

Tip: If you have QuickTime Player Pro, you can use the View→Play All Movies command to begin playback of all open movies at the same instant. It's a handy way to compare the quality of two or more copies of the same exported movie, each prepared with a different codec.

- **Play the movie backward**. You can play your movie backward—but not always smoothly—by pressing ⌘-left arrow, or by Shift-double-clicking the movie itself. (You must keep the Shift button pressed to make the backward playback continue.) There's no better way to listen for secret subliminal messages.

- **Loop the movie**. When you choose View→Loop and then click Play, the movie plays endlessly from beginning to end, repeating until you make it stop. (Loop Back and Forth makes it loop backward, from end to beginning.)

- **Play Selection Only (Pro only)**. View→Play Selection Only, of course, plays only what you highlighted on the scrubber bar.

- **Play All Frames (Pro only)**. If you try to play a very large movie that incorporates a high frame rate (many frames per second) on a slow Mac, QuickTime Player skips individual frames of the movie. In other words, it sacrifices smooth motion to keep the video in sync with the soundtrack.

  But if you choose View→Play All Frames and then play the movie, QuickTime Player says, "OK, forget the soundtrack—I'll show you every single frame of the movie, even if it isn't at full speed." You get no sound at all, but you do get to see each frame of the movie.

QuickTime Player Pro

If you spent the $30 to upgrade to the Pro version of QuickTime Player, you unlock a number of additional features. Some of these are playback tricks described in the previous section; others are especially useful for iMovie work. Read on.

FREQUENTLY ASKED QUESTION

QuickTime Player 7 vs. QuickTime Player Pro

What's with all these dimmed menu commands that say PRO beside them?

That's Apple's subtle way of saying, "Just *look* at all you'd get if you upgraded your free player to the Pro version! All of these features await you!"

If you're convinced, then for $30, Apple will sell you a password that turns your copy of QuickTime Player into QuickTime Player Pro. (To obtain this password, call 888-295-0648, or click the Upgrade Now button to go to *www.apple.com/quicktime/buy*.)

To record your password, choose QuickTime Player→Registration. Your password gets stored in your Home →Library→Preferences folder, in a file called QuickTime Preferences. (Remember that when you upgrade to a new Mac.)

Once you upgrade, you gain several immediate benefits—not the least of which is the permanent disappearance of the "upgrade now" advertisement. Now you have QuickTime Player Pro, and you can edit your movies as described later in this chapter.

You can also import many more sound and graphics formats, and—via the File→Export command—convert sounds, movies, and graphics into other formats.

Oh—and all those dimmed commands come back to life and lose the little PRO logos.

Undo	⌘Z
Redo	⇧⌘Z
PRO Cut	⌘X
Copy	⌘C
PRO Paste	⌘V
PRO Delete	
PRO Select All	⌘A
PRO Select None	⌘B
PRO Trim to Selection	
PRO Add to Movie	⌥⌘V
PRO Add to Selection & Scale	⌥⇧⌘V
Find	▶
Special Characters...	⌥⌘T

Presenting Your Movies

After going to the trouble of editing down your footage (as described in Part 1) and exporting it as a QuickTime movie (as described in Chapter 14), what you may want to do most of all is *show* the movie to other people. Even the non-Pro version of QuickTime Player can play movies, of course, but the Pro version offers a much better showcase for your work: the View→Present Movie command.

"Presenting" your movie is the best possible way to watch a QuickTime movie on your screen. The QuickTime Player blacks out the screen, automatically magnifies the movie (by choosing a lower resolution) so that it fills more of the screen, and devotes all the Mac's power to playing the movie smoothly (Figure 16-7). (To interrupt the movie, press ⌘-period.)

Tip: Don't buy QuickTime Pro just for this feature. It comes free with the also-free QuickTime Player X (page 354).

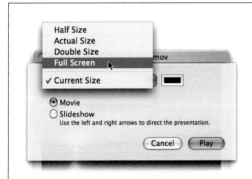

Figure 16-7:
The Present Movie command makes your movie fill the playback screen (although enlarging your video makes it grainier and coarser, which is why Apple gives you a choice here).

Editing Movies

The most powerful feature in the Pro version of QuickTime is its ability to *edit* QuickTime movies. You can rearrange scenes, eliminate others, and save the result as a new movie with its own name. It's more powerful than the Trim feature in QuickTime Player X (page 356).

All of this is perfectly possible within iMovie itself, of course, but sometimes you want to edit a QuickTime movie you exported from iMovie—to make it shorter for emailing, for example.

Tip: QuickTime Player can open all of iMovie's favorite movie formats (page 49). In fact, you can find all the clips that iMovie knows about—every last shred of video in your Event browser—tucked away in your iMovie Events folder (see page 59), ready for double-clicking to examine in QuickTime Player. This trick may come in handy if you want to edit a clip you already imported, using some feature that's available only in QuickTime Player but not in iMovie.

Selecting footage

Before you can cut, copy, or paste footage, you need a way to specify just *what* footage you want to manipulate. QuickTime Player Pro's solution: the two tiny L-shaped handles beneath the horizontal scroll bar, visible in Figure 16-8.

Figure 16-8:
QuickTime Player Pro has a little-known subtitling feature, complete with the freedom to choose a type style. Copy some formatted text from a word processor; highlight a slice of footage in QuickTime Player, and choose Edit→"Add to Movie." The copied text appears as a subtitle on a black band, beneath the picture, as shown here.

These are the "in" and "out" points of your footage, exactly like the crop handles in iMovie. By dragging these handles, you enclose the scene you want to cut or copy.

Tip: You can get more precise control over the selection procedure by clicking one of the L-shaped handles and then pressing the right or left arrow key, just as you can with the scrubber bar under iMovie's Monitor window. Doing so expands or contracts the selected chunk of footage by one frame at a time.

You may also prefer to select a piece of footage by Shift-clicking the Play button. As long as you hold down the Shift key, you continue to select footage. When you release the Shift key, you stop the playback, and the selected passage appears in gray on the scroll bar.

Once you highlight some of footage, you can proceed as follows:

- Jump to the beginning or end of the selected footage by pressing Option-right or -left arrow key. (This doesn't work if one of the handles is highlighted.)

- Deselect the footage by dragging the two L-shaped handles together again.

- Play only the selected passage by choosing View→Play Selection Only. (The other Movie menu commands, such as Loop, apply only to the selection at this point.)

- Drag the movie picture out of the Player window and onto the desktop, where it becomes a *movie clip* that you can double-click to view.

- Cut, copy, or clear the highlighted material using the commands in the Edit menu.

Tip: If you paste some copied text directly into QuickTime Player Pro, you get a 2-second title (such as an opening credit) at the current frame, professionally displayed as white type against a black background (Figure 16-8). QuickTime Player retains the font, size, and style of the text. You can paste a graphic image, too; again, you get a 2-second "slide" of that still image.

If you find it easier, you can also drag a text or picture *clipping file* directly from the desktop into the QuickTime Player window; once again, you get a 2-second insert. To make the text or picture appear longer than 2 seconds, drag or paste it several times in a row.

In either case, you specify the fonts, sizes, and styles of your low-budget titling feature by formatting the text *before* you copy it from your word processor. (This feature requires a word processor that preserves formatting on the Clipboard. Most modern text processors, including Stickies, TextEdit, and Word, and most email programs, do so.)

Pasting footage

After you cut or copy footage, you can move it elsewhere in the movie. Specify where you want the pasted material to go by first clicking or dragging in the horizontal scroll bar, so that the black playhead marks the spot; then choose Edit→Paste. The selection triangles (and their accompanying gray scroll bar section) show you where the new footage has landed. (That makes it easy for you to promptly choose Edit→Cut if you change your mind.)

There are several variations of the Paste command at your disposal, too. They work like this:

- The Edit→"Trim to Selection" command is like the "Trim to Selection" command in iMovie, in that it eliminates the outer parts of the movie—the pieces that *aren't* selected. All that remains is the part you first selected.

- The Edit→"Add to Movie" command adds whatever's in the Clipboard so that it plays *simultaneously* with the selected footage—a feature that's especially useful when you add a *different kind* of material to the movie. (See Figure 16-8.)

- If you highlight some footage and then choose Edit→"Add to Selection & Scale," whatever you paste in the highlighted region gets stretched or compressed in time, speeding up or slowing down both the audio and video until the pasted bit fits. The effect can be powerful, comical, or just weird. (Can you say, "Alvin and the Chipmunks"?)

Tip: You can edit sounds exactly as you edit movies, using precisely the same commands and shortcuts. Use the File→Open command in QuickTime Player Pro to locate a sound file you want to open. It opens exactly like a QuickTime movie, except with only a scroll bar—no picture.

Exporting Edited Movies

After you finish working on a sound or movie in QuickTime Pro, you can send it back out into the world in any of several ways.

The Save As command

If you choose Edit→Save As, QuickTime offers you only two options, both of which can be confusing:

- **Save as a reference movie**. You'll almost never want to use this setting, which produces a very tiny file that contains no footage at all. Instead, it's something like an alias of the movie you edited. It works only as long as the original, unedited movie remains on your hard drive. If you try to email the newly saved file, your unhappy recipient won't see anything at all.

- **Save as a self-contained movie**. This option produces a new QuickTime movie—the one you just finished editing. Although it consumes more disk space, it has none of the drawbacks of a "reference movie" file.

The Export command

Usually, your primary interest in using QuickTime Pro will be to export its edited clip, either for use in iMovie or other programs (PowerPoint, web pages, and so on).

When you find yourself in that situation, choose File→Export. The resulting dialog box should look familiar: It's the Save As dialog box that appears when you save an iMovie project as a QuickTime movie. This is your opportunity to specify the size, frame rate, color depth, special effects, and many other aspects of the movie you're about to spin off.

This is also where you can convert the QuickTime movie into some other format: AVI (Windows movie), Image Sequence (which produces a very large collection of individual graphics files, one per frame), and so on—or convert only the soundtrack to AIFF, System 7, or WAV (Windows) formats, for example.

How to use QuickTime Player with iMovie

But as an iMovie fan, what you'll probably want to do most often is open your iMovie clips in QuickTime Player Pro, make changes to them, and then save them for further use in iMovie.

In that case, you'll probably adopt a routine like this:

1. **In iMovie, Control-click (or right-click) the clip you want to edit. From the shortcut menu, choose "Reveal in Finder."**

   You switch to the desktop, where the movie file's icon is highlighted and waiting in whatever window it calls home.

2. **Option-drag the movie icon to your desktop to make a copy of it. Double-click the copy.**

   The movie clip opens before you in QuickTime Player. Edit it as described in this chapter. (The following pages walk you through some rather spectacular special-effect edits.)

   When you finish editing, go on:

3. **Choose File→Save.**

   You now have an edited version of the clip on your desktop.

4. **Switch back to iMovie. Choose File→Import Movies, then navigate to the desktop and open the edited movie.**

   After you indicate which Event you want it to join, the edited video becomes a new iMovie clip, which you can use to replace the original in your project, if you like. After the import, you can delete the one you saved to the desktop in step 2.

So why did you edit a copy, and not just save changes to the original clip?

Because if you edited one of iMovie's clips behind its back, iMovie wouldn't be able to update the tiny filmstrip movie that it uses to represent your video while you're editing. (It creates that filmstrip movie only when you import video the official way.) And if the clip and its filmstrip don't match, you can't export the results—they're locked in iMovie forever.

Advanced QuickTime Pro: Track Tricks

As far as QuickTime Player is concerned, a piece of footage is nothing more than parallel *tracks* of information: audio and video. Most movies have only two tracks—one video and one audio—but there's nothing to stop you from piling on multiple audio tracks, overlapping video tracks, and even specialized layers like a text track or an animation track.

The key to understanding the multiple simultaneous tracks in a QuickTime movie is the Movie Properties dialog box (Figure 16-9). It opens when you choose Window→Show Movie Properties (⌘-J).

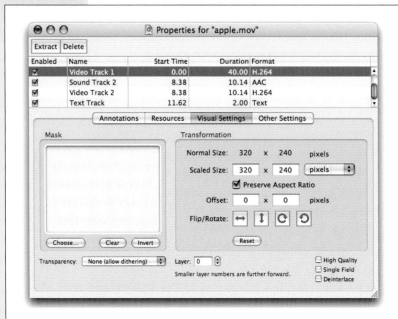

Figure 16-9:
The Movie Properties dialog box shows you all the parallel streams that go by when you play a movie: the various video, sound, and even text tracks. The Visual Settings tab is particularly useful for iMovie fans, because it lets you do things you can't do in iMovie (like flip a movie 90 degrees).

Here's some of the fun you can have at this point:

- **Turn off tracks.** Turn off the Enabled checkbox for any track you want to hide or mute. This fascinating command highlights an intriguing feature of Quick-Time Player Pro—its ability to embed more than one audio or video track into a single movie. If you really wanted to, you could create a movie with six different soundtracks, all playing simultaneously.

  Or maybe you created two different versions of a movie—one with throbbing, insistent background music, and one with New Age noodling. Using this option, you can quickly and easily try watching your movie first with one soundtrack, and then with the other.

- **Extract Tracks.** Click a track name and click the Extract button (top left). "Extract" actually means *copy and separate* into a new Player window. (If you double-click a soundtrack, it appears as nothing but a scroll bar with no picture.) At this point, you can copy some or all of the extracted track so you can paste it into another movie.

- **Delete Tracks.** As the name implies, this button removes the selected track from the movie. For example, after experimenting to see which of several soundtracks you prefer (as described above), you'll want to delete the rejected versions before you save the final movie.

Now that you know the general workflow, here are a few recipes that illustrate how iMovie + QuickTime Player Pro = Fun and Creativity.

Flip a Clip

So you're making a gag movie of your buddy at work. You have a shot of him leaving the starting line in a potato-sack race at the office retreat. You want to splice in some old footage of Olympic track star Carl Lewis breaking through the tape, making it look like that's your buddy at the finish line. Only one problem: Your buddy is running from left to right in the shot, and Carl Lewis, in his shot, is running from right to left. How will you ever make that look right?

By fixing it first:

1. **Open the clip in QuickTime Player Pro.**

   See the steps on the previous two pages.

2. **Choose Window→Show Movie Properties (⌘-J).**

   The Properties dialog box appears (Figure 16-9).

3. **Click Video Track, and then click Visual Settings.**

   You can now apply all kinds of freaky changes to the video track. The simple Rotate commands are available in iMovie itself—but not the *Flip* commands.

4. **Click the first Flip button (the first arrow button visible in Figure 16-9).**

   As you watch, your entire video picture flips into a mirror image of itself.

5. **Save the edited movie. Switch back into iMovie and import the QuickTime file as described on page 49.**

   Suddenly, you're a master at comedy.

The Video Wall

QuickTime Player isn't fussy. It's perfectly happy to accept two, three, four, or more videos, all pasted into the same clip. You can move, scale, and shrink them independently, creating a video-wall effect like the one shown in Figure 16-10.

To create this effect, just repeat the preceding steps, over and over again. The trick, of course, is keeping track of which videos are on top, so you can control the overlapping.

Actually, it's not terribly difficult if you have good concentration and an assistant with a notebook; see Figure 16-10.

Figure 16-10:
Each time you paste another layer of video, it becomes a new track, listed independently in the Properties palette. (You might want to rename each track to help you keep them straight. Do that by double-clicking a track's name.) To specify the front-to-back layering of your videos, choose a layer's name, and then click Visual Settings. Use the Layer control, circled here, to move this video track closer to the front of the stack. (Lower-numbered tracks cover up higher-numbered ones.)

Part Three: iDVD '11

3

Chapter 17: iDVD Basics

Chapter 18: DVD Menus, Slideshows, and the Map

Chapter 19: Designing iDVD Themes

Chapter 20: Advanced iDVD

iDVD Basics

iDVD—the program, the legend—turns iMovie movies and iPhoto slideshows into Hollywood-style DVDs you can watch on your TV. iDVD lets you design a DVD's main menu, add playback controls, and otherwise dress up iMovie movies to give you dynamic, interactive DVDs that look amazingly professional. iDVD handles the technology, you control the style.

Not only does iDVD offer lots of pro-style features and effects, but you can even burn widescreen DVDs—discs that play your movie in the wide, rectangular, cinematic proportions of today's digital TV screens.

And the cost of entry to do all this? For software, all you need is iDVD. For hardware, you need a DVD recorder, either built into, or connected to, your Mac. Pretty much every recent Mac, except for the MacBook Air, includes a DVD recorder.

Why iDVD?

Don't look now, but Apple thinks that the era of DVDs has passed. The real action, he believes, is on the Internet. iDVD, according to Steve Jobs, is "for people who still want to make DVDs." (His subtext: "Those losers!")

But don't tell that to the 120 million U.S. families who don't have high-speed Internet access—or any Internet access at all—and therefore can't see online video. These people aren't on YouTube; they can't see your MobileMe gallery. But they almost certainly have DVD players. And producing your movies on DVD offers a wealth of benefits: The sleek discs are small, light, and easy to mail. They last a long time—decades, if you believe the manufacturers—if you stick to brand-name blanks like Verbatim and Imation, and keep the burned discs in a cool, dry place.

Getting iDVD

If you own iMovie '11, you already have iDVD—Apple includes both programs in its iLife suite.

Note: iDVD wasn't updated *at all* in the '11 version of the iLife suite. No new themes. No new features. It's precisely the same software that came with iLife '08. Yes, that's *two* versions ago.

You don't have to worry about iDVD's system requirements; if you can run iMovie, you can run iDVD. But here again, faster computers work a lot better than slower ones. Even though the iDVD in iLife '11 has the same version number as the one that appears in iLife '08, Apple says it requires Mac OS X 10.6.4 or later.

What You're in For

In the following chapters, you'll learn how to integrate movie clips, still pictures, and sound into a movie in very flexible ways; customize Apple's stock design templates; and unlock iDVD's darkest secrets. But what most people do at first is usually much simpler: They create a movie in iMovie, and then hand it off to iDVD so they can burn it. Or they burn a DVD directly from their camcorder, using iDVD's OneStep DVD feature (see page 398).

This chapter guides you through both these rituals. Most of what you're about to read, though, covers the iMovie-to-iDVD sequence, which entails six broad steps:

1. **Prepare your audio, video, and pictures.**

   In addition to movies, iDVD can incorporate audio and graphics files into your shows. iDVD doesn't, however, give you any way to *create or edit* these files. You have to prepare them in other programs, like iMovie, first.

2. **Insert chapter markers.**

   In a commercial Hollywood DVD, you can jump around in a movie without rewinding or fast-forwarding through it, thanks to the movie's *scene menu* or *chapter menu*. A chapter menu is a set of bookmarks that let you jump to a specific scene in a movie. (Although this chapter is about iDVD, you actually add your chapter markers in iMovie; see "Phase 2: Insert Chapter Markers".)

3. **Export a finished iMovie video to DVD.**

   iMovie '11 has a "Share to iDVD" function that makes sticking your home movie onto a DVD very convenient.

4. **Design the menu screens.**

   In iDVD terms, a *menu* isn't a list of commands that drops down from the top of the screen. Instead, it's a screen full of buttons that you click with your TV's remote to control the movie's playback. One button, called Play, starts playing the movie. Another, called Scene Selection, might take you to a second menu screen full of individual "chapter" buttons, so your audience doesn't have to start watching a movie from the beginning if they don't want to.

DVD menu design is at the heart of iDVD. The program lets you specify where and how each button appears onscreen, and lets you customize the menu's look with different backgrounds and title treatments.

5. **Add your movies to a DVD.**

Remember those videos you exported in step 3? Now that you've got a handsomely designed menu screen ready and waiting, you can drop them into place.

6. **Burn your DVD.**

To create a DVD, iDVD compresses your movie into the universal DVD file format called *MPEG-2*, and then copies the results to a blank recordable DVD. This process, called *burning*, lets you produce a disc that plays back either in a computer or on most set-top DVD players.

This chapter covers the details of these six steps.

Phase 1: Prepare Your Video

For the most professional results, prepare your video in iMovie (or other video-editing program) before you import it into iDVD. Here are a couple of key issues to keep in mind.

Overscanning and You

Every day, millions of TV viewers are blissfully unaware that they're missing the big picture. In TV's early days, the little cathode-ray guns inside the TV picture tube created an image by painting one line of the picture at a time, then turning around and heading back in the opposite direction, painting the second line. To make sure the screen was painted edge to edge, these early TVs overshot the edges of the screen—they *overscanned* the screen, to use the technical term.

Today, TV technology is much improved, but standard-definition tube TVs still overscan. The amount they do varies, but you may be missing as much as 10 percent of a picture beyond the left and right edges of the screen (and often beyond the top and bottom of the screen, too).

TV producers are careful to keep a movie's action and titles in a part of the frame that's least likely to be lost to overscan. If you plan to edit your film, this so-called "TV-safe" area is your concern, too. The overscanning effect means that when you show your iMovie productions on a TV, you'll lose anything that's very close to the edges of the frame. In particular, broadcasters refer to two danger zones of a video image: the *title-safe area* and the *action-safe area* (see Figure 17-1).

Title-safe boundary   Action-safe boundary

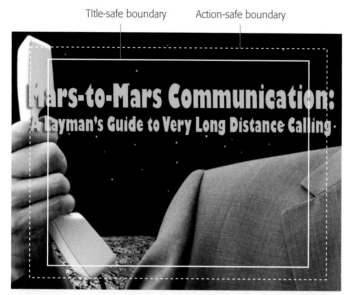

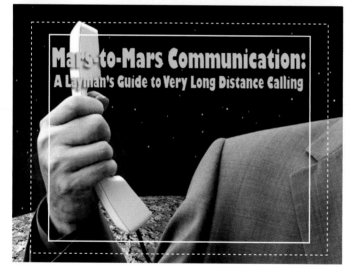

Figure 17-1:
Top: Your TV may crop objects that appear outside the title-safe area. North American picture-tube TV sets will almost certainly crop out objects beyond the action-safe area, so avoid recording key visual elements there.

Bottom: For maximum safety, keep key elements within the more restrictive title-safe area, though you can let non-vital portions (like the knuckles and cord in this example) stray into the action-safe area.

Note: Flat-panel TV sets, like plasmas and LCDs, don't have picture tubes, and therefore don't overscan.

The title-safe area

When a TV chops off parts of your movie's title, making it difficult or impossible to read, your audience can't help but notice. In some old versions of iMovie, you had to be careful when you created onscreen credits and titles: If you chose the largest font size, they could wind up getting lopped off at the outer limits of the screen. In iMovie '11, however, you don't have to worry: The program doesn't let a title expand into the outer 10 percent on either side of the title-safe area.

COMPLAINT DEPARTMENT

What About HDTVs?

It's pretty amazing that a cheapo program like iMovie lets you edit and play high-definition video. Ahead of the curve, baby!

Well, sort of. Once you finish editing your hi-def movie, where are you going to play it? You can send it to the Web, or you can view it on your Mac—but weirdly enough, Apple doesn't have any suggestions for getting your hi-def movies onto your hi-def *television*. (Sure, you can burn a DVD, but most DVDs aren't hi-def; Blu-ray discs, described below, are the exception.)

It isn't that Apple's ignoring HDTVs. The problem is that its answer—sending your hi-def movie to the TV over Apple TV—is, in Steve Jobs's words, "a hobby." Even though the latest version of Apple TV costs only $100, not many people have it, and most people may never get it as long as the Apple TV remains an Apple hobby. (That said, if you *do* have Apple TV, it can play 720-pixel high-def video files from your Mac, so it's at least an option.)

So without an Apple TV, how *do* you get your hi-def home movies onto your HDTV? There are dozens of answers, none great. Here's a brief rundown of the most prominent methods.

- **Connect your computer to your HDTV**. With the right cable and the right connections, you may be able to treat your HDTV as an external monitor for your Mac. Usually, you'll connect the DVI port on the Mac to the VGA jack on a TV, so you'll need (what else?) a DVI-to-VGA cable. (Some HDTVs have DVI

ports instead of VGA, which means that a plain old DVI cable fits the bill.) Amazon.com has cables galore, so you shouldn't have trouble finding one.

Of course, the problems with this approach are that (a) your computer and TV might not be in the same room, and (b) you have to run back to the Mac to control movie playback. Laptop owners win this round.

- **Use your Xbox 360/PS3/Tivo HD/[Insert Device Name Here]**. Each of these living-room-connected machines is capable of playing back videos. But copying your videos onto their hard drives isn't a simple process. Let Google be your friend in hunting down the step-by-steps. Almost certainly, you'll spend a lot of time exporting your movies via QuickTime, so get to know Chapter 14 well.

- **Burn a Blu-ray Movie**. The screamingly obvious solution, of course, is, "Burn your movie to a Blu-ray DVD, and then play that on your TV!" How ironic, then, that, at least at this writing, Macs don't come with Blu-ray-burning drives. And even if they did, you can't use iDVD to burn them—you'd have to buy another company's Blu-ray DVD burner and another company's software—like Toast (*www.roxio.com*), for example.

The whole thing, alas, is complicated and expensive. Steve Jobs wasn't kidding when he called Blu-ray a "bag of hurt."

The action-safe area

Professional broadcasters also refer to the *action-safe* area of the screen. It's not quite as restrictive as the title-safe area, because your audience can usually figure out what's going on even if the action is slightly clipped at the outer edges of the screen. Still, it's vital that critical action remain within the central portion of the screen.

Imagine, for example, a science-fiction video. A mysterious enemy teleports your hero and his sidekick to a moon of Jupiter. The sidekick throws something to the hero—something that can save the day. In Figure 17-1 at top, for example, what's in the hero's hand may be obvious to you, but most TV viewers would have a hard time guessing that it's a handset because most of it falls outside the action-safe area.

In Figure 17-1 bottom, the sidekick's hand and the phone he throws appear completely within the action-safe area. Even if the TV winds up chopping off the outer edges of the picture, you've preserved the visual story, and your hero can safely call home.

Note: Readers and their lawyers will please forgive the science of this example in that (a) there's no such thing as teleportation; (b) there's no air to breathe on the moons of Jupiter, let alone to talk with; (c) the hero and his colleague would die almost instantly from catastrophic depressurization; and (d) even assuming the hero could make the call out, the speed of light ensures that it would take hours for his message to reach earth. When writing computer books, authors are limited to the royalty-free art collections they have on hand. The art used here appears courtesy of Ulead's Royalty-Free Media collection.

You can keep your action within the action-safe area in two ways:

- **Frame correctly to begin with**. Keeping important visual features and motion away from the edges of your video as you record it is by far the easiest solution.

- **Resize the footage**. You can resize your video and center it within a frame using iMovie's Crop tool (page 191). This approach, however, may degrade your video quality (see page 192).

Phase 2: Insert Chapter Markers

If you've ever rented or bought a movie on DVD, you're already familiar with *chapters*, better known as scenes (Figure 17-2).

DVD chapters let viewers skip to predefined starting points within a movie, or pick up watching where they left off, either by using the scene menu or by pressing the Next Chapter or Previous Chapter buttons on the remote control.

As part of its effort to de-emphasize the DVD, Apple took the chapter-marker feature out of iMovie '08—and, as a result of the ensuing uproar, restored it in iMovie '09 (where it remains in '11), better than ever.

Figure 17-2:
*Most DVDs have
something called a
scene menu, like this
one (from the movie
"Ronin"), which lets
viewers jump di-
rectly to their favorite
scenes in a movie.
Your DVD scene
menus probably
won't be quite this
elaborate, but you get
the idea.*

Actually, you can mark a scene *four* ways. And even though iMovie '11 can claim top
chapter-marking prowess, all four options have their place:

- **Use iMovie '11**. Hands down the easiest and most convenient way to mark a
  chapter. This will probably be your method of choice 99 percent of the time.

- **Export the movie to iMovie 6**. If you ended up with your movie in iMovie 6
  (the reasons and method are covered on page 302), you can head straight from
  there to iDVD. The older version of iMovie has a really great chapter-adding
  feature.

- **Export the movie to GarageBand**. GarageBand has convenient chapter-adding
  features, too—*and* a "Send to iDVD" command just like iMovie's. If you use
  GarageBand to edit your audio tracks anyway (see "GarageBand Basics" on page
  257), it might make sense to add your chapters here.

- **Use iDVD's automatic chapter-marker feature**. iDVD can add markers to a
  movie *for* you—but it places them at even intervals, like every 4 minutes. You
  don't have the freedom to place the markers where you want them—at logical
  scene breaks, for example.

You'll learn the first chapter-marking method on the following pages. You can find
out about the other three in this chapter's free downloadable appendix, "More Chapter Markers," available on this book's Missing CD page at *http://tinyurl.com/33blf68*.

Tip: Any DVD markers you create will work on an Apple TV or anything else that plays QuickTime files: iTunes, iPhones, iPads, iPods, Front Row, QuickTime Player, DVD Player (the Apple program), and most commercial DVD players.

Markers in iMovie '11

Chapter markers in iMovie '11 work something like sticky notes in a book: You grab one, stick it where you want it, and then name it. It's about as easy as it gets.

Before you begin, turn on iMovie's Advanced Tools (choose iMovie Preferences and then, on the General tab, turn on Show Advanced Tools).

Now, if you examine the upper-right corner of the project window closely, you'll find two little stowaways:

- **Comment markers.** The tiny brown speech bubble represents *comment markers*. The idea here is to let you annotate your movie. It can remind you of further work you want to do ("Add a different song here"), identify someone in the video (in a way that won't actually appear during playback), and so on.

- **Chapter markers.** The tiny orange bubble with the white arrow inside represents *chapter markers*—and within your project, you can see the ones that survived the transition from iMovie to iDVD.

You'll find both kinds of markers handy when you work on longer projects, because a pop-up menu (Figure 17-3) lets you jump directly to a marker, without having to scroll and hunt.

Figure 17-3:
To insert a chapter marker, drag one from the "tray" above the Project window to the appropriate spot in your project. Rename it by double-clicking the text to highlight it, and then type in whatever label you want. You can quickly select any of your markers (and even project titles) using the handy marker menu that sits next to the marker tray.

To add either of these markers, drag your mouse from one of the appropriate marker "trays" to the spot in your project you want to mark. Once you release the mouse, a small rectangular marker appears in the filmstrip, numbered sequentially (Figure 17-3).

Tip: You're not stuck with the numbers that iDVD automatically assigns marker labels. Double-click a marker to rename it;. Type in "Day 3: Disney," for example, or "Mom Takes a Spill." The chapter names you choose show up in your DVD menus.

If your project is long and the chapter markers plentiful, they become an efficient navigational tool. There's a tiny pop-up menu above the project-area scroll bar. Click the ▼ to reveal a list of all your markers, both comments and chapters. Choose one to jump to that spot (and highlight the chosen marker).

Tip: You can insert chapter markers without dragging them from the tray to your movie. Control-click (or right-click) any spot in a filmstrip and, from the shortcut menu, choose Add Chapter Marker. iDVD inserts the marker at the playhead, which is incredibly handy if you're skimming a project and you find the precise spot for the next marker.

Chapter-marker pointers

A few things to note about chapter markers:

- **When you move, copy, or erase clips, chapter markers go along for the ride**. iMovie associates chapters with individual clips.

- **There's a "secret" unlisted chapter**. iMovie and iDVD always create one more chapter than you see on the iDVD Chapters list. This extra chapter corresponds to the very beginning of your movie (00:00:00), and starts out with the label "Start." (You don't see it until you arrive in iDVD.)

Tip: To get rid of the secret "Start" chapter, create your own chapter marker at the very beginning of a project. That marker will then appear in the chapter list.

- **iDVD menu screens can fit up to 12 buttons each**. That's "up to," because the actual number depends on the *theme* you pick.

Phase 3: Export from iMovie '11

If you skipped the chapter-marking fun in Phase 2 above, sending your masterpiece to iDVD is just one menu click away: choose Share→iDVD. iMovie takes the time to encode your movie into a format that iDVD recognizes. Once that's done, iDVD opens, creates a new project, and plugs your movie into the DVD menu.

Note: Behind the scenes, what format do you guess Apple uses to encode your movie? None other than the Apple Intermediate Codec, the same format used to encode AVCHD footage for editing (see page 8) and the same format iMovie uses to prepare a clip to go fast, slow, or in reverse (see page 157).

Export Your Movie as a File

Sharing to iDVD via the menu command has one potentially annoying outcome: it always inserts your movie into a new project. That's not a big deal if you're starting from scratch, but if you want more than one iMovie on a single DVD, the "Share to iDVD" command doesn't cut it.

Happily, this isn't the only way to insert a movie into iDVD. You can incorporate additional movies into an *existing* DVD—but only if you first export those movies as QuickTime files.

Follow the instructions on page 303, which show you how to create a QuickTime movie in the Apple Intermediate Codec movie format (the one that lets you edit in iMovie [see page 48]).

Tip: Save exported movie files in your Movies folder. That way, iDVD will have easy access to them, as described later in this chapter.

Phase 4: Design the Menu Screen

Once you add any chapter markers you want in iMovie, export your video and open up iDVD.

The opening screen gives you four options (Figure 17-4, top):

- **Create a New Project**. In iDVD, "project" refers to the DVD you're designing, not the movie itself (unlike iMovie, where your "project" *is* the movie).

POWER USERS' CLINIC

Export Movies from Final Cut

If you're reading this book, you're probably using iMovie to edit your movies. But iMovie is not Apple's only video-editing program. You may be using one of its two more powerful programs, Final Cut Express or Final Cut Pro. And there's no reason you can't turn those movies into DVDs using iDVD, too.

In either version of Final Cut, click the sequence (movie) you want to export, and then choose File →Export→QuickTime Movie. In the Save dialog box that appears, choose Chapter Markers from the Markers pop-up menu (if, of course, you've actually added these markers). Turn off "Make movie self-contained."

From the Setting pop-up menu, choose NTSC DV (the North American video standard) or PAL (Europe). Navigate to your Movies folder, and then click Save. Final Cut creates a tiny QuickTime file—called a reference movie—on your hard drive, which is much smaller and faster than a full, self-contained QuickTime movie. As long as you don't delete the original movie files you used in your Final Cut project, iDVD knows exactly what to do.

Finally, go to iDVD and add the movie to your menu screen as described in Chapter 18.

- **Open an Existing Project**. Just burning a DVD doesn't mean the end of your project. You can open it up again later to burn another copy of that DVD, or to make changes to it and *then* burn it.

- **Magic iDVD**. This feature, too, avoids any iMovie involvement. But this time, Magic iDVD creates a disc using a bunch of pictures, movies, and music files as its raw material. See "Magic iDVDs" on page 399.

- **OneStep DVD** is a one-click way to dump a videotape onto a DVD right from your camcorder, bypassing iMovie altogether. See "OneStep DVDs and Magic iDVDs" on page 397.

To create a DVD for the first time, click "Create a New Project." You now have three choices to make (Figure 17-4, bottom):

- **Name the project**. What you type here won't appear on the DVD; it's just a file name for organizational purposes on your Mac.

- **Choose where to save it**. iDVD suggests your Documents folder, but you can choose anywhere you like.

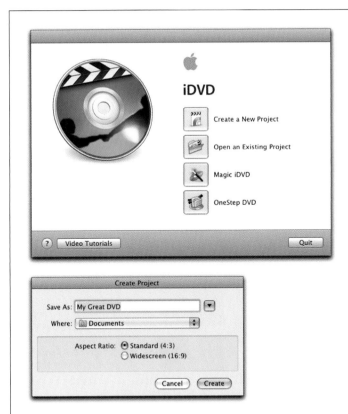

Figure 17-4:
Top: You can choose from four options on iDVD's main screen. Or you can ignore this dialog box and choose a command from iDVD's File menu, like Open Recent.

Bottom: Choose a name, location, and aspect ratio for your movie.

- **Choose an aspect ratio**. This is actually a pretty big decision: iDVD is asking what shape TV you'll play the DVD on.

  If you choose the standard aspect ratio (4:3), the DVD will perfectly fit traditional, squarish TV screens. If you play the video on a widescreen set, you'll see black vertical bars on either side of the picture.

  If you choose Widescreen (which has a 16:9 aspect ratio), the opposite will happen: The DVD will look fantastic on—and completely fill—high-def TV screens, but will have *horizontal* letterbox bars if you play it on older, standard sets.

Tip: You can always change your mind about the aspect ratio later by choosing Project→"Switch to Standard (4:3)" or "Switch to Widescreen (16:9)."

Once you make your choices, click Create.

Note: If you created your project in iMovie '11, iMovie 6, or GarageBand, you may not see the options shown in Figure 17-4. Instead, you might see a predesigned menu screen like the one shown in Figure 17-5. If you added chapter markers to your project, for example, you'll find two buttons: Play (meaning "Play the movie from the beginning") and Scene Selection. On the finished DVD, the latter button takes your audience to a second screen, which is filled with individual buttons for the chapters you created. In fact, this second screen may well have arrows that lead to *third and fourth* screens, since iDVD themes can vary in the number of buttons they have per screen.

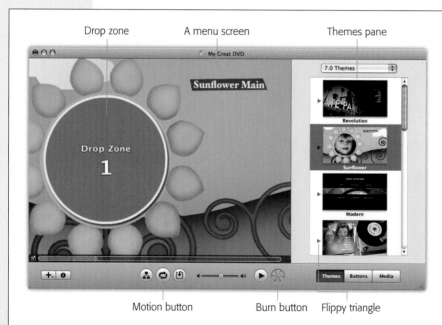

Figure 17-5:
In iDVD, you add, edit, and manipulate the buttons, pictures, movies, and titles that make up the menus for your DVD. The "drawer" on the right side of the screen is a permanent fixture, always open and always on the right. It's the area identified here as the Themes pane.

All About Themes

The look of the DVD menu screen now before you is based on a *theme*: a unified
design that governs how your DVD's menus look and behave, complete with attractive backgrounds, coordinated typography, and background music (Figure 17-5).

Tip: If the Apple logo appears in the lower-right corner of your iDVD Project, you can intervene. Choose
iDVD→Preferences and turn off "Show Apple logo watermark."

---

iDVD comes with more than 150 themes. Each includes a main menu screen, a
chapter navigation screen, and an Extras screen (for bonus DVD features you add
with iDVD).

It takes a lot of individual design decisions to make a theme. For example:

- **Background image or video**. Whatever art appears in the background, whether
  that's still images or video clips, is part of the theme. The movement of the desert in the Anime Pop theme is one example of video in action.

Tip: iDVD livens up many of its themes with looping animations (like the rotating petals in the Sunflower
theme); many themes have music, too. The Motion button (⟳) turns the animation and music on and
off (it doesn't affect your finished DVD, however).

- **Button type**. The buttons in an iDVD project can take the form of either little
  graphics or text phrases that your audience clicks with the TV's remote control.

- **Button look**. The look of your buttons can vary. Text buttons may have simple
  backgrounds; graphic buttons may have borders.

- **Button positions**. Each menu can accommodate up to 12 buttons, depending
  on the theme you choose, and you can't change their positions.

- **Drop zones**. *Drop zones* are areas into which you drag a favorite video clip
  (and sometimes more than one) that plays continuously in the background on
  the main menu screen. If you've ever seen a Hollywood DVD, you've seen this
  effect. One key scene from the movie plays over and over, looping until you
  choose one of the buttons on the menu screen—or go quietly insane. *Dynamic*
  drop zones move across the screen, passing in front of each other, providing
  amazing visual effects.

- **Text boxes**. Text boxes let you freely add text to your menu screens. You could
  use one, for example, to provide instructions for your viewers, copyright notices, or details about what they're about to see.

- **Font selections**. Themes also specify the color, font size, and typeface of menu
  titles and buttons.

Figure 17-6 shows two very different looks for the same project. The difference lies
only in the chosen theme.

Choosing a Theme

iDVD starts up with a very cool-looking, high-tech, black-on-black theme called Revolution Chapters (Figure 17-6, bottom), but goodness knows, you're not stuck with that. A range of canned themes awaits your inspection. To see them, make sure you have the Themes button (lower-right corner) selected. Then choose a theme *set* from the pop-up menu at the top of the Themes palette. iDVD has four built-in sets, each named for the version of iDVD that first included them: 7.0 Themes, 6.0 Themes, 5.0 Themes, and Old Themes (from iDVD 3 and 4).

With most themes, you can click the flippy triangle (Figure 17-5) to reveal all the screens that make up a theme *family*—complementary menus for the Scene Selection screen, a DVD Extras page, and so on. If you bought additional themes online, you'll see them in this pop-up menu, too. Use the menu to switch between themes, or choose All to see all the themes in a single, scrolling list. Go through the list of themes, clicking each one to see what it looks like in the main work area, or just rely on the thumbnail icons to get a sense of the theme's flavor.

Figure 17-6:
iDVD themes can create strikingly different menu screens for similar projects.

Top: The Forever theme (shown in the 4:3 aspect ratio) displays gracefully sliding photos (or videos) in the drop zones as the windows float from right to left; a string quartet plays, too.

Bottom: The Revolution Chapters theme (shown in its widescreen, 16:9 shape) has a stunning, high-tech look. It features two counter-rotating cylinders, one bearing your project's name and the other displaying what you've put into the drop zones.

Tip: When you peruse the Themes pane, it looks like all the iDVD 7.0 and 6.0 themes apply only to wide-screen movies. If you created your movie in the standard 4:3 format and you select one of these themes, iDVD displays a warning box asking if you want to keep your project's 4:3 format or *change* it to the 16:9 format. That gets annoying fast. (Yes, you could turn on "Do not ask me again," but then iDVD will use the widescreen format without even asking you.)

For best results as you try different themes for your project, do so in widescreen mode to avoid being interrupted by that warning. You can always switch to the 4:3 version of a theme later by choosing Project→"Switch to Standard (4:3)."

If your movie has no chapters, your DVD menu consists of only a single screen—the main menu you've been looking at the whole time—it takes on your chosen theme instantly. A movie that has chapter markers in it, however, has at least one additional menu screen: your Scene Selection screen. In that case, when you click a theme thumbnail, iDVD asks if you want to apply the theme family to the entire project, so that the main menu and the Scene Selection menus match; this is almost always what you want. Figure 17-7 shows how.

Figure 17-7:
As a rule, always use a single theme family for your entire project. When this message appears, turn on "Do not ask me again," and then click OK. Doing this ensures that every screen in your project looks consistent. Good idea, good design.

Tip: You can also apply a theme to all the menus later by choosing Advanced→"Apply Theme to Project." Or you can apply a theme only to the *submenus*—not the main screen—by choosing Advanced→"Apply Theme to Submenus."

When you're happy with your theme, you're ready to proceed with your iDVD design work. (If you later wonder what you were thinking when you chose a theme, you can change it at any time until you actually burn the DVD; see page 386.)

Tip: You can buy additional themes, or download free samples, from other companies (like *http://www. DVDThemePAK.com*). Install them by creating a folder called Favorites in your Library folder (the one in the main hard drive window, not the one in your Home folder), and then putting your new themes inside.

The Inevitable Paragraphs About Aspect Ratio

As you probably know, there are two popular *aspect ratios*—screen shapes—for televisions these days: the standard 4:3 format and the widescreen ratio (see "Aspect Ratios: The Missing Manual" on page 62). iDVD can create DVDs in either format; see Figure 17-8. You're asked to choose which format you want when you first create a project, and you can switch to the other format at any time, using the Project menu.

Figure 17-8:
Each of the "widescreenable" themes comes in two formats: a standard 4:3 version (top) and a widescreen version (bottom). The question is: What happens if you create a widescreen DVD, and then play it on a 4:3 standard television? To find out easily, choose View→Show Standard Crop Area. iDVD responds by dimming the outer right and left edges of the picture, showing you what part of the picture you'll lose on a traditional television set. What you'll discover is that Apple has cleverly designed the widescreen themes so that all the important stuff—drop zones, buttons, titles, and so on—are close enough to the center that a standard TV won't chop them off. In fact, in most cases, there's very little difference between the 4:3 version of a theme (top) and the not-chopped-off portion of a widescreen theme (bottom). The bottom line: Choosing widescreen format for a DVD generally means that the menus will play beautifully on both standard and widescreen TV sets. But the video on the DVD is another matter.

Now, it turns out that Apple cleverly designed all the iDVD 7.0 and 6.0 themes to look great on *both* standard and widescreen TV sets. Figure 17-8 explains all. So if the menu screens will look good regardless of TV shape, why not just choose widescreen format for *every* DVD you make?

That's because the *video* on your DVD isn't so accommodating. If you shot it in widescreen, and play it back on a standard set, you'll probably wind up with letterbox bars above and below your movie. And if you shot it in the standard 4:3 format, playing it on a widescreen set results in black bars on the sides. The bottom line: Choose the aspect ratio for your DVD that matches the aspect ratio of the video you're going to burn.

Drop Zones: The Basics

Drop zones let you use video, slideshows, or still images on your menu screens. They're purely decorative, designed to entertain your audience as they study their menu choices. (You embed the videos or pictures by *dropping* them onto the designated *zones* in the menu template—hence the name.) Not every theme has drop zones, but most of the iDVD 7.0, 6.0, and 5.0 themes do. As if you couldn't guess, the words "Drop Zone" (Figure 17-9) indicate where the drop zones are.

Figure 17-9:
Double-click any drop zone, or click the Drop Zone Editor button, to bring up the interactive drop zone editor shown here. Note that drop zones aren't always perfect rectangles or squares, so your video or photo may get clipped around the edges. You can fill drop zones with individual photos, bunches of photos (for a slideshow effect), or movies.

Drop Zone Editor   Open Drop Zone Editor   Media button

Tip: If you don't see the telltale phrase "Drop Zone" followed by a number, choose iDVD→Preferences. Click the General tab, and then turn on "Show drop zone labels." (Turning off this checkbox only hides the words "Drop Zone," not the drop zones themselves.)

Note that you may not immediately see all of a theme's drop zones at once; several themes take their time in parading drop zones onto the screen (or rotating through them). To see all the drop zones at once, click the Show Drop Zones button below the screen (Figure 17-9).

Filling drop zones

iDVD gives you four ways to fill these empty gray spaces with videos and pictures:

- **Drag directly onto the full-size rectangle**. This technique is shown at the top of Figure 17-9. Most of the time, you'll drag videos or pictures from the Media Browser. (Click the Media button at the lower-right corner of iDVD, and then click either Photos or Movies at the top.)

- **Drag onto the drop zones in the drop zone editor**. To open iDVD's drop zone editor, click the Editor button shown in Figure 17-9. You'll see dotted-line thumbnails for all the drop zones show up beneath the menu screen so you don't have to wait for iDVD to cycle through them.

Tip: If you have a series of drop zones lined up along the bottom of the screen, you can use them as navigational bookmarks; click one, and the drop zone on the theme screen above displays that moment in the animation.

- **Let iDVD fill the zones**. Choose Project→Autofill Drop Zones. iDVD loads photos or movies—of its own choosing—into the drop zones.

- **Choose a picture or movie from your hard drive**. Control-click (or right-click) a drop zone; from the shortcut menu, choose Import. Find and open a movie, slideshow, picture, or folder full of pictures. iDVD uses that material to fill the drop zone.

Drop zones: the details

No matter how you view drop zones, here's how things work:

- **Hiding drop zones**. Drop-zone animation can be stunning, but filling the zones can take time and tweaking. When you're in a hurry, or when you actually prefer the theme *without* the zones, you can remove them. Choose View→Inspector (or press ⌘-I), and then turn off "Show drop zones and related graphics."

- **Adding to a drop zone**. Drag any video, photo album, image, or collection of images right onto a drop zone outline to install it there. You can drag icons out of the Finder, or directly out of the Media pane.

Note: If you drop an album of photos in a drop zone, you'll get a mini-slideshow, right there within the drop zone. The slideshow can display up to 99 images. (More on dragging images out of the Photos pane in Chapter 19.)

- **Replacing items in a drop zone**. Just drag something new onto the zone.

- **Removing items from a drop zone**. To empty a drop zone, drag the image or video away from the spot, just as you'd drag something off of the Mac OS X dock or sidebar. A cute little puff of smoke confirms the picture or movie's disappearance.

- **Turning on motion**. If you add a video to a drop zone and it doesn't seem to play, click the Motion button (⟳) at the bottom of the iDVD window, or press ⌘-J. (Note that turning off Motion also turns off any background audio track and brings motion menus and motion buttons to a standstill.)

Note: The on/off status of the Motion button has no effect on your final DVD, which always plays a theme's animations and soundtrack.

- **Editing a drop-zone slideshow or movie**. If you popped a movie or slideshow into a drop zone, you have some additional editing powers available to you—like deciding in what order the photos appear in the slideshow, or which part of the movie loops within the zone. (See page 389 for more on drop zone editing.)

Redesigning the Theme

You can change every tiny aspect of your theme—if you have the time and patience. Turn to Chapter 19 for a full discussion on creating and editing themes.

Phase 5: Add Your Movies

See "Adding Movies" on page 403 for details on the many ways to put movies and pictures onto your DVD.

Phase 6: Burning Your DVD

You're almost ready to burn a DVD. Before you go using up a blank disc, however, test it to make sure that it works on your virtual DVD player, otherwise known as your Mac.

Previewing Your Project

iDVD's Play button (▶) lets you test your DVD pre-burn to avoid unpleasant surprises. The program simulates a DVD player in what it calls Preview mode. You even get a simulated remote control to help you navigate through the DVD's menus, movies, and so on, as shown in Figure 17-10. To return to iDVD's edit mode, click Exit or Stop (■).

Tip: Instead of using the arrow buttons on the virtual remote to highlight and click screen buttons, use your mouse—you'll find thait's not only less clumsy, but also a decent indication of how your DVD will play back on computers that can play DVDs.

Figure 17-10:
To "click" your onscreen buttons, use the arrows on the remote to highlight the one you want, and then click the Enter button in the middle of the remote. Click the ⏮or ⏭ buttons to skip back or forward by one chapter, or hold them down to rewind or fast-forward.

Checking for Errors

A DVD is a complex beast. Behind the scenes, there's all kinds of programming and linking going on—and any number of things could result in a DVD that doesn't work right after you burn it.

Before you proceed, click the DVD Map icon (identified and explained on page 408). On the DVD map that appears, ■ or ⚠ show up on any screen where problems await. For example:

- You created a slideshow, but forgot to add slides to it.
- You created a new menu screen, but didn't add anything to it.
- You haven't filled in all the drop zones.

Work through these alerts, resolving the problems one by one.

Maximum DVD Playback Time

When a DVD-burning program goes to work, it faces an important decision. Given that a blank single-layer DVD contains a limited amount of space (4.7 GB or so), how much data can it afford to devote to each frame of video?

iDVD offers three approaches. (You make your choice for the *current* project by choosing Project→Project Info, or for *future* projects by choosing iDVD→Preferences, and then clicking the Projects button.) As Figure 17-11 shows, your options, from good to better quality, are:

- **Best Performance**. "Best performance" refers to how quickly iDVD burns your disc. If you choose this option, your video will look fantastic, and your Mac can burn the disc relatively quickly. That's because iDVD doesn't optimize the movie—meaning it doesn't analyze the video to cut out extraneous data, like the parts of a movie that don't change from one frame to the next. As a result, iDVD burns an exact replica of your movie down to the byte, so you can only burn movies that last a maximum of 60 minutes for standard DVDs. (You get about 120 minutes for dual-layer DVDs; see "The Burn" on page 396.)

GEM IN THE ROUGH

Secrets of the Theme Scrubber

iDVD's scrubber bar (the thin white scroll bar beneath the menu screen) lets you preview the animation for a theme. You can let the preview play automatically (click the ⟳ button) or you can drag the scroll handle to zip through it, watching how the theme changes over time. To move through the animation one frame at a time, press the keyboard arrow keys.

Many themes, including the one shown in Figure 17-5, include a "play once" introduction—a preliminary animation that plays before your menu buttons appear. iDVD represents this preview segment with a crosshatched area of the scrubber bar (it's on the far left of the bar). Some themes also have a crosshatched area at the *end* of the scrubber, a "play-out" portion that helps link back to the beginning of the loop.

At times, you might want to turn off that introductory animation—for example, when you're designing secondary menu screens (like the Scene Selection screen). If you turn off the checkbox to the left of the scrubber, you hide the crosshatched section of the bar. You also eliminate the introductory portion, both as it plays in iDVD and on your final, burned DVD. Now, only the main, looping portion of the menu-screen animation plays. (You can always restore

the intro by turning the checkbox back on again.) Similarly, the checkbox at the right end of the scrubber hides the play-out animation.

Speaking of scrubber-bar secrets: If you turn off the Motion (⟳) button at the bottom of the iDVD screen, you bring the menu's animation to a halt. (This step doesn't affect the motion in the finished DVD.) Once you turn the animation off, you can manually control the scrubber, dragging its playhead anywhere you want. Oh, and you can choose View→Hide Motion Playhead to tuck the scrubber bar out of sight and View→Show Motion Playhead to bring it back.

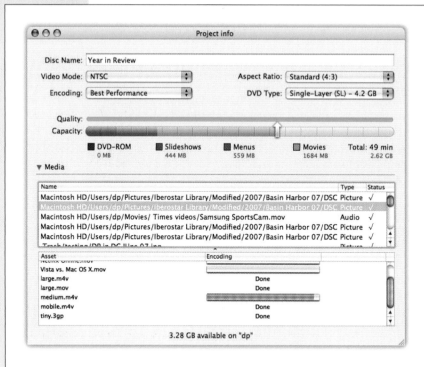

Figure 17-11:
This panel gives you detailed information on the DVD you're about to burn: how much material is on the disc, the aspect ratio, the DVD format (single- or dual-layer), and so on. Note: As the white arrow moves from green (excellent) into yellow, orange, and then red on the Quality graph, the video quality goes down. The more stuff you cram into your DVD, the more iDVD has to compress it, lowering the quality. If you change the encoding setting for a one-hour video from Best Performance to Professional, you'll see that the Pro option gives superior results.

The Best Performance option thinks like this: "Since I don't have to fit very much video on this disc, then hey—I can devote the maximum amount of data to each frame of video, for great quality. But I'm allotting the same amount of data to every frame, rather than trying to save space by analyzing the footage and seeing where I can conserve. Not having to calculate how much data I need for each frame will save me time and make the burning process go quickly."

Tip: Part of what makes this method burn your disc so fast is that it does a lot of advance work in the background *while* you're designing your DVD. That's good because it saves you time, but bad because, on slower Macs, it can make iDVD feel sluggish. If your Mac bogs down, choose Advanced→"Encode in Background" and then turn off that feature.

Before you burn a disc, confirm that a checkmark appears next to each *asset* (that is, each picture, movie, soundtrack, or what-have-you).

- **High Quality**. This option writes 120 minutes of video to a standard (single-layer) DVD (and nearly 4 hours of video for double-layer blanks). The tradeoff: It takes a lot longer to burn your DVD, because iDVD performs a deep analysis on your movie before burning.

That analysis tells iDVD to use more or less data to describe each frame of your movie, depending on how much action takes place in that frame. iDVD employs the same trick to conserve bytes on its DVD as Hollywood movie studios use: *variable bit-rate (VBR) encoding.* iDVD conserves data for frames that need it the most. The trouble is, this analysis takes a long time. That's why High Quality discs take longer to burn than Best Performance discs.

Put another way, the High Quality option makes iDVD think, "I'm going to use every micron of space on this blank DVD. I'll analyze the amount of video I have, and divide it into the amount of space available on the DVD. The amount of data I use to describe an individual frame of video will vary from project to project, and it will take me a lot longer to burn the DVD because I have to do so much analysis. And I can't get started on that analysis until the movie is ready to be burned (background encoding, described in "OneStep DVDs, Magic iDVDs" on page 397, isn't available with this setting). But at least my human will get two hours of great-looking video per disc."

- **Professional Quality**. Use this advanced encoding method for the really important stuff. It takes twice as long as High Quality to burn a DVD, because iDVD takes *two* passes through your material, one frame at a time. That's *double* variable bit-rate encoding. The result is better, richer color and, especially, sharper-looking photo slideshows. The Professional method can fit two hours of video onto a single-layer blank DVD—and produces truly amazing-looking discs.

One Last Techie Look

Part of iDVD's job is to *encode* (convert) your movies, music, and pictures into the MPEG-2 format that standard DVDs use. It's actually a big, hairy job, one that Apple and iDVD try to hide from you for fear of freaking you out. Nonetheless, if you inspect what's going on with your encoding before burning a disc, you'll be a better person for it.

To do so, open the Project Info window (choose Project→Project Info, or press Shift-⌘-I). The dialog box that appears shows how close you are to filling up the DVD with your movies, menus, and other elements. Figure 17-11 has the details.

Tip: If you click the tiny storage-space readout at the right end of the graph ("4 GB," for example), it cycles among different displays: how many minutes' worth of material your DVD will have, and how many separate tracks (individual playable bits) you've set up.

Shopping for Blank DVDs

iDVD can burn most kinds of blank DVDs. As you shop, pay close attention to what you're buying:

- **DVD-R.** You can record on these single-sided blanks only once—permanently. Of all these formats, DVD-R is the least expensive and the one that will play on the most DVD players. (Capacity: 4.2 GB, or 2 hours of video.)

- **DVD+R.** At one point, this competing format caused no end of grief to people whose Macs could burn only DVD-R discs—and weren't paying attention to that miniscule + sign when they bought their blanks. Today, all Macs can burn DVD+R just as easily as DVD-R, and all but the most ancient DVD players can play both types.

- **DVD-RW or DVD+RW (Rewritable).** Same idea, except that you can erase these and use them again. (When you insert a DVD-RW you've used before, iDVD automatically offers to erase it.) Some older DVD players can't play these, though.

- **DVD+R DL (Double Layer).** This kind of blank holds 7.7 GB—close to 4 hours of video. All current Macs can record onto these blanks, and all current DVD players can play them. Older Macs may not be able to record these discs, however.

Tip: To find out if your Mac can burn double-layer discs, choose Project→Project Info. If the DVD Type pop-up menu offers a choice of "Double-Layer (DL)," you're one of the lucky ones.

The Burn

When you finish editing your menus and testing your virtual DVD thoroughly, it's time to proceed with your burn. This is the moment you've been waiting for.

1. **Choose File→Save Project (⌘-S).**

    This might be a good opportunity to confirm that your hard drive has some free space, too. iDVD needs *twice* the amount of free space that your project itself takes up. Use the Project Info graph (Figure 17-11) as your guide.

2. **Click the Burn button twice.**

    See Figure 17-12.

Figure 17-12:
The first time you click on the gray, closed Burn button, it "opens," revealing a throbbing yellow-and-black button. Click this button and iDVD begins the encoding and burning process, which can take hours.

3. **Insert a blank DVD when your Mac asks for it.**

   Be sure you use the correct kind of disc for your DVD burner. For example, don't attempt to burn 1x or 2x blanks at 4x speed.

4. **Wait.**

   It can take iDVD a *very* long time to process all your audio, video, and photos, encoding them into the proper format for a DVD. Your wait time depends on how complex your project is, how fast your Mac is, and which encoding setting you chose. The bottom line is that burning a DVD is usually measured in hours, not minutes.

   For best results, make sure that no background programs are busy—downloading email, playing iTunes music, and so on—while you burn a disc. A busy computer may introduce video glitches (like dropped frames) during the burn.

   Eventually, though, a freshly burned DVD pops out of your drive.

Tip: After your new DVD pops out, a message says, "Your disc has been created. If you want to create another DVD, insert another disc now." Sure enough, you can spin out multiple copies of your project by inserting blank discs each time you see this prompt. The beauty part is that iDVD records the copy of your project without going through the time-consuming process of encoding your data again.

OneStep DVDs and Magic iDVDs

If you've read this far, you know that even a simple iMovie-to-iDVD transfer can involve quite a bit of effort and learning. That's why Apple came up with not one, but two ways to shorten the distance between your camcorder and a finished DVD:

- **OneStep DVD.** This is a one-click way to dump a videotape to DVD. You just plug in a camera and record directly to a DVD, bypassing iMovie altogether. The result is exactly like the camcorder cassette, with the same footage in the same order as you shot it on your camcorder.

  In effect, OneStep DVD turns a *tape* camcorder into a DVD camcorder. It's a handy way to offload footage from a bunch of tapes, either because blank DVDs are cheaper than tapes, or because tapes have a more limited shelf life.

- **Magic iDVD.** Here again, the idea is to automate a lot of the grunt work involved in designing a DVD. But this time, instead of using raw material straight from your camcorder, Magic iDVD knits together existing files on your hard drive. Choose a bunch of pictures, movies, and music files, and boom—iDVD produces the disc for you.

  The result doesn't have to be a finished product. You wind up with an iDVD project that you *could* burn right away, but that you're also welcome to edit and fine-tune.

The following is a walk-through of both features.

OneStep DVD

As noted above, OneStep DVD transfers the video footage in your camcorder to a virtual DVD on your Mac. It's very simple—and very limited. For example:

- iDVD can record video from only a prerecorded MiniDV tape in a camcorder or a movie file on your hard drive. It can't record from the TV, a cable box, an analog-to-digital converter box, or your digital camcorder's video pass-through feature. It also can't record from a *hi-def* tape camcorder or any tapeless camcorder.

- You can't edit the video before you write it to disc, nor can you choose which parts to include.

- You can't customize your project in any way. The resulting DVD won't have a theme, a menu screen, or buttons. Instead, it will be an autoplay DVD—a disc that begins playing automatically when you insert it into a DVD player.

Note: Like iMovie, OneStep DVD doesn't play well with 12-bit audio, which is the standard audio-recording setting for some digital camcorders. Record your video using the 16-bit setting (which you change in the camcorder's menus); otherwise, your audio and video may drift apart on the DVD.

Here's how you use OneStep to copy a tape onto a DVD:

1. **Insert a recorded DV tape into your camcorder, and connect the camcorder to your Mac using a FireWire cable. Turn on the camcorder and set it to VCR or Play mode.**

   Chapter 1 ("Importing from a Tape Camcorder" on page 31) has details.

2. **In iDVD, choose File→OneStep DVD.**

   If your Mac's DVD drive has a slide-out tray, it opens automatically.

Tip: If, instead, you choose File→"OneStep DVD from Movie," you're telling iDVD you want to record to disc a QuickTime movie that's on your hard drive. iDVD turns that movie into a DVD that plays automatically and instantly in "kiosk mode," where the DVD's main screen automatically appears when you pop the disc into a player, ready for your key click.

---

3. **Insert a blank recordable DVD.**

   Close the DVD tray, if necessary.

4. **Wait.**

   iDVD takes over your camera, automatically directing it to rewind, play back, and then stop (Figure 17-13).

Tip: You don't have to let iDVD rewind your tape to the beginning. You can specify where you want the transfer to begin by cueing up the tape in the camcorder before you begin the steps above. Then, the instant iDVD begins rewinding the tape, press Play on the camcorder. You've convinced OneStep that the tape has just been rewound completely, and iDVD starts the capture process.

Ordinarily, iDVD imports video until the end of the tape, or until it sees 10 seconds of blank tape, whichever comes first. But you can override this feature, too. Whenever you feel that you've transferred enough of the tape, press the Stop button on your camcorder to end the capture process. OneStep moves right ahead to the compression and burning stages.

Figure 17-13:
The OneStep DVD feature automates capturing, preparing, processing, and burning a DVD from the contents of your camera's tape. One-Step doesn't actually record the disc until it encodes the video, which can take minutes or hours after capture. You can click the Cancel button any time during the encoding process to quit without burning, no harm done.

After iDVD finishes capturing your video, it takes the normal amount of time to compress your video and burn it to disc, so schedule the whole thing for a time (a *long* time) when you won't need your Mac. Go get coffee, found a new religion, or do something else that will occupy you as the tectonic plates move on inexorably and California continues its long, slow slide into Alaska.

Magic iDVDs

The magic of Magic iDVD all happens in a single dialog box, shown in Figure 17-14. It's a fun, easy way to put together a project for iDVD, or to even skip the whole editing thing and put together an instant DVD. You choose the movies and photos you want to include, choose the theme (menu design) you prefer, and then click Create Project to produce a new, ready-to-edit (or ready-to-burn) iDVD project.

Figure 17-14:
Using Magic iDVD is just like going shopping. "I'll take these movies, that slideshow, those audio clips, that theme... and wrap them up to go, please." Select the media you want to use, and then drop them into the labeled wells ("Drop Movies Here" is one, for example). Click the Create Project button to start a new project using all your selections, or click the Burn button to create an instant DVD.

Magic iDVD isn't *completely* on autopilot, however. You have to exhibit just a tiny bit of effort:

- **Name your DVD**. Edit the text box to the right of DVD Title.

- **Choose a theme**. iDVD displays all its themes in a horizontal scrolling list; the pop-up menu above the list groups them by iDVD version (7.0, 6.0, and so on). (See "Choosing a Theme" on page 386 for details on themes.)

- **Add movies**. Click the Movies tab (top right), and then drag the icons of the videos you select onto the movie wells. (You can also switch to the Finder, and drag the videos into the wells right from the desktop.) If you drop in several movies at once, iDVD reassigns them to their own individual wells.

- **Add slideshows** Click the Photos tab (top right), and then drag pictures onto a Photos cell. You're creating a slideshow here, so don't drag *individual* photos. Either drag albums from your iPhoto list or select *batches* of photos and drag them en masse onto a well. To add music to this new slideshow, click the Audio tab to view your iTunes master list. Now you can drag either an individual song or a complete playlist onto any well where you've installed some pictures. A ◀)) icon appears superimposed on that cell.

- **Remove stuff if necessary**. If you change your mind about something, you can remove a movie or slideshow by dragging its icon out of a well (or by selecting a well, and then pressing the Delete key). And what about audio? The only way to remove audio from a slideshow is to remove the slideshow itself. You can, however, *change* the audio by dropping a new music track on top of an occupied slideshow well.

- **Preview your DVD**. Click the ▶ button to see what iDVD has built for you using the raw ingredients you fed it (Figure 17-15).

Figure 17-15:
A Magic iDVD has only two buttons on its main menu: Movies and Slideshows. It autofills all drop zones with selections it makes from the movies and pictures you've included.

- **Create a new iDVD Project—or burn, baby, burn**. If it all seems close enough to something you can use, click Create Project. iDVD builds a standard iDVD project containing all the elements and choices you set up in the Magic iDVD window. You're free to edit, rearrange, delete, or otherwise tweak the elements and you've saved a lot of time. Alternatively, if the preview makes you think that what iDVD has done is just perfect—or good enough—click the Burn button twice. iDVD asks you for a blank DVD. The rest is just a matter of waiting.

DVD Menus, Slideshows, and the Map

C hapter 17 shows you how easy it is to convert a single iMovie project into a genuine DVD. But iDVD is capable of far more. You can use it, for example, to create a single disc that contains *six* of your greatest iMovie masterpieces. Or you can create a *slideshow* DVD, which happens to be one of the world's greatest ways to display digital photos. (You can even incorporate movies *into* that slideshow.) And you'll never know joy like that of designing your own navigation menus, complete with menus within menus.

This chapter shows you how, by doing a few more things in iDVD, you can gain far more power and freedom when you create your DVD menus.

Adding Movies

When you get right down to it, all iDVD really does is add window dressing—menus, buttons, and so on—to movies, photos, and music you create in *other* programs. Take movies, for example. As Chapter 14 makes clear, you can move an iMovie project into iDVD via the Media Browser. But that's just one of the ways to add movies to your project. You can also:

- Use the File→Import command.
- Drag movies into the iDVD window from your desktop.
- Choose movies from the Media Browser.

The following pages take you through these tasks.

The Import Command

iDVD's File→Import command lets you embed video, pictures, audio, and background movies onto whatever menu screen you're editing; see Figure 18-1.

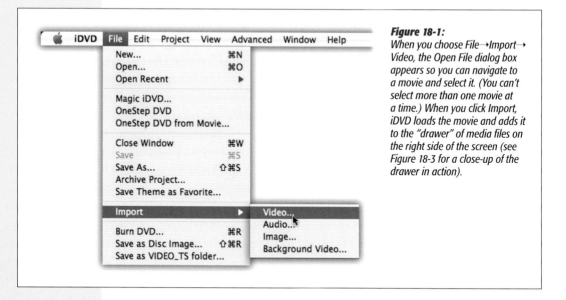

Figure 18-1:
When you choose File→Import→Video, the Open File dialog box appears so you can navigate to a movie and select it. (You can't select more than one movie at a time.) When you click Import, iDVD loads the movie and adds it to the "drawer" of media files on the right side of the screen (see Figure 18-3 for a close-up of the drawer in action).

The Finder

Another great way to embed a movie on a menu screen is to drag it there, either right off the desktop or from an open folder window. Figure 18-2 tells all.

The Media Browser

Dragging files from the Finder is great, but it assumes that you know where your movies are. If you're a little fuzzy on where you stored your movie files, iDVD can help. Click the Media button, and then click the Movies button at the top (see Figure 18-3).

Tip: iDVD's Media Browser displays the movies in your Movies folder, but you can tell it to list movies in *other* folders on your Mac, too. Choose iDVD→Preferences, click the Movies tab, click Add, and then navigate to and select the additional folder you want iDVD to monitor for movies. Repeat for additional movie folders.

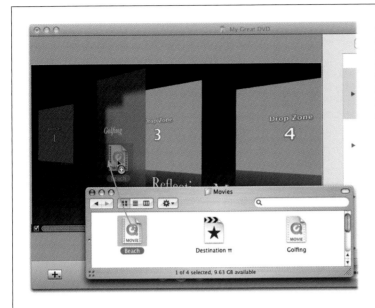

Figure 18-2:
Here's a quick way to add a movie to one of your menu screens: Position the Finder window that contains the movie so you can see both it and the iDVD menu screen at the same time. Then drag the movie to a drop zone.

Figure 18-3:
The Media Browser lists all the logical places your Mac stores movies: your iMovie projects folder, movie files in your Movies folder, camera movies from iPhoto, and non-commercial videos from iTunes. Click the flippy triangle next to one of these folders to see what's in it. Drag the movie you want onto the menu screen to make it part of your DVD-in-waiting.

Submenus ("Folders")

Depending on the theme you choose, iDVD may impose a limit of 6 or 12 buttons per menu screen. Fortunately, that doesn't mean you're limited to 12 movies per DVD. You can add more movies by creating *submenus*—menus that branch off of the main menu. You can even make *sub*-submenus (see Figure 18-4).

You may have seen submenus if you created an iMovie DVD with more than a handful of chapter markers; iDVD automatically adds submenus when you go over a menu screen's button limit.

You can add submenus on your own, too. Whenever you choose Add Submenu from the + pop-up menu at the lower-left corner of the screen, iDVD adds a submenu button to the current menu screen. In some themes, especially those that began life in previous versions of iDVD, this button looks like an actual folder; in most, it's simply a new text button. Behind the scenes, though, this button represents a second menu screen, a blank canvas with room for yet another 6 or 12 buttons.

Navigating Submenus

Navigating iDVD folders while building your project is pretty easy, once you master these tips:

- **Open submenus by double-clicking**. Double-click any placeholder folder or submenu button to "open" it—that is, to bring up the menu screen it represents.

- **Return by clicking the back arrow**. Each submenu screen includes a back arrow. Click it to return to the parent menu.

- **Names may not match**. A folder/submenu button's label doesn't have to reflect the title that appears on the corresponding screen (for example, a button labeled "My Early Years" can lead to a menu screen titled, "When I Was Young"). You can edit the text in both places individually.

WORKAROUND WORKSHOP

Temporary Buttons

When you try to add more buttons to a menu screen than iDVD can handle, the program gracefully announces that you've added too many buttons. If you click OK, iDVD eliminates the new button you tried to add. If you click Temporarily Allow—often a more convenient choice—iDVD permits you to add those extra buttons for now, so you have the convenience of (for example) cutting and pasting them to other menu screens.

But with great power comes great responsibility. iDVD wants you to understand that you can't actually burn a DVD with too many buttons on a menu screen. If you forget to dispose of the extra buttons before clicking the Burn button, another warning message appears, and your burning efforts come to a grinding halt. Avoid over-buttoned menus by creating generous and well-thought-out submenus.

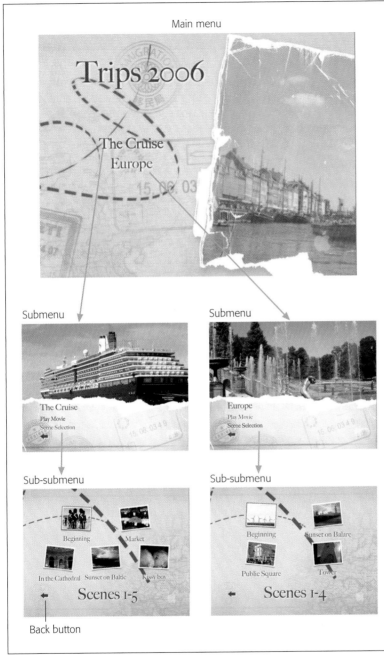

Main menu

Submenu

Submenu

Sub-submenu

Sub-submenu

Back button

Figure 18-4:
An iDVD menu screen can't hold more than 6 or 12 buttons. If you want to place any more, you'll have to branch off into submenu screens, or even sub-submenu screens. This DVD has two movies, each of which has chapters within them. When your audience clicks a movie's name (with the TV remote control), they go to a submenu screen that has a Play button on it (which plays the whole movie) and a Scene Selection button (to open yet another menu screen, this one displaying the movie's chapters so your audience can choose a point to begin playback). These submenus give you the room you need to create buttons that make it easier for your audience to navigate your DVD. As your projects grow more complex, you must use folders (submenus) to add enough space to showcase all your pictures and movies.

- **Themes don't have to match**. Each menu screen can have its own theme. If you change a screen's theme and want to apply it to an entire project, choose Advanced→"Apply Theme to Project." To apply a theme to just the submenus below the currently displayed menu, choose Advanced→"Apply Theme to Submenus" instead.

- **Mind your minutes**. The more folders and themes you add to your project, the closer you come to iDVD's limit of 15 minutes of video for menu screens (see the note below). Reaching that limit isn't such a remote possibility, either; 1-minute video loops on seven menu screens take up nearly all your available space, even if you use the same background video on every menu.

Note: The total durations of *all* the videos on *all* your menus can't exceed 15 minutes. Weird, huh? If you try to add a menu that would exceed this limit, iDVD displays a message that says, "Total menu duration exceeds 15 minutes." Click Cancel to eliminate the new menu you tried to add, or click Ignore to add the menu despite the warning, with the understanding that you'll have to solve the space issue manually before you burn the DVD. Or click Fix to make iDVD shorten the menu's loop so that it fits within the remaining video menu space on your disc.

The DVD Map—and Autoplay

As you can see, menus and submenus can build up with alarming rapidity. At times your projects may grow out of control; pretty soon, you feel like Hansel and Gretel with not enough bread crumbs.

iDVD's media map pretty much eliminates these navigational problems. It's a living, interactive diagram of your DVD, with icons that represent your DVD's menus, videos, and slideshows, and reveals how they're connected. As your menu and button layouts grow more complex, you can use the map screen to keep track of your menu structure.

To view the map, click the Map button at the bottom of the main iDVD window. iDVD highlights the element you were working on (see Figure 18-5). When you finish working with the map, click the Map button again, or click Return.

Main menu   Flippy triangle (collapses this tree limb)

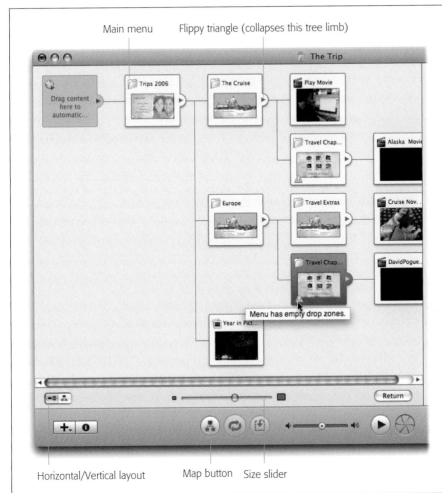

Horizontal/Vertical layout   Map button   Size slider

Figure 18-5:
You can view the map either as a horizontal or vertical tree. Use the size slider to adjust the icons' size. Option-drag the background to scroll the whole window diagonally—a much faster method than adjusting the scroll bars individually. Open a menu or slideshow for editing by double-clicking its icon. Watch out for yellow exclamation points, which indicate problems you should fix before you burn your DVD.

Tip: On iDVD's map, each menu tile includes a flippy triangle. Click it to expand or collapse that limb of the menu tree—you'll find it easier to navigate complex projects.

Editing in the Map

The map is interactive; you can even design and edit your DVD from this single screen. For example:

- You can delete a bunch of menu screens or other elements all at once. Select them by Shift-clicking them individually (Shift-click a second time if you select an icon by mistake), and then press the Delete key.

- Similarly, you can quickly apply new themes to your menu screens without ever leaving the map. Click the Themes button on the Themes pane, select the relevant menu icons, and then select a new theme.

  You can even add new menu screens and slideshows from the Map screen. Start by highlighting a menu screen's icon on the map. When you choose Project→Add Submenu or Project→Add Slideshow, you'll see that iDVD now links that screen to a secondary screen. At that point, you can specify *which* movies or *which* photos you want on those new screens by clicking Media, then either Photos or Movies, and then dragging your selections onto the newly created Map tile.

- iDVD lets you change characteristics of multiple menu screens simultaneously using the Map. Just Shift-click to choose the menu icons you want, choose View→Show Inspector (⌘-I) to open the Inspector palette, and then make any changes you like. You're editing all those menu screens at once.

- Watch out for the yellow triangle exclamation points. When you see one, point to it with your cursor, as shown above. You'll see that iDVD has identified some problem with that menu screen—it may contain no buttons at all, for example, or it's got drop zones that you haven't filled.

Autoplay

The Autoplay tile is the key to a *great* iDVD feature: It lets you create DVDs that start playing instantly when you insert them into a DVD player. No menus, no remote control—just instant gratification.

Hollywood DVDs use this Autoplay behavior to display video *before* the menu screen appears. You know—a bright red FBI warning, previews of coming attractions, or maybe just a quick snippet of the movie on the DVD. You can do that, too, or you can use Autoplay to create a DVD that *never* gets to the menu screen—a DVD consisting of *only* Autoplay material. That is, you insert the DVD, and it plays from start to finish automatically. You might design a project this way for the benefit of, for example, technophobic DVD novices whose pupils dilate merely contemplating using a remote control. Or you could design an autoplay DVD for a kiosk, or just to avoid mucking around with menu designs.

The key to this feature is the Autoplay tile, the very first one in Map view (at the top or the left, depending on whether you opted for a vertical or horizontal tree); see Figure 18-6. Whatever you drag onto it will play automatically when the DVD is inserted, before your viewers even touch their remote controls.

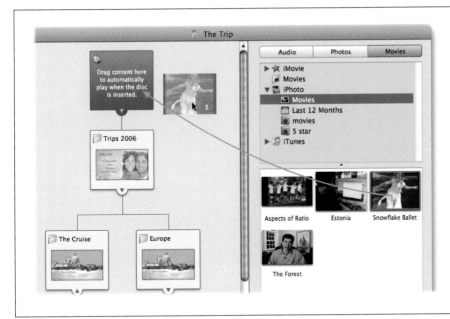

Figure 18-6:
*If you decide to
add or replace
your Autoplay
material, just drag
new stuff right
onto it. Or, to
eliminate the Au-
toplay segment,
drag it right off
the tile. It disap-
pears in a tiny
puff of Mac OS X
cartoon smoke.*

You can drag three kinds of media onto the Autoplay tile:

- **A video clip**. Click the Media button, and then click Movies at the top of the pane. Drag the movie you want directly onto the Autoplay tile to install it there.

- **A still image**. Click the Media button, but this time click Photos at the top. Now iDVD shows your complete iPhoto collection, including all your albums. To use an image as a startup screen, drag it onto the Autoplay tile. (You can add audio to the startup screen, too, just as you'd add audio to a slideshow—by dragging an audio file from the Audio section of the Media pane.)

Tip: If you tinker with the graphics tools in a program like Photoshop, or even PowerPoint or Keynote, you could come up with a decent replica of the standard FBI warning that appears at the start of a commercial DVD. You could precisely duplicate the wording and typographical look—or you could take the opportunity to do a hilarious spoof of the usual warning.

- **A slideshow**. Once you open your iPhoto collection as described above, you can drag an entire iPhoto album onto the autoplay icon, and the disc will autoplay as a slideshow. Alternatively, you can click and ⌘-click just the photos you want, and drag them en masse onto the autoplay icon. In fact, you can even drag photos—as a group or in a folder—right out of the Finder and onto this icon.

To control how long your still image remains on the screen, or how quickly your autoplay slideshow advances, double-click the Autoplay tile. You arrive at the Autoplay slideshow editor, a screen just like the one shown on page 415, where you can adjust the timing, transitions, and even the audio that plays behind your picture(s).

Note that unless you also turn on looping, described next, the DVD will eventually have to show *something* after it plays the Autoplay material. For that reason, it's a good idea to designate a basic main-menu screen in iDVD—something that will appear after the DVD finishes its Autoplay cycle.

Looping

If you highlight the button for a movie, slideshow, or Autoplay tile—either in Map view or on a menu screen—and then choose Advanced→Loop Movie (or Loop Slideshow), you unleash another raft of possibilities. You can make a DVD that repeats the highlighted material (a slideshow or movie) over and over again—in other words, one that *never* gets to the menu screen.

That's a great way to create a self-running, self-repeating slideshow of digital photos to play on a TV at a party or wedding reception. You could also use it to create a self-looping kiosk display at a trade show.

In any case, the DVD will loop endlessly—or at least until it occurs to someone in your audience to press the Menu or Title button on the physical DVD player's remote. Clicking the Menu button redisplays the previous menu screen; the Title button returns viewers to the main menu.

DVD Slideshows

Even with Internet photo-sharing services like Flickr, Picasa, and MobileMe, DVDs can still be one of the world's best delivery mechanisms for digital photos. Your friends sit there on the couch. They click the remote control to walk through your photos (or, if you choose, they let the slideshow advance automatically). Instead of passing around a tiny pile of fragile 4×6 prints, your audience gets to see your photos at TV-screen size, looking sensational—accompanied by a custom soundtrack if you choose.

In iDVD, you can incorporate *movies* into your slideshows, too. Sure, this feature may seem to violate the very definition of a slideshow, but whatever—the ability to mix stills and videos adds a lot to the visual record of your life.

If you've embedded movies into an iDVD menu screen, installing photos will seem like a piece of cake. Once again, you can do so several ways, each with its own advantages:

- **iPhoto albums**. Click Media, and then click Photos. iDVD presents your entire iPhoto picture collection, including any albums you created to organize them.

  The great thing about this system is that iPhoto albums contain well-defined image progressions. That is, you presumably dragged the photos into an emotionally satisfying sequence, and that's exactly how iDVD presents the pictures—as they appear in the album, from first image to last.

- **Folder drag-and-drop.** If the pictures you want aren't in iPhoto, you can drag a folder full of them right off the desktop (or from a Finder folder) and onto an iDVD menu screen. iDVD creates a slideshow from the images, all right, but it puts them into an unpredictable sequence.

- **Slideshow Organizer.** iDVD features a special window called the Slideshow Organizer, in which you can add photos to a slideshow and drag them into any order you like. This approach takes a little work, but it gives you the freedom to import images from many sources without having to organize them beforehand.

Note: A DVD slideshow (*any* DVD slideshow, not just those produced by iDVD) can contain at most 99 slides, and one DVD can contain at most 99 slideshows. The designers of the DVD format obviously recognized that there's a limit to the patience of home slideshow audiences.

---

iPhoto Albums

You can use either of two approaches to create iDVD slideshows from your iPhoto album collection. One begins in iPhoto, the other in iDVD.

Starting in iPhoto

As part of the much-appreciated integration of iPhoto, iTunes, iMovie, and iDVD, iPhoto offers a menu choice that exports albums and slideshows to iDVD. In the iPhoto Source list, click the album or slideshow you want to export, choose Share→iDVD…, and then wait as iPhoto transfers the data.

Now, although the steps to embed the iPhoto entities called *albums* and *slideshows* are the same, the way they work in iDVD differs.

- If you export an iPhoto *slideshow* (a set of photos to which you've applied music, panning and zooming effects, crossfades, and even individual, per-slide timings), iDVD treats the result as a movie. When a viewer presses the Enter or Play button on the TV's remote, he'll see a canned slideshow, with all the pictures in the sequence, and with the timings *you* specified; they'll have no control over the show. You can work with a slideshow movie as you would any other movie you import.

- If you export an *album* (a "folder" full of photos, assembled and arranged by you), iDVD treats the result as a *slideshow*—a collection of pictures that your DVD audience can peruse, one at a time, using the arrow buttons on the remote control. The rest of this discussion applies to these types of DVD slideshows.

When you add an album slideshow to iDVD, it uses the name of the album as the label for the resultant submenu button. Double-click the label to view the list of pictures inside, change their sequence, and make other adjustments, as described on page 415.

Tip: If, while in iPhoto, you make changes to your album—by adding photos or rearranging them, for example—click iPhoto's iDVD button again. Instead of adding a second copy of the (now-edited) slideshow to your DVD project, iDVD is smart enough to update your project's existing slideshow. As a result, you can update your albums as often as you like without any adverse affects on your iDVD project. Note, however, that you *don't* enjoy this luxury when you use the Photos pane within iDVD. Dragging an album out of the Photos pane onto a menu a second time gives you a second copy.

Starting in iDVD

If you don't want to work in iPhoto, there's an even easier way to turn iPhoto albums into living slideshows. Just click the Media button, and then the Photos button, and voilà: iDVD presents you with tiny thumbnails of every digital photo in your collection. You even get to see the list of albums, exactly as they would appear in iPhoto (Figure 18-7). From here, you can drag either albums or arbitrary groups of selected thumbnails onto a menu screen to create a slideshow.

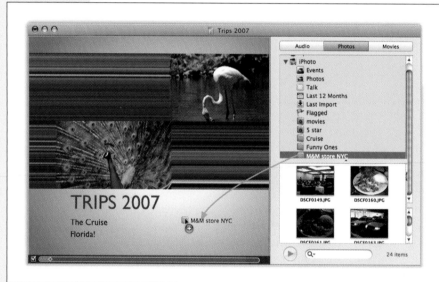

Figure 18-7:
To add a new slideshow from iDVD, drag an album or batch of selected photos from the Photos pane onto your iDVD workspace. The usual multiple-selection tricks apply: ⌘-click several albums or photos in turn to select groups of them.

Drag Folders from the Finder

Suppose you don't keep all your pictures in iPhoto (hey, it could happen). In that case, you may prefer to drag a folder of photos out of the Finder and onto an iDVD menu screen. (Make sure the folder contains nothing but pictures and movies. If it contains any other kind of document, or even other folders, iDVD may complain that it can't handle an "Unsupported File Type: Unknown Format.")

The folder shows up on the menu screen as a new slideshow button. You're ready to edit your slideshow, as described below.

Add a Slideshow, Worry About the Pictures Later

If all your photographic masterpieces aren't already together in iPhoto or even in a Finder folder, you can bring them into iDVD individually.

To do that, start by creating a new slideshow folder: From the + pop-up menu (lower-left corner of iDVD), choose Add Slideshow (or choose Project→Slideshow, or press ⌘-L). iDVD creates a new, empty slideshow. Double-click it to enter the Slideshow Editor described next.

The Slideshow Editor

No matter how you get your slideshow into iDVD, you edit it by double-clicking the drop zone to open iDVD's Slideshow Editor. Once there, double-click the Drop Zones icon ( ) to call up the Slideshow Editor's editing screen. See Figure 18-8 for a quick tour.

Figure 18-8:
The Slideshow Editor's editing screen lets you build and customize your slideshows. Each slide or movie appears in order, as a numbered thumbnail; you can move the slides or movies around by dragging them, delete the ones you don't want, or add new ones by dragging them from the desktop or the Media pane of the Customize drawer. The buttons in the lower-left corner let you switch between displaying your media in list view and icon view (shown here). Click Return (lower-right corner) to go back to iDVD's menu-editing mode.

Adding or omitting slides and movies

To add new pictures to your slideshow, do one of the following:

- **Drag from the Finder**. Drag an image, a selection of images, a folder of images, or some movies directly onto the editing screen.

- **Click Media, and then click Photos or Movies**. Drag a picture, a set of several shots, an iPhoto album, or a movie onto the editing screen.

- **Import an image**. Choose File→Import→Image. Navigate to any picture file, select it, and then click Open.

Tip: Before clicking Open, you can highlight several photos to bring them all in at once. If the photos you want appear consecutively in the list, click the first one, and then Shift-click the last one to highlight all of them. If not, ⌘-click each photo you want to import. Either way, click Open to import them into iDVD simultaneously.

To remove a picture or movie from a slideshow, select it in the editing screen and then press the Delete key. You can remove a whole bunch of pictures or movies simultaneously by first Shift-clicking them or ⌘-clicking them, exactly as described in the previous tip.

Reordering slides and movies

To change the sequence of slides and movies, just drag them around. Once again, you can select multiple thumbnails at once and then drag them en masse.

Renaming slides or movies

Click the name below each thumbnail to open a name-editing box.

Slideshow Settings

iDVD offers some useful options when you click the Settings button at the bottom of the Slideshow Editor window:

- **Loop slideshow**. If you turn on the "Loop slideshow" checkbox, the slideshow repeats endlessly, or until someone in your audience presses the Menu or Title button on their DVD's remote control.

- **Display navigation**. When you check this option, your DVD displays navigation arrows on the screen as your slideshow plays. Viewers can click these buttons with their remote controls to move back and forth within your slideshow.

  Being able to navigate your slideshow gives viewers a feeling of flexibility and control, but you may consider the majesty of your photography marred by superimposed triangle buttons. If that's the case, leave "Display navigation" unchecked; your audience can use the < and > buttons on their remotes to navigate.

- **Add image files to DVD-ROM**. When iDVD creates a slideshow, it scales your photos to 640×480 pixels. That's ideal for a standard television screen, which, in fact, can't display any resolution higher than that. But if you intend to distribute your DVD to somebody who's computer savvy, you may want to give them the original, full-resolution photos. They won't see the higher resolution of these photos when they insert the disc into a DVD player. But when they insert your DVD into their *computers*, the DVD works as a disc with files on it and they'll see a folder filled with the original, high-res photos, for purposes like printing, using as Desktop wallpaper, and so on. (In other words, you've created a dual-format disc that's both a DVD-video disc and a DVD-ROM.)

- **Show Titles and Comments**. You can add comments for each image in your slideshow—and then, at your discretion, have them appear onscreen during the slideshow.

  When you click Settings and then turn on "Show titles and comments," you're telling iDVD to display photo names and comments in *both* the Slideshow Editor *and* on the TV screen when the DVD plays. Once you do this, you can click the gray "Add comments" text below each slide title to add custom text.

Note: The comments feature can be great if you've named your pictures, say, "Martha gives Dad a kiss," but not so great for pictures named "IMG_NK01219," "IMG_NK01222," and so on. If you display photo titles and comments, keep them succinct, meaningful, and easy-to-read.

- **Duck audio while playing movies**. In iDVD, you can nestle movies right in among your still photos; they begin playback automatically during the slideshow. But what happens if you added background music to your slideshow—and it drowns out the dialog in your movie? Or worse, what happens if the video has a music track of its own—now you've got two clashing soundtracks. This option avoids these clashes by automatically lowering your slideshow music whenever a movie plays.

Slideshow Options

Other Slideshow Editor features include:

- **Slide Duration**. Use this pop-up list to specify how much time each slide spends on the screen: 1, 3, 5, or 10 seconds, "Fit to Audio," or "Manual."

  Manual, of course, means that your audience has to press their remote control's Next button to change pictures.

  Fit to Audio appears in the pop-up menu only after you add a song or playlist to your slideshow. If you do, iDVD determines the timing of your slides automatically—by dividing the length of the soundtrack by the number of slides in your show. In other words, if you have a 60-second song and 20 slides in a show, each slide sits onscreen for 3 seconds.

Tip: "Fit to Audio" offers a nifty way to create a simple, no-fuss DVD "mix tape" that you can play on your home theater system. Drop a song into the Audio well (see the next page) but add only one photograph, which may be the album art for that song or a graphic showing the song's title. Make a series of "slide-shows" this way. Once you burn the whole thing to a DVD, you can play a song in its entirety as the DVD displays the album cover on the screen. (If you add an album instead of just one song, you can display the album's art during playback.)

- **Transition**. You can govern how one slide morphs into the next with any of several graceful transition effects—Dissolve, Cube, and so on. Try each style for yourself by selecting a transition and then watching your slideshow. (Click ▶ to start the show; click it again to return to the editor.) Viewing just a few slides shows you how the transitions work.

   The transition you specify here affects all the slides in a show; you can't set transitions on a slide-by-slide basis. Note, too, that transitions *add* to the time your slides spend on the screen. If you choose 3 seconds for the slide duration, each slide actually hangs around for nearly 5 seconds when you factor in the time it spends morphing.

Slideshow audio

Music has a profound impact on the effect of a photo slideshow—you can't appreciate how dramatic that is until you watch the same slideshow without music.

The easiest way to add music to a slideshow is to click Media, and then click the Audio button at the top of the pane. Conveniently enough, iDVD displays your entire iTunes music collection, complete with any playlists you created, as well as any GarageBand pieces you composed (Figure 18-9).

When you find suitable musical accompaniment, drag it out of the GarageBand or iTunes list and onto the Audio well (also shown in Figure 18-9). You can even drag an entire playlist into the well; the DVD will play one song after another according to the playlist, so that the music won't die ignominiously in the middle of the slide show. You can also drag a sound file from any Finder window or from the desktop onto the Audio well.

Note: When it's empty, the Audio well looks like a small speaker (◀»). When it's occupied, an icon identifies the kind of audio file you have; it might say, for example, AIFF, AU, or MP3. When you add a playlist rather than a single song, the type of icon iDVD displays varies, usually showing the file type of the first song in the playlist.

To try out a different piece of background music, drag a new song or audio file onto the Audio well. And if you decide that you don't want music at all, drag the file directly out of the Audio well and onto any other part of the screen. An animated puff of smoke confirms your decision.

Figure 18-9:
The Music list includes your iTunes tunes, plus any music you created using GarageBand. Customizing your soundtrack makes for a great DVD because you can tailor it to the mood and the length of your slideshow. (Your GarageBand pieces show up in iDVD only after you open Garage-Band's Preferences, click the General tab, and then turn on "Render an audio preview when saving." Oh, and one more thing: iDVD won't see your GarageBand pieces unless you keep them in your Home→Music→ GarageBand folder.)

Leaving the Slideshow Editor

To return to iDVD's menu editor, click the Return button at the bottom-right of the Slideshow Editor.

Burning Your Slideshow

Once you design a slideshow DVD, previewing and burning it works exactly as described beginning in "The Burn" on page 396.

Since most people have never thrilled to the experience of viewing a digital-camera slideshow on their TV sets, a few notes are in order:

- Your viewers can use the Next and Previous buttons on the TV's remote control to move forward and backward through the presentation, no matter what timing you originally specified when you designed the show.

- They can also press the **II** button to freeze a picture onscreen for greater study (or while they go to the bathroom). Both the slideshow and music stop until they click the Pause or Play button again.

- If your audio selection or playlist is shorter than the slideshow, the song starts over again.

- Your viewers can return to the main menu screen by clicking the Menu button on the TV remote.

- When the slideshow is over, the music stops and the main menu screen reappears.

Designing iDVD Themes

S ome of Apple's iDVD themes offer great visual backgrounds but weak audio. Others provide terrific sound but so-so text. Some create a nearly perfect package, while others seem broken beyond repair. Fortunately, in the end, it doesn't matter, because iDVD lets you adapt themes to your taste and save your creations as *Favorites* themes.

Favorites let you move beyond canned themes and presets to create truly customized DVD menus. You can change the fonts and colors on buttons and titles, adjust the length of a looping background video, move buttons around the screen and change their styles, move text around the screen, substitute new background art or background patterns, replace or remove the audio loop that plays when the main menu is onscreen, and much more. Let this chapter be your guide.

Tip: Here's one thing you'll notice in this chapter, and in iDVD in general: Learning the ⌘-I keystroke is incredibly useful. That's the shortcut for the View→Show Inspector command. It opens a floating black panel, illustrated often in this chapter, filled with formatting options specific to the theme element you selected: a button, a text block, or the menu screen itself. (You hide this panel the same way you launched it: with another ⌘-I.)

---

iDVD's Built-In Themes

iDVD's built-in themes vary in complexity. Some offer completely realized presentations. Others provide little more than colors and fonts, leaving it up to you to mold them into a full-fledged theme. Either way, the built-in themes, both old and new, provide an excellent jumping-off point for your DVDs.

You call up all five theme collections—7.0 Themes, 6.0 Themes, 5.0 Themes, Old Themes, and Favorites—from the Themes pop-up menu. As you study the scrolling list, you'll notice that:

- **iDVD gathers all your Favorites themes in one place**. When you choose Favorites from the pop-up menu at the top of the Themes pane, iDVD lists all the themes you created. (This list is empty when you start out using iDVD.) If you bought themes from other companies (like *www.dvdthemepak.com*) iDVD lists them individually in the pop-up menu.

- **You can view all the theme sets at once**. To view just one theme set, select its name from the Theme Set pop-up menu. To view all the themes, choose All instead.

- **The ribbon means "Favorite."** A gray prize ribbon appears in the lower-left corner of certain themes. It lets you know that the theme is a Favorite—a theme you created yourself. You'll find out how to create Favorites later in this chapter.

Editing Buttons

When Apple first introduced iDVD, its flamboyant buttons generated a lot of excitement. Each one could display a small video or photo, offering visual previews of the linked material.

Times have changed. These days, text buttons have quietly replaced that old button design. In the 7.0 and 6.0 theme collections, *no* main-menu buttons display videos or pictures; all are simple text labels.

If you choose an older theme so your buttons have some pizzazz, you don't have to be content with the stock button position or style. You can move the buttons around, change their labels, and so on.

Changing Button Names and Fonts

To change the label on a button, click the button name once, pause, and then click it a second time to open the editing box. As shown in Figure 19-1, you can both retype the name and change the type size and font.

Keep these points in mind when you work with iDVD text:

- **Be succinct**. DVD screens are small, so there's not much room for long and involved text.

- **Be discreet**. Don't let one text box overlap another.

- **Spell-check**. Nothing reflects a lack of attention to detail more than a lovingly crafted masterpiece called "For Mouther's Day."

Tip: If your buttons' text labels start to crash into each other, try making the text wrap into a narrow column, so that it's several lines long. Just press Return to start a new line.

Figure 19-1:
In iDVD, little font, size, and style menus appear right beneath any text box or button you're editing. You can use only one text style per text box, however.

Button Styles

When you cycle through menu buttons using the arrow keys on your DVD player's remote, how does a commercial Hollywood DVD indicate which option you selected? Easily; a selected button exhibits some kind of highlighting—it lights up, changes color, gets underlined, or sprouts an indicator bullet. You'll find all these options, and more, in iDVD's Buttons panel (Figure 19-2).

But wait, there's more. Just because a theme comes with text-only buttons doesn't mean you have to be content with that. The Buttons panel lets you turn plain-jane text buttons into picture- or movie-preview buttons. Here's how you do that:

1. **Select the buttons you want to change.**

   Most of the time, you want to choose Edit→Select All Buttons (⌘-A) so that all the buttons on a menu screen match. But you could, in theory, make different buttons highlight in different ways.

2. **Click Buttons (lower-right corner of the screen).**

   The Buttons panel appears, filled with design options (Figure 19-2).

3. **Choose a button style from the pop-up menu at the top.**

   The first three choices (Text, Bullets, and Shapes) create text-only buttons, and they're somewhat inconsistent. For example, the options in the Text and Bullets categories affect only what happens when a viewer selects a button using the TV's remote control. That is, when the button is simply sitting there, unselected, it has *no* special graphic treatment—it's just words on the screen. But when someone selects the button, the button displays either a fancy underline (in the Text style) or a bullet shape next to its label (in Bullet style, shown at the lower left in Figure 19-2).

The Shapes panel, on the other hand, adds a colorful background to all your buttons, both selected and unselected (lower right in Figure 19-2). You can't, however, control the button's "selected" look; iDVD builds that treatment into the Shapes style (it's usually a starburst that appears next to the button's name).

If you choose any of the bottom four commands from the pop-up menu, you turn the buttons into picture- or movie-preview buttons. Figure 19-2 shows you how to do that.

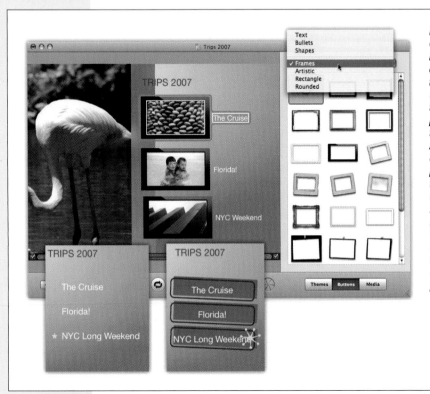

Figure 19-2:
Choose the button or buttons you want to change (top). Click the Buttons button (lower right). To turn text buttons into picture or movie buttons, choose Frames, Artistic, Rectangle, or Rounded from the pop-up menu. Click the shape you want; the selected buttons sprout picture or movie previews. (To turn them back into text-only buttons, choose Text, Shapes, or Bullets from the pop-up menu.)

4. **Click the button style you want.**

   You've now changed the text or picture/movie style for the selected buttons, including what graphic they use to indicate they're selected. But you haven't yet decided what *color* highlighting those selected buttons will have.

5. **Click an empty spot on the menu screen. Choose View→Show Inspector (⌘-I).**

   The floating Menu Info window opens.

6. **Click the Highlight button.**

   Now the Color Picker dialog box opens.

7. **Choose the color you want for the highlighting.**

   You're changing the color of the highlighted element—the underline, bullet, or starburst—that appears when someone selects the button. (See "General Guidelines" on page 216 for details on using the Color Picker.)

8. **Click the ▶ button to try out your new buttons.**

   iDVD starts up its DVD-player simulation mode, complete with virtual remote control.

Justification, Drop Shadows, and Thumbnail Size

iDVD gives you a floating palette dedicated exclusively to button editing. To open it, click a button and then choose Show→Inspector (or press ⌘-I). As shown in Figure 19-3, this panel looks different depending whether you're editing text-only buttons or picture/video buttons.

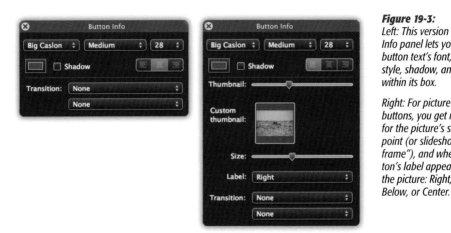

Figure 19-3:
Left: This version of the Button Info panel lets you control the button text's font, size, color, style, shadow, and alignment within its box.

Right: For picture or video buttons, you get more options—for the picture's size, looping point (or slideshow "poster frame"), and where the button's label appears relative to the picture: Right, Left, Above, Below, or Center.

Repositioning Buttons

Each theme comes with predetermined locations for your buttons. (In fact, internally, iDVD stores layout maps for each theme's buttons: one that specifies button positions if the theme has *three* buttons, another for *four* buttons, and so on.)

iDVD lets you move your buttons around just by dragging them, and you can easily align them with the overlaid guidelines (see Figure 19-4).

Tip: In general, buttons snap into alignment automatically. But if you really, truly want free rein to drop buttons anywhere (even though the result might be a little ugly), click anywhere on the background of the menu, and then choose Show→Inspector (or press ⌘-I). In the Menu Info panel, click "Free positioning."

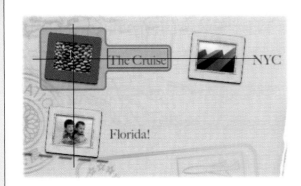

Figure 19-4:
As you drag buttons around, you'll know when you've got them lined up with each other. Horizontal or vertical guidelines appear, as shown here, and you feel a subtle snapping when you line up an element with something else on the screen.

Removing Buttons

To remove a button from a menu screen, click it once, and then press the Delete key.

Tip: To remove a series of buttons, you can click the first button and then Shift-click the last one to highlight all the buttons in between. Or ⌘-click individual buttons to highlight only those.

Of course, if you're removing a button to put it on a different menu screen, you can use the Cut and Paste commands in the Edit menu.

Editing Picture and Movie Buttons

In some themes—including all the iDVD 6.0 and 7.0 main-menu screens—the buttons on your menu screen are just bits of text.

But in some of the older themes, and in the chapter screens of some of the newer ones, iDVD creates buttons that are actually tiny pictures or movie clips that preview the slideshow or movie that's in store. And you can turn any text-only buttons *into* picture or movie buttons easily enough, as shown in Figure 19-2 (for details, see "Justification, Drop Shadows, and Thumbnail Size" on page 425).

Here's how you control what appears on these preview buttons.

1. **Click the preview button once, pause, and then click it a second time.**

   Don't just *double-click*; you'll open another menu screen or movie if you do that.

   Some button-formatting controls appear above the button, as shown in Figure 19-5.

Figure 19-5:
You control where a video loop begins on a button preview here. For buttons that link to movies, you get to pick the starting frame. For buttons that link to slideshows, you pick which photo appears on the button.

2. **Drag the slider to the spot you want.**

   The slider lets you navigate through your entire movie or slideshow, from start to end. Pinpoint where you want the button's video playback to begin or, if you're creating a slideshow button, choose the one photo you want to appear on the button itself (called the *poster frame*). Then again, if your button links to a movie, it doesn't have to have an animated preview. You can turn on the Still Image checkbox to choose a poster frame for the movie, something that doesn't actually play.

Tip: You have yet a third option for the button image: Rather than pick a scene from your movie or slideshow, you can use any graphic you want. To do that, select the button, choose View→Show Inspector, and then drag any graphics file right onto the "Custom thumbnail" image, either from the Finder or the Media panel. You'll see the button change instantly.

---

3. **Click anywhere on the background to deselect the button.**

   Turn on the Motion button (↻) to see the video play in the menu button.

Editing Text

Although most people focus primarily on iDVD's drop zones, video buttons, and so on, text also plays a critical role. It's a dependable, instantly recognizable part of a DVD menu system.

The text you can fiddle with falls into two categories (in addition to button labels, of course):

- **Menu titles** help viewers figure out where they are in your DVD menu system by providing clues: "Our Vacation" or "Pictures (Week 1)," for example. The title of a menu usually appears at the top of the screen, although you can put it anywhere you like.

- **Text boxes** can appear anywhere on your screen, too. You fill them with whatever explanatory text you think is appropriate: instructions, introductions, a description of your project, and so on.

Tip: In iDVD, as in life, brevity is the soul of captions.

You can customize your text using a boatload of techniques. Each one changes the selected text on only the *currently displayed* DVD menu screen.

- **Create a text box**. To add a block of text, choose Project→Add Text (⌘-K). Double-click the placeholder text and type away to create your own label, title, or instructions.

- **Select the text box**. Click the text box once (if you see the text formatting controls onscreen beforehand, click anywhere on the screen to dispense with them, and then click the text box). iDVD highlights the box. Now you can drag it to move it, press Delete to *remove* it, Shift-click another text box to highlight both at once, use the Copy command so you can paste them onto another menu screen, and so on.

- **Change the text**. To highlight a piece of text, double-click anywhere inside the text box. iDVD highlights the entire phrase, meaning you can just begin to type, replacing the entire text blob, without first dragging across it. (Of course, if you want to edit only *part* of the existing text, drag across that text with your mouse first.) Press Return or Enter when you finish.

- **Choose a font, size, weight, color, and alignment**. Whenever you edit text, a mini-formatting palette automatically appears. Use it to change the text's typeface and size (Figure 19-6, top). For more options, use the Text Info palette (shown at bottom in Figure 19-6).

  You're not allowed to mix and match fonts *within* a text box, but each *text block* (each button label, title, or text box) can have a different look.

- **Add (or remove) a drop shadow**. Use the Shadow checkbox in the Text Info palette to add a faint shadow behind and below your text, which creates an easier-to-read, almost 3-D effect.

- **Position the title or text box**. You can drag titles and text boxes anywhere you like on the screen. Be careful not to park one where the *overscanning* effect of older TVs (see "Phase 1: Prepare Your Video" on page 375) might chop off some letters. To avoid this problem, choose View→Show TV Safe Area before you drag, taking care to keep the text inside the superimposed guidelines.

Editing Backgrounds

Menu-screen backgrounds provide a look and atmosphere that defines the entire screen. As a result, choosing a new background can add a unique twist to an existing theme.

Here's what you can use as a replacement for the Apple-supplied backgrounds.

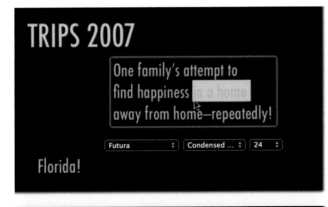

Figure 19-6:
Two ways to format a text block.

Top: When you highlight a piece of text to edit it, you get this miniature pop-up panel of font options.

Bottom: If you hit ⌘-I, you get a more complete formatting panel, which now includes shadow, color, and justification options.

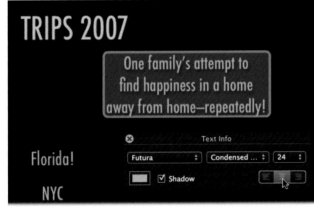

A Still Photo

Yep, you can replace the background that came with the Apple theme. In some cases, this simple action makes the theme look *completely* different.

Note: iDVD never distorts a photo that you embed as a background. If it's not the right shape for your TV, iDVD adds black letterbox bars to fill the gap. If you really care, you can prepare the photo in a program like Photoshop or Graphic Converter before installing it as a menu graphic. The dimensions for a *standard TV set* are 720×540 pixels; for a *widescreen set*, use 854×480. (For the PAL system used in Europe, use 768×576 for standard TVs, and 1024×576 for widescreens.)

To bring this change about, drag a photo from the Media Browser (click Media, then Photos) or the Finder into any of these three spots:

- **Any empty spot on the menu**. Avoid the drop zones.

- **The Menu Info panel**. See Figure 19-7 for details on working with the Menu Info panel, also known as the Inspector panel.

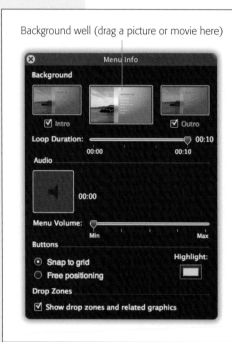

Background well (drag a picture or movie here)

Figure 19-7:
Click a blank spot on the menu screen, and then press ⌘-I to open the Inspector window to customize the screen itself. You can now drag a new photo into the Background well shown here.

- **The Drop Zone editor**. You met this handy row of drop-zone wells in Chapter 17, but it harbors a little secret: Another version of the Background well lurks at the left side. See Figure 19-8.

A Group of Photos

You can also drag an album full of photos, or just a handful of random ones, onto any of the Background areas described above. They become a slideshow that plays when the menu is onscreen.

To make this work, drag the photos into the Drop Zone editor's Background well (Figure 19-8). You can't drag them into an empty spot on the menu, or into the Inspector panel.

A Movie

If the idea of a static photo background doesn't pop your cork, you can create moving, animated, *video backgrounds*, just like the ones on many commercial Hollywood DVDs.

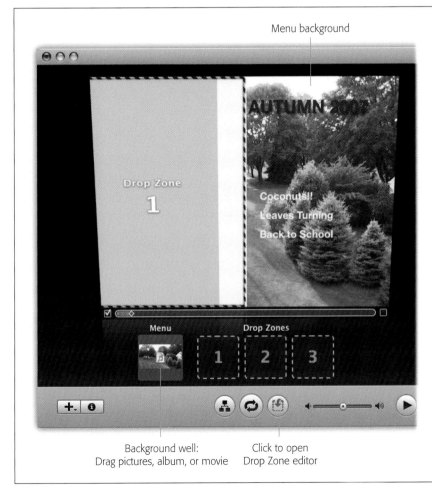

Menu background

Background well:
Drag pictures, album, or movie

Click to open
Drop Zone editor

Figure 19-8:
To change the menu background, open the Drop Zone editor. The icon is a background-image "well." Drop a picture or movie here and it becomes the menu screen's new, improved background. Drag the icon out of this well to reinstate the original background.

Here again, Apple gives you several places to drop your movie:

- **Any empty spot on the menu.** Avoid the drop zones. Drag a movie's icon directly onto the background—but as your cursor arrives, press the ⌘ key. A shortcut menu sprouts from your cursor, offering two choices: "Add movie" or "Replace background." Can you guess which one to click? (Hint: "Replace background.")

- **The Inspector panel.** See Figure 19-7 again.

- **The Drop Zone editor.** See Figure 19-8 again.

Once you add the movie background, you can control how *much* of it loops on the menu screen. Click anywhere on the background, press ⌘-I to open the Menu Info panel (shown in Figure 19-7), and then adjust the Loop Duration slider.

Some Notes

Before you delve into the exciting new world of background replacement, keep these points in mind:

- **Your video will loop**. Your background video file will play, then restart and play again as long as your audience leaves the menu onscreen. There's no way to make a video background play just once. Unless you take special care when you create your video background, you'll see sudden, sharp, sometimes distracting transitions when one loop cycle ends and the next one begins. See "Designing Video Loops in iMovie" on page 433 for help.

- **Video tends to move**. If you're not careful, video can hide or overwhelm your titles, buttons, and drop zones. "Audition" your videos and make sure they work with your menus before you burn a disc. In particular, watch for moving objects and scenes that are too bright or too dark.

- **One menu only**. The background-replacement techniques described above change only the current menu screen. To apply the change to *all* your menu screens, choose Advanced→Apply Theme To Project.

Note: Remember, iDVD limits the total duration of *all* the videos on *all* your menus to 15 minutes.

Menu Audio

Some of Apple's canned themes come with music soundtracks, and some don't. For example, if you want some music to play during the otherwise silent Shelves theme, you have to add it yourself.

You can also *replace* the music that comes with any of Apple's themes. In the case of musically challenged themes like Anime Pop, this ability is a true blessing, possibly saving lives and sanity. Adding a menu-screen soundtrack is a heck of a lot like installing a menu-screen background movie.

What to Drag

You can drag an audio file or QuickTime movie, either from the Finder or from the iDVD Music pane (click Media in the lower-right, and then Audio at the top). For example, you can drag a song—or even a whole playlist—out of your iTunes list. If you use a QuickTime movie, iDVD harvests only the soundtrack, not the video.

Where to Drag

Once again, you can drag audio into any of three spots:

- **The existing background**. That is, you can drag an audio file or movie directly into an empty spot on the menu, as shown in Figure 19-9. (Avoid the drop zones.)

- **The Menu Info panel**. Click an empty spot on the menu screen, and then press ⌘-I to open the Menu Info panel. You'll see an Audio well at the center (see Figure 19-7), where you can drag an audio or movie file in or out.

- **The Drop Zone editor**. You can drag an audio file onto the same spot where you'd drop a background *movie*. See Figure 19-8.

Incidentally, iDVD doesn't do much to help when your background video and background audio are different lengths. If the music is too short, it repeats until the video finishes playing, cutting off the music if necessary to start the music in sync with the next video loop. If the *music* is too long, the video continues looping until the music ends, cutting off the video mid-repeat. Use the Duration slider in the Menu Info panel (Figure 19-7) to set the loop time, which applies to both sound and video.

Or, if you're really a perfectionist, you could always use GarageBand to match the soundtrack length to the video. Create a nice fade-out at the end of the audio, and a fade-in at the beginning, so that the looping won't be jarring.

POWER USERS' CLINIC

Designing Video Loops in iMovie

Background videos don't have to jump between the end of one play-through and the beginning of the next. If you're willing to take a little time in iMovie, you can eliminate these sudden visual changes. Consider these techniques:

Fade Out/Fade In. Create a smooth fade-out at the end of a clip, and a smooth fade-in at the beginning, using the Fade Through Black transition described on page 136 in Chapter 5.

Use Cross-Dissolve. If you prefer, you can design your movie loop so that the end cross-dissolves into the beginning of the next loop. Go to the final frame of your movie and use the yellow handles to choose the last 4:02 (four seconds, two frames) of video. Right-click the clip and choose Split Clip from the pop-up menu. Now drag this newly created 4:02 clip to the front of your movie, and add

a 4-second cross dissolve between the clip and the original start of your movie; finally, export your work.

You can choose a different length for the crossfade; just make sure that the clip you move to the front of your movie lasts at least two frames longer than the desired transition time. This technique works particularly well on stock footage, such as windswept grass, fish in an aquarium, and so forth.

You may discover a couple of drawbacks to this method. First, the starting and ending audio and video will overlap, and you may not like the results. Second, the background video will, unfortunately, start with the crossfade. There's no way yet to make it start playing from an un-crossfaded spot, unless you do some clever cutting and pasting in iMovie. iDVD '12, perhaps? (Probably not.)

Figure 19-9:
If you've got a decent music collection in iTunes, adding background music is easy. Keep in mind that some of the most satisfying and appropriate soundtracks are those you create yourself, using GarageBand. Any finished compositions you export from GarageBand show up in the iTunes list, too. (In fact, Apple created the soundtracks included with iDVD in GarageBand! It's a company that eats its own dog food, as the saying goes.)

Tip: Remember, this technique affects the background music of the currently displayed menu screen only. To apply the change to *all* your menu screens, wrap up by choosing Advanced→Apply Theme To Project. And don't forget to stay below your total menu-length budget of 15 minutes.

Replacing Menu Audio

To replace a custom audio file with another, repeat the steps you used to embed the music to begin with. iDVD replaces the current track with the new one.

Removing Menu Audio

To remove audio, drag it out of the Audio well (in either the Menu Info panel or the Drop Zone editor). Puff! When an Audio well is empty, iDVD displays ◀ᴼ in it.

If you want to remove *all* the audio from your menu screen, you may have to drag twice: Your first drag removes custom sounds, and the second one removes the theme sound, if one exists.

Adjusting Menu Audio Volume

You can control your menu screen's audio volume using the slider in the Menu Info panel (Figure 19-7). Don't forget to check your audio before burning; this slider affects the final DVD.

Saving Favorites

After applying all the techniques described so far in this chapter, you may end up creating masterpieces of adapted iDVD themes. Fortunately, iDVD lets you save and reuse these modified themes. Here's how to go about it:

1. **Choose File→"Save Theme as Favorite."**

   A Save dialog box appears at the top of the window.

2. **Type a name for your new theme. Turn on "Shared for all users," if you like.**

   If you're the only person who uses your Mac, never mind. But if you share a Mac with other students, co-workers, or family members, each of whom has a Mac OS X *account*, the "Shared for all users" option makes your theme available to other people who use the machine. (Otherwise, your masterpiece appears in the list only when *you* use iDVD.)

   When you save a Favorite, you no longer need to keep the original theme on which it was based, as far as iDVD is concerned. Feel free to discard, rename, or move the original theme files from their locations on your hard drive. (The box below offers the details.)

3. **Turn off "Replace existing" if you want to create a new entry in the theme list.**

   If you turn *on* "Replace existing," iDVD treats your adapted theme as a replacement for the one you based it on.

4. **Click OK.**

   iDVD saves your theme as a new Favorite. You'll be able to apply it to other DVDs in the future by choosing its name from the Themes pane. (Choose Favorites from the pop-up menu to see its listing.)

Secrets of the Theme Files

Whenever you save a new Favorite theme, iDVD does a fair amount of administrative work. Behind the scenes, it creates a new theme file on your hard drive. If you decided to share your theme with other account holders (see step 2 above), iDVD stores the file in the Library→iDVD→Favorites folder. If not, it winds up in your Home→ Library→iDVD→Favorites folder. Unlike regular themes, whose names end with the suffix .theme, Favorites use a .favorite file extension.

Why is this important to know? Because it tells you how to remove a saved Favorite: Just drag the .favorite file out of the secret folder and into the Trash. The next time you open iDVD, that Favorite no longer appears in the Themes pane pop-up menu.

It's also worth noting that when you create a Favorite, iDVD copies all relevant materials, including background audio and video, to the newly created theme. (Don't believe it? To view this material, navigate to the saved .favorite file. Control-click or right-click its icon; from the shortcut menu, choose Show Package Contents. Then open the Contents→Resources folder.)

Advanced iDVD

Although iDVD appears to be a simple, straightforward tool for wrapping videos, photos, audio, and menus into a single, neat package, there's more power lurking inside than you might expect. You can see, change, and control things you never knew you could—if you're willing to try new and unusual approaches. Some of these approaches require add-on software. Others demand nerves of steel and a willingness to dive into hidden iDVD files.

In this advanced chapter, you'll discover how some of these sideways (and backward and upside-down) methods can expand your iDVD disc-development repertoire.

iDVD: The DVD-ROM Maker

At their core, DVD discs are nothing more than storage devices. You most often associate them with media files—movies, songs, and so on—but they can store boring old data files, too, like Microsoft Word documents or email messages. In fact, iDVD sets aside a portion of every DVD you create for data files, namely housekeeping files that the DVD uses to work properly. In DVD lingo, this area is called the DVD-ROM portion of your disc, and iDVD's ability to add data files to it may be its least-known feature. (The files won't show up on a DVD player, by the way—only on a computer.)

With iDVD, you can store any kind of data you want in the DVD-ROM portion of a disc. Here are just a few ways you can use this feature to enhance your disc:

- **Store documents that relate to your DVD contents**. A disc's DVD-ROM area provides the perfect place to store documents related to your DVD. You might, for example, include the script you used to film a movie, or different versions of the movie that eventually led to a final event invitation, extended family narratives, copies of email and other correspondence, and so on. One of the most common uses for the DVD-ROM portion of a disc is to store full-resolution versions of the digital photos featured in a slideshow. Remember: TV sets aren't much good for displaying text, but a DVD-ROM and a computer can come to the rescue.

- **Store web pages**. Web pages are perfect additions to the DVD-ROM disc area. You can create a self-contained website related to your DVD and add the files to the disc. Viewers can open these files with an ordinary web browser. For example, a DVD with a training video can contain supplementary lessons in HTML (web page) format.

- **Store email-quality versions of your video**. Use the DVD-ROM area of your disc to store small, compressed versions of your video, or "wallet-size" pictures from a slideshow, suitable for email. Now your audience can share their movie experience with other people.

Adding Files to the DVD-ROM Area

iDVD's DVD-ROM file management couldn't be simpler. Just drag icons out of the Finder and into the DVD-ROM Contents window (go to Advanced→Edit DVD-ROM Contents), as shown in Figure 20-1.

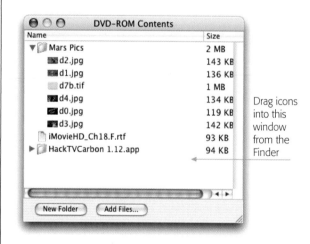

Figure 20-1:
By using the Add Files button or by dragging, you can store documents, folders, programs, and other computer files on a DVD—even one that has movies or other media on it. Recipients can access these files with a computer. In other words, iDVD can burn DVDs that go beyond the realm of simple videos.

Drag icons into this window from the Finder

Organizing DVD-ROM Contents

The DVD-ROM Contents window lets you organize your files in several ways:

- **Add folders**. Click New Folder to add a folder to your list.

- **Remove things**. Either drag files or folders right out of the list, or select them and then press the Delete key. (Dragging out of the list gives you the cool puff-of-smoke animation.)

- **Move items into or out of folders**. You can drag files onto folder icons to file them there—or drag them out again to move them elsewhere or delete them entirely.

- **Create subfolders**. Drag one folder onto another to create subfolders.

- **Rename a folder**. Double-click the name of a folder to select and edit it. Press Return or Enter when you finish typing.

- **List/hide folder contents**. You can click a folder's flippy triangle to see what's inside it, exactly as you would in Finder list views.

Uncover Your DVD Project File

Behind the scenes, iDVD stores all the pieces of your project inside the .dvdproj file you created when you first saved your work. However, .dvdproj isn't a true "file," even though it looks like a single icon on your desktop. It's actually a *package* of files—disguised as a Mac OS X folder—that contains many subfolders and files. To peek inside, follow these steps:

1. **Quit iDVD.**

   Never mess with your project files when you have iDVD running.

2. **Control-click (or right-click) the project file. From the shortcut menu, choose Show Package Contents.**

   You'll find your projects in iDVD's default project folder (Users→[your account name]→Documents, unless you specified a different destination). You've now opened that "file" in a folder window.

3. **Open the Contents→Resources folder.**

   You're in. Here are all the different files that make up your DVD (see Figure 20-2 for an example).

So what is all this stuff?

- Your **ProjectData** file stores all the settings for your DVD project, in the form of a binary *property list*. It tells iDVD how to put together the menus, sound files, graphics, and other pieces that comprise your DVD.

Tip: If you're an inquiring soul, drag the ProjectData icon onto the icon of a binary XML editor, like Apple's (free) Property List Editor. Turns out ProjectData is just a humble XML file, and—as long as you're careful not to make or save any changes—you can pass an enlightening afternoon studying its contents to discover how your DVD is structured.

- iDVD stores compressed video files—the ones that your audience will actually see—in the **MPEG** folder. If you really want to, you can play one of these files right on your Mac: Copy it to the desktop, add an .m2v suffix to its file name, and watch it using a program that can play MPEG-2 files (like VLC, a free movie player available at *http://www.videolan.org/vlc*).

Figure 20-2:
Your .dvdproj file stores all the movies, sounds, graphics, and data associated with your iDVD project in a series of hidden subfolders and files.

- If you're using an older theme, one where the buttons display little pictures or videos, you'll see that a **Thumbnails** folder stores the tiny QuickTime videos that play on the buttons. Double-click one of them to play it in QuickTime right on your Mac.

iDVD doesn't fill the remaining folders until it actually burns your DVD. At that point, it uses these folders to store intermediate files as it works. For example:

- In the **Menu** folder, iDVD stores MPEG-2 (.m2v) files that represent the video loops used on your menu screens, complete with buttons, thumbnails, and so on.

- As you could probably guess, the **Slideshow** folder stores all the digital pictures and movies you chose for your slideshows, and the **Audio** folder contains all the sound files. (You could double-click one of the sound files to play it in Quick-Time, if you really wanted to.)

- The **Overlay** folder holds *menu overlays* (videos that animate buttons when your viewers highlight them) and *motion overlays* (animations that play on top of drop zones—the Theater theme curtains or the Brush Strokes paint effect, for example).

Automator and iDVD

As any power user can tell you, Automator is one of the best (and lesser known) features of the Mac operating system. It's a scripting (code-writing) program that automates all kinds of repetitive actions, and all without you writing a single line of code. Building an Automator action is basically a matter of drag and drop. If you find yourself using iDVD regularly, for a wedding movie business, for example, or real estate walkthrough DVDs, definitely give Automator a serious look.

Note: Teaching you how to use Automator is beyond the scope of this book, but you can learn quite a bit from the handy video tutorials at *http://automator.us/leopard/video/index.html*. (The videos are narrated by a creepy computer voice, but if you can watch these without getting nightmares later, they're well worth the time.)

Here are the Automator actions Apple created just for iDVD (Figure 20-3):

- **Add Movie to iDVD Menu**. Sticks a movie into an iDVD project menu. You might use this action if you're processing movie files to eventually burn to a DVD.

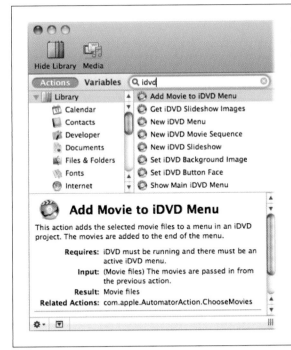

Figure 20-3:
Automator, Mac OS X's simple scripting tool, contains a list of actions made just for iDVD. To find the iDVD actions quickly, type "iDVD" into the search field.

- **Get iDVD Slideshow Images**. If you want to use Automator to do some work on the photos in an iDVD slideshow, this action retrieves the file names and locations of the photos. Then you can use other Automator actions to edit the images (flip them, crop them, make thumbnails from them, and so on).

- **New iDVD Menu**. Just as it says in the name, this command creates a new iDVD menu.

- **New iDVD Movie Sequence**. This action creates playback menus when you put a group of movies on a single DVD. You can specify how many movies you want to appear on each menu.

- **Set iDVD Background Image**. As you learned in Chapter 19, you can create a custom background for iDVD menus. This action takes an image you specify and automatically creates an iDVD menu background.

- **Set iDVD button face.** Remember how you can make iDVD buttons that have pictures or movies on them? This action uses a selected picture or movie on all the buttons in the current iDVD menu.

- **Show Main iDVD Menu.** If you're automating a number of steps in an Automator sequence, this action takes you back to the main menu of an iDVD project, should the need arise.

Archiving Your Project

Ordinarily, iDVD doesn't store any videos, photos, or sounds in your iDVD project file. It remains a tiny, compact file that stores only *pointers* to those files, which reside elsewhere on your hard drive. That's why, if you delete or move one of those media files, iDVD mildly freaks out—its pointers become invalid.

In early versions of iDVD, you couldn't transfer a project from one Mac to another for this very reason. And that meant that you couldn't *design* a DVD on one Mac (one that lacked a DVD burner, for example), and then *burn* it on another. You also couldn't back up your project file, content that you included all of its pieces.

Fortunately, in more recent versions of iDVD, Apple came up with a solution. The Archive Project command lets you completely "dereference" a project, meaning the project file will *contain* every file used in your project: movies, photos, sounds, theme elements, and DVD-ROM files. Your project file becomes completely self-contained, ready for backup or transfer to another computer. (It's also now really, really huge.)

Follow these steps to produce an archive:

1. **Save your project.**

   If you forget this step, iDVD reminds you.

2. **Choose File→Archive Project.**

   The Save As panel shown in Figure 20-4 appears.

3. **Turn checkboxes on or off, if you like.**

   "Include themes" copies your theme files into the project—something that's unnecessary if you use standard Apple themes. But if you use themes from other companies, ones you designed, or modified versions of Apple originals, turn on this checkbox. "Include encoded files" is the more important option, because it's very unlikely that all your sounds, photos, and movies are also on the destination Mac.

Turn the boxes on and off to see how much space you'll use/recover.

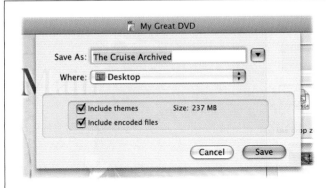

Figure 20-4:
The Archive Project's Save As panel lets you specify whether you want to include themes and encoded files as part of your archived project. You can save quite a bit of disk space by leaving these options unchecked. The Size indicator to the right of "Include themes" tells you how much space your project will occupy.

4. **Name the archive file, choose a folder location for it, and then click Save.**

    Wait as iDVD builds the new archive. This can take a few minutes, so be patient. You may be working with *very* large files.

Archived projects look like any other projects in that they use the same .dvdproj extension. But inside, they're very different. For proof, simply open it as a package (Control-click its icon; from the shortcut menu, choose View Package Contents). Inside its Contents→Resources folder, you'll find new folders called Assets and Themes, which store the extra archived elements (Figure 20-5).

Figure 20-5:
When iDVD archives a project, it adds folders to the project bundle. The Assets folder stores original copies of your audio and video files (in the "av" sub-folder), DVD-ROM content (in "data"), and images (in "stills"). If you choose to save themes, they show up in the Themes folder.

Note: To turn your photos and videos into DVD-compatible files, iDVD must *encode* (convert) them into a format called MPEG. Depending on your Preferences settings, iDVD may constantly be working on this time-consuming task in the background, or it may do the job only when you burn a DVD. Either way, an archived project also stores any MPEG files iDVD creates. They save you time when you burn a DVD, but they make the archive's file size balloon like a blimp.

If you'd rather make the archive file smaller, choose Advanced→Delete Encoded Assets before saving the archive. iDVD removes the encoded MPEG files—but you'll pay for this gesture in re-encoding time when you're ready to burn your discs.

Copying an Archive to a Different Mac

Suppose you designed a DVD using a Mac that lacks a DVD burner. Now, as Apple intended, you used the Archive command to prepare it for transfer to a Mac that *does* have a burner.

Transfer the archived project using any convenient method: copy it across a network, transfer it using iChat, copy it onto an iPod, or whatever. (It's too big for email, of course, but you could instead post it on a website for downloading.) The project opens normally on the other machine, with all of its pieces intact, ready to touch up and burn.

Disk Images

Thanks to a handy iDVD feature, you can save your project as a computer file called a *disk image.* You may have run into the disk-image (.dmg or .img) format before; it's a favored storage format for software you download. It's popular because you get a single, self-contained file that *contains* many other files, arrayed inside exactly as though they were on a disk. When you open a disk-image file, in fact, it turns into a little hard-disk icon on your desktop, with all its contents tucked inside.

Note: Don't confuse a disk image with a project archive; they're two very different beasts. A disk image is a virtual disk, a bit-for-bit copy of the data that would appear on an actual, physical DVD—it just happens to be stored on a hard drive rather than a DVD.

Project archives, in contrast, contain all the source material that iDVD uses for that project. The only thing that can read or "play back" a project archive is iDVD itself.

To turn an iDVD project into a disk image, first save the project. Then, choose File→"Save as Disc Image" (Shift-⌘-R). Choose a file name (for example, *Summer Fun.img*) and a location, and then click Save. Now wait as iDVD compresses your movie and saves it to disk. All this takes just as long as it would to burn an actual DVD, so now's your chance to catch up on some magazine reading.

When it's all over, you'll find a new .img icon—a disk image—on your desktop. Disk images are amazingly high-octane, cool stuff for two reasons:

- **You don't have to burn a disc to watch your movies.** Mac OS X's DVD Player program (go to Applications→DVD Player) can play back a disk image just as though it's a real DVD. You see all the menus, slideshows, and other iDVD features you've grown to love.

As shown in Figure 20-6, the trick is to open the Video_TS folder. Never heard of it? Well, it's an important folder on *every DVD ever made*—it's where all the video files reside—and there's one on your disk image, too.

Figure 20-6:
Apple's DVD Player program (Applications→DVD Player) can play back disk images as well as physical DVDs. In the Finder, double-click a disk image to create a virtual DVD on your desktop. Now launch DVD Player and choose File→Open DVD Media, as shown at top. In the dialog box that appears, navigate to the disk image (remember, this is a virtual disc, so you'll find it under Devices in the Finder), choose the Video_TS folder, and then click Choose. Press the space bar to start playback.

Tip: Playing back a disk image is a handy way to test a DVD's integrity; after all, you don't want to use up a perfectly good blank disc by burning an incomplete DVD. The tip doesn't work for dual-layer DVDs, though, because disk images don't indicate where the "break" is between dual layers.

- **You can burn a new copy whenever you want, without waiting.** You can use Roxio Toast (a beloved commercial burning program) or Mac OS X's own Disk

Utility program to burn a disk image onto a real DVD—without having to go through the excruciating multi-hour encoding process again. Figure 20-7 provides the amazingly simple instructions for this long-sought solution.

Figure 20-7:
Double-click your disk image in the Finder to make its virtual disk appear. Then open Disk Utility (in your Application→Utilities folder), click the virtual disk, and then choose Images→Burn. Disk Utility prompts you to insert a blank DVD. Do so, and then click Burn.

Professional Duplicating

Maybe you organized a school play and you want to sell copies of the performance to parents as a fundraiser. Maybe you want to send out "new baby" videos to your family circle. Or maybe you used iDVD to create a video brochure of your small business's products and services.

In each of these cases, burning a DVD one at a time on your Mac looks like a time-consuming, expensive hassle. Furthermore, home DVD burners use a laser to record your bits and bytes on an organic dye, which deteriorates over time. Commercial DVDs stamp the digital signals directly into the plastic.

Accordingly, when you want to make more than a handful of copies of your DVD, you might want to enlist the aid of a *DVD service bureau*. DVD service bureaus are middlemen between you and the large replication plants, which don't deal directly with the public.

Technically, these companies offer two services:

- **Duplication**. Duplicated discs are copies of your original DVD. Service bureaus use banks of DVD burners, five or 10 at a time, that churn out copy after copy on DVD-Rs (the same kinds of blanks you want to use). You pay for materials and labor, usually by the hour. (Discs with less data burn more quickly, producing more discs per hour.) This is the way to go if you need fewer than 100 copies of your disc. (On the other hand, remember that some DVD players don't play DVD-R discs.)

- **Replication**. Replication is designed for huge numbers of DVDs, 200 and up. In this process, the company actually presses the DVDs just the way Hollywood movie studios do—and the results play back in virtually every DVD player.

  Service bureaus replicate your discs in factories. They take the data from your master DVD-R and press 4.7 GB "DVD-5" discs—standard DVDs, not DVD-Rs. You can also replicate to dual-layer discs; just ask your salesman for details. Expect to pay about a dollar per disc for a run of 1,000 discs. Smaller runs will cost more per disc, larger runs less, but $400 is about the least you'll pay for a replication job.

Note: DVD service bureaus often call themselves *replicators*, even though they offer both duplication and replication.

Prepare to Copy

All DVD service bureaus accept DVD-R masters of the sort that iDVD burns. Nevertheless, keep these tips in mind:

- **Submit two**. Always submit two copies of your master. It costs you almost nothing in materials and time, and can save your project if one disc fails.

- **Use name brands**. Burn your masters on the best-quality discs available. Brand-name blanks, like Verbatim, Maxell, and TDK, are less likely to lead to duplication problems. (One replicator complains that if you hold those cheapie 30-cent discs up to the light, you can see light pass right through them!)

- **Use DVD-Rs**. Despite the format wars in DVD standards (DVD-R vs. DVD+R), the -R standard is better for replication. Many factories, in fact, don't accept +R discs, which leads to manufacturing problems.

- **You don't need a DVD burner**. If your Mac doesn't have a DVD burner, most service bureaus can create a master DVD from a disk image (which you can create directly from iDVD). You'll pay a little extra for the conversion.

- **Collect your copyright documentation**. Every replicator will ask you to sign a copyright release stating that you have permission to use the material on your disc. (If you're not asked about this, run away screaming. It's a red flag that you're dealing with an unsavory replicator.)

As a rule, anything you videotape is yours. You own it. If you use music from a friend, then a simple signed and dated letter will do: "Casey is my friend and has the right to use my music." If you use royalty-free material, make a note of it. And if you use music you bought from the iTunes music store (or ripped from a commercial music CD), well, you may be on thin ice.

Choosing a Replicator

When choosing a service bureau or replicator, start by getting references—preferably for *recent* projects. Do your legwork and make the calls. You can also check with the Better Business Bureau to see if a service bureau has a history of customer complaints.

Tip: Choose a licensed replicator. Replicators and manufacturers must pay a small royalty on every DVD they produce, because DVDs are copyrighted technology. Some factories, even in the U.S., operate with questionable practices—some pay all their fees, some pay part of their fees, some don't pay fees at all. Reputable service bureaus don't work with gray-market replicators.

Take cost into account when you pick a service bureau, but keep in mind that you often get what you pay for. It may be worth paying extra to find a technically savvy replicator who will ask the right questions, hold your hand as needed, and make sure that your project turns out right.

Working with Replicators

When you submit a work order to a replicator, be *very* specific. Unless you specify Amray cases (the Blockbuster-style cases, with a little plastic hub-and-button that holds the DVD in place) and cigarette-stripped shrink wrap (standard clear plastic wrapping, so named because you pull a strip to open it, just as on a pack of cigarettes), you may end up with DVDs shoved into CD jewel cases. Sit down with your salesperson and go through all the options, from packaging to turnaround time.

Complex packaging takes more time and costs more. Consider ordering your discs in bulk paper sleeves or "slimline" cases (the most basic DVD delivery cases), without printing on them, to save on costs and time. To save even more money, you may be able to set up a deal where you pay to replicate 1,000 discs but package only 200 of them.

Fulfillment

If you're interested in *selling* your DVD masterpieces, you may want to hire yet another company to package, mail, and collect payment for them. *Fulfillment* companies—many run by DVD service bureaus—build a basic website, take orders, and mail out your discs. All you have to do is provide your iDVD masters, sign the contracts, pay the setup bills—and start working on your Oscar acceptance speech.

Making DVDs Last

Your homemade DVDs (which are "burned" using dyes) probably won't last the 100 years expected of commercial DVDs (which are etched with lasers). But don't get too depressed by the occasional article about homemade DVDs "going bad" in a matter of months. Most cases of "DVD rot" come down to one of two things: problems created during manufacturing or poor handling by their owners.

There's not much you can do about manufacturing errors, apart from buying name-brand blank DVDs. As for handling, these tips should ensure that your recordable DVDs will last for years:

Store your discs in a cool, dry place. DVD-Rs are sensitive to both temperature and humidity. In an ideal world, DVDs would love to live in a cupboard that's 68 degrees Fahrenheit with 30 to 50 percent humidity. In the real world, room temperature is fine as long as temperature swings aren't a fact of life. Recordable DVDs hate large changes in humidity, too.

Keep your discs out of the light. Prolonged exposure to ultraviolet light degrades the organic dyes in the recordable layer, possibly making the data on your discs unreadable. Regular light may also hurt your discs, primarily through heat.

Don't flex your discs. With their laminated polycarbonate layers, recordable DVDs are very sensitive to bending or flexing. In fact, the quickest way to destroy your disc is to bend it. So don't. Store your discs in soft envelopes or in cases where you pinch a center hub to release the DVD. Don't store them in CD jewel boxes that have "buttonless" snap-on hubs—you have to bend the discs too much to free them.

Hold discs by the edges. Fingerprints, scratches, and dust on the disc surface interfere with a laser's ability to read data. DVDs are much more sensitive than CDs in this regard, because the data is crammed together so much more tightly.

Don't stick on labels. Adhesive labels throw off the disc's balance—and might even ruin your drive when the heat makes the glue melt. Instead, use a CD-safe marker to write on your DVD-Rs.

Part Four: Appendixes

4

Appendix A: iMovie '11, Menu by Menu

Appendix B: Troubleshooting

Appendix C: Master Keyboard Shortcut List

Appendix D: Visual Cheat Sheet

iMovie '11, Menu by Menu

As you've certainly noticed by now, iMovie doesn't look like a standard Mac program. Part of its radical charm is that it represents almost all its functions onscreen. There simply aren't many menu commands. But don't get complacent: You'll miss some great features if you don't venture to the top-of-screen menu bar much.

Now, documenting iMovie menu commands is tricky because they're constantly changing. The command that says Select All Events one minute might say Select All another, and Select Entire Clip a minute after that. The wording is always of the same gist—delete things, select things, and so on—but it changes according to the situation.

Here's a rundown of the commands in iMovie's menus:

iMovie Menu

In Mac OS X, Apple names the first menu (after the menu) for the program you're using—in this case, iMovie.

About iMovie

This command opens the About box, containing the requisite Apple legal information. There's really only one good reason to open this window: It's the easiest way to find out exactly which version of iMovie you have.

Preferences

Opens the Preferences window (Figure A-1). (*Keyboard shortcut*: ⌘-comma.)

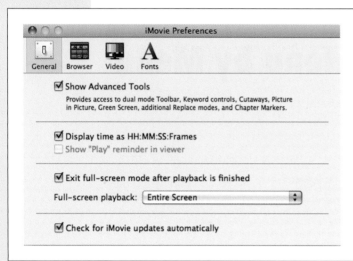

Figure A-1:
You can get to this box quickly by pressing ⌘-comma, which isn't so hard to learn considering it's also the keystroke that opens the Preferences box in iPhoto, iTunes, GarageBand, and most other Apple and Microsoft programs. What isn't typical, though, is the way Apple has split apart four sets of preferences. In this box, you'll find options that govern the entire iMovie program. In the Project Preferences box, you set options independently for each movie-editing project.

Here's a tour.

General Tab

- **Show Advanced Tools**. This may not be Apple's finest interface-design moment, but whatever: When you turn on this option, a motley assortment of additional features shows up in random iMovie places. On the central toolbar, the Keyword button appears. "Paint to select" editing becomes available (page 91). So does "Paint to reject" or "Paint to mark as Favorite" editing (page 113).

  This option reveals additional drag-and-drop menu options that show up when you drop one clip onto another. Specifically, the options are Cutaways (page 103), Green Screen (page 159), Picture-in-Picture (page 165), and additional replace options (page 89).

  And in the Video Adjustments panel, individual sliders appear for red, green, and blue color intensity (page 182).

- **Display Time as HH:MM:SS:Frames**. Ordinarily, iMovie shows you the lengths of clips and selections using seconds—for example, "8.5s," meaning 8.5 seconds.

  Experienced video editors, however, are used to looking at *timecode* displays, which take the form of minutes:seconds:frames—for example, "02:08:15." If you turn this checkbox on, iMovie adds the number of frames to all time readouts. So instead of "8.5s," you'll see "8:15." (There are 30 frames per second in North American video.)

- **Show "Play" reminder in viewer**. From the day you first tried iMovie, you might have noticed the message that appears in the Viewer window whenever you point to a filmstrip: "Press the space bar or double-click to Play." Apple wanted to make really, really sure that you knew how to play your video.

  Once you get that technique under your belt, though, you might feel that this message is unnecessary. You can turn it off with this checkbox. (The box automatically turns off if you turn on Advanced Tools.)

- **Exit fullscreen mode after playback is finished**. Pretty much what it says. If you turn this option on, every time you finish playing back a movie in full-screen mode, you return to iMovie. If it's off, then you stay in full-screen mode for more playback experimentation.

- **Fullscreen playback size**. See page 94 for details on this option.

- **Check for iMovie updates automatically**. If you turn this option on, then iMovie sends out an electronic feeler each time you open it and you're online, to see if a new update is available. If so, you're invited to download and install it.

Browser Tab

- **Show date ranges in Event Library**. If you turn this option on, each Event in your Event list sprouts, in tiny lettering, a legend like "Oct 25, 2007-Nov 1, 2007," to let you know the time period covered by the video inside.

- **Use large font for project and Event lists**. You guessed it: This option enlarges the type size in these two lists.

- **Always show active clip badges**. Many of the changes you can make to a project clip (things like stabilization, color changes, and volume adjustments) result in a tiny badge appearing on the top-left corner of the clip. Unchecking this option makes those invisible until you move your mouse cursor over a clip.

- **Always show clip durations**. When your mouse pointer hovers over a clip, iMovie displays the clip's length. Checking this box makes the little timecode show up permanently, no matter where your mouse is.

- **Use project crop setting for clips in Event Browser**. You can read about the aspect-ratio problem on page 63. And you can read about how you want your project to *handle* the aspect-ratio problem on page 64.

  But the choice you make for handling mis-fitting footage in your *project* doesn't do anything in the *Event Browser*. That is, setting up letterbox bars for the project itself doesn't create letterbox bars as you peruse your source clips in the Event Browser—unless you turn on this option. Then the Event Browser displays your clips with the same Crop or Fit setting you selected for the project.

- **Automatically stabilize clips that have been analyzed**. Once iMovie analyzes clips in the Event Browser (page 176), it can automatically stabilize them as you add them to your project. Leave this unchecked, and iMovie won't stabilize project clips unless you tell it to via the Inspector.

- **Apply rolling shutter correction for clips that have been analyzed**. Just as with stabilization, iMovie can automatically fix the rolling shutter problem (page 181) when you add clips to your project. If this box stays unchecked, you'll need to turn on the rolling shutter fix in the Inspector.

- **Show Fine Tuning controls**. The "buttons" referred to here are shown in Figure 3-13 (page 101). They appear when you point to a filmstrip without clicking. And when you click one of these little buttons, you get the orange vertical clip-cropping handles that let you lengthen or shorten a clip by up to 1 second.

  If the appearance of that little button confuses you or clutters up your life, you can hide it by turning it off. Even then, you can still make those orange clip-cropping handles appear when you want them—just by pressing the Option and ⌘ keys.

- **Double-click to: Edit/Play**. If you choose Edit, double-clicking a clip brings the Inspector out of hiding, letting you make changes to the clip. If you select Play, double-clicking works just like pressing the space bar; iMovie starts playing the clip from the playhead on.

- **Clicking in Event browser…** These three options let you control what happens when you click a filmstrip in the Event Browser. On a freshly installed copy of iMovie, you get a 4-second selection. But you can also opt to have one click select the entire clip or deselect everything (because you prefer to drag to make selections, not click).

Video Tab

- **Import HD video as: Large/Full**. Page 37 offers a full description of this option, which pertains solely to video you import from high-definition camcorders.

Fonts Tab

This tab gets full treatment on page 212.

Provide iMovie Feedback

This command takes you to a web form on Apple's site where you can register complaints, make suggestions, or gush enthusiastically about iMovie. (Don't expect a return call from Steve Jobs, however.)

Register iMovie

This links to yet another Apple web page. Registering iMovie simply means giving Apple your contact information so you can access Apple's online support documents, receive upgrade notices, get special offers, and so on. There's no penalty for not registering, by the way. Apple just wants to know more about who you are, so that it can offer you exciting new waves of junk mail.

Check For Updates

If iMovie isn't set to check for Apple patches and bug-fix updates automatically, you can make it check manually on your command, using this option.

Hide iMovie, Hide Others, Show All

These aren't iMovie commands—they're Mac OS X's.

In any case, they determine which of the various programs running on your Mac are visible onscreen at any given moment. The Hide Others command is probably the most popular of these three. It zaps away the windows of all other programs—including the Finder—so that the iMovie window is the only one you see.

Tip: If you know this golden Mac OS X trick, you may never need to use the Hide Others command: To switch into iMovie from another program, hold down the Option and ⌘ keys when clicking ★ in the Dock. Doing so simultaneously brings iMovie to the front and hides all other programs you have running, producing an uncluttered, distraction-free view of iMovie.

Quit iMovie

This command (*keyboard shortcut*: ⌘-Q) closes iMovie after offering you the chance to save any changes you made to your project file. The next time you open iMovie by double-clicking its icon, the program reopens whatever project document you were working on.

File Menu

As in any Mac program, the File menu serves as the program's interface to the rest of the Macintosh world. It lets you import movies and video, manage Events, create or duplicate projects, or quit the program.

New Project

Creates a new project in the Projects list, ready for filling with video snippets from the Event Browser.

New Folder

Creates a simulated file folder in the Projects list, into which you can drag individual projects. It's a tool for managing long project lists as your editing skills grow.

New Event

Creates a new event in the Events list, which you can create before importing any video. This also lets you reorganize your Events just how you want them (page 65).

Duplicate Project

Creates a duplicate of the project you're working on. This is a great trick for generating alternate versions—a shorter edit, a raunchier one, and so on.

Tip: iMovie HD had a cool option for exporting just the selected clips in a project, which comes in handy when you need to ship out only part of your movie. If you're pining for that feature, you can just create a duplicate of your project and trim it down to exactly what you want to export.

The great thing about creating and duplicating projects is, of course, that you don't use up any more hard drive space. A project is, behind the scenes, simply a tiny text file; it doesn't store any video. The instructions in that text file just refer to the video that iMovie actually stores in your Events.

Import from Camera

This is just another way to bring up the import screen you read about on page 31.

Import Movies/Camera Archive/iMovie HD Project

You read about importing movies on page 49, camera archives on page 44, and iMovie HD projects on page 47.

Project Properties

This command opens the all-important Project Properties dialog box (Figure A-2), which is a lot like Preferences except that the options you set here apply only to one project—the one you're working on.

- **Aspect Ratio**. This pop-up menu specifies the movie-frame proportions of your project, as described on page 62.

- **Frame Rate**. You read about frame rates on page 19 when you read about the difference between NTSC and PAL. This menu, when not grayed out, gives you the opportunity to adjust the frame rates for your project. Unless you're dealing with a mix of the two formats, you really shouldn't need this menu.

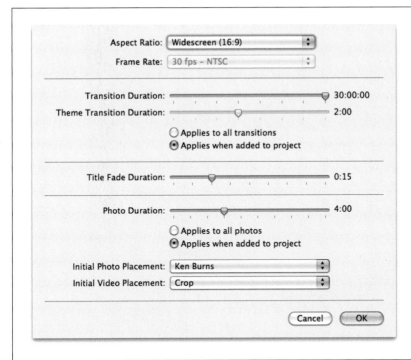

Figure A-2:
This is the preferences dialog box for the project you're working on. Commit the corresponding keystroke to memory: ⌘-J (it stands for proJect—get it?).

- **Transition Duration**. Drag this slider left or right to determine how long a newly added transition takes.

- **Theme Transition Duration**. This slider works the same as above, but affects the specially animated transitions iMovie uses with its themes (page 141).

- **Applies to all transitions**. If you opt for this choice, the duration slider affects all transitions—those already placed and those you have yet to place. (It means that you'll lose all custom duration adjustments you applied to transitions in the project.)

- **Applies when added to project**. This one means "Leave the durations of the transitions I already adjusted alone, but make all incoming transitions this long."

- **Title Fade Duration**. This slider controls how long the text of your titles takes to fade in and out during their appearances in your movie.

- **Photo Duration**. When you first drag a photo into your storyboard, it turns into a "still video" clip. This slider lets you specify how long those clips play when you first put them in the storyboard. (You can always adjust their timing later, of course.)

- **Applies to all photos**. Just as with the equivalent setting for transitions, if you pick this option, the duration slider affects all photos, those already placed and those you have yet to place. (It means that you'll lose all custom duration adjustments for the photos in your project.)

- **Applies when added to project**. This one means "Leave the durations of the *photos* I already adjusted alone, but make all incoming photos this long."

- **Initial Photo Placement**. This pop-up menu tells iMovie how to handle photos that don't exactly fit the aspect ratio of your movie project. It can either crop them (enlarge to fill the frame), fit the frame ("Fit in Frame") by adding letterbox bars, or execute the Ken Burns effect (perform a slow zoom and pan across them).

- **Initial Video Placement**. Similarly, this pop-up menu controls what happens when you add mis-fitting video to a project. iMovie can either enlarge it to fit the frame (Crop) or add letterbox bars ("Fit in Frame").

Project Theme

This command opens the Theme settings for your project, which you learned about in chapter 5. Get to it by pressing Shift-⌘-J.

- **Project Theme**. This is where you choose a theme for your project, if any. Page 139 has a lot more information about themes.

- **Automatically add (pick a transition)**. Here, you control whether or not iMovie automatically puts in transition effects between the clips in your project—and if so, which transition, and how long you want it to last. Details are on page 133. If you pick a theme, this menu turns into a plain ol' checkbox, and iMovie chooses the theme titles and transitions for you.

Move to Trash

To delete most things in iMovie, like transitions, titles, or sound clips, you just click the item and then press the Delete key.

Things that represent more effort, however, like projects, Events, and imported video, require more effort to delete—and those steps always begin with this command, whose wording changes to reflect whatever you have highlighted (for example, "Move Event to Trash" or "Move Entire Clip to Trash").

They wind up in the Macintosh Trash, as described on page 119, so you can recover them if you change your mind (until you empty the trash, that is).

Move to Rejected Clips Trash

This saves you a trip to the Rejected Clips view (page 119). Select this and any clips you already rejected will go directly to the Macintosh trash without passing Go.

Space Saver

This command is another way to reclaim a lot of disk space. It rounds up all your unwanted or unused video and purges it from your hard drive; details are on page 121.

Consolidate Media

Collects media for a given project so that it all lives on a single drive. More on this on page 61.

Merge Events

iMovie generally splits imported video into Events—shots you filmed on the same day. You may sometimes find it useful, however, to combine several Events into a single Event, like the three days' worth of video you took during a single weekend getaway.

To use this command, first highlight the Events you want to merge. (Click one, and then ⌘-click each additional one.) Then choose this command. iMovie asks you to name the new, combined Event.

Split Event Before Selected Clip

Conversely, you may sometimes want to split an Event in two. That's the purpose of this command. Highlight a filmstrip within the Event, and then choose this command; iMovie creates a second Event containing the selected filmstrip and everything that followed it. If you called the first event Vacation, iMovie calls the second one Vacation 1.

Adjust Clip Date and Time...

You'll use this command to fix any event footage that just didn't happen when iMovie thinks it happened. To set iMovie straight on footage dates, follow the instructions on page 68.

Analyze Video

This menu item tells iMovie to examine a clip for stabilization (page 176), rolling shutter fix (page 181), and people-finding (page 117). Don't plan on analyzing a lot of footage unless you have an extra month or two. (It takes a long time.)

You'll also find, buried in this menu, Mark Camera Pans. Choosing this analyzes your footage for left or right pans (swings of the camera from right to left or left to right), and then marks the pans with Pan Left and Pan Right keywords. Pretty nifty.

Optimize Video Full/Large

Some cameras store video in processor-intensive formats, notably the H.264 format. On even moderately speedy Macs, these clips look jittery during scrubbing, ruining one of iMovie's coolest features. To smooth things over, you can use this menu item to convert your clips to the Apple Intermediate Codec (see page 48). The resulting files take up a lot more disk space than H.264, but they scrub much more smoothly. Use the Full option to preserve HD footage in full quality, or the Large option to use Apple's HD-lite. (Read more about this choice on page 37.)

Page Setup, Print Project

It might seem peculiar to find a Print command in a video-editing program. But there are times when the Print command might be helpful:

- You're working on a long project that doesn't fit into the iMovie window. By making a printout, you can see the big picture.

- You might want to share a visual representation of your project, identifying particular transitions, clips, or titles for someone who isn't sitting in front of your screen with you.

- Your Event Browser is overflowing with clips, and you're sorting through them, trying to decide which to trim or delete.

In all of these cases, you can print your Events or projects for handy reference.

Tip: Use the Print Preview button to get an accurate view of your output before you commit it to ink and paper.

Note, however, that:

- The Print command prints whatever project or Event(s) you have selected, so be sure to select the proper ones in the left-side list before you begin. (Remember, you can select more than one project or Event by ⌘-clicking them.)

- The Print command respects the magnification levels you use to view your clips. That is, the half-second zoom means a lot of frames on your printed page; the 30-second zoom means very few.

- iMovie attempts to fit everything on a single page. If it can't, it reduces the thumbnail sizes of the entire printout as much as necessary, all in an effort to fit the number of "preferred" pages you specified (Figure A-3).

- When you print Events, you get a divider on the printout that identifies each Event.

- If you choose, you can also include favorite, keyword, and reject markings in your printout (Figure A-3).

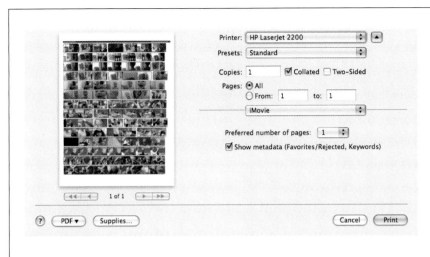

Figure A-3:
If you choose iMovie from the third pop-up menu, you discover that two handy options have been lurking. "Preferred number of pages" determines iMovie's target maximum for the printout. But if your project won't fit in this number of pages even with tiny thumbnails, iMovie prints out the additional pages required. The "Show metadata" checkbox will include keyword, favorite, and reject markings in the printout.

Edit Menu

The Edit menu and Clip menu contain all the editing commands described in Chapters 2 and 3. In fact, along with the various drag-and-drop editing techniques described in this book, the commands in these two menus are the only tools you need to build your movies.

Undo

In iMovie, you can take back not only the last edit you make, not only the last 10, but an infinite number of steps, all the way back to the last time you opened iMovie. The ability to change your mind, or to recover from a particularly bad editing decision, is a considerable blessing.

The wording of this command changes to show you which editing step you're about to reverse. It might say Undo Merge Events, Undo Split, and so on. *Keyboard shortcut*: ⌘-Z.

Redo

We're only human, so it's entirely possible that sometimes you might want to undo your Undo.

For example, suppose you just used the Undo command a few times, retracing your steps back to a time when your movie was in better shape, and then decide that you've gone one step too far. That's when the Redo command is useful; it tells iMovie to undo your last Undo, so you can step forward in time, redoing the steps you just undid. (If you haven't yet used the Undo command, then iMovie dims Redo.) *Keyboard shortcut*: Shift-⌘-Z.

Cut, Copy, Paste

You can use the Cut, Copy, and Paste commands just as you would in any other program: to move stuff around. You can cut, copy, and paste whatever you select: entire filmstrips or just chunks of them.

For example, you can cut a selection from a clip and paste it into another spot, or you can copy a selection and paste it into another project.

Cut, Copy, and Paste also work when you edit text, such as the names of your clips or the text for your credits and other titles.

Paste Adjustments

Once you painstakingly edit the look of a clip (for color correction, for example), a photo (to use a Ken Burns effect, for example), or some audio (to boost the volume, for example), you can rapidly enhance a bunch of other footage in the same way. Just copy the first clip, and then, after selecting the other clips, use the Paste Adjustments commands. You have a lot of options:

- **Video**: Color changes
- **Audio**: Volume changes
- **Crop**: Crop, fit, or Ken Burns changes
- **Cutaway/Picture-in-Picture/Green Screen**: Unique characteristics (such as fade and opacity) of these clips
- **Video Effect**: Video effect changes
- **Audio Effect**: Audio effect changes
- **Stabilization**: Stabilization and zoom changes
- **Rolling Shutter**: Rolling shutter setting changes
- **Speed**: Timing changes
- **Map Style**: Type of map changes

Delete Selection, Delete Entire Clip (Reject, Reject Entire Clip)

More ways to get rid of stuff. If you select only a portion of a filmstrip, you can use the Delete Selection command (or press the Delete key) to snip out just that segment. Or add the Option key to get rid of the entire clip, even though only a piece is highlighted.

In the Event Browser, these commands say Reject instead of Delete, but only because rejecting, in iMovie, is the first step toward deleting footage for good. The box on page 121 has the details.

Select All Events

This command is a chameleon. It always means "Select All," but the wording changes.

- If you select a portion of a clip in the Event Browser, it says Select Entire Clip.
- If you select an Event in the Events list, it says Select All Events.
- If you highlight a clip in the storyboard, the command says Select All (meaning all filmstrips).
- If you highlight some text in a text box, the command says Select All (meaning all text in this box).

Keyboard shortcut: ⌘-A.

Select

You have even more selection options available to you under Edit→Select.

Select None

Memorizing this command (or better yet, its keyboard equivalent, Shift-⌘-A) is an excellent idea. It deselects everything, including clips and pieces of clips. That's useful when, for example, you want to use one of the "clip-painting" techniques described on page 91, which require that you have nothing highlighted.

Select to Playhead

If you started to select part of a clip, and want to extend your selection to where your playhead is, simply press Shift-A and iMovie draws the yellow selection box out to your playhead. This trick works on either end of a partial selection (either before or after what you've already selected), but it doesn't work beyond the end of a single clip.

Select Video Clips/Transitions/Photos/Maps/Backgrounds/Animatics

This super useful set of selection menus lets you select all the project elements of a certain type. For example, if you choose Edit→Select→Photos, iMovie selects all the photos in your project, allowing you to change their timing or crop settings all in one go.

Transition Overlap

Every transition you add between two clips uses up bits of those clips to execute the transition, as explained on page 132. Because iMovie takes a few frames of each clip during a transition, adding transitions actually makes your project shorter, unless you adjust this menu setting. Leave it on "All – Maintain Clip Range" and transitions continue to use up clip frames. Change it to "Half – Maintain Project Duration" and iMovie goes and grabs extra bits of the clips from the original footage, enough to keep your projects from getting shorter.

Note: The Half setting doesn't work if there's no extra footage for iMovie to grab.

Spelling

iMovie uses Mac OS X's built-in spell checker to check iMovie titles only (Chapter 8).

Special Characters

You're creating a subtitle for an interview with the CEO of "I've Got a ¥en™" Productions. But how the heck do you type the ¥ symbol—or the ™ symbol? Easy one. You choose this command and double-click the symbol you want from the palette arrayed before you. *Keyboard shortcut*: Shift-⌘-S.

Clip Menu

This menu offers the remaining editing tools you need for your projects.

One-Step Effects

The first seven menu items in the Clip menu are covered in detail starting on page 170. Go there to learn what each of these do.

Duplicate Last Title

There's no way to copy and paste titles in iMovie, so this command makes up for that (in part). If you are doing a bunch of similar titles over a series of clips, just do the first title as usual (page 204), then select the next clip in your project and choose Clip→Duplicate Last Title. iMovie inserts a title identical to the last one you created. This isn't as flexible and handy as a Copy-and-Paste duet, but it's better than nothing.

Trim to Selection

Use this command to trim excess ends off a storyboard clip after you isolate a portion of it using the triangular handles under the Scrubber bar. *Keyboard shortcut:* ⌘-B.

Trim Clip End

You can fine-tune a clip's length with these commands—or, more practically, with the keyboard equivalents, Option-left arrow or Option-right arrow. Each press makes the clip one frame shorter or longer. (You're changing either the beginning or the end of the clip, whichever is closest to your cursor.)

Split Clip

It's often convenient to chop a clip in half, or even into three pieces; this command does the trick. Make a selection in any storyboard filmstrip; iMovie splits the clip at the beginning of the yellow selection border. (If the border doesn't go all the way to the end of the clip, you'll wind up with *three* pieces.)

Join Clip

If, having split a clip as described above, you want to *rejoin* the pieces, place them consecutively in the storyboard, and then use this command. This won't join clips that were never part of one clip to begin with.

Extend Over Next Clip

Leveraging the cool ability to reference the original footage rather than just cutting it up into pieces and adding it to your storyboard (as explained on page 97), use this nifty menu command by selecting a clip and then choosing this from the menu. iMovie extends the clip you selected so that its length matches that of the clip behind it, and then it replaces that clip entirely.

Detach Audio

This handy command takes the sound from the selected project clip and puts it in as a sound effect (page 234), still synced up with the clip. It also mutes the clip from which you took the audio.

Mute/Unmute Clip

This completely silences a clip or restores the volume setting if you already muted the clip. Saves you a trip to the Inspector, so learn the *keyboard shortcut:* Shift-⌘-M.

Remove Volume Adjustments

This puts a clip's volume back to its original, unmodified state.

Add Beat Marker

Tells iMovie to use that marker as a reference point for the "Snap to Beats" feature, covered on page 235. This command only works when you have an audio track open in the Clip Trimmer.

Arrange Music Tracks

This command refers to background music tracks, the sort of floating background audio that plays from the beginning of the project (page 228). If you set up more than one of these tracks, this command opens a window (page 232) that lets you change their sequence.

Unpin Music Track

Again, page 228 has more details. But this command applies to background music tracks you dragged horizontally to pin them to specific video frames. And it means "Un-pin this puppy, so that it floats freely against the left side of the project."

View Menu

This menu is mostly about changing the way iMovie displays your video clips while you work.

- **Favorites Only, Favorites and Unmarked, All Clips, Rejected Only**. These commands hide or show filmstrips in your Event Browser, according to how you branded them: as favorite clips, rejected clips, or neither (Chapter 4). If you're ever looking for a filmstrip that you're sure you once had, check this menu; they may just be hidden.

- **Group Events by Disk, Group Events by Month, Show Most Recent Events at Top, Show Separate Days in Events**. All these options control the way iMovie lists your Events at the left side of the window. Chapter 2 has details.

- **Play, Play Selection, Loop Selection, Play from Beginning, Play Around Current Frame, Play Full Screen**. These are pretty much self-explanatory, no? For details, see page 93. And learn the keyboard shortcuts.

- **Reveal in Event Browser.** This handy option lets you click a clip in the storyboard, and then jump to the corresponding raw source clip in the Event Browser. Seeing the original clip gives you a lot more information; for example, you can see how much of the clip you've used, whether or not you've used pieces of the clip elsewhere in the project (as indicated by the orange stripes), whether or not you applied any cropping or color correction to the master clip, and so on.

- **Snap to Ends**. Wow, talk about obscure. When you're dragging an audio stripe, photo stripe, or text stripe in the storyboard, would you like iMovie's assistance in lining it up with the exact beginning of the filmstrip? If so, turn on this option. You'll feel and see a little snap of your cursor as you drag the stripe close to the clip end.

- **Snap to Beats**. This causes certain editing behaviors in iMovie to respect beat markers you add to an audio track. Read page 235 to get the process down pat.

- **Audio Skimming**. When you skim (see page 77), iMovie generally plays the audio simultaneously, which may sound fragmented and disturbing. Turn off this option if you'd rather skim in silence.

- **Playhead Info**. When you turn this option on, a balloon pops out of the playhead when you move it, identifying the date and time you shot the video, and pinpointing your cursor's location from its beginning point.

Text Menu

You'll find this menu useful only when you edit movie titles. All of its commands affect your typography, and all of them are described in Chapter 8.

Share Menu

In theory, anyway, the whole point of video editing is to produce a finished flick that you want to show somebody. This menu offers you eight ways to export your finished product:

- **Media Browser** gets your movie into other Apple software like Keynote, GarageBand, or iWeb.

- **iTunes** is the first step toward landing your movie on an iPod, iPhone, or Apple TV.

- **iDVD** burns your movie to DVDs, with custom menus and all.

- **MobileMe Gallery** is the custom photo- and movie-sharing site available to MobileMe subscribers.

- **YouTube** is YouTube, the world's most popular free video-sharing website.

- **Facebook** is where 500 million people waste time.

- **Vimeo** is the slicker, less cluttered version of YouTube.

- **CNN iReport** is where you kickstart your journalism career.

- **Podcast Producer** is a tool that comes with Mac OS X Server, simplifying the process of creating and sharing your podcasts with the world.

- **Export Movie**. Like Share→Media Browser, this command offers a dialog box that lists four canned screen sizes. But like Share→ "Export using QuickTime" (described below), it offers you a chance to store the resulting file with a name and folder location of your choice.

- **Export using QuickTime** turns your movie into a video file on your hard drive. But unlike Export Movie, this command gives you access to dozens of Quick-Time options that confer infinite control over frame size, frame rate, audio compression, video compression, and more.

- **Export Final Cut XML**. If you have one of Apple's more powerful video-editing programs, like Final Cut Express or Final Cut Pro, you'll be grateful for this option. It turns your entire iMovie project into an XML file—an exported project file. Later, you can open up this file in Final Cut to finish editing it with a far more powerful suite of tools. See Figure A-4 for some caveats and limitations.

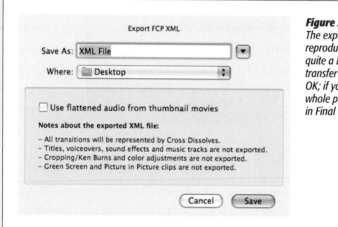

Figure A-4:
The exported project file doesn't completely reproduce your iMovie work. As noted here, there's quite a bit of stuff that doesn't make it through the transfer alive (music, titles, and so on). But that's OK; if you plan ahead, you'll never miss them. The whole point is to dress up your project's rough cut in Final Cut anyway.

Tip: The exported file doesn't actually contain any video. It's just a description of your project—your edits—and references to the original, captured video files that sit in your iMovie '11 Events folders. Final Cut therefore works from the original, unmodified clips, preserving all their quality.

You'll also find Republish and Remove commands here, for when you want to edit an already published masterpiece or for when it's outlived its usefulness.

Chapters 13 through 15 cover all these exports in detail.

Window Menu

This window is fairly standard in Mac OS X programs. The Minimize and Zoom commands are almost always present; they let you minimize iMovie (hide its window by collapsing into a Dock icon) or expand the window to fill your screen.

But iMovie's Window menu is quite a bit more detailed than the basics.

Precision Editor

This opens the Precision Editor tool described on page 105.

Clip Trimmer

This opens the Clip Trimmer tool described on page 100.

Clip Adjustments, Video Adjustments, Audio Adjustments

Each of these menu commands takes you to the Inspector and chooses the corresponding tab.

Cropping, Ken Burns, and Rotation

This just offers a menu command for all the cropping tool stuff covered on page 272.

Show Projects Full-screen, Show Events Full-screen

Goes straight to the full-screen preview mode (page 94), previewing either your projects or your event footage.

Hide/Show Commands

These are the Hide/Show commands for the various panels of iMovie: **Project Library, Event Library, Keyword Filter, Viewer, Music and Sound Effects, Photos, Titles, Transitions,** and **Maps and Backgrounds**. It's great to remember that these exist when you try to make room on your screen to edit your movie.

Viewer

The **Viewer** command is a bit different. There's no way to hide the Viewer window—it would be a little tough trying to edit a video without being able to see it—but these three sub-commands let you change its size.

Tip: You can also make the Viewer almost any in-between size by dragging iMovie's central toolbar up or down.

Swap Event and Projects

Finally, this command flips the top and bottom halves of the editing screen, so that the storyboard is now on the bottom. The advantage is that there's no Viewer window taking up the bottom-left of iMovie's screen, so you get a more expansive workspace.

Viewer on Secondary Display

If you're lucky enough to have a second display hooked up to your Mac, you can use it to show the preview window, making a lot more room for your projects and events.

Help Menu

iMovie doesn't come with a manual—if it did, you wouldn't need this book. Instead, you're expected to learn its functions from the online help.

Search

This search box does two things when you type in text:

- If the text appears in a menu command, the command shows up in the resulting list. Pointing to the list item will even open up and highlight the corresponding menu command.

- If the text appears in the Help documentation, it provides a link to the corresponding help article, which opens in the Help window. (See next.)

iMovie Help

Choose this command to open the iMovie '11 Help window, where you'll see a list of iMovie help topics (Figure A-5).

You can use this Help program in either of two ways:

- Keep clicking colored links, burrowing closer and closer to the help topic you want. You can backtrack by clicking the left arrow button at the top of the window, exactly as in a web browser.

- Type a search phrase into the top window, such as *cropping,* and then click Search (or press Return), as shown in Figure A-5.

Either way, you'll probably find that the iMovie online assistance offers a helpful summary of the program's functions, but it's a little light on "what it's for" information, illustrations, tutorials, speed, and jokes.

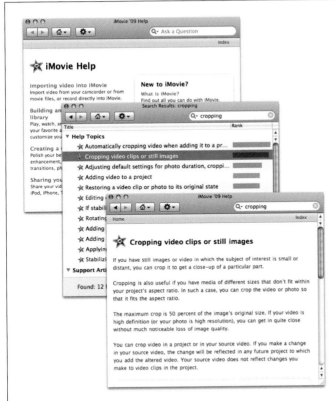

Figure A-5:
The Help Center's first screen offers big-ticket links like "What is iMovie?" and "Sharing Your Video Project." Most people, however, start by typing a phrase into the search box and then clicking Search (top). You get a list of Help pages that the Mac thinks might contain the information you want (middle). The Relevance graph indicates how confident the Help program is. (A longer bar means more occurrences of your search phrase relative to the text on that help page.) Double-click a topic to read the corresponding help page (bottom). Click the Back button at the top of the screen to return to the list of topics.

Welcome to iMovie

Opens the Welcome screen that appeared the first time you launched iMovie.

Keyboard Shortcuts

This is really just another link into the iMovie Help system, but a particularly valuable one. It takes you to a table showing about 50 keyboard shortcuts in iMovie. (They're among the listings in Appendix C of this book.)

Supported Cameras

This takes you to a handy web page Apple designed to list all the cameras iMovie supports. You can use this to plan your next camera purchase.

Service and Support

Opens your web browser and takes you to Apple's iMovie help website. Which, by the way, is a pretty great resource for asking questions and getting answers.

Drag and Drop Menu

This is the menu that appears when you drag and drop footage onto underlying clips in your project (Figure A-6). The full list only appears if you turn on Advanced Tools in iMovie's preferences, which was covered in this appendix on page 454.

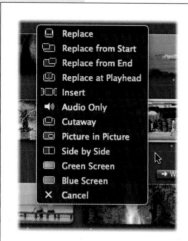

Figure A-6:
This unique menu only appears when you drop a clip from the Event Library onto another clip in your project. The long version of this menu only appears when you turn on Advanced Tools in the iMovie Preferences (page 88).

Replace

Entirely replaces the underlying clip with the footage you're adding, no matter how long either one is.

Replace from Start

Lengthens or shortens an added clip so that it matches the length of the replaced clip, starting from the beginning of the replacement clip and extending forward. So if the replaced clip is 10 seconds long and the selection replacing it is only 5 seconds long, iMovie adds another 5 seconds to the *end* of the video chunk you're adding.

Replace from End

The same as "Replace from Start," but resizes the added clip starting from the end of selection and extending backward. If a clip being replaced is 10 seconds long, but the selection replacing it is only 5 seconds long, iMovie will add 5 seconds to the *beginning* of the selection.

Replace at Playhead

The same as the other "Replace from" options, but places the start of your selected footage at the project playhead and extends or shortens the footage at the beginning and end of your selection to fill the space left by the replaced clip.

Insert

Cuts the underlying clip at the playhead into two pieces, and plugs the added footage in between.

Audio Only

Adds just the audio track from the footage being dragged and dropped. The audio appears as a little blue banner running under your project clips.

Cutaway

Superimposes your added footage over the underlying clip, which continues to live underneath.

Picture in Picture

Places the added footage in a little box just like many TVs offer for watching two channels at once. This is covered in greater detail on page 165.

Side by Side

Places the added footage in the left or right half of the screen (page 169).

Green Screen/Blue Screen

For footage shot with a green screen or blue screen background, superimposes everything *but* the green/blue stuff onto the underlying footage, making it appear as if the green screen subject is in the same place as the underlying footage. Also covered on page 159.

Cancel

Hey, we all make mistakes.

Troubleshooting

A pple does amazing things with each new version of iMovie. They add features new not just to iMovie, but new to consumer video editing, period. And you know what happens with brand-spanking-new features, right? Right: glitches.

Here's an impressive compendium of the problems you may run into—and the world's best attempts at solving them.

Two Golden Rules

If there's any common wisdom at all about iMovie, here it is—a pair of golden rules that will stave off a huge number of problems down the road:

- **Use the latest version**. Each ".01" or ".1" iMovie upgrade zaps a whole host of bugs and glitches. The updates are free, so when your Software Update program advises you that one is available, jump at the chance to install it.

- **Set your camcorder to 16-bit audio**. The typical tape camcorder can record its audio track using either 12-bit or 16-bit audio. The factory setting is 12-bit, which gives people who aren't computer owners a chance to overlay a second audio track without erasing the original camera sound. Trouble is, 12-bit audio may slowly drift out of sync with the video when you burn your finished project to a DVD.

   Use your camera's menu system to switch to 16-bit audio. You, an iMovie aficionado, can easily overlay additional audio using your computer, so you give up nothing—except a lot of frustration. (Make this change *now*, before you record anything important.)

General iMovie Troubleshooting

Let's start general, shall we?

Weird Inconsistent Problems

When a program's preferences file becomes scrambled, all kinds of peculiar behavior can result. Buttons and functions don't work. Visual anomalies appear. Things just don't work right.

If iMovie starts having a bad hair day, suspect its preferences file. Quit the program, open your Home→Library→Preferences folder, and throw away the files called *com.apple.iMovie9.plist* and *com.apple.iApps.plist*.

The next time you run iMovie, it automatically builds a new preferences file. This file will have the original factory settings (for the options in, for example, the Preferences dialog box), but at least it will be healthy and whole.

Tip: The same advice applies to iDVD. If the program begins flaking out on you, unexpectedly quitting or otherwise acting odd, open your Home→Library→Preferences folder and throw away the file called *com.apple.iDVD.plist*.

Keeping Your Hard Disk Happy

Remember the old expression "If Mama ain't happy, ain't nobody happy"? Well, if your hard disk isn't happy, iMovie won't be happy, either.

Here's a short list of maintenance suggestions. A little attention every week or so may help keep minor hard drive problems from becoming major problems:

- After installing or updating any software, use Disk Utility to repair permissions. (Disk Utility is in your Applications→Utilities folder. Click the First Aid tab, click your hard drive, and then click Repair Permissions.)

- Back up, back up, back up. Oh, and have a good back up? Use, for example, the Time Machine backup software built right into Mac OS X. It can back up your entire hard drive onto another hard drive, automatically, hourly, completely. Since hard drives are dirt cheap these days—a $60 drive would probably cover you—there's little reason not to set up this automatic backup system.

Tip: Don't worry about arcane things like defragmenting your hard drive or manually running the background maintenance jobs. Modern Macs (with OS version 10.5 or later) do all this on their own.

Starting Up and Importing

Trouble getting going? Here's some advice.

iMovie Doesn't See the Tape Camcorder

Try these checks, in this order:

Make sure you set your camera to VCR or VTR or whatever the setting is called that plays back your tape. Check the FireWire cable connections. Turn the camcorder off and then on again. Quit iMovie, turn the camcorder on, and then reopen iMovie. Restart the Mac. Try a different FireWire cable.

Do you have a high-def tape camcorder (that uses the so-called HDV format)? If so, delve into the menus and make sure that the camcorder's output matches what you recorded.

See, these camcorders can record either standard-definition or high-definition video on the same tape. But when you connect the camcorder to a TV or a Mac, it has to know which format to transmit.

Usually, you get a choice of DV (which means standard definition, 4:3), HDV (high definition, widescreen, 16:9), and Auto. But Auto doesn't always work. If you're having problems, choose DV or HDV manually.

iMovie Doesn't See the Tapeless Camcorder

First, note that some camcorders refuse to enter PC connection mode unless you plug them into a power outlet. They won't even consider entering PC mode when running on battery. (The camcorder's fear is that it will run out of battery power in the middle of the transfer, possibly corrupting and ruining some of your video scenes.)

Second, keep in mind that your Mac can't import video from AVCHD-format camcorders (see "AVCHD, MPEG-2, and Other Such Jargon" on page 8) unless it has an Intel processor. Check your camcorder's box or manual—or just read the logos on its body—to find out if it's an AVCHD camcorder. Back on your computer, choose →About This Mac to see if you have an Intel Mac. (You'll actually see the word Intel on the resulting information screen. All Mac models developed since January 2006 have Intel processors.)

Finally, try plugging the USB cable into one of the USB jacks on the Mac itself, rather than into the USB jack on the Mac's keyboard. (The one on the keyboard is for low-powered gadgets only.)

If you double-check all three of these conditions, quit iMovie and reopen it. Now, at long last, the Import screen should appear.

Video Looks Interlaced

You know the cool iMovie Preview window (page 36), where you get to see and even play the thumbnails for the video on tapeless camcorders before you actually import any video? Sometimes, that preview playback looks awful. It might be jerky or have nasty interlace lines, for example.

Rest assured that this is all just a problem with the preview. Once you actually import this footage, it'll look fine.

No Sound from Tape Camcorder

If you're used to the old iMovie, you might wonder why you can't hear anything as you import footage from your tape camcorder. That's because iMovie no longer plays audio through the Mac when you import. If you want to hear the soundtrack as you import, leave the camcorder's screen open so you hear the audio from the camcorder itself.

iMovie Crashes on Startup

If you can't even make it past the startup phase, start by deleting the preference files as described earlier (page 478).

Also consider rebuilding your iPhoto library; iMovie checks in with iPhoto every time you open it, and if there's something wrong with your iPhoto library, iMovie chokes. To rebuild the iPhoto library, quit iPhoto, and then reopen it while holding down the ⌘ and Option keys. In the resulting dialog box, you see several diagnostic options. Turn on all five, click the Rebuild button, and then wait a very long time. When it's all over, iMovie should be much happier about doing business with a clean, fresh iPhoto library.

Can't Import from DVD Camcorder

See the note on page 45.

Dropouts in the Video

A *dropout* is a glitch in the picture. DV dropouts are always square or rectangular. They may be blotches of the wrong color or may be multicolored. They may appear every time you play a particular scene, or may appear at random. In severe circumstances, you may get lots of them, such as when you try to capture video to an old FireWire hard drive that's too slow. Such a configuration may also cause tearing of the video picture.

Fortunately, dropouts are fairly rare in digital video. If you get one, it's probably in one of these three circumstances:

- **You're using a very old cassette.** Remember that even DV cassettes don't last forever. You may begin to see dropouts after rerecording on the tape 50 times or so.

- **You're playing back a cassette that was recorded in LP (long-play) mode.** If you recorded the cassette on a different camcorder, dropouts are especially likely.

- **It's time to clean the heads on your camcorder.** The electrical components that actually make contact with the tape can become dirty over time. Your local electronics store sells head-cleaning kits for just this purpose.

If you spot the glitch at the same moment on the tape every time you play it, then the problem is on the tape itself. If it's there during one playback but gone during the next, the problem more likely lies with the heads in your camcorder.

Note: Different DV tape manufacturers use different lubricants on their tapes. As a result, mixing tapes from different manufacturers on the same camcorder can increase the likelihood of head clogs. It's a good idea, therefore, to stick with tapes from one manufacturer (Sony, Panasonic, or Maxell, for example) when possible.

Editing

Once you learn the program's ins and outs, there's not much that can go wrong during editing.

Can't Drag Certain Photos into the Movie

If you open the Media Browser and try to drag an iPhoto photo into your movie but you get a "The file could not be imported" error message, it's probably a RAW file. (That's a high-end photo file format created by semiprofessional SLR cameras and intended for processing later on a computer.)

The solution: Return to iPhoto. Make a tiny change to the photo, like a small crop or brightness adjustment. When you exit editing mode, iPhoto applies the change and, in the process, turns the RAW photo into a JPEG or TIFF-format photo, which iMovie can import.

Can't Use Audiobooks in Soundtrack

Yep, you can't use an audiobook as an iMovie soundtrack. They show up in the Media Browser, all right, but if you drag them into iMovie, nothing happens. Them's the breaks.

Filmstrips Don't Reflect Changes

It's true: If you crop a filmstrip or apply color adjustments to it, you'll see the changes on playback—but not on the filmstrip itself. iMovie always displays its original film-strip, no matter what changes you make to it.

That can be a little upsetting when, for example, you rotate a photo 90 degrees and you don't see the change in the filmstrip. But there's nothing you can do about it.

Thumbnails Are Blank or Corrupted

Sometimes the thumbnail files iMovie creates when it imports video (see "Automatic Scene Detection" on page 36) get corrupted during the import process. Sometimes, just skimming an event-with-corrupted-thumbnails even locks up your computer. To fix the problem:

1. Quit iMovie.

2. Open Home→Movies→iMovie Events→[Your Event Name].

3. Move the folder called iMovie Thumbnails to the Trash.

4. Restart iMovie.

iMovie notices the missing thumbnails and makes new ones. If the problem repeats itself, even with new thumbnails, you may need to trash the entire Event and import your footage again. Make sure you still have the footage before you trash the Event!

Exporting

When it's all over, certain roadblocks may stand between you and your adoring fans.

"Compatible Version of iDVD Required"

If you get the above message when you try to export a movie, you probably renamed or moved one of the iLife programs.

Don't do that. They're supposed to have their original names (iMovie, iPhoto, iDVD, iWeb, iTunes), and they're supposed to be in your Applications folder.

YouTube Turns You Down

If you export a movie to YouTube that has exactly the same duration as one you already posted, YouTube may see the second movie as a duplicate and refuse to accept it—even if the two movies have different names.

The solution is simply to change the duration of the second movie, even if it's by only one frame.

Text Chopped Off on DVD

You create a movie in iMovie and add some good-looking titles and credits—yet when you send the movie to iDVD for burning, you discover that the text is getting chopped off by the TV.

Unfortunately, iMovie '11 doesn't seem to know about the TV-safe area that iDVD knows about (page 375). It's left to you to figure out how to avoid these margin areas of the screen. For example, keep your titles short and centered. And don't use subtitles at all, so they won't get chopped off at the bottom. Or just make your own title designs, as described on page 427.

Where to Get Help

You can get personal iMovie help by calling Apple's help line at (800) 500-7078 for 90 days after you buy the iLife DVD, iMovie from the Mac App Store, or a new Mac. (Technically, you can call within the first 90 days of *ownership*, but the clock really doesn't start until your first call.) After that, you can either buy an AppleCare contract for another year of tech-support calls ($170 to $350, depending on your Mac model), or pay $50 per individual call!

Beyond 90 days, however, consider consulting the Internet, which is filled with superb sources of fast, free technical help. Here are some of the best places to get your questions answered:

- **Apple's own iMovie discussion forum**. Here, you can read user comments, ask questions of knowledgeable iMovie fanatics, or hang out and learn good stuff (the link appears on *www.apple.com/support/imovie*).

- **iMovie List**. There's a mailing list—several, actually—dedicated to iMovie and only iMovie. These lists are perfect places to ask questions without embarrassing yourself. Sign up by visiting *www.egroups.com* and searching for *imovie*.

- **Official iMovie help pages**. Apple doesn't freely admit to bugs and problems, but there's a surprising amount of good information in its official iMovie answer pages (*www.apple.com/support/imovie*).

- **Official iMovie tutorials**. Apple offers step-by-step instructions and movies at *www.apple.com/ilife/video-showcase/#imovie*.

Master Keyboard Shortcut List

As you know, iMovie '11 was conceived with a single goal in mind: speed, baby, speed. And part of gaining speed is mastering keyboard shortcuts, so you don't waste time puttering around in the menus. So here it is, by popular, frustrated demand: the master list of every secret (or not-so-secret) keystroke in iMovie '11. Clip and post it to your monitor (unless, of course, you got this book from the library).

Tip: There are also a million shortcut menus—the contextual menus that appear when you Control-click (or right-click) almost anything on the screen. Most of the time, the commands you find there just duplicate what's in the menus. Learning the keyboard shortcut is still faster.

Panes, Panels, and Windows

Minimize iMovie	⌘-M
Show/Hide Music and Sound Effects	⌘-1
Show/Hide Photos pane	⌘-2
Show/Hide Titles pane	⌘-3
Show/Hide Transitions pane	⌘-4
Show Hide Maps, Backgrounds, and Animatics pane	⌘-5
Show/Hide Inspector	I
Show/Hide Inspector Video Adjustments tab	V

Show/Hide Inspector Audio Adjustments tab	A
Show/Hide Keywords window	K
Show/Hide Crop/Ken Burns/Rotation window	C
Show/Hide Voiceover window	O
Viewer size small/medium/large	⌘-8, ⌘-9, ⌘-0
iMovie Preferences window	⌘-, (comma key)
Project Properties	⌘-J
Project Theme	Shift-⌘-J

Event Browser and Storyboard

Scroll to top/bottom	Home/End
Scroll up/down	Page Up/Page Down
Show clip time/date	⌘-Y
Project Properties	⌘-J
Project Theme	Shift-⌘-J
iMovie Help	Shift-⌘-?
New project	⌘-N
Delete project	⌘-Delete
Print Event Browser or storyboard	⌘-P
View Favorite and Unmarked event footage	⌘-L

Playback

Play from cursor	space bar
Play the 1 second on either side of the cursor	[(left bracket key)
Play the 3 seconds on either side of the cursor	] (right bracket key)
Play selected footage	/
Loop selected footage	Option-/
Play project (or Event) from start	\ (backslash)
Play projects full-screen	⌘-6
Play events full-screen	⌘-7
Play selection full-screen	⌘-G
Exit full-screen mode	Esc
Lock playhead	Hold down Control key

Editing

Import from camera	⌘-I
Export as file	⌘-E
Select all (or whole filmstrip)	⌘-A
Expand selection to playhead	Shift-A
Deselect all	Shift-⌘-A
Cut, Copy, Paste	⌘-X, ⌘-C, ⌘-V
Paste copied adjustments	Shift-⌘-V
Paste video adjustments only	Option-⌘-I
Paste audio adjustments only	Option-⌘-A
Paste crop/Ken Burns adjustments only	Option-⌘-R
Paste cutaway, green screen, or picture-in-picture adjustments only	Option-⌘-U
Paste video effect adjustments only	Option-⌘-L
Paste audio effect adjustments only	Option-⌘-O
Paste stabilization adjustments only	Option-⌘-Z
Paste rolling shutter adjustments only	Option-⌘-T
Paste speed adjustments only	Option-⌘-S
Paste map style adjustments only	Option-⌘-M

Working with Clips

Add selection to storyboard	E
Mark selection as a Favorite	F
Mark selection as a Reject	R (or Delete, in Event Browser only)
Unmark selection	U
Shift selection border	arrow keys (left, right)
Restore one hidden frame to clip	Option-right arrow (cursor near end of clip) or Option-left arrow (cursor near beginning)
Shorten clip by 1 frame	Option-left arrow (cursor near end of clip) or Option-right arrow (cursor near beginning)
Trim to Selection	⌘-B
Open Precision Editor	⌘-/
Open Clip Trimmer window	⌘-R
Apply numbered keyword	1, 2, 3, 4…

Remove all keywords from selection	0 (zero)
Undo	⌘-Z
Redo	Shift-⌘-Z
Split clip	Shift-⌘-S

Music and Audio

Show/Hide Music and Sound Effects	⌘-1
Show/Hide Inspector Audio Adjustments tab	A
Show/Hide Voiceover window	O
Audio during skimming on/off	⌘-K
Mute/Unmute clip	Shift-⌘-M
Turn on/off Snap to Beats	⌘-U
Add Beat Marker	M

Editing Titles

Show/Hide Titles panel	⌘-3
Show/Hide Fonts panel	⌘-T
Bold	Shift-⌘-B
Italic	Shift-⌘-I
Underline	Shift-⌘-U
Outline style	Shift-⌘-O
Increase/decrease type size	⌘-plus sign, ⌘-minus sign
Left-, center-, right-justified text	⌘-{, ⌘-|, ⌘-}
Tighter/looser spacing (kerning)	Option-⌘-left arrow, Option-⌘-right arrow
Cut, Copy, Paste	⌘-X, ⌘-C, ⌘-V
Copy text formatting	Option-⌘-C
Paste text formatting	Option-⌘-V

Visual Cheat Sheet

iMovie, as you've probably gathered, is completely different from any other program you've seen before—including previous versions of iMovie. You'll find it filled with handy visual cues as to what's going on. But, especially at first, learning all those cues can seem like a full-time job.

iMovie is teeming with thin banners over and under your filmstrips (in green, blue, or purple); horizontal colored lines drawn right across them (in red, green, and orange); little white "badges" huddled in the corners of filmstrips; faint corner badges that appear only when you *point* to a filmstrip; gigantic green or purple bubbles lying behind your entire project map; and on and on.

You practically need a cheat sheet to remember what they're all for—and here's where you'll find it.

Crop badge
Double-click to
edit crop, Ken
Burns, or
rotation settings

**PiP Effect
(blue border)**
Similar in appearence
to Cutaways (gray
border) and Green
Screen effects (green
border)

Red stripe
Rejected footage

Yellow banner:
Theme title

Brown banner:
Comment marker

Map clip
Animated travel
map

Sun badge
Color adjustments
applied. Double-click
to edit

Interclip icons
Above: Theme transition
Below: Regular transition

Speaker badge
Volume adjusted.
Double-click
to edit

Gear bad
Click to m
adjustme

Green bubble
Background music

Purple Banner
Recorded narration

Purple bubble
Background music
(Pinned to clip)

Hand badge
Stabilization is applied.
Black (small shake)
Orange (moderate shake)
(Red (heavy shake)
Red w/line (too shaky)

Orange stripes
Footage has been
used in project

Green stripe
Footage has been
marked as Favorite

Blue stripe
Footage has been
marked with
keyword(s)

Index

Symbols

4:3 format, 62, 272, 387
8mm cassettes, importing movies from, 51–53
11 kHz, 8 bits, 348
11 kHz, 16 bits, 348
16:9 format, 62, 272, 387
16-bit audio, 477
22 kHz, 16 bits, 348
30 fps, 342
44.1 kHz, 16 bits, 348
2010, 2009, 2008… (Events Library), 65

A

AAC codec, 347
AAC files, 224
About iMovie, 453
Action (movie trailer), 287
Add Beat Marker, 468, 488
Add Freeze Frame, 99
Add Movie to iDVD Menu, 441
Add selection to storyboard, 487
Add Still Frame to Project, 99
Adjust Clip Date and Time…, 461
Advanced Drag and Drop, 87, 102
advanced editing, 295–306
  choosing next shot, 298
  continuity, 297–298
  iMovie 6, 295, 302–306
    exporting to tape, 302
    plug-ins, 303
    transferring from iMovie '11, 303–304
    transferring to iMovie '11, 304–306
    video special effects, 302
  modern film theory, 296–297
  popular editing techniques, 299–302
    cutaways and cut-ins, 300
    establishing shots, 299

    intercutting, 302
    parallel editing, 302
    reaction shots, 300
    shot variety, 299
    tight editing, 299
  theory, 295
  when to cut, 298
Advanced Tools, 163, 380
Adventure (movie trailer), 288
Aged Film effect, 154
AIFF files, 224
albums, video photo, 262
Align, 210
All Clips, 468
alpha-channel PNG file, 218
Always show active clip badges, 455
Always show clip durations, 455
ambient sound, 246
AMR Narrowband, 347
analog inputs, 9
analog tapes, importing movies from, 51–53
Analyze for stabilization and/or people, 34
Analyze Video, 461
analyzing performances, 5
Animatics, 150–151, 485
  building storyboard, 150
  showing/hiding, 485
  storyboards
    printing for filming, 151
Animation codec, 349
Apple Intermediate Codec, 37, 44, 48, 349
Apple Lossless, 347
Apple's help line, 483
Apple TV, 312
Applies to all photos, 460
Applies to all transitions, 459
Applies when added to project, 459, 460

Apply numbered keyword, 487

Apply rolling shutter correction for clips that have been analyzed, 456

Apply Theme to Project (iDVD), 387

Archive Project, 442

Arrange Music Tracks, 233, 468

arrow-key trick, 85

aspect ratios, 62–64, 272, 458
- 4:3 format, 387
- 16:9 format, 62, 387
- changing, 64
- Crop, 64
- Fit in Frame, 64
- high-def TV, 62
- iDVD, 384, 388–389
- Initial Video Placement pop-up menu, 64
- mismatched, 63–64
- odd, 343
- problem, 455
- Project Properties dialog box, 64
- Standard (4:3), 62
- standard TV, 62
- Switch to Standard (4:3), 387
- Widescreen (16:9), 62

audio, 223–260
- AAC files, 224
- adding from Finder, 227
- adding to storyboard, 225–228
  - Music and Sound Effects browser, 225–227
- adjustments, 471
- AIFF files, 224
- Arrange Music Tracks, 233
- background music (see background music)
- beat markers (see beat markers)
- camcorders, 224
- Clip Trimmer (see Clip Trimmer)
- during skimming on/off, 488
- effects (see Audio Effects)
- enhancing, 255–256
- equalizer, 256
- extracting from video, 244–246
- files not listed in iMovie audio browser, 229
- Floating Music Tracks, 234
- free music, 233
- GarageBand (see GarageBand)
- importing music from a CD, 224
- iTunes tracks, 224
- keyboard shortcuts, 488
- kinds of, 223–224
- MP3 files, 224
- multiple clip adjustments, 252–253
- narration (see narration)

- Picture-in-Picture (PiP), 168
- pinned music (see sound effects)
- Pinned Music Tracks, 233
- removing adjustments, 253
- sound effects (SFX) (see sound effects (SFX))
- sources, 224
- Split Clip, 254
- Unpin Music Track, 234
- volume adjustments, 246–252
  - adjusting overall clip volume, 249–252
  - ducking, 250
  - Fade In, Fade Out, 251
  - Normalize Clip Volume, 251
  - other volume tools, 249
  - rubber-banding, 247–249
  - Volume slider, 250
- WAV files, 224

audiobooks, troubleshooting, 481

audio codecs, 338
- AAC, 347
- IMA 4:1, 347
- QDesign Music 2, 347

Audio Effect option (Paste Adjustments), 464

Audio Effects, 253–255
- applying, 253–254
- applying to part of clip or song, 254
- Cathedral, 255
- Cosmic, 255
- Echo, 255
- Muffled, 254
- Multitune, 255
- Pitch Down/Up, 255
- Robot, 255
- Shortwave Radio, 255
- Small/Medium/Large Room, 255
- Split Clip, 254
- Telephone, 255

Audio folder, 440

Audio Only, 475
- ambient sound, 246
- echo, making, 245
- narration, 246
- reusing sound, 245

Audio option (Paste Adjustments), 464

Audio Skimming, 469

Automatically add (pick a transition), 460

Automatically play movies when opened, 360

Automatically stabilize clips that have been analyzed, 456

automatic correcton, 187–188

automatic scene detection, 36

Automatic Transitions, 127
- adjusting, 134
- turning off, 134

Automator, iDVD, 441–442
  Add Movie to iDVD Menu, 441
  Get iDVD Slideshow Images, 441
  New iDVD Menu, 442
  New iDVD Movie Sequence, 442
  Set iDVD Background Image, 442
  Set iDVD button face, 442
  Show Main iDVD Menu, 442
Autoplay, iDVD, 410–412
AVCHD, 8, 479
AVCHD Lite, 9
AVI files, 339

B

background music, 224, 227, 228–234
  beat markers, 236
  deleting, 234
  Floating Music Tracks, 234
  Pinned Music Tracks, 233
  pinning and unpinning, 229–232
  rearranging unpinned music, 232
backgrounds, 266–267, 485
  cutaways, 267
  showing/hiding, 485
  video effects, 267
backing up, projects, 56
Baseline, 211
Beat Marker, 488
beat markers, 235–240
  adding video clips, 238
  background music, 236
  beat warning, 240
  Flip at Beat Markers, 173
  inserting, 236
  Jump Cut at Beat Markers, 171
  Phase 1: Add your Background Music, 236
  Phase 2a: Insert Beat Markers, 236
  Phase 2b: Tapping Out Beats, 237
  Phase 3: Add Your Video Clips, 238
  Precision Editor, 239
  Snap to Beats, 236, 238, 239, 240
  Split at Beat Markers, 172
  transitions, 240
Bigger, 210
Black & White effect, 155
Bleach Bypass effect, 155
Blockbuster (movie trailer), 288
Blue Screen effect, 159–165, 475
Blur filter (QuickTime), 156
Bold, 210, 488
Boogie Lights title style, 202
brightness, 186–187
broadcast segments, 5
building the movie, 75–108

Add Freeze Frame, 99
Add Still Frame to Project, 99
Clip Trimmer, 100–101
comment markers, 98
copying and pasting movie, 96
cutaways, 103–105
  adjusting, 104
  removing, 105
full-screen playback, 94–95
Phase 1: Review Your Clips (Skim +
  Play), 75–79
  filmstrips, 76–77
  playback, 78–79
  skimming, 77–78
Phase 2: Select the Good Bits, 79–85
  4-second chunks, 80–81
  adjusting selection, 82
  deselecting, 84
  dragging, 80
  entire clips, 81
  highlighting all filmstrips, 82
  highlighting consecutive clips, 82
  highlighting random icons, 82
  multiple clips, 82
  playing selection, 83
  removing clip from selection, 82
  selecting specific project elements, 84
Phase 3: Build the Storyboard, 85–91
  adding to end, 85–86
  adding to middle, 87
  advanced insert options, 87–90
  orange stripe, 91
  Replace, 89
  Replace at Playhead, 89
  Replace from End, 89
  Replace from Start, 89
Phase 4: Fine-Tune the Edit, 93
Phases 2 to 3 (Alternate): Paint-to-Insert,
  91–92
Precision Editor, 105–107
rearranging movie, 95–96
shortening or lengthening clips, 97–102
  Clip Trimmer, 100–101
  fine-tuning with Extendo buttons,
    101–102
  ripple editing, 97
  selecting piece to delete, 98
  selecting piece to keep, 99
Split Clip, 99, 102–103
  at playhead, 103
storyboard playback, 93–94
  one-second (or 3-second) playback, 93
  selection playback, 93
  whole-storyboard playback, 93

building the movie (*continued*)
  Trim to Playhead, 99
  Trim to Selection, 99
Bulletin Board theme, 139
burning DVDs, 375
  maximizing playback time
    Best performance, 393
    High Quality, 394
    Professional Quality, 395
  (see also iDVD, Phase 6: Burning Your DVD)
burning slideshows, 419
Burns, Ken, 273
business videos, 4
Buttons panel, 423
buttons, Temporarily Allow, 406

C

camcorders, 5–23
  16-bit audio, 477
  audio, 224
  AVCHD, 8
  AVCHD Lite, 9
  DVD, 6, 17, 45
  hard-drive camcorders, 6, 17
  high definition format, 7
  high-def tape camcorder, 479
  iFrame, 9
  long-term storage problems, 17–23
  memory cards, 6, 17, 40
  MPEG-1 and MPEG-2, 7
  recording live from, 45–47
  tape, 17
    troubleshooting, 479
  tapeless, 6–23
    troubleshooting, 479
  useless features, 15–23
    date/time stamp, 16
    digital zoom, 16
    special effects, 15
    title generator, 15
  worthwhile features, 9–23
    analog inputs, 9
    built-in light, 13
    CCDs (charge-coupled devices), 11
    FireWire, 9
    FlexiZone, 14
    HD inputs, 10
    image stabilizer, 11
    manual controls, 12
    minutes-remaining readout, 13
    night-vision mode, 14
    optical zoom, 12
    progressive-scan CCDs, 15
    Push Focus, 14
    remote control, 13
    scene modes, 13
    still photos, 14
Camera Archive, 44
Cancel, 475
Cartoon effect, 154
Cathedral (Audio Effect), 255
CCDs (charge-coupled devices), 11
CDs, importing music from, 224
Centered title style, 200
channels, 184
  individual channel sliders, 189–190
chapter markers, 374, 378–381
  GarageBand, 379
  iDVD's automatic chapter-marker feature, 379
  iMovie, 379, 380
    comment markers, 380
  tips, 381
  ways to mark chapters, 379
cheat sheet, 489
Check for iMovie updates automatically, 455
Check for Updates, 28, 457
Circle Close transition, 135
Circle Open transition, 127, 135
Clicking in Event browser…, 456
Clicking in Event browser deselects all, 87
Clicking in Event browser selects, 81
Clip Adjustments, 471
clip-flagging, 109–124
  deleting footage for good, 119–121
  Favorites, 109
    hiding/showing, 112–113
    one-step method, 110–112
    two-step method, 110
    unmarking, 112
  keywords, 109, 113–116
    editing keyword list, 115
    painting onto clips, 115
    People, 118
    removing, 116
    select-then-apply method, 116
  Movie Trailers storyboard, 109
  People, 109, 117–118
    analyzing for people, 117
  Rejects, 109
    hiding/showing, 112–113
    one-step method, 110–112
    two-step method, 110
    unmarking, 112
  selecting marked footage, 112
Clip menu, 466–475
  Add Beat Marker, 468
  Arrange Music Tracks, 468
  Detach Audio, 467
  Duplicate Last Title, 466
  Extend Over Next Clip, 467

Join Clip, 467
Mute/Unmute Clip, 467
One-Step Effects, 466
Remove Volume Adjustments, 468
Split Clip, 467
Trim Clip End, 467
Trim to Selection, 467
Unpin Music Track, 468
clips
    keyboard shortcuts, 487
    making smaller, 70
clip time/date, showing, 486
Clip Trimmer, 100–101, 227, 235, 232
    inserting beat markers, 236
Clouds title style, 203
CMOS light-sensor chip, 181
CNN iReport (Share menu), 469
CNN's iReport, 313
    exporting to, 324–327
        after iReport is online, 326
codecs
    audio (see audio codecs)
    video (see video codecs)
color balance, 188–189
color channels, 184
color correction, 182–191
    channels, 184
    color balance, 188–189
    histogram, 185
    Phase 1: Select the Clip, Find the Frame, 182
    Phase 2: The Video Adjustments Panel, 183
    Video Adjustments panel, 183–184
        automatic correcton, 187–188
        Brightness slider, 186–187
        Contrast slider, 186–187
        copying and pasting adjustments, 191
        Exposure slider, 184–185
        individual channel sliders, 189–190
        Levels slider, 185
        removing or editing adjustments, 190
        Saturation, 189
        White Balance, 188
Color Picker, 204, 218
Colors dialog box, 218
    Color palettes, 218
    Color sliders, 218
    Color wheel, 218
    crayons, 218
    Image palettes, 218
    RGB and HSV, 218
colors, TV-safe, 215
Color Tint filter (QuickTime), 156
Comic Book theme, 139
comment markers, 98
Compatible Version of iDVD Required, 482

compressed video, 335
compression, video, 335–337
    spatial compression, 335–336
    temporal compression, 336–337
Consolidate Media, 61–62, 461
continuity, 297–298
contrast, 186–187
Convert Entire Clip, 157, 158
Copy, 464, 487
copyright law, 233
copyright notices (see titles)
Copy text formatting, 488
Copy the clips (Consolidate Media), 61
Copy the events (Consolidate Media), 61
Cosmic (Audio Effect), 255
Create a New Project (iDVD), 382
credits (see titles)
credits sequences, 277
Crop
    aspect ratios, 64
    showing/hiding, 486
Crop option (Paste Adjustments), 464
cropping, 272–273, 471
Cropping tool, 175, 191–195
    adjusting or removing a crop, 195
    steps, 193–195
    uses for, 192
Cross Blur transition, 136
Cross-Dissolve (iMovie), 433
Cross Dissolve transition, 136
crossfade transition, 125, 136
Cross Zoom transition, 136
Cut, 464, 487
Cutaway option (Paste Adjustments), 464
cutaways, 475
    adjusting, 104, 269
    advantages over filmstrips, 269–270
    and cut-ins, 300
    backgrounds, 267
    building the movie, 103–105
    cropping, fitting, and rotating, 273
    poking holes in, 270
    projects, 268–270
    removing, 105
    timing changes, 272
    transparency, 269

D

data rate, 344
dates, Events, 66, 265
Date/Time title style, 203
Day into Night effect, 155
Delete Encoded Assets, iDVD, 444
Delete Entire Clip, 465
Delete project, 486

Delete Selection, 465
deleting clips, 119–121
deleting partial clips, 121
Deselect All, 487
Detach Audio, 467
digital zoom, 16
dimensions (see aspect ratios)
disk images, iDVD, 444–446
    burning new copy, 445
    playing back, 445
disk space, reclaiming, 41
Display as List, 264
Display Time as HH:MM:SS:Frames, 454
dissolve transition, 125, 136
Documentary (movie trailer), 288
Document color, 215
Doorway transition, 136
Double-click to: Edit/Play, 456
Drag and Drop, Advanced, 87, 102
Drag and Drop menu, 474–475
    Audio Only, 475
    Cancel, 475
    Cutaway, 475
    Green Screen/Blue Screen, 475
    Insert, 475
    Picture in Picture, 475
    Replace, 89, 474
    Replace at Playhead, 89, 475
    Replace from End, 89, 474
    Replace from Start, 89, 474
    Side by Side, 475
Dream effect, 155, 171
Drifting title style, 201
Drop Box folder, importing movies, 50
dropouts, 480
Drop shadow, 215
Drop Zone editor, 431, 433
drop zones, 385, 389–391
    adding to, 390
    editing a drop-zone slideshow or movie, 391
    filling, 390
    hiding, 390
    removing items, 391
    replacing items, 391
    turning on motion, 391
ducking, 250
Duplicate Last Title, 466
Duplicate Project, 458
durations, photo, 271–272
DVD camcorders, 6, 17
    importing movies, 45
DVD-R, 396
DVD+R, 396
DVD+R DL (Double Layer), 396
DVD-RW or DVD+RW (Rewritable), 396

DVDs
    blank, 396
    extending life of, 449
    (see also iDVD)
DVD service bureaus, 446
    choosing, 448
    duplication, 447
    fulfillment, 448
    preparing to copy, 447
    replication, 447
    working with, 448
dvdthemepak.com, 422
DV/DVCPRO-NTSC codec, 349
DV-PAL, DVCPRO-PAL codecs, 349

E

Echo (Audio Effect), 255
echo, making, 245
Echo title style, 201
Edge Detect filter (QuickTime), 156
editing, troubleshooting, 481–483
    audiobooks, 481
    filmstrips, 482
    photos won't drag into movie, 481
    thumbnails, 482
editing movies
    advanced editing (see advanced editing)
    keyboard shortcuts, 487
editing titles, keyboard shortcuts, 488
Edit menu, 463–475
    Cut, Copy, Paste, 464
    Delete Entire Clip, 465
    Delete Selection, 465
    Paste Adjustments, 464
    Redo, 463
    Reject, 465
    Reject Entire Clip, 465
    Select, 465
    Select All Events, 465
    Select None, 465
    Select to Playhead, 465
    Select Video Clips/Transitions/Photos/Maps/
        Backgrounds/Animatics, 465
    Special Characters, 466
    Spelling, 466
    Transition Overlap, 466
    Undo, 463
Educational Map, 148
effects
    audio (see Audio Effects)
    narration, 240–241
    QuickTime filters, 156
    transitions (see transitions)
    video (see video effects)
egroups.com, 483

Emboss filter (QuickTime), 156
Epic Drama (movie trailer), 288
equalizer, 256
establishing shots, 299
Event browser
    Clicking in Event browser deselects all, 87
    clip-flagging (see clip-flagging)
    printing, 486
    stabilization, 177
Event Browser, 30
    keyboard shortcuts, 486
Event Library, 30
Events, 65–69
    Consolidate Media, 61
    dates, 66, 68, 265
    definition of, 39
    deleting, 69
    fine-tuning, 65–66
    font size, 66
    Group Events By Disk, 66
    Group Events by Month, 66
    hiding Events list, 69–70
    importing movies, 39
    iPhoto, 264
    Merge Events, 461
    merging, 68
    Most Recent Events at Top, 66
    renaming, 68
    Select All Events, 465
    Show date ranges in Events Library, 66
    Show Separate Days in Events, 66
    sort order, 66
    Split Event Before Selected Clip, 461
    splitting, 66–67
    stabilization, 177
    Swap Event and Projects, 472
Events Library
    2010, 2009, 2008…, 65
    iPhoto Videos, 65
    Last Import, 65
Exit full-screen mode, 486
Exit full-screen mode after playback is
    finished, 455
Expand selection to playhead, 487
Export as file, 487
Export Final Cut XML, 470
exporting movies, 356
    CNN's iReport (see CNN's iReport, exporting
      to)
    custom Web pages (see Web, exporting
      movies)
    Facebook (see Facebook, exporting to)
    from iMovie '11, 381–382
    high-definition video, 351
    Media Browser, 328

MobileMe (see MobileMe, exporting to)
    QuickTime Player Pro, 366–367
    QuickTime (see Export using QuickTime)
    to iTunes, 309–311
    troubleshooting, 482–483
      Compatible Version of iDVD
        Required, 482
      truncated text, 483
      YouTube, 482
    Vimeo (see Vimeo, exporting to)
    YouTube (see YouTube, exporting to)
exporting still frames, 279–282
    QuickTime Player Pro, 282
    resolution problem, 279–280
exporting to tape, 302
Export Movie, 470
Export using QuickTime, 338–348, 470
    Audio settings, 346–348
      AAC codec, 347
      AMR Narrowband, 347
      Apple Lossless, 347
      IMA 4:1 codec, 347
      QDesign Music 2 codec, 347
    AVI files, 339
    Filter dialog box, 344–345
    mono/stereo settings, 348
    Movie Settings box, 340
    Rate and Size settings, 347–348
    Size button, 345
    Standard Video Compression Settings dialog
      box, 340–344
      Compression Type pop-up menu, 340
      Data Rate section, 344
      Frame Rate box, 341
      frames per second, 341–344
      key frames, 343
      Quality slider, 344
exposure, 184–185
Extendo buttons, 101–102, 149
Extend Over Next Clip, 467

F

Facebook, 313
    exporting to, 322–323
      after movie is online, 322
    posting to, 322
Facebook (Share menu), 469
Fade In, Fade Out (volume), 251
Fade Out/Fade In (iMovie), 433
Fade Through Black transition, 127, 136
Fade Through White transition, 136
fade to black, 276
Fade to Black effect, 171
Far Far Away title style, 203
Fast Forward effect, 171

Favorite event footage, viewing, 486
Favorites
    clip-flagging, 109
        hiding/showing, 112–113
        one-step method, 110–112
        two-step method, 110
        unmarking, 112
    iDVD themes, 435–436
    marking clips as, 82
    rejecting everything but, 122
Favorites and Unmarked, 113, 468
Favorites Only, 112, 468
File menu, 457–475
    Adjust Clip Date and Time…, 461
    Analyze Video, 461
    Consolidate Media, 461
    Duplicate Project, 458
    Import from Camera, 458
    Import Movies/Camera Archive/iMovie HD
        Project, 458
    Merge Events, 461
    Move to Rejected Clips Trash, 460
    Move to Trash, 460
    New Event, 458
    New Folder, 458
    Optimize Video Full/Large, 462
    Page Setup, 462
    Print Project, 462
    Project Properties, 458–475
    Project Theme, 460
        Automatically add (pick a transition), 460
    Space Saver, 461
    Split Event Before Selected Clip, 461
Film Grain effect, 154
Film Noir (movie trailer), 288
Film Noise filter (QuickTime), 156
filmstrips, 70, 76–77
    cropping, fitting, and rotating, 273
    playhead, 77
    projects, 267–268
    secrets of, 78
    selecting all clips, 82
    timing changes, 271
    troubleshooting, 482
    versus cutaways, 269–270
Filmstrip theme, 139
film theory, 296–297
filtering photos, 263
filters (see effects)
Final Cut, 470
    exporting movies from, 382
Finder
    adding audio from, 227
    adding movies in iDVD, 404
    dragging video from, 49
    Photos browser, 265–266

FireWire, 9
FireWire cable, 31
FireWire jacks, 31
Fit in Frame, aspect ratios, 64
Fit to Audio (Slideshow Editor), 417
Flash effect, 172
FlexiZone, 14
Flip at Beat Markers effect, 173
Flipped effect, 154
Floating Music Tracks, 234
folders
    drag-and-drop, 413
    Photos browser, 267
Font Panel
    iMovie, 212
    showing/hiding, 488
    System, 213–216
        Collections, 213
        Document color, 215
        Drop shadow, 215
        Family, Typeface, 214
        Line Spacing, 216
        Outline, 216
        Size, 214
        Strikethrough, 214
        Text color, 215
        Underline, 214
fonts, 210–219
    Align, 210
    Baseline, 211
    Bigger, 210
    Bold, 210
    choosing favorite fonts and colors, 213
    general guidelines, 216–217
    Italic, 210
    Justification, 211
    Kern, 211
    Ligature, 211
    Outline, 210
    Smaller, 210
    Underline, 210
font size, Events, 66
footage stabilizer, 34, 42
Formal title style, 203
Four Corners title style, 201
frame-accurate editing, 83
frame rate, 458
    QuickTime, 334
frames per second, QuickTime, 341–344
    8, 10, 341
    12, 15, 342
    24, 25, 342
    29.97, 342
    30, 342

free music, 233
freeplaymusic.com, 233
freeze-frame effect, 276, 278
Friendship (movie trailer), 288
Front Row, 312
fulfillment, 448
full-screen mode
    exiting, 486
    playing events in, 486
    playing projects in, 486
    playing selection in, 486
    Show Events Full-screen, 471
    Show Projects Full-screen, 471
Fullscreen playback size, 455

G

Gain sliders, 190
GarageBand, 28
    basics, 257–259
    chapter markers, 379
    editing audio, 257–260
    Music and Sound Effects, 225
    Preferences, Render an audio preview when
        saving, 419
    prerecorded loops, 260
    recording live instrument or voice, 260
    recording MIDI instrument, 260
    Render an audio preview when saving, 225
    scoring, 259
Get iDVD Slideshow Images, 441
global transitions, 127
Glow effect, 155
Gradient title style, 203
Green Screen effect, 159–165, 475, 487
    adding effects to, 165
    getting the shot, 162–163
    how it works, 162
    inserting, 163–164
    key frame, 165
    preparing, 161
    removing, 165
Green Screen option (Paste Adjustments), 464
Group Events By Disk, 66, 468
Group Events By Month, 66, 468

H

H.264 codec, 349
hard disk
    maintenance suggestions, 478
    troubleshooting, 478
hard-drive camcorders, 6, 17
Hard Light effect, 155
HD inputs, 10
HDTV, 377
HDV format, 479

Heat Wave effect, 155
help
    iMovie discussion forum, 483
    iMovie List, 483
    official iMovie help pages, 483
    official iMovie tutorials, 483
Help menu, 472–475
    iMovie Help, 472
    Keyboard Shortcuts, 473
    Search, 472
    Service and Support, 474
    Supported Cameras, 473
    Welcome to iMovie, 473
Hide iMovie, 457
Hide Others, 457
Hide/Show Commands, 471
high definition camcorders, 7
high-definition camcorders, 35, 42
high-definition video, 37
    exporting, 351
high-def tape camcorder, 479
histogram, 185
Hold Last Frame effect, 172
Holiday (movie trailer), 288
home movies, 3
Horizontal Blur title style, 202
how Keyword Filter, 118
HSV, 218

I

iDVD
    adding movies, 403–405
        Finder, 404
        Import command, 404
        Media Browser, 404–406
    adding movies to DVD, 375, 391
    Apply Theme to Project, 387
    archiving project, 442–444
        copying archive to a different Mac, 444
    aspect ratios, 384, 388–389
    Audio folder, 440
    Automator, 441–442
        Add Movie to iDVD Menu, 441
        Get iDVD Slideshow Images, 441
        New iDVD Menu, 442
        New iDVD Movie Sequence, 442
        Set iDVD Background Image, 442
        Set iDVD button face, 442
        Show Main iDVD Menu, 442
    Autoplay, 410–412
        slideshow, 411
        still image, 411
        video clip, 411

iDVD (*continued*)

burning DVDs, 375
(see also iDVD, Phase 6: Burning Your DVD)
buttons, Temporarily Allow, 406
Buttons panel, 423
chapter markers, 374, 378–381
automatic, 379
GarageBand, 379
iMovie, 379
tips, 381
ways to mark chapters, 379
Create a New Project, 382
Delete Encoded Assets, 444
designing menu screens, 374
(see also iDVD, Phase 4: Design the Menu Screen)
disk images, 444–446
burning new copy, 445
playing back, 445
Drop Zone editor, 431, 433
drop zones, 389–391
adding to, 390
editing a drop-zone slideshow or movie, 391
filling, 390
hiding, 390
removing items, 391
replacing items, 391
turning on motion, 391
DVD-ROM maker, 437–439
adding files, 438
adding folders, 438
listing/hiding folder contents, 439
moving items into or out of folders, 439
removing files and folders, 439
storing documents, 437
storing email-quality versions of your video, 438
storing web pages, 438
subfolders, 439
DVD service bureaus, 446
choosing, 448
duplication, 447
fulfillment, 448
preparing to copy, 447
replication, 447
working with, 448
exporting
from iMovie '11, 381–382
iMovie video to DVD, 374
movies from Final Cut, 382
getting, 374
Inspector panel, 431
looping, 412

Magic iDVD, 383, 397, 399–402
adding movies, 400
choosing theme, 400
naming DVD, 400
new iDVD Project, 401
previewing DVD, 401
removing movie or slideshow, 401
slideshows, 400
map, 408–412
editing, 410
Menu folder, 440
MPEG files, 444
MPEG folder, 440
OneStep DVD, 383, 397–399
Open an Existing Project, 383
Overlay folder, 440
Phase 1: Prepare Your Video, 375–378
overscanning, 375–380
Phase 2: Insert Chapter Markers, 378–381
ways to mark chapters, 379
Phase 3: Export from iMovie '11, 381–382
Phase 4: Design the Menu Screen, 382–391
aspect ratios, 388–389
background image or video, 385
buttons, 385
drop zones, 385, 389–391
fonts, 385
text boxes, 385
themes, 385
themes, choosing, 386–387
themes, redesigning, 391
Phase 5: Add Your Movies, 391
Phase 6: Burning Your DVD, 391–397
blank DVDs, 396
burning, 396–397
checking for errors, 392
encoding, 395
maximizing playback time, 392–395
previewing project, 391
Play button, 374
preparing audio, video, and pictures, 374
professional duplicating, 446–449
ProjectData file, 439
project files, 439–440
reasons for using, 373–374
Resources folder, 439
Scene Selection button, 374
scrubber bar, 393
Shapes panel, 424
Share to iDVD, 374
Show Apple logo watermark, 385
Show drop zone labels, 389
Show Standard Crop Area, 388
Slideshow folder, 440
slideshows, 412–419

adding image files to DVD-ROM, 417
audio, 417, 418
Autoplay, 411
burning slideshow, 419
creating a new slideshow folder, 415
folder drag-and-drop, 413, 414
iPhoto albums, 412, 413–414
Loop slideshow, 416
Magic iDVD, 400
navigation, 416
settings, 416–417
Show titles and comments, 417
Slideshow Editor (see Slideshow Editor)
Slideshow Organizer, 413
still image, Autoplay, 411
submenus, 406–408
naming, 406
opening, 406
returning, 406
themes, 408
time limit, 408
themes
buying additional, 387
Magic iDVD, 400
menu screens, 385
redesigning, 391
scrubber bar, 393
Thumbnails folder, 440
time limit, 408
video clip, Autoplay, 411
iDVD (Share menu), 469
iDVD themes, 421–436
audio, 432–435
adjusting volume, 435
dragging audio file or QuickTime
movie, 432
Drop Zone editor, 433
Menu Info panel, 433
removing files, 434
replacing files, 434
where to drag, 433–434
built-in, 421–422
Favorites, 422
ribbon, 422
viewing all theme sets at once, 422
editing backgrounds, 428–432
Drop Zone editor, 431
group of photos, 430
Inspector panel, 431
movie, 431–432
notes, 432
still photo, 429–430
editing buttons, 422–427
Buttons panel, 423
changing names and fonts, 422

justification, drop shadows, thumbnail
size, 425
picture and movie buttons, 426–427
removing, 426
repositioning, 425
Shapes panel, 424
styles, 423–425
editing text, 427–428
changing text, 428
drop shadows, 428
font, size, weight, color, and
alignment, 428
menu titles, 427
positioning title or text box, 428
text boxes, 427
Favorites, 435–436
Menu Info panel, dragging audio or movie
file, 433
QuickTime movies, 432
secrets of theme files, 436
Show Inspector, keyboard shortcuts, 421
iFrame, 9
iLife Sound Effects, 225
IMA 4:1 codec, 347
image stabilizer, 11
iMovie
adding locations, 149
analyzing performances, 5
broadcast segments, 5
business videos, 4
Camera Archive, 44
chapter markers, 379, 380
comment markers, 380
Check for Updates, 28
clip-flagging (see clip-flagging)
converting movie trailers to regular iMovie
project, 292–294
crashes, 480
Cross-Dissolve, 433
Event Browser (see Event Browser)
Event Library (see Event Library)
Events (see Events)
exporting from iMovie '11, 381–382
Fade Out/Fade In, 433
Font Panel, 212
footage stabilizer, 34, 42
getting into, 29–30
home movies, 3
importing movies (see importing movies)
interviews, 4
minimizing, 485
Official iMovie help pages, 483
official iMovie tutorials, 483
on a new Mac, 27
on existing Mac, 28

iMovie (*continued*)
    Photos browser (see Photos browser)
    playhead, 30
    Project Library, 29
    Project Library (see Project Library)
    projects (see projects)
    project storyboard (see storyboard)
    QuickTime Player Pro, 366
    storyboard (see storyboard)
    the application, 27–28
    timeline, 72–74
    toolbar, 30
    training films, 4
    transferring project from iMovie 6 to
        iMovie '11, 304–306
    transferring project from iMovie '11 to
        iMovie 6, 303–304
    troubleshooting
        peculiar behavior, 478
    turning photos into video, 5
    uses for, 3–23
    video loops, 433
    video photo albums, 4
    Viewer, 29
    Web movies, 4
    work area, 69–73
        hiding Events list, 69–70
        hiding projects, 69–70
        making video clips smaller, 70
        swapping clip areas, 71
        timeline, 72–74
        Viewer, adjusting or relocating, 70
iMovie 6, advanced editing, 295, 302–306
    exporting to tape, 302
    plug-ins, 303
    transferring from iMovie '11, 303–304
    transferring to iMovie '11, 304–306
    video special effects, 302
iMovie '08, 2
iMovie discussion forum, 483
iMovie Help, 472, 486
iMovie List, 483
iMovie menu, 453–475
    About iMovie, 453
    Check For Updates, 457
    Hide iMovie, 457
    Hide Others, 457
    Preferences, 454–456
        Browser tab, 455–475
        Fonts tab, 456
        General tab, 454–455
        Video tab, 456
    Provide iMovie Feedback, 456
    Quit iMovie, 457
    Register iMovie, 457
    Show All, 457

iMovie Preferences window, 486
iMovie Sound Effects, 225
Import command, adding movies in
        iDVD, 404
Import from camera, 487
Import from Camera, 458
Import HD video as: Large/Full, 456
importing movies, 27–54
    Analyze for stabilization and/or people, 34
    Apple TV, 312
    dragging video from Finder, 49
    Drop Box folder, 50
    DVD camcorders, 45
    Events, 39
    footage stabilizer, 34, 42
    from old analog tapes, 51–53
        Approach 1: Use a Camcorder with Pass-
            Through Conversion, 51
        Approach 2: Record onto Your DV
            Camcorder, 51–52
        Approach 3: Use a Media Converter, 52
        Approach 4: Use a Digital8 Camcorder, 53
    from tape camcorders, 31–36
    Front Row, 312
    high definition, 37
    iPhone, 44
    iPod Touch, 44
    old iMovie projects, 47–49
    stabilization, 176
    tape camcorders
        automatic scene detection, 36
        footage stabilizer, 34
        high-definition, 35
    tapeless camcorders, 36–43
        footage stabilizer, 42
    to iPod, iPhone, iPad, 311–312
    troubleshooting, 480
importing music from a CD, 224
importing photos, 261–263
    integrated succession of photos, 262
    QuickTime image formats, 265
Import Movies/Camera Archive/iMovie HD
        Project, 458
Increase/decrease type size, 488
Initial Photo Placement, 460
Initial Video Placement, 460
Initial Video Placement pop-up menu, 64
Insert, 475
Inspector
    Audio Adjustments tab, 486, 488
    changing Travel Map timing, 148
    photo durations, 271
    removing video effects, 157
    showing/hiding, 485

Speed slider, 158
Video Adjustments tab, 485
Inspector panel, 431
Instant Replay effect, 171
intercutting, 302
interlaced, 480
interlacing, 279
interviews, 4
iPhone, importing movies, 44
iPhoto, 28
    albums, 412–414
    Events, 264
    looping in slideshows, 262
    slideshows, 413
    video photo albums, 262
iPhoto Videos (Events Library), 65
iPod, iPhone, iPad, importing movies, 311–312
iPod Touch, importing movies, 44
iSight camera, recording live from, 45–47
Italic, 210, 488
iTunes
    exporting movies to, 309–311
    Music and Sound Effects, 226
    QuickTime Player X, 354
iTunes (Share menu), 469
iTunes tracks, 224
iWeb, 28
    exporting movies, 327, 328–331
        editing or deleting page, 331
        when you are done, 330

J

jellyroll footage, 181–182
    Rolling Shutter adjustments, 181
Join Clip, 467
Jump Cut at Beat Markers effect, 171
Justification, 211

K

Ken Burns effect, 195, 273–275, 471
    showing/hiding, 486
Kern, 211
kerning, 488
keyboard shortcuts, 473, 485–488
    Show Inspector, 421
key frames
    Green Screen effect, 165
    QuickTime, 343
Keyword Filter, 118
keywords
    clip-flagging, 109, 113–116
        editing keyword list, 115
        painting onto clips, 115
        People, 118
    removing, 116
    select-then-apply method, 116
    Rejects, 122
Keywords window, showing/hiding, 486

L

Last Import (Events Library), 65
layered effect, 277
Left, 488
Lens Flare filter (QuickTime), 156
Lens Flare title style, 202
letterbox bars, 64
levels, 185
Ligature, 211
Line Spacing, 216
Lock playhead, 486
Loop Movie, 412
Loop selected footage, 486
Loop Selection, 468
Loop Slideshow, 412
Love Story (movie trailer), 288
Lower Third title style, 200
Lower title style, 201

M

Mac
    FireWire jacks, 31
    iMovie on a new, 27
    iMovie on existing, 28
macmall.com, 28
macwarehouse.com, 28
Magic iDVD, 383, 397, 399–402
    adding movies, 400
    choosing theme, 400
    naming DVD, 400
    new iDVD Project, 401
    previewing DVD, 401
    removing movie or slideshow, 401
    slideshows, 400
Map, Background, and Animatic browser, 266
Maps, showing/hiding, 485
Map Style option (Paste Adjustments), 464
Mark selection as a Favorite, 487
Mark selection as a Reject, 487
Maximum Zoom slider, 179
Media Browser, 328, 329
    adding movies in iDVD, 404–406
Media Browser (Share menu), 469
memory-card camcorders, 6, 17
memory cards, 40
Menu folder, 440
Menu Info panel, dragging audio or movie file, 433
Merge Events, 461

Minimize iMovie, 485
MobileMe, 313
  Allow movie to be downloaded, 321
  exporting to, 319–322
    after movie is online, 321
    getting movie into MobileMe Gallery, 319
  getting account, 319
  Hide Movie on my Gallery home page, 321
  QuickTime Player X, 354
MobileMe Gallery, 469
  deleting movie, 322
  editing and republishing video, 321
  getting movie into, 319
  watching video, 321
modern film theory, 296–297
Mosaic transition, 137
Most Recent Events at Top, 66
motion blur, 177
Motion JPEG codec, 349
Move the events (Consolidate Media), 61
Move to Rejected Clips Trash, 460
Move to Trash, 460
movies
  adding in iDVD (see iDVD, adding movies)
  building (see building the movie)
  changing speed of footage, 157–159
  chapter markers (see chapter markers)
  creating still images from footage, 276–279
    creating cool titles, 276
    credits sequences, 277
    freeze-frame effect, 276, 278
    layered effect, 277
    still frame, 277
  cropping, 272–273
  dimensions (see aspect ratios)
  effects (see video effects)
  exporting from Final Cut, 382
  extracting audio from video, 244–246
  fitting, 272–273
  fixing shaky footage, 178–181
  hiding shaky footage, 179
  Loop Movie, 412
  pixelated images, 273
  QuickTime Player (see QuickTime Player)
  rotating, 272–273
  transitions (see transitions)
  video effects (see video effects)
  video stabilization (see stabilization)
movie trailers, 283–294
  Action, 287
  Adventure, 288
  audio adjustments, 290
  Blockbuster, 288
  building, 289–292
  catalog, 287–289

  clip's color settings, 290
  converting to regular iMovie project, 292–294
  customizing, 290–293
  Documentary, 288
  Epic Drama, 288
  Film Noir, 288
  Friendship, 288
  Holiday, 288
  Love Story, 288
  outlines, 285
  Pets, 288
  Romantic Comedy, 289
  Shot List, 286
  Sports, 289
  Spy, 289
  starting new project, 284
  Storyboard, 286
  Supernatural, 289
  Travel, 289
  video and/or audio effects, 291
  what is a movie trailer?, 283
Movie Trailers storyboard, clip-flagging, 109
MP3 files, 224
MPEG-1 and MPEG-2, 7
MPEG-2, 479
MPEG-4 Video codec, 350
MPEG files, 444
MPEG folder, 440
Muffled (Audio Effect), 254
Multitune (Audio Effect), 255
Music
  keyboard shortcuts, 488
  showing/hiding, 485, 488
Music and Sound Effects, 225–227
  adding audio from Finder, 227
  free music, 233
  GarageBand, 225
  iLife Sound Effects, 225
  iMovie Sound Effects, 225
  iTunes, 226
  playback controls, 226
  sound effects, 231
music (see audio)
Mute/Unmute Clip, 467, 488

N

narration, 224, 240–244
  adding new information, 242
  Audio Only, 246
  effects, 240–241
  identifying scenes, 241
  reminiscence, 241

Voiceover, 241–244
    choosing sound source, 242
    deleting, shortening, or moving
        stripe, 244
    Noise Reduction, 243
    Play project audio, 243
    setting input level, 242
    Voice Enhancement, 243
Negative effect, 155
New Audio Recording (QuickTime
    Player X), 357
New Event, 458
New Folder, 458
New iDVD Menu, 442
New iDVD Movie Sequence, 442
New Movie Recording (QuickTime
    Player X), 357
New Project, 57, 486
New Screen Recording (QuickTime
    Player X), 357
News theme, 139
NightShot, 14
night-vision mode, 14
Noise Reduction, 243
nonlinear editing software, 1
Normalize Clip Volume, 251
NTSC standard, 19

O

official iMovie help pages, 483
official iMovie tutorials, 483
Old World effect, 155
OneStep DVD, 383, 397–399
One-Step Effects, 170–173, 466
    Dream, 171
    Fade to Black, 171
    Fast Forward, 171
    Flash, 172
    Flip at Beat Markers, 173
    Hold Last Frame, 172
    Instant Replay, 171
    Jump Cut at Beat Markers, 171
    Rewind, 171
    Sepia, 171
    Slow Motion, 171
    Split at Beat Markers, 172
    White, 171
Open an Existing Project (iDVD), 383
Open Clip Trimmer window, 487
Open Precision Editor, 487
optical zoom, 12
Optimize Video Full/Large, 462
orange stripe, 91
Organic Main and Organic Lower title
    style, 202

Outline, 210, 216
Outline style, 488
Overlap title style, 201
Overlay folder, 440
overscanning, 375–380
    action-safe area, 378
    title-safe area, 377

P

Page Curl transition, 137
Page Setup, 462
PAL, 19
Panels keyboard shortcuts, 485
Panes keyboard shortcuts, 485
Paper title style, 203
parallel editing, 302
Paste, 464, 487
Paste Adjustments, 464
Paste audio adjustments only, 487
Paste audio effect adjustments only, 487
Paste copied adjustments, 487
Paste crop/Ken Burns adjustments only, 487
Paste cutaway, 487
Paste map style adjustments only, 487
Paste rolling shutter adjustments only, 487
Paste speed adjustments only, 487
Paste stabilization adjustments only, 487
Paste text formatting, 488
Paste video adjustments only, 487
peculiar behavior, 478
People (clip-flagging), 109, 117–118
    analyzing for people, 117
    keywords, 118
Pets (movie trailer), 288
Photo Album theme, 139, 142
Photo Duration, 459
Photo - JPEG codec, 349
photos
    creating still images from footage, 276–279
        creating cool titles, 276
        credits sequences, 277
        freeze-frame effect, 276, 278
        layered effect, 277
        still frame, 277
    pixelated images, 273
    turning photos into video, 5
    video photo albums, 4
Photos browser, 263–267
    backgrounds, 266–267
    Display as List, 264
    filling entire, 265
    Finder, 265–266
    folders, 267
    opening photos, 264
    previewing photos, 264
    tips, 264–265

Photos pane, showing/hiding, 485
Picture-in-Picture option (Paste
    Adjustments), 464
Picture-in-Picture (PiP), 165–169, 475
    adjusting size and position, 166–167
    changing appearance, 167–168
    inserting, 166
    mixing audio, 168
    moving and trimming PIP clip, 169
    removing, 169
pinned music (see sound effects)
Pinned Music Tracks, 233
pinning and unpinning background
    music, 229–232
Pitch Down/Up (Audio Effect), 255
pixelated images, 273
Pixie Dust title style, 202
Play, 468
Play Around Current Frame, 468
playback, 78–79
    keyboard shortcuts, 486
playback window, QuickTime, 334
Play button (iDVD), 374
Play events full-screen, 486
Play from Beginning, 468
Play from cursor, 486
Play Full Screen, 468
playhead, 30, 77
Playhead Info, 79, 469
Play project (or Event) from start, 486
Play projects full-screen, 486
Play selected footage, 486
Play Selection, 468
Play selection full-screen, 486
Play sound in front most player only, 361
Play the 1 seconds on either side of the
    cursor, 486
Play the 3 seconds on either side of the
    cursor, 486
PNG files, alpha-channel, 218
Podcast Producer, 469
pointers, 56
Precision Editor, 239, 471
    building the movie, 105–107
Preferences, 454–456
    Advanced Tools, 163, 380
    Browser tab, 455–475
        Always show active clip badges, 455
        Always show clip durations, 455
        Apply rolling shutter correction for clips
            that have been analyzed, 456
        Automatically stabilize clips that have
            been analyzed, 456
        Clicking in Event browser…, 456
        Double-click to: Edit/Play, 456

Show date ranges in Event Library, 455
Show Fine Tuning controls, 456
Use large font for project and Event
    list, 455
Use project crop setting for clips in Event
    Browser, 455
Clicking in Event browser deselects all, 87
Clicking in Event browser selects, 81
Fonts tab, 213, 456
Gain sliders, 190
GarageBand, 225
    Render an audio preview when
        saving, 419
General tab, 454–455
    Check for iMovie updates
        automatically, 455
    Display Time as HH:MM:SS:Frames, 454
    Exit fullscreen mode after playback is
        finished, 455
    Fullscreen playback size, 455
    Show Advanced Tools, 454
    Show "Play" reminder in viewer, 455
QuickTime
    Automatically play movies when
        opened, 360
    Play sound in front most player only, 361
Show Apple logo watermark, 385
Show date ranges in Events Library, 66
Show drop zone labels, 389
Use large font for Project Library and Event
    Library, 66
Video tab, 456
prerecorded loops (scoring), 260
Print Event browser or storyboard, 486
printing, storyboards, 151
Print Project, 462
ProjectData file, 439
Project Library, 29, 57–62
    Consolidate Media, 61–62
    projects
        creating new, 57–58
        deleting, 59
        duplicating, 58
        folders, 59
        moving, 60
        renaming, 58
        undeleting, 60
Project Properties, 458–475, 486
Project Properties dialog box, 64
    adjusting length of transition, 130–131
    Applies to all photos, 460
    Applies to all transitions, 459
    Applies when added to project, 459, 460
    Aspect Ratio, 458
    Frame Rate, 458

Initial Photo Placement, 460
Initial Video Placement, 460
Photo Duration, 459
Theme Transition Duration, 459
Title Fade Duration, 459
Transition Duration, 459
projects, 55–56
   adding photos, 267–272
      cutaways, 268–270
      filmstrips, 267–268
   aspect ratios, 62–64
   backing up, 56
   choosing video clip, 56
      pointers, 56
   creating new, 57–58
   deleting, 59
   duplicating, 58
   folders, 59
   hiding, 69–70
   moving, 60
   Project Library (see Project Library)
   renaming, 58
   Swap Event and Projects, 472
   undeleting, 60
project storyboard (see storyboard)
Project Theme, 460, 486
   Automatically add (pick a transition), 460
Provide iMovie Feedback, 456
Pull Focus title style, 202
Push Focus, 14

Q

QDesign Music 2 codec, 347
QuickTime
   AMR Narrowband, 347
   Apple Lossless, 347
   audio codecs, 338
      AAC, 347
      IMA 4:1, 347
      QDesign Music 2, 347
   Automatically play movies when opened, 360
   compressed video, 335
   compression
      spatial, 335–336
      temporal, 336–337
   data rate, 344
   exporting to (see Export using QuickTime)
   frame rate, 334
   frames per second, 341–344
   high-definition video, 351
   image formats, 265
   key frames, 343
   playback window, 334
   Play sound in front most player only, 361

QuickTime Player 7 vs. QuickTime Player
   Pro, 362
   saving, 350
   understanding, 333–338
   video codecs, 348–350
      Animation, 349
      Apple Intermediate Codec, 349
      DV/DVCPRO-NTSC, 349
      DV-PAL, DVCPRO-PAL, 349
      H.264, 349
      Motion JPEG, 349
      MPEG-4 Video, 350
      Photo - JPEG, 349
QuickTime effect, 217
QuickTime Player 7 (Free Version), 358–362
   audio level meters, 358
   changing screen size, 361
   controls, 358–360
      hidden, 360
   counter, 360
   Fast-Forward, 360
   hidden controls, 360
   Jump to Start, Jump to End, 360
   looping movie, 362
   Play All Frames (Pro only), 362
   playback tricks, 360
   playing more than one movie, 361
   playing movie backward, 361
   Play Selection Only (Pro only), 362
   Play/Stop button, 359
   resize handle, 358
   Rewind, 360
   scroll bar, 359
   selection handles, 360
   volume, 360
QuickTime Player Pro, 353, 362–367
   editing movies, 363–366
      Add to Movie command, 365
      Trim to Selection command, 365
   exporting edited movies, 366–367
      Export command, 366
      Save As, 366
      using with iMovie, 366
   exporting still frames, 282
   flipping clips, 369
   multiple videos in same clip, 369
   pasting footage, 365
   Play All Frames, 362
   Play Selection Only, 362
   presenting movies, 363
   selecting footage, 364
   tracks, 367–370
      deleting, 368
      extracting, 368
      turning off, 368

QuickTime Player X, 353, 354–358
    New Audio Recording, 357
    New Movie Recording, 357
    New Screen Recording, 357
    recording in, 357–358
    sharing, 354–356
        iTunes, 354
        MobileMe, 354
        YouTube, 355
    trimming movies, 356–357
QuickTime video filters, 156
Quit iMovie, 457

R

Raster effect, 154
reaction shots, 300
recording live from camcorder or iSight
        camera, 45–47
Redo, 80, 463, 488
Register iMovie, 457
Reject and Review, 122
Rejected Clips window, 122
Rejected Only, 113, 468
Reject Entire Clip, 110, 465
rejecting categories of clips, 122
Rejects, 465
    clip-flagging, 109
        hiding/showing, 112–113
        one-step method, 110–112
        two-step method, 110
        unmarking, 112
    deleting footage for good, 119–121
    keywords, 122
    marking clips as, 82
reminiscence (narration), 241
remote control, 13
Remove all keywords from selection, 488
Remove Volume Adjustments, 468
Render an audio preview when saving, 225,
        419
Replace, 474
Replace at Playhead, 475
Replace at Playhead (Drag and Drop), 89
Replace (Drag and Drop), 89
Replace from End, 474
Replace from End (Drag and Drop), 89
Replace from Start, 474
Replace from Start (Drag and Drop), 89
replication, 447
resolution, still frames, 279–280
Resources folder, 439
Restore one hidden frame to clip, 487
Reveal in Event Browser, 468
Reverse effect, 157–159
Rewind effect, 171

RGB, 218
right-justified text, 488
ripple editing, 97
Ripple transition, 138
Robot (Audio Effect), 255
Rolling Shutter adjustments, 181–182
Rolling Shutter option (Paste
        Adjustments), 464
Romantic Comedy (movie trailer), 289
Romantic effect, 155
rotating, 272–273
rotating video, 175, 195–197
    adjusting or removing rotation, 197
Rotation, 471
Rotation window, showing/hiding, 486
Roxio Toast, 445
rubber-banding, 247–249

S

sampling, 347
Saturation, 189
Save for Web command, 356
scene modes, 13
Scene Selection button (iDVD), 374
Sci-Fi effect, 155
scoring in GarageBand, 260
Scrapbook theme, 139
scrolling, 486
Scrolling Credits title style, 201, 209–210
scrubber bar (iDVD), 393
Search, 472
Select, 465
Select All Events, 465
Select All (or whole filmstrip), 487
Select None, 465
Select to Playhead, 465
Select Video Clips/Transitions/Photos/Maps/
        Backgrounds/Animatics, 465
Sepia effect, 171
Sepia Tone effect, 155
Service and Support, 474
Set iDVD Background Image, 442
Set iDVD button face, 442
Shapes panel, 424
Share menu, 469–475
    CNN iReport, 469
    Export Final Cut XML, 470
    Export Movie, 470
    Export using QuickTime, 470
    Facebook, 469
    iDVD, 469
    iTunes, 469
    Media Browser, 469
    MobileMe Gallery, 469
    Podcast Producer, 469

Vimeo, 469
YouTube, 469
Share to iDVD, 374
sharing
  QuickTime Player X, 354–356
    iTunes, 354
    MobileMe, 354
    YouTube, 355
  YouTube (see YouTube, exporting to)
Sharpen filter (QuickTime), 156
Shift selection border, 487
Shorten clip by 1 frame, 487
Shortwave Radio (Audio Effect), 255
Shot List, 286
Show Advanced Tools, 88, 454
Show All, 457
Show Apple logo watermark, 385
Show clip time/date, 486
Show date ranges in Event Library, 455
Show drop zone labels, 389
Show Events Full-screen, 471
Show Fine Tuning controls, 456
Show/Hide Crop/Ken Burns/Rotation
    window, 486
Show/Hide Fonts panel, 488
Show/Hide Inspector, 485
Show/Hide Inspector Audio Adjustments
    tab, 486, 488
Show/Hide Inspector Video Adjustments
    tab, 485
Show Hide Maps, 485
Show/Hide Music and Sound Effects, 485, 488
Show/Hide Photos pane, 485
Show/Hide Titles, 485, 488
Show/Hide Transitions pane, 485
Show/Hide Voiceover window, 486, 488
Show Inspector, keyboard shortcuts, 421
Show Main iDVD Menu, 442
Show Most Recent Events at Top, 468
Show only Favorites, 112
Show "Play" reminder in viewer, 455
Show Projects Full-screen, 471
Show Separate Days in Events, 66, 468
Show Standard Crop Area (iDVD), 388
Side by Side, 475
Side-by-Side effect, 169–170
  changing appearance, 170
Sideways Drift title style, 201
skimming, 77–78
Slide Duration (Slideshow Editor), 417
Slideshow Editor, 415–419
  adding or omitting slides and movies, 416
  audio, 418
  exiting, 419
  Fit to Audio, 417

Manual, 417
options, 417–419
renaming slides or movies, 416
reordering slides and movies, 416
Slide Duration, 417
Transition, 418
Slideshow folder, 440
Slideshow Organizer, 413
slideshows
  iDVD, 412–419
    adding image files to DVD-ROM, 417
    audio, 417, 418
    Autoplay, 411
    burning slideshow, 419
    creating a new slideshow folder, 415
    folder drag-and-drop, 413, 414
    iPhoto albums, 412, 413–414
    Loop slideshow, 416
    Magic iDVD, 400
    navigation, 416
    settings, 416–417
    Show titles and comments, 417
    Slideshow Editor (see Slideshow Editor)
    Slideshow Organizer, 413
  iPhoto, 413
  looping, 262
  Loop Slideshow, 412
Slo-Mo effect, 170
Slow Motion effect, 171
Smaller, 210
Small/Medium/Large Room (Audio
    Effect), 255
Snap to Beats, 236, 238, 239, 240, 469, 488
Snap to Ends, 469
Soft Bar title style, 203
Soft Edge title style, 202
sort order (Events), 66
sound, troubleshooting, 480
sound effects, 223, 224, 234–235
  adding or removing, 231
  adjusting length, 235
  attaching multiple, 235
  showing/hiding, 485, 488
soundtracks, QuickTime, 339
Space Saver, 121–123, 461
spatial compression, 335–336
Special Characters, 466
Speed option (Paste Adjustments), 464
Speed slider (Inspector), 158
Spelling, 466
Spin In, Spin Out transitions, 138
Split at Beat Markers effect, 172
Split Clip, 99, 254, 467, 488
  at playhead, 103
  building the movie, 102–103

Split Event Before Selected Clip, 461
Sports (movie trailer), 289
Sports theme, 139
   customizing, 144–146
Spy (movie trailer), 289
stabilization, 175, 176–182
   degress of, 178–180
   Event browser, 177
   Events, 177
   fixing shaky footage, 178–181
   hiding shaky footage, 179
   jellyroll footage, 181–182
      Rolling Shutter adjustments, 181–182
   Maximum Zoom slider, 179
   motion blur, 177
   notes, 179
   red squiggles across bottom of clip, 180
   removing, 180
   selected clips, 176
Stabilization option (Paste Adjustments), 464
Standard (4:3), 62, 272
still frames, 277
   exporting, 279–282
      QuickTime Player Pro, 282
      resolution problem, 279–280
Storyboard, movie trailers, 286
storyboard playback
   one-second (or 3-second) playback, 93
   selection playback, 93
   whole-storyboard playback, 93
storyboards, 29
   adding audio to storyboard, 225–228
      Music and Sound Effects browser,
         225–227
   Animatics
      building storyboard, 150
      printing for filming, 151
   building, 85–91
      adding to end of storyboard, 85–86
      adding to middle, 87
      advanced insert options, 87–90
      orange stripe, 91
      Replace, 89
      Replace at Playhead, 89
      Replace from End, 89
      Replace from Start, 89
   keyboard shortcuts, 486
   printing, 486
   titles, 204–206
Strikethrough, 214
subtitles (see titles)
Supernatural (movie trailer), 289
Supported Cameras, 473
Swap Event and Projects, 472
Swap transition, 138

Switch to Standard (4:3), 387
System Font Panel, 213–216
   Collections, 213
   Document color, 215
   Drop shadow, 215
   Family, Typeface, 214
   Line Spacing, 216
   Outline, 216
   Size, 214
   Strikethrough, 214
   Text color, 215
   Underline, 214

T

tape camcorders, 17
   high-definition, 35
   importing movies, 31–36
      automatic scene detection, 36
      footage stabilizer, 34
   troubleshooting, 479
tapeless camcorders, 6–23
   importing movies, 36–43
      footage stabilizer, 42
   memory cards, 40
   troubleshooting, 479
Telephone (Audio Effect), 255
temporal compression, 336–337
Temporarily Allow, 406
Text color, 215
Text menu, 469
themes, 139–146
   adjusting transition's length, 142–144
   Bulletin Board, 139
   changing, 141
   choosing, 139–140
   Comic Book, 139
   customizing, 141
   Filmstrip, 139
   iDVD
      buying additional, 387
      Magic iDVD, 400
      menu screens, 385
      redesigning, 391
      scrubber bar, 393
   News, 139
   Photo Album, 139, 142
   removing, 146
   Scrapbook, 139
   Sports, 139
      customizing, 144–146
themes, iDVD (see iDVD themes)
Theme Transition Duration, 459
thumbnails
   sizing, 264
   troubleshooting, 482

Thumbnails folder, iDVD, 440
Ticker title style, 202
tight editing, 299
Tighter/looser spacing (kerning), 488
timeline, 72–74
timing changes, photos, 271–272
Title Fade Duration, 459
Title Fade Duration slider, 221
titles
    adjusting timing, 207–208
    Boogie Lights, 202
    Centered, 200
    changing start or end points, 220
    Clouds, 203
    Color Picker, 204
    creating cool titles, 276
    custom, 217–221
    customizing, 141
    Date/Time, 203
    deleting, 220
    Drifting, 201
    Echo, 201
    editing, 220
    Far Far Away, 203
    Font Panel, 212
        system, 213–216
    fonts (see fonts)
    Formal, 203
    Four Corners, 201
    Gradient, 203
    Horizontal Blur, 202
    keyboard shortcuts, 488
    Lens Flare, 202
    Lower, 201
    Lower Third, 200
    moving, 220
    Organic Main and Organic Lower, 202
    Overlap, 201
    Paper, 203
    Pixie Dust, 202
    positioning, 204–206
    Pull Focus, 202
    Scrolling Credits, 201, 209–210
    setting up, 199–210
    Sideways Drift, 201
    Soft Bar, 203
    Soft Edge, 202
    storyboard, 204–206
    styles, 200–204
    theme-based, 204
    Ticker, 202
    Torn Edge, 203
    typing text, 208
    Upper, 201
    using graphics, 261

Vertical Drift, 201
Zoom, 202
Titles panel, showing/hiding, 485, 488
toolbar, 30
Torn Edge title style, 203
training films, 4
Transition Duration, 459
Transition Duration slider
    Applies to all transitions, 130
    Applies when added to project, 130
    number of seconds, 131
Transition Overlap, 466
transitions, 199
    about, 125–126
    appropriate, 127
    Automatic Transitions, 127, 133–135
        adjusting, 134
        turning off, 134
    beat markers, 240
    changing, 129
    Circle Close, 135
    Circle Open, 127, 135
    consistency, 127
    Cross Blur, 136
    Cross Dissolve, 136
    crossfade, 125
    Cross Zoom, 136
    deleting, 129
    dissolve, 125
    Doorway, 136
    dropping into place, 129
    duration, 129–133
        how length of movie is affected, 132–133
        not getting what you want, 131
    Fade Through Black, 127, 136
    Fade Through White, 136
    global, 127
    individual effects, 127–129
    Mosaic, 137
    Page Curl, 137
    Project Properties dialog box
        adjusting length of transition, 130–131
    Ripple, 138
    Spin In, Spin Out, 138
    Swap, 138
    themes (see themes)
    ways to transition, 127
    when not to use, 126–127
    Wipe Down, Up, Left, Right, 138
Transition (Slideshow Editor), 418
Transitions pane, showing/hiding, 485
Travel Maps, 146–149
    adding, 146–147
    changing style, 148
    changing timing, 148–149

Travel Maps (*continued*)
 Extendo buttons, 149
 Inspector, 148
 shortening a map, 149
 changing travel points, 147
 Educational Map, 148
 Watercolor Map, 148
Travel (movie trailer), 289
Trim Clip End, 467
Trim to Playhead, 99
Trim to Selection, 99, 100, 467, 487
troubleshooting, 477–484
 16-bit audio, 477
 dropouts, 480
 editing, 481–483
  audiobooks, 481
  filmstrips, 482
  photos won't drag into movie, 481
  thumbnails, 482
 exporting, 482–483
  Compatible Version of iDVD
   Required, 482
  truncated text, 483
  YouTube, 482
 hard disk, 478
 iMovie crashes, 480
 iMovie discussion forum, 483
 iMovie List, 483
 importing, 480
 no sound, 480
 official iMovie help pages, 483
 official iMovie tutorials, 483
 peculiar behavior, 478
 photos won't drag into movie, 481
 tape camcorders, 479
 tapeless camcorders, 479
 versions, 477
 video looks interlaced, 480
 where to get help, 483
turning photos into video, 5
Turn on/off Snap to Beats, 488
TV-safe colors, 215
type size, increasing/decreasing, 488

U

Underline, 210, 214, 488
Underwater background, 266
Undo, 80, 463, 488
Unmarked event footage
 viewing, 486
Unmark selection, 487
Unpin Music Track, 234, 468
updates
 Check for iMovie updates automatically, 455
 Check for Updates, 28
 Check For Updates, 457

Upper title style, 201
Use large font for project and Event list, 455
**Use large font for Project Library and Event
 Library,** 66
**Use project crop setting for clips in Event
 Browser,** 455

V

versions, 477
Vertical Drift title style, 201
VHS, importing movies from, 51–53
Video Adjustments, 471
Video Adjustments panel, 183–184
 automatic correcton, 187–188
 Brightness slider, 186–187
 Contrast slider, 186–187
 copying and pasting adjustments, 191
 Exposure slider, 184–185
 histogram, 185
 individual channel sliders, 189–190
 Levels slider, 185
 removing or editing adjustments, 190
 Saturation, 189
 White Balance, 188
video codecs, 348–350
 Animation, 349
 Apple Intermediate Codec, 349
 DV/DVCPRO-NTSC, 349
 DV-PAL, DVCPRO-PAL, 349
 H.264, 349
 Motion JPEG, 349
 MPEG-4 Video, 350
 Photo - JPEG, 349
video compression (see compression, video)
Video Effect option (Paste Adjustments), 464
video effects, 153–174
 adjusting, 157
 Aged Film, 154
 applying, 155–157
 backgrounds, 267
 Black & White, 155
 Bleach Bypass, 155
 Blue Screen, 159–165
 Cartoon, 154
 changing speed of footage, 157–159
  removing changes, 159
 Day into Night, 155
 Dream, 155
 Film Grain, 154
 Flipped, 154
 Glow, 155
 Green Screen, 159–165
  adding effects to, 165
  getting the shot, 162–163
  how it works, 162

inserting, 163–164
key frame, 165
preparing, 161
removing, 165
Hard Light, 155
Heat Wave, 155
list of, 154–155
Negative, 155
Old World, 155
One-Step Effects, 170–173
    Dream, 171
    Fade to Black, 171
    Fast Forward, 171
    Flash, 172
    Flip at Beat Markers, 173
    Hold Last Frame, 172
    Instant Replay, 171
    Jump Cut at Beat Markers, 171
    Rewind, 171
    Sepia, 171
    Slow Motion, 171
    Split at Beat Markers, 172
    White, 171
Picture-in-Picture (PiP), 165–169
    adjusting size and position, 166–167
    changing appearance, 167–168
    inserting, 166
    mixing audio, 168
    moving and trimming PIP clip, 169
    removing, 169
Raster, 154
removing, 157
Reverse, 157–159
Romantic, 155
Sci-Fi, 155
Sepia Tone, 155
Side-by-Side, 169–170
    changing appearance, 170
Slo-Mo, 170
Vignette, 155
X-Ray, 155
video loops in iMovie, 433
Video option (Paste Adjustments), 464
video photo albums, 4
video special effects, 302
video stabilization (see stabilization)
Viewer, 29, 471
    adjusting or relocating, 70
Viewer on Secondary Display, 472
Viewer size small/medium/large, 486
View Favorite and Unmarked event
    footage, 486
View menu, 468–475
    All Clips, 468
    Audio Skimming, 469

Favorites and Unmarked, 468
Favorites Only, 468
Group Events by Disk, 468
Group Events By Month, 468
Loop Selection, 468
Play, 468
Play Around Current Frame, 468
Play from Beginning, 468
Play Full Screen, 468
Playhead Info, 469
Play Selection, 468
Rejected Only, 468
Reveal in Event Browser, 468
Show Most Recent Events at Top, 468
Show Separate Days in Events, 468
Snap to Beats, 469
Snap to Ends, 469
Vignette effect, 155
Vimeo, 313
    exporting to, 323–324
        after movie is online, 324
Vimeo (Share menu), 469
visual cheat sheet, 489
Voice Enhancement, 243
Voiceover, 241–244
    choosing sound source, 242
    deleting, shortening, or moving stripe, 244
    Noise Reduction, 243
    Play project audio, 243
    setting input level, 242
    showing/hiding, 486, 488
    Voice Enhancement, 243
volume adjustments, 246–252
    adjusting overall clip volume, 249–252
    ducking, 250
    Fade In, Fade Out, 251
    Normalize Clip Volume, 251
    other volume tools, 249
    rubber banding
        finding rubber band, 247
        using rubber band, 248–249
    rubber-banding, 247–249
    Volume slider, 250

W

Watercolor Map, 148
WAV files, 224
Web
    CNN's iReport (see CNN's iReport)
    exporting movies, 327–331
        freehand way, 327
        iWeb, 327, 328–331
    Facebook (see Facebook)
    MobileMe (see MobileMe)
    posting movie on your site, 331

Web (*continued*)
    Vimeo (see Vimeo)
    YouTube (see YouTube)
Web movies, 4
Welcome to iMovie, 473
White Balance, 188
White effect, 171
Widescreen (16:9), 62, 272
Window menu, 471–475
    Audio Adjustments, 471
    Clip Adjustments, 471
    Clip Trimmer, 471
    Cropping, 471
    Hide/Show Commands, 471
    Ken Burns, 471
    Precision Editor, 471
    Rotation, 471
    Show Events Full-screen, 471
    Show Projects Full-screen, 471
    Swap Event and Projects, 472
    Video Adjustments, 471
    Viewer, 471
    Viewer on Secondary Display, 472
Windows keyboard shortcuts, 485
Wipe Down, Up, Left, Right transitions, 138

X

XML files, 470
X-Ray effect, 155

Y

YouTube, 313, 469
    alternative, 313
    deleting movie, 318
    exporting to, 314–319
        after movie is up, 317–319
        editing and republishing, 318
        first time, 314–317
        HD, 315
        play back size, 315
        posting videos, 317
        watching video, 317
    HD videos, 316
    QuickTime Player X, 355
    Tell a Friend feature, 317
    troubleshooting, 482

Z

zoom
    digital, 16
    tip, 13
    zoom, 12
Zoom title style, 202

Colophon

Nellie McKesson provided quality control for *iMovie '11 & iDVD: The Missing Manual*. The book was proofread and composited in Adobe InDesign CS4 by Dessin Designs (*www.dessindesigns.com*).

The cover of this book is based on a series design originally created by David Freedman and modified by Mike Kohnke, Karen Montgomery, and Fitch (*www.fitch.com*). Back cover design, dog illustration, and color selection by Fitch.

David Futato designed the interior layout, based on a series design by Phil Simpson. The text font is Adobe Minion; the heading font is Adobe Formata Condensed; and the code font is LucasFont's TheSansMonoCondensed. The illustrations that appear in the book were produced by Robert Romano using Adobe Photoshop and Illustrator CS.

Get even more for your money.

Join the O'Reilly Community, and register the O'Reilly books you own.It's free, and you'll get:

- 40% upgrade offer on O'Reilly books
- Membership discounts on books and events
- Free lifetime updates to electronic formats of books
- Multiple ebook formats, DRM FREE
- Participation in the O'Reilly community
- Newsletters
- Account management
- 100% Satisfaction Guarantee

Signing up is easy:

1. **Go to: oreilly.com/go/register**
2. **Create an O'Reilly login.**
3. **Provide your address.**
4. **Register your books.**

Note: English-language books only

To order books online:

oreilly.com/order_new

For questions about products or an order:

orders@oreilly.com

To sign up to get topic-specific email announcements and/or news about upcoming books, conferences, special offers, and new technologies:

elists@oreilly.com

For technical questions about book content:

booktech@oreilly.com

To submit new book proposals to our editors:

proposals@oreilly.com

Many O'Reilly books are available in PDF and several ebook formats. For more information:

oreilly.com/ebooks

O'REILLY®

Spreading the knowledge of innovators   www.oreilly.com

Buy this book and get access to the online edition for 45 days—for free!

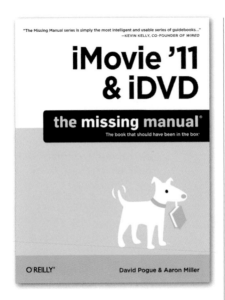